D1352666

Civil Litigation

SUSAN CUNNINGHAM-HILL

KAREN ELDER

OXFORD

UNIVERSITY PRESS

OXFORD
UNIVERSITY PRESS

Great Clarendon Street, Oxford, OX2 6DP,
United Kingdom

Oxford University Press is a department of the University of Oxford.
It furthers the University's objective of excellence in research, scholarship,
and education by publishing worldwide. Oxford is a registered trade mark of
Oxford University Press in the UK and in certain other countries

Sixth edition 2013
Seventh edition 2014
Eighth edition 2015

Impression: 1

Published in the United States of America by Oxford University Press
198 Madison Avenue, New York, NY 10016, United States of America

British Library Cataloguing in Publication Data
Data available

ISBN 978–0–19–876591–2

Printed in Great Britain by
Bell & Bain Ltd., Glasgow

MH16567978290241

CONTENTS

As indicated, the litigation train features both at the beginning of chapters, commencing in Chapter 6, and on the Online Resource Centre. The former illustrates a small section of the train relevant to the chapter, whilst the latter denotes three different levels of detail of the train, as follows, uncovered by the click of the mouse.

1. The first level displays the train in its entirety.
2. The second level sets out a variety of generic subheadings for each individual stage on the train.
3. The third level details the substantive information for each subheading.

online resource centre

The final part of the vocational approach—linked to both case studies—is the video clips that appear on the Online Resource Centre. The clips should be viewed as learning aids in that they seek to illustrate, in a practical way, aspects of civil practice. The videos are not necessarily a depiction of how cases always proceed, and they should not be regarded as definitive examples of how advocacy should be conducted. Commentary is included on the clips, as well as 'top tips' from the advocate's and the court's perspectives. The participants relied on the documentation and information provided for the case studies as presented at the end of chapters and as featured on the Online Resource Centre. The filming was based around a 'general framework for filming' document, but all participants devised the detail of their own script. It is important to remember that case law used to support legal submissions and the interpretation of the CPR in these clips may have changed since the filming of these videos. It is a timely reminder, therefore, that, when preparing for advocacy in practice, thorough research of the current law on both substantive and procedural matters is always required.

1.3 RESEARCH SOURCES

Legal research is an important part of your studies, but it is also a crucial skill that you will be required to exercise in practice. An accurate, relevant, and up-to-date research report to your supervising fee earner (covering both primary and secondary sources, primarily in electronic resources) will reflect well on you. The Online Resource Centre provides invaluable links to related websites from which you can access further useful information. Here, we include a summary of useful practitioner resources which can be found both in text format and (in part) in electronic format.

online resource centre

1.3.1 PRACTITIONER WORKS

There is a proliferation of widely available resources for civil litigators which primarily focus on the CPR, Practice Directions, and Protocols, with useful commentaries on their application in practice. We seek to mention those works most commonly used by civil litigators in practice.

- *Blackstone's Civil Practice* (Oxford University Press)
- *The White Book* (Sweet and Maxwell)
- *The Green Book* (Butterworths)

1.3.2 JOURNALS AND NEWSLETTERS

Articles contained in journals and newsletters allow practitioners to keep up to date with current issues in all areas of the law. There are general legal journals, such as the *Solicitor's Journal* and the *Law Society Gazette*, which contain legal news, letters, commentaries, and a legal update on a variety of topical legal matters. The journals and newsletters pertinent to civil litigation are *Litigation Funding* (Law Society Publishing) and *Civil Procedure News* (Sweet & Maxwell).

1.4 **A MATTER OF STYLE**

The use of the masculine he/his should be taken to include she/her. It is not intended to cause offence by adopting the masculine as the general descriptive phrase in this manual. Further, in using the masculine, we do not want to give the impression that all advocates and judges are male; far from it—the female stake in litigation practice on both sides of the bench is ever increasing!

1.5 **THE CIVIL PROCEDURE RULES (CPR)**

The CPR represents the cornerstone of the English and Welsh civil legal system. The CPR are also supported by Pre-Action Protocols, which provide guidance in relation to the pre-action behaviour of parties and High Court Guides (the supplemental information in respect of court practice in the High Court).

All of these aim to provide a comprehensive procedural code that will govern the conduct of all civil cases in all civil courts in this country, and will represent your primary source for the study and practice of civil litigation. The CPR have an explicit foundation in the concept of the 'overriding objective', which is looked at in some detail in Chapter 2, along with the whole philosophy of the civil courts system.

1.6 **PROFESSIONAL CONDUCT**

1.6.1 **INTRODUCTION**

A very important and pervasive area of practice is the professional conduct rules that govern the solicitors' profession and other legal practitioners alike. These are contained in the Solicitors' Regulation Authority (SRA) Handbook 2011 (the SRA Handbook).

1.6.2 **AN OUTCOMES-FOCUSED REGULATION (OFR)**

Our professional conduct rules are based on what has been described as an 'outcomes-focused regulation'. It is designed to be more flexible, in that there could be several ways or actions that could show a firm as compliant, and it represents a move away from the traditional prescriptive rules whenever appropriate.

Legal practitioners are required to meet a number of mandatory conduct 'Outcomes'. This will be explained in more detail later. The basic idea, however, is that instead of following detailed rules 'for the sake of it', legal practitioners will be able to ensure compliance with the conduct rules by demonstrating certain activities that can be used to show that they comply with the mandatory Outcomes.

This approach, whilst flexible, will necessitate greater judgment by legal practitioners (although at the same time allowing greater freedom) as to the systems and procedures they need to put into place to ensure that the Outcomes are met.

Here we intend to give a general introduction to OFR within the context of civil litigation, but do not attempt to explain how the rules will operate in great detail, nor how they will apply to different subject-specific areas of practice. The SRA website (http://www.sra.org.uk) contains further detailed information, including a great deal of useful explanatory material and videos. We do not have copyright permission to replicate any part of the SRA Handbook, and we would recommend that you read this section and the relevant chapters with the SRA Handbook to hand to enable you to cross-refer to the detail of the Rules.

1.6.3 **THE SRA HANDBOOK**

The SRA Handbook applies to all individuals and firms regulated by the SRA. It is very important for all legal practitioners to familiarize themselves with the contents of the SRA Handbook, which is set out as follows:

- The Principles
- The SRA Code of Conduct—Outcomes and Indicative Behaviours (IBs)
- The Accounts Rules
- Authorization and Practising Requirements
- Client Protection
- Disciplinary and Costs Recovery
- Specialist Services

In this manual, we will be dealing only with the Principles, the Outcomes, and the IBs of the SRA Code of Conduct.

1.6.4 **THE PRINCIPLES**

The Principles are the starting point of the OFR regime. They set out the key requirements expected of all SRA regulated firms and individuals. There are ten mandatory Principles and the Outcomes are designed to achieve adherence to these fundamental Principles.

The Principles apply throughout the SRA Handbook—they are all-pervasive. The SRA Handbook states that the mandatory Principles are the starting point when considering any ethical dilemma. The SRA has called them 'the Principles against which all actions will be judged'.

The ten Principles are set out at the beginning of the SRA Handbook and can be found at http://www.sra.org.uk/solicitors/handbook/handbookprinciples/content.page. The SRA Handbook elaborates on each one, with guidance for legal practitioners.

1.6.5 **THE SRA CODE OF CONDUCT**

1.6.5.1 Structure of the Code—Outcomes and Indicative Behaviours (IBs)
The Outcomes are set out in five sections and each section has several chapters, as shown in Table 1.1. There are separate Outcomes for each chapter (see paragraph 1.6.5.2).

1.6.5.2 How to approach your compliance with the Code
Legal practitioners must first look at the Principles to ascertain which Principle or Principles apply to a chosen situation and then see which Outcomes are relevant to the work they do. The Outcomes in each chapter describe what legal practitioners are expected to achieve to comply with the Principles in specific contexts. They must then consider both in the context of their practice, and ensure that there are appropriate systems and processes in place to meet the Outcomes. Guidance is given as to how each Outcome may be achieved. This is provided by means of non-mandatory IBs, which are again numbered, and appear below the relevant Outcomes in each chapter. These provide examples of behaviours that may establish whether a relevant Outcome has been achieved. The suggested IBs in each chapter are not an exhaustive list. An individual or firm may choose a different method from those listed by which to demonstrate that they have achieved, or complied with, an Outcome. If the method is not on the list of IBs, the SRA may require the individual or firm to demonstrate how the Outcome was achieved and to provide evidence of this.

Some chapters are further supplemented by non-mandatory guidance notes.

IBs may perhaps be seen as the 'low risk' way of meeting the Outcomes. The SRA states that its enforcement approach will focus on breach of the main Principles and failure to

TABLE 1.1 THE OUTCOMES OF THE SRA CODE OF CONDUCT

Section 1—You and your client	Chapter 1—Client care
	Chapter 2—Equality and diversity
	Chapter 3—Conflicts of interests
	Chapter 4—Confidentiality and disclosure
	Chapter 5—Your client and the court
	Chapter 6—Your client and introductions to third parties
Section 2—You and your business	Chapter 7—Management of your business
	Chapter 8—Publicity
	Chapter 9—Fee sharing and referrals
Section 3—You and your regulator	Chapter 10—You and your regulator
Section 4—You and others	Chapter 11—Relations with third parties
	Chapter 12—Separate businesses
Section 5—Applications, waivers, and interpretation	Chapter 13—Application and waivers provisions
	Chapter 14—Interpretation
	Chapter 15—Transitional provisions

meet the mandatory Outcomes. The SRA states that the responsibility for compliance lies with the partnership, LLP, individual owners, managers, and other regulated individuals.

The Code of Conduct can be found at http://www.sra.org.uk/solicitors/handbook/code/content.page.

1.6.6 **HOW WE DEAL WITH PROFESSIONAL CONDUCT IN THIS MANUAL**

Because professional conduct is a pervasive aspect of being a practitioner, we have aimed to achieve an integrated approach to this difficult area. We have sought to do this in two different ways:

- by dispersing text boxes dealing with professional conduct issues throughout the chapters at appropriate intervals; and

- in later chapters, by dealing substantively with key areas of the CPR that feature in general litigation practice, including client care (particularly costs information to the client), conflict, disclosure, confidentiality, and advocacy and litigation services.

We would therefore suggest that you keep an eye out, in the relevant chapters, for the specific areas of professional conduct. It is not our intention to cover all aspects of your professional conduct duties, only those we feel are most applicable to legal practice in a dispute resolution department, and these are contained in all the Principles and in Section 1, Chapters 1 to 6 of the SRA Code of Conduct.

Further, due to the flexibility of the rules, where we discuss any part of the SRA Handbook (as described earlier) in later chapters, our suggested highlighted Principles, Outcomes, or IBs are not intended to be the only relevant answer; rather, they are a guide as to the most relevant and pertinent responses to an issue. Consequently, you may have your own suggestions to add.

2 A MODERN LITIGATION APPROACH

Relevant parts of the CPR: 1

2.1 INTRODUCTION

The study and practice of what is commonly referred to as 'civil litigation' is probably somewhat misleading. A more accurate description would be 'dispute resolution', as there is now an emphatic move away from resolving disputes through the court system. Consequently, whilst students and practitioners are required to know how to conduct a case within the court framework, they are also expected to have an understanding of the philosophy and alternatives to litigation if they are to act in accordance with their professional obligations.

As we progress through the 21st century and embrace the many fundamental changes to the way in which we practise, we observe that certain features of our current practice merit mention at this stage: the growing importance of time limits and the rise of the number of litigants in person.

This chapter addresses the following:

- how we litigate in the 21st century;
- the concept of the overriding objective; and
- human rights and civil litigation.

2.2 CIVIL LITIGATION REFORM

2.2.1 WHAT IS THE PURPOSE OF CIVIL LITIGATION?

Civil litigation encompasses the 'machinery' and the 'mechanics' of how legal and equitable rights are asserted, determined, and enforced through the courts in the absence of agreement between the parties. The rules being upheld by the courts have their base in Christian and commercial ethics: what is good, but also what may have been agreed.

The courts therefore exist to do justice between persons who come to them. It has, however, been a long-term criticism of the courts that the very processes designed to ensure that justice may be achieved through the courts can also cause a delay and expense.

2.2.2 THE CPR AND REFORM

To promote the quest for justice in a timely, cost-efficient way, the manner in which we have conducted civil litigation has been in a constant state of flux, with Lord Woolf's complete overhaul of civil procedure in 1998 and Lord Jackson's review for improvement in 2010. The reforms implemented by Lord Jackson primarily in 2012 and 2013 are unlikely to be the last, however, as the Civil Justice Council is constantly seeking to refine the litigation process. Indeed there are suggestions from the Civil Justice Council that further, yet unparticularized reforms are inevitable particularly in relation to the cost of litigation.

2.2.3 THE KEY FEATURES OF CIVIL PRACTICE IN THE COURTS

Civil litigation practice in the courts is conducted in accordance with the CPR. The ethos of this practice is set out below:

- The CPR have a fundamental objective—that is, a stated reason for their existence: the 'overriding objective': all cases must be conducted justly, fairly, expeditiously, and proportionately, and in compliance with court rules, practice directions, orders, and procedures. The whole culture, or ethos, of litigation has as its aim to be less adversarial and more inquisitorial. See paragraph 2.3 in this chapter.

- The changes to litigation seen over the last few years, and the ways in which it can be funded by either claimants or defendants, can play a major part in the way an action may progress. These effects need to be understood so that the client can be fully aware of the implications of the way their or the opponent's case is being funded. See Chapter 3. Financial considerations are a key factor to take into account—the issue of 'proportionality' as regards costs is a keyword. See Chapter 4.

- There is a fundamental expectation that parties will attempt to resolve their dispute by making offers to settle or entering into an ADR process rather than proceeding to trial and to persist in their settlement attempts. See Chapters 5 and 15.

- Pre-Action Protocols indicate what steps (of 'best practice') should be taken before an action is commenced. See Chapter 8.

- The systems of judicial case and costs management once proceedings have been issued ensure that the courts govern the progress and ambit of an action. Cases are also 'tracked' by the court—to the small claims track, the fast track, or the multi-track. See Chapter 12.

- The disclosure of documents and both lay and witness evidence is controlled by the court, and the parties have an onerous duty to the court to comply with any requirements ordered. See Chapters 16, 17, and 18.

- Trials deal with relevant issues only and the trial judge will usually expect the parties to provide chronologies, skeleton arguments, and reading plans to promote expediency at trial. See Chapter 19.

As the CPR are updated several times a year, all legal representatives need to keep a careful eye on these regular updates issued by the Ministry of Justice, available online at http://www.justice.gov.uk/courts/procedure-rules/civil/update, and they should also review recent cases emanating from such rule changes in the senior courts.

2.2.4 **LITIGANTS IN PERSON (LIP)**

Litigants in person are known as unrepresented parties, self-represented litigants, or self-represented parties. Today, LIPs must deal with a legal system that is designed primarily for legal representatives and as a result, the system is often complex and obscure for them. They may feel (and often are) at a disadvantage. Consequently they should be treated in a way that redresses that disadvantage and achieves fairness to ensure that cases are dealt with justly pursuant to the overriding objective (see paragraph 2.3) and that the right to a fair trial is maintained in accordance with Art. 6, European Convention on Human Rights (ECHR).

Legal representatives should therefore approach opposing LIPs with an understanding of these issues and of the courts' approach to LIPs. There are limits to what an LIP can and cannot do in litigation and that can depend on whether the LIP is an individual, a company, or a protected party such as a child. However, generally they can conduct their own litigation and represent themselves at trial (sometimes with lay assistance).

As you are now much more likely to come across an LIP as an opponent, you need to be aware of your duties, if any, to an LIP. A legal representative does not generally owe a duty of care to any opposing party to litigation, whether represented or not. Indeed, the legal representative's duty is to protect his own client's interests against the opposite party. That said, a legal representative's professional conduct duties do have some relevance to his dealings with an opposing LIP. All legal representatives must of course comply with the SRA Code of Conduct as discussed in Chapter 1 at paragraph 1.6.

Within the SRA Code of Conduct, the Law Society practice note sets out the Law Society's view as to best practice for legal representatives dealing with LIPs and gives guidance in relation to applicable provisions in the SRA Code. The mandatory Principles must still be adhered to but the following should also be considered:

- Legal representatives must not take advantage of LIPs (Outcome (O) 11.1).

- Clients must receive the best possible information about the costs of their matter (O 1.13). You should explain to the client at the outset the additional costs that can arise when proceedings become more protracted, and any other potential adverse costs implications as a result of having an LIP as the opposing party.

- Legal representatives must comply with court orders that place obligations on them (O 5.3). They must inform the client of circumstances in which the legal representative's duties to the court outweigh their obligations to the client (O 5.5).

The CPR apply equally to LIPs but in reaching a case management decision, the court may well take into account the fact that a party is an LIP. Clients should be made aware of this, so that they know what the matter is likely to involve in terms of time and cost.

In addition to our professional conduct rules and the CPR acknowledging the existence of LIPs and how best to assist them, legal representatives can greatly assist the efficient progress of the litigation where one party is an LIP. Offering an LIP some practical assistance may in fact assist the client to progress the litigation. To this end, in June 2015 guidelines were prepared by the Bar Council, the Law Society, and CILEx to assist legal representatives when dealing with LIPs. Legal representatives can also help the court in directing attention to matters that need to be addressed at case management conferences and directions hearings where there is an LIP. Examples of assistance that could be considered (if in the interests of the client) include:

- providing a web link to a procedural rule, or a link to or copy of an authority (not just the citation);

- preparing all bundles and drawing orders where it would normally be for the opposing party to do, unless the LIP confirms he will do it;

- where a particular pre-action protocol applies, sending a copy of that protocol with the letter of claim;
- allowing the LIP sufficient time to get to grips with material, such as costs information for possible agreement (IB 11.1, SRA Code), and providing skeleton arguments and other documents in good time before a hearing;
- providing details of sources of support for LIPs (such as the Citizens Advice Bureau and the Personal Support Unit. The judiciary has published a handbook to assist LIPs that covers the entire court process and gives advice on how best to approach each stage of litigation);
- defining the issues by filing and serving a list of issues as a matter of course;
- allocating responsibilities between the parties;
- explaining the steps to be taken and time limits. This can help to avoid future misunderstandings and delay;
- ensuring that the costs involved are fully explained;
- ensuring adequate time estimates for hearings. This helps to avoid unnecessary adjournments where hearings take longer due to the participation of an LIP who is unfamiliar with procedure.

It is the general experience of those in practice who run cases where an LIP is the opposing party that litigation can take longer to conclude either by way of settlement or trial and that costs can accrue somewhat unnecessarily. By acknowledging your opponent as an LIP, this will undoubtedly reduce those timeframes and legal costs.

2.3 THE OVERRIDING OBJECTIVE

This is the very first (and fundamental) Part of the CPR, entitled '*The Overriding Objective*':

1.1 (1) The Overriding Objective of these Rules is to enable the court to deal with cases justly and at proportionate cost.

  (2) Dealing with a case justly and at a proportionate cost includes, so far as is practicable—

   (a) ensuring that the parties are on an equal footing;

   (b) saving expense;

   (c) dealing with the case in ways which are proportionate—

    (i) to the amount of money involved;

    (ii) to the importance of the case;

    (iii) to the complexity of the issues; and

    (iv) to the financial position of each party;

   (d) ensuring that it is dealt with expeditiously and fairly;

   (e) allotting to it an appropriate share of the court's resources, while taking into account the need to allot resources to other cases; and

   (f) enforcing compliance with rules, practice directions, and orders.

This 'overriding objective' is critical. It is the cornerstone of the CPR. The overriding objective is to be the starting point for all proceedings commenced and as the case proceeds. It is the rule to which all legal representatives will return whenever assistance is required in interpreting the CPR or in seeking to justify a step in the action.

2.3.1 WHAT IS THE EFFECT OF THE OVERRIDING OBJECTIVE?

The effect of the aims set out in the overriding objective means that interpretation of the rules must be purposive rather than a close analysis of individual words. The application of the rules and the use made of them by litigants must 'in general' be justifiable in terms of the aims of the overriding objective. Words will, wherever possible, be given their natural meaning.

Words such as 'may' clearly imply a discretion, but words such as 'must' or 'should' do not. Care needs to be taken, however, even when seeing such words in a rule.

 Example

Whilst the word 'may' is included in a rule, implying a discretion, it may not be clear from the rule who has that discretion. In *McPhilemy v Times Newspapers Ltd (No 2)* [2000] 1 WLR 1732 the discretion in the word 'may' in CPR 32.5(5)—'any other party *may* put the witness statement in as evidence' (the rule relates to provisions applying when a party has served a witness statement, but later elects not to call that witness or use the statement at trial)—is with the court, not the 'other party', as mentioned in the rule. This is not obvious from the words of the CPR.

2.3.1.1 Dealing with a case justly, fairly, expeditiously, and proportionately, and in compliance with the court rules, practice directions, orders, and procedures

The court's primary concern must be to create justice, but this 'justice' must be further defined in terms of the need for a case to be: conducted without undue delay; fair to the parties; and proportionate to the value (or importance or complexity) of the action. Where the aims of the overriding objective seem, in certain circumstances, to contradict each other, the need to achieve 'justice' will override any apparent contradiction. So, for example, if a party requires an extension of time, this may contradict the aim to deal with cases expeditiously. In these circumstances, the aim to give 'justice' may override the need for expeditiousness if, on the particular facts, it is appropriate and 'just' to do so.

We can generally say that dealing with a case 'justly' involves an analysis of the remaining aims. Dealing with a case 'proportionately' will sometimes mean that what may be appropriate or 'just' in one case will not be appropriate or 'just' in another: for example, where the value or importance of one case is less than that of another. Proportionality is most often applied to the financial value of an action and the sum of costs that should (proportionately) be utilized to seek justice, but it can equally be applied to situations concerning the importance of the case or the availability of judicial time.

Where cases are to be dealt with 'expeditiously', this means not only 'efficiently' and within the rules, but also in a way that saves costs. 'Saving costs' also incorporates the concept of what is proportionate—that is, what is a suitable level of expenditure for that case.

We could add a further 'aim' to the CPR: that of requiring the parties and their legal representatives to cooperate wherever possible. This need to have a less adversarial, more cooperative litigation system is clearly anticipated in the greater importance given to other forms of dispute resolution by the CPR. It also implies a need for legal representatives to be less combative in their dealings with one another, and to cooperate with each other and the court in assisting a case to proceed efficiently.

2.3.1.2 What advice should be given to clients concerning the overriding objective?

It is important that clients should be advised at the outset of *their* retainer of their obligations and duties, and the expectations of the court in conducting actions within the aims of the overriding objectives. In advising clients about these aims, the client should also be advised of the possible consequences of a failure to abide by the overriding objective. These may include costs and/or interest sanctions, which may be applied as a penalty for the failure. Proportionality of costs is also something that will need to be highlighted to clients at the outset. This is discussed in more detail in Chapter 4, paragraph 4.3.

2.4 **THE COMPUTATION OF TIME**

Litigation is frequently about working within a framework of rules with associated time limits. As a legal representative, you will therefore need to know how to calculate a period of time for filing (lodging with the court) or serving (on a third party) that is either specified by the CPR and its Practice Direction (PD) or by a judgment or order of the court. However, CPR 3.9 permits the court to place emphasis on the efficient and proportionate conduct of litigation when considering whether a party who has exceeded a time limit set by the court should be able to avoid the penalty of missing a deadline. The manner in which the courts have applied CPR 3.9 has fluctuated since CPR 3.9 was introduced into the CPR in 2013. Initially, many parties were either struck out, had to pay additional costs, or were unable to rely on evidence. However, in more recent times the court has moved away from such a robust application. A fuller discussion on relief from sanctions and CPR 3.9 can be found in Chapter 12 at paragraph 12.9, where the emergence of important case law on this point is examined. However, as a starting point, legal representatives must fully understand how time limits are calculated and whether such time limits can in fact be complied with.

We intend to deal with general time computation and not specific time limits imposed by the CPR, statute, or any service requirements. Those time limits are dealt with in the appropriate chapters later in the manual.

2.4.1 **PERIODS OF TIME EXPRESSED AS A NUMBER OF MONTHS**

If you must do something within 'four months', this implicitly means four calendar months (CPR 2.10).

For example, if you were to issue a claim form on 1 March, it would have to be served within four months after the date of issue—that is, on or before 1 July.

2.4.2 **PERIODS OF TIME EXPRESSED AS A NUMBER OF DAYS**

The key issues for you to be aware of here are the meaning of 'clear days' and the difference between 'more than five days' or 'less than five days'.

2.4.2.1 'Clear days'
Periods of time expressed in days, whether more or less than five days, implicitly mean 'clear days'. What this means is that in calculating the number of days in which you must do something, you must not include the day on which the period begins, and if the end of the period is defined by reference to an event such as a hearing, then you must not include the day of the event (CPR 2.8(2) and (3)).

For example, if your particulars of claim must be served within 14 days of service of the claim form and the claim form was served on 2 November, then the last day for service of the particulars of claim is 16 November.

2.4.2.2 'More than five days'
If a time period is stated to be more than five days, then bank holidays and Saturdays and Sundays are included.

For example, taking the case of the particulars of claim above, the weekends in November are included in the 14-day calculation.

2.4.2.3 'Less than five days'
Some periods of time are expressed to be five days or less, but bank holidays, Christmas Day, Good Friday, and weekends are excluded (CPR 2.8(4)).

For example, if you are to serve an application notice three days before a hearing and the hearing is on 20 February (a Monday), then the last day for service will be 14 February (a Tuesday).

Practical Considerations

Calculating time in these instances can be crucial, so ensure that you read the part of the CPR, judgment, or order carefully. There are occasions on which a step has to be taken within a period of days described as being 'beginning with' a certain day. If that is the case, then that start day is included in the computation of time.

2.4.2.4 An important exception
The main exception to the above points is where you are calculating the deemed date of service (see Chapter 9, paragraph 9.7.1).

2.4.2.5 Filing documents when the court office is closed
CPR 2.8(5) states that where the period of time for filing a document ends on a day on which the court office is closed, the document will be filed in time if it is done on the next day on which the court is open.

2.5 THE IMPACT OF HUMAN RIGHTS LEGISLATION ON CIVIL LITIGATION

2.5.1 HOW ARE THE CPR INTERPRETED?

When construing the rules, the courts primarily seek to give the words their natural meaning. Where the meaning is clear, the courts do not have the power to interpret a different meaning. However, if the application of the natural meaning of a rule applying traditional rules of construction means that a party's human rights would be infringed, the Human Rights Act 1998, s. 3(1), provides that 'so far as it is possible to do so, . . . [the words] must be read and be given effect in a way that is comparable with the Convention Rights'. The court therefore has the power to interpret the CPR in the light of human rights legislation.

2.5.2 WHAT ARE THE MAIN PROVISIONS OF THE EUROPEAN CONVENTION ON HUMAN RIGHTS (ECHR) THAT HAVE A DIRECT IMPACT ON THE CPR AND THE LITIGATION PROCESS?

Articles 6, 8, and 10 of the ECHR are those that have the most direct impact on the CPR and that you, as a legal representative, will encounter most frequently in litigation practice.

2.5.2.1 Article 6—the right to a fair hearing
Article 6 makes it clear that any provision that restricts a person's right to submit his claim to a judge may breach the 'right to a fair hearing'. There are many situations in which a person's rights are restricted in this way: for example, where the dispute must be submitted to a tribunal (such as in employment disputes) or to an administrative process (that is, in setting the sum of maintenance that a parent must pay to the other parent with care of the child where the parents are divorced). When this occurs, three questions need to be considered to establish whether the restriction is one that contravenes the right to a fair hearing, as follows:

1. Does the case involve a determination of the person's civil rights and obligations?
2. Is the administrative determination of the person's rights subject to control by the courts?
3. Is the restriction of the person's right to access to the courts proportionate?

In nearly all of the situations in which we see the law apparently restricting a person's right to a fair hearing, we will see that they do not breach Art. 6 once the above three questions are considered.

2.5.2.2 Article 8—the right to respect for private and family life

Private and family life includes the relationship between spouses, parents and children, unmarried couples and their children, grandparents and grandchildren, and a person's sexual orientation, personal identity, and private space.

Article 8 may be invoked to protect personal and private information, correspondence, telephone conversations, and relationships between people. A balance sometimes has to be struck between the protection provided by Art. 8 and the right to a fair hearing under Art. 6. Where the confidentiality involves children (for example, in a family law hearing), it is generally thought that Art. 8 will take precedence, but where the confidentiality involves adults (for example, in the need for proper and fair disclosure in a civil action), Art. 6 will take precedence. In the latter situation, there are clear limits to any precedence of Art. 6. This has been clearly demonstrated in *Jones v University of Warwick* [2003] 1 WLR 954, in which video evidence of the claimant in personal injury actions has been held to be 'fair' where the video evidence is obtained secretly but in public places, but not fair if obtained secretly and of the claimant in his own home.

In *Long Beach Ltd and Denis Christel Sassou Nguesso v Global Witness Ltd* [2007] EWHC 1980 (QB), the court examined the balance to be achieved between the claimants' right to privacy under Art. 8 and the rights of the defendant to freedom of expression under Art. 10. The findings in this case were significantly influenced by the fact that the documents (over which the claimants sought the right to privacy) had already come into the 'public' domain as a result of the court proceedings and the public interest in publication.

2.5.2.3 Article 10—the right to freedom of expression

Article 10 provides a qualified right to freedom of expression. The right is qualified by the need to protect another individual's rights or reputation. This Article has altered the common law test applied in the grant of injunctions. A practical review of injunctions is contained in Chapter 14, paragraph 14.7 and there is an Additional Chapter 'Injunctions and other Equitable Remedies' available on the Online Resource Centre.

 online resource centre

Also, in defamation claims, there may be proceedings to restrain publication of information that would invade the privacy of another person. *Douglas v Hello! Ltd* [2001] QB 967, the case involving Michael Douglas and Catherine Zeta Jones, involved a breach of the couple's right to privacy of photographs taken of their wedding. In these cases, a balance has to be made between the potentially competing interests of protecting private and family life under Art. 8, and the right to freedom of expression and the protection of the rights and reputation of persons under Art. 10.

It is often a question of balancing the right of privacy with the right of freedom of expression. This balancing exercise was also considered in the case *HRH Prince of Wales v Associated Newspapers Ltd* [2006] EWCA Civ 1776, concluding that where it was obvious that the information was private (as it was here, being contained within a private diary), Art. 8 will prevail.

2.5.3 RAISING HUMAN RIGHTS LEGISLATION IN CIVIL LITIGATION

2.5.3.1 Jurisdiction

Claims under the Human Rights Act 1998, s. 7(1)(a) in respect of a judicial act must be brought in the High Court. Other civil claims under the Human Rights Act 1998 can be brought in the County Court or the High Court.

Deputy district judges and masters (whether sitting in the High Court or in a County Court) cannot hear claims under the Human Rights Act 1998.

2.5.3.2 Statements of case

Form N1 (the claim form) and notices of appeal have boxes on the printed form in which the claimant must state whether a Human Rights Act 1998 point is being raised in the action or in the appeal. If it is, then full particulars of the point must be set out in the particulars of claim or appeal claim. See Appendix 3 for an example of a completed claim form used to commence a civil claim.

2.5.3.3 A declaration of incompatibility

The court may not make a declaration of incompatibility under the Human Rights Act 1998, s. 4, unless 21 days' notice has been given to the Crown (Human Rights Act 1998, s. 5, and CPR 19.4A(1)). Where this occurs, directions requiring notice will usually be made at the first opportunity and a Minister, or other person permitted by the Human Rights Act 1998, is entitled to be joined on application by the Minister or by direction of the court.

2.5.3.4 Claims for damages for a breach of a human right

Where a claim is made for damages for a breach of a human right, notice must be given to the Crown.

2.6 THE SINGLE COUNTY COURT

The Crime and Courts Act 2013 established the single County Court by making provision for the removal of geographical jurisdictional boundaries from the county courts. This single County Court will sit at various locations within England and Wales in a way similar to the High Court, and will have a single seal and a single identity to indicate its national jurisdiction. The courthouses in which it will convene will act as 'hearing centres' with court administrative offices attached to them.

The introduction of the single County Court required prevalent consequential amendments throughout the CPR, for example the renaming of individual county courts as County Court hearing centres.

KEY POINTS SUMMARY

- Understand that litigation today is underpinned by the overriding objective.

- Be aware of the impact of the CPR on how you conduct the resolution of a dispute for your clients.

- Check your time limits when calculating periods of time and beware that missing a deadline could result in severe sanctions.

- Take account of human rights issues when proceeding with a claim.

SELF-TEST QUESTIONS

1. What role does the court have in the conduct of litigation?

2. What underpins the whole ethos of civil practice in the courts?

3. When a part of the CPR indicates when an order should be complied with by reference to a number of days, is the date of the order and/or the date by which the order must be complied with included in calculating the number of days?

online
resource
centre

Suggested answers to these self-test questions can be accessed in the Student Resources section of the Online Resource Centre.

3 COSTS INFORMATION TO THE CLIENT AND FUNDING OPTIONS

3.1 INTRODUCTION

When a legal representative takes instructions from a client at the outset of a new matter, he is obliged to give to the client the best information possible about the likely costs of pursuing and ultimately resolving the dispute, as well as discussing with the client the best way of funding the action. This advice needs to be reviewed with the client throughout the duration of the matter.

This funding advice is inextricably linked to a legal representative's professional conduct duties highlighted in the SRA Code of Conduct 2011 ('the Code'). The law in relation to costs and funding has undergone a fundamental overhaul in line with the Legal Aid, Sentencing and Punishment of Offenders Act 2012 ('LASPO 2012'). Some of the proposed reforms on costs and funding are still nevertheless a 'work in progress'. This chapter will focus on the following:

- what information your client needs to know about costs in accordance with the SRA Handbook's Principles and its Chapter 1 on Client Care in the Code, and, in order to meet these professional obligations, the advice to be given;

- the different types of funding options currently available that may or may not be offered to a client.

3.2 **THE SRA HANDBOOK**

Before proceeding further with this section, you may wish to refresh your memory on the intention behind the Code (contained in the SRA Handbook), and how this is to be used by those in legal practice. You may therefore need to refer to the Code itself concurrently with paragraph 1.6 in Chapter 1 of this manual. The Code contains, amongst other things, the rules setting out what information a legal representative should give to his client about his services, including costs. The Code is particular to solicitors, but essentially applies to all those in legal practice. The relevant Principles and Chapter 1 on Client Care are the parts upon which we are going to focus, particularly the Outcomes and Indicative Behaviours (IBs) as they relate to information and advice that will be given to a client about costs.

 Professional Conduct

The Principles and Outcomes must be taken seriously as they are mandatory. The IBs are non-mandatory but provide useful guidance on how to comply with the Principles and Outcomes.

3.2.1 **THE TEN PRINCIPLES**

The ten mandatory Principles underpin the Code. They define the fundamental, ethical, and professional standards that the SRA expects of all legal practitioners. Your starting point when faced with an ethical dilemma is always to have regard to the Principles. When two or more Principles conflict, the one which takes precedence is the one which best serves the public interest in the particular circumstances, especially the public interest in the proper administration of justice.

3.2.2 **THE SRA CODE OF CONDUCT 2011: CHAPTER 1—CLIENT CARE**

This chapter contains reference to the Outcomes and IBs relevant to issues concerning client care. Remember that the Outcomes are mandatory but the IBs are not. The latter are examples of behaviour that may establish that an Outcome or Principle has or has not been complied with. The overarching theme of client care is to provide a proper standard of service to each individual client. This is likely to encompass:

- ensuring your client has all the information he needs to enable him to make an informed decision about the service he needs from you;
- considering how you are going to provide that service; and
- advising how much it is going to cost.

Chapter 1 of the Code deals with many other issues, such as complaints, but for the purpose of our manual, we are focusing on the costs and funding information that needs to be provided to your client.

The key features to note about costs and funding advice to clients are as follows:

- That it provides the best possible information on costs and funding at the outset, and throughout the matter. In practice, therefore, information on costs should be discussed at the first client meeting and confirmed in a follow-up letter, along with the options available as regards funding (if any).
- Costs should be reviewed regularly and costs updates should be given, preferably in writing. These should not just be given in relation to the amount of costs but also in relation to the likelihood, or not, of the recoverability of those costs. Regular reviews of the initial

position on costs should therefore be undertaken and reported to the client with reasons for any change in relation to previous cost information. This may include not only changes to an hourly rate, or change of a fee earner dealing with the matter, but also changes of strategy that have occurred.

- The costs information to be given is surprisingly detailed. Costs estimates are required to be prepared for the client not only at the outset of the retainer, but at pertinent stages of the litigation, along with details of likely disbursements to be incurred. Costs estimates or formal 'costs budgets', the latter being required for most multi-track claims (for more details on the nature and use of costs estimates and costs budgets, see Chapter 4—The Nature, Extent, and Recovery of Legal Costs; Chapter 12—Case Management; and Chapter 20—Assessment of Costs Proceedings), are both also a mandatory requirement for provision to the court. Where costs estimates or costs budgets are prepared for the court they will have to be justified and they will be scrutinized by the court at later stages of an action when costs are being considered or when applications for certain directions orders are being sought.

- General information on costs is very likely to be contained in the client care letter and as such it is primarily the costs calculations that need to be communicated to the client and updated at later dates.

 Practical Considerations

Case law has emphasized the need for legal representatives to comply with their professional conduct obligations and has highlighted the importance of keeping detailed attendance notes of any discussions about costs as well as a written record of the costs information that has been provided to the client. By doing this, you will satisfy the relevant Outcomes and IBs.

3.2.3 HOW DOES THE LEGAL REPRESENTATIVE COMPLY IN PRACTICE WITH THE PRINCIPLES AND CHAPTER 1 OF THE SRA CODE OF CONDUCT 2011?

In order not to fall foul of your professional conduct obligations here, the Code's requirements must be dealt with at the outset of a new matter as indicated earlier. This is considered further at Chapter 6, paragraph 6.2, where more professional conduct duties, in addition to providing information on costs and funding, are discussed.

As the matter progresses, the legal representative has a continuous duty to update the client about costs and funding, as well as to ensure that he complies with the specific requirements under the Civil Procedure Rules (CPR) on costs. These, to a degree, overlap with the general provision of costs information to the client in Chapter 1 but are more prescriptive and involve the cost information being provided to the court as indicated earlier, either in the form of costs estimates in fast-track cases or in the form of costs budgets in most multi-track claims. The courts have become increasingly robust in ensuring that costs incurred in an action are 'proportionate', 'justified', and 'fair'. Where costs incurred are considered not to be proportionate, justified, or fair, the likelihood is that they will not be recoverable or may not be allowed at all.

Additionally, clients involved in litigation need to be aware of the following issues. These will impact on the costs information that needs to be given to them.

- The loser generally pays the winner's costs—but this is not always the case, because costs are ultimately at the discretion of the court.

- The court will look at the conduct of the parties when making a decision about who pays costs.

- What options, other than litigation, there are for resolving their dispute, such as mediation or another form of alternative dispute resolution (ADR).

- The fact that litigation is expensive.

- There should be a review of the cost–benefit analysis at key stages in the litigation, such as at disclosure, or when witness statements are exchanged. At these, and at other times, there should be an analysis of the case as it has progressed and this may include a review of the merits of the case (in relation to) the total costs of the action so far incurred as well as the costs that are to be incurred from then on, together with a review of the client's resources or the terms of a funding or insurance agreement, the opponent's ability to pay any judgment against him, and the likelihood of enforcing a judgment against the opponent.

- Costs are quantified on two bases: standard and indemnity (defined in Chapter 4, paragraph 4.3.2).

- Costs are assessed pursuant to either a summary assessment or a detailed assessment. (These procedures are set out in Chapter 20 'Assessment of Costs Proceedings'.)

 Costs

It is extremely difficult to provide an estimate of the overall likely cost of a matter to the client. If a precise figure cannot be given at the outset, the legal representative should explain the reason to the client and proceed in one of the following ways:

- Agree either a maximum figure by way of a cost cap to be reviewed.
- Identify a stage when a more meaningful costs estimate can be given.
- Consider whether it would be more appropriate to provide a fixed fee for a defined phase of the claim. For example, Phase I could include specific steps between first instructions and the commencement of the pre-action protocol phase. A carefully calculated fee is agreed with the client and when the end of the first phase is completed, a Phase II fixed fee could be agreed up until a further stage in the action if appropriate, or alternatively a costs estimate or cap could then be provided to the client. Fixed fees, costs estimates, and caps can be used consecutively in any phase of an action, but if using a fixed fee or costs cap, then these must be expressly agreed with the client in advance.

3.2.4 WHAT ARE THE CONSEQUENCES IF YOU BREACH THE PRINCIPLES OR OUTCOMES OF THE SRA CODE OF CONDUCT 2011?

The Principles and the Outcomes have a statutory effect as well as a disciplinary effect. Essentially, this means that a breach of their requirements may render you liable to pay damages to the client and to a reduction of the bill, as well as conditions being placed on your practising certificate (if you are a solicitor), a fine, a suspension, or even being struck off the Roll. These sanctions are all separate from the client's right to pursue a negligence claim against you, if appropriate.

3.3 METHODS OF FUNDING A CLAIM AND IMPORTANT CHANGES

When you take initial instructions from your client, you will need to consider in some detail with him how he is going to fund his claim or his defence of a claim. There are a number of options that may or may not be available to your client, but it is best to sit down with your client and discuss each option with him and whether an option is available to him or not, with reasons, so as to find the most appropriate method of funding.

The most common methods of funding offered by legal practices are set out in the following paragraphs. Many of these methods stand alone or can be combined depending on your client's needs and the assessed risk in each case for both client and practice.

Most legal practitioners will not offer any type of funding arrangement if the prospects of success are below 60 per cent. For a comparison of these different methods of funding see Table 3.1 at the end of this chapter.

3.3.1 'BEFORE THE EVENT' (BTE) INSURANCE

Many clients have existing insurance in respect of motor vehicles and property or even as a perk of a credit card facility. Under the terms of these policies, the client may have (sometimes unbeknown to him) legal expenses insurance that may cover payment of some or all of his own and his opponent's legal costs of a civil action, if necessary.

A legal representative should ask his client to check all existing insurance policies to ascertain whether such cover is provided, the extent of the cover, and whether it is appropriate. If your client is relying on such a policy to fund an action, it may be appropriate for the legal representative himself to look at the terms of the policy to identify the existence and ambit of those terms, as many BTE policies have intricate and sometimes difficult-to-understand policy exclusions or limits of indemnity of £25,000. This may not be sufficient to cover many multi-track cases. If your client has the benefit of BTE, then there is a presumption that he will use it rather than seek another method of funding.

3.3.2 PRIVATE FUNDS

Private funds are the traditional method of paying for litigation, and the client's ability to pay privately very much depends on his own resources available from capital and income. It is more usual for commercial clients to pay privately than individuals, although in either case it makes the provision of costs information to your privately paying client even more pertinent.

The client will pay the legal representative's costs of conducting the case at an agreed hourly rate, plus disbursements and VAT. (For a full discussion on how those costs are made up and assessed, see Chapter 4, paragraphs 4.3.2 and 4.4.) In accordance with the terms of the retainer set out in the client care letter, the client will usually be billed on an interim basis every month for work done.

 Professional Conduct

The client should be informed at the outset, in compliance with Outcome 1.3, that if he is successful, his costs are likely to be more than any amount of costs recoverable from his opponent. This is for several reasons:

- the opponent will always attempt to compromise your costs as a matter of principle;

- you will usually advise your client to accept, with your client's express authority, a lesser amount for your costs to avoid the further expense and time commitment of a detailed assessment of those costs;

- in pursuing a claim on behalf of your client in accordance with your professional conduct obligations and doing the best for your client, you will almost certainly spend time on the case that will simply be irrecoverable if the matter proceeds to a detailed assessment: for example, attending on the client for an hour when your opponent may successfully argue that 30 minutes was reasonable, or spending six hours drafting and reviewing your client's witness statement when three-and-a-half hours may have been reasonable. Some aspects of your advice to your client in litigation are also rarely recoverable—for example, the time spent in advising him of the best method of funding available and your client care obligations to him in general.

In litigation, when a costs recovery order has been made in your client's favour, this will not generally cover the time spent on certain aspects of the case and thus, although it is work properly done on the file (for example, interviewing or taking a statement from a witness that you ultimately decide not to use) and is work for which your client should pay, it will not be part of the costs of the action.

In practice, there is an unwritten rule that there is usually to be expected, in most cases, a shortfall of at least 20–30 per cent in the recovery of costs.

3.3.3 UNION AND ASSOCIATION FUNDING

If your client is a member of a trade union or other association, he may have funding in place by virtue of his membership to cover his own legal fees, and possibly his opponent's legal fees if he loses. It is incumbent on the legal representative to ask the client at the first meeting whether he is a member of a union or association.

It may well be that further enquiries are needed to ascertain relevant cover, but care must be taken by the legal representative to ask the client in a clear and unambiguous manner about membership details. If it is the case that the client has union funding, it is very likely that the union will insist, in accordance with the terms of membership, that panel solicitors be appointed to represent the client. In this case, you must inform the client that if he is to take advantage of this, then he must terminate any retainer that he has with you and you must forward to the client any relevant documentation. The benefit to the client of having union-backed funding is that the client does not have to concern himself with any part of his ultimate damages award being diverted to his legal representative, as is the position under CFAs and DBAs (see paragraphs 3.3.5 and 3.3.8).

3.3.4 PUBLIC FUNDING (LEGAL AID)

Public funding (now also more commonly known as Legal Aid) in civil matters is effected through the Legal Aid Agency (LAA).

The way in which legal aid works today is that it is only solicitors' practices that have a contract with the LAA that can undertake legally aided work.

In order to be eligible for legal aid, the client has to satisfy a financial eligibility test and a merits test before the level of service from the LAA is decided upon. Details of all of the materials governing public funding can be found in the Legal Aid Agency Manual at http://www.justice.gov.uk/legal-aid. If public funding is available, it can be offered, subject to the satisfaction of the means and merits test, on a partial contribution basis by the client out of his disposable capital or income paid to the LAA on a monthly basis, or the client can be wholly publicly funded with no contribution.

However, there are a number of excluded categories of work that cannot be funded by the LAA and these include (not exhaustively) all personal injury work (save for some instances of obstetric clinical negligence cases) and matters of a property, trust, probate, or commercial nature—that is, essentially, most areas of civil and commercial litigation. Due to these far-reaching exclusions, LAA funding is not looked at in any detail in this manual.

3.3.5 CONDITIONAL FEE AGREEMENTS (CFAs)

The way in which CFAs operate has been substantially changed by the implementation of Lord Jackson's 2010 Review. In this section, we provide a basic outline of the purpose and effect of both the old and new CFAs in the civil courts on the basis that it will still take another year or two for the new regime of CFAs, with their different cost implications, to come to fruition by way of settlement or court hearing. It will only be at that point that the courts will then be able to address the workability of the new CFAs and adjudicate on any inherent issues that may arise. As we are only some three years from the date of their inception at the time of writing this edition, only time will tell whether the new CFAs are to be a viable and profitable method of funding for clients and legal representatives alike.

3.3.5.1 What are CFAs?

A CFA is essentially an agreement for litigation services under which the legal representative's fees and expenses, or any part of them, are payable only in particular circumstances, those circumstances being the success of a client's claim (Courts and Legal Services Act 1990, s. 58). CFAs are available to claimants and defendants, and can stand alone or be used in conjunction with other forms of funding.

There are a number of different types of CFA, depending on the fee agreement between the client and the law firm. The most common types of CFA are those with a success fee and a discounted CFA with no success fee.

3.3.5.1.1 *CFA with a success fee*

Position until 1 April 2013

Up until 1 April 2013, a CFA with a success fee was the most common form of funding, particularly for personal injury claims. These operated on the basis that the client and the law firm entered into a legally binding agreement where the client paid no legal costs to his legal representative throughout the duration of his case. If the client was successful, the legal representative was then entitled to charge an agreed percentage uplift to his base costs (these are the normal legal costs based on an hourly rate), known as an 'additional liability' or 'success fee'. Therefore, in the event of a 'win' for the client, the usual order for payment of the successful client's costs would be for the losing opponent (in personal injury litigation this is usually an insurance company) to pay most of those reasonable base costs, disbursements, and part of the success fee, which was either fixed, agreed by the parties, or ultimately set by the court. Consequently, the client was very likely to retain most if not all of the damages awarded.

If the client lost, however, then the general rule on costs would be that the losing client would not secure an order that the opponent pay his base costs, disbursements, and part of the success fee. In these circumstances, there was no charge to the client for the base costs incurred and no success fee was levied, although the legal representative was usually (this will depend on the terms of the CFA—please see the Example scenarios to understand this point) entitled to the payment of disbursements from his client.

 Practical Considerations

The terms of payment from the client to the legal representative whether he won or lost ultimately depended on the terms of the CFA. For example, some CFAs required payment of disbursements to be paid by the client as the case progressed. Other firms made decisions to pay the disbursements as they arose and to recoup them (at trial or settlement) from the client or the opponent, depending on whether the case was successful or not.

 Example of the operation of a CFA with a success fee for a successful claimant

A claimant client and legal representative entered into a CFA with a success fee of 50 per cent representing the risk element alone (see paragraph 3.3.5.2.1 for an explanation of the calculation of the success fee) in respect of personal injuries sustained in a road traffic accident. The client agreed to pay all the disbursements himself. The client was successful and recovered damages of £30,000. The base costs incurred by his legal representative were £20,000 plus VAT. The opponent was ordered to pay the claimant's costs. The claimant therefore retained all his damages payment of £30,000 and secured a payment from the opponent in respect of his disbursements. The claimant's legal representative claimed base costs of £20,000 plus a success fee of £10,000, making a total of £30,000 plus VAT for legal costs from the opponent.

 Example of the operation of a CFA with a success fee for a losing claimant

Taking the facts of the previous example, if the client lost his action, he would be unlikely to secure an order for costs in his favour. Therefore, as he had lost, he would recover no damages and he would not secure the return of the disbursements paid by himself. However, he would not be required to pay the £20,000 to his legal representative, nor would he be asked to pay the £10,000 success fee.

Position from 1 April 2013

From 1 April 2013, the basis of the legally binding CFA agreement is the same until the point where the client succeeds. Now, whilst the client can still recover most of his reasonable base costs and disbursements from the losing opponent if a costs order is made in his favour, he is not permitted to seek to recover any part of the success fee from the opponent. The client must bear this himself. In personal injury cases, the success fee (inclusive of VAT) can be set at a figure up to 100 per cent of the base costs, but the amount recoverable is limited to 25 per cent of the damages recovered by the client (excluding future pecuniary losses) and is net of any state benefits received by the client. In all other cases the success fee can be no greater than 100 per cent of the legal representative's fees. A copy of the Law Society model CFA for personal injury and clinical negligence claims and Guidance leaflet can be found on the Online Resource Centre.

online
resource
centre

 Example of the operation of a CFA with a success fee for a successful claimant

Continuing with the previous example, the legal representative can still agree a success fee of 50 per cent but is limited to recovering no more than 25 per cent (of the relevant damages recovered at £30,000) inclusive of VAT from his client in the personal injury claim. Therefore, the claimant would secure payment from the opponent in respect of his disbursements. The claimant's legal representative would claim base costs of £20,000 plus VAT from the opponent and assess the success fee at £10,000 being 50 per cent of the base costs. However that £10,000 represents more than 25 per cent of the damages recovered by the client and as such the legal representative will be limited to claiming a success fee of £7,500 inclusive of VAT from his client. Consequently, the client would only retain £22,500 of his damages payment.

 Example of the operation of a CFA with a success fee for a losing claimant

Taking the facts of the previous example, if the client lost his action, he is again unlikely to secure an order for costs in his favour. Therefore, as he had lost, he would recover no damages and he would not secure the return of the disbursements paid by himself. However, he would not be required to pay the £20,000 to his legal representative, nor would he be asked to pay the £7,500 success fee.

There are a number of exceptions to the new rule that the success fee can no longer be recovered from the opponent and these are as follows:

- in defamation, publication, and privacy cases—deferred for the foreseeable future; and
- in diffuse mesothelioma cases—under further review by the Lord Chancellor.

In these situations, even after CFAs with success fees have been entered into after 1 April 2013, if the client is successful, the success fee can be recovered from the opponent, but this will be subject to the usual arguments or scrutiny by the court on what that level of success fee should be.

However, these changes are not retrospective and as such, any CFA with a success fee entered into before 1 April 2013 will fall under the old regime, meaning that part of the success fee, in principle, can be recovered from the opponent in the event the client wins and secures a costs order in his favour.

3.3.5.1.2 *Discounted CFAs*

These appear to be unaffected by the 1 April 2013 changes. Whilst discounted CFAs more commonly feature in commercial cases, they are less common than CFAs with success fees. They operate on the basis that an enhanced percentage on base costs is charged to the client as the litigation progresses and that the client pays as he goes along. If the client is successful, then there is no further enhancement, but if the client loses, then the legal costs are reduced and a reimbursement may be made to the client.

With the demise of legal aid in civil litigation, part of the aim of the expansion of the use of CFAs for funding purposes was to provide access to justice, and to encourage the risks of litigation to be shared between the client litigant and the person most able to assess the level of that risk—the legal representative. A legal representative is unlikely to take on an action if he stands too great a risk of not being paid if the action is lost.

3.3.5.2 The success fee

The success fee is the additional liability or enhancement to the legal representative's base costs. Both the way in which this has been calculated and the ability to recover this from the opponent have seen major changes since 1 April 2013. There are a number of categories of success fee:

3.3.5.2.1 *The discretionary success fee—how is it calculated?*

Position until 1 April 2013

Primarily, there were two aspects to the calculation of the success fee. The success fee used to represent the risk factor to the legal representative of taking on the litigation and the fact that the legal representative is, in effect, postponing being paid his legal costs until the resolution of the claim. Whatever percentage was attached to each of these elements, the global success fee including risk and postponement could not have been more than 100 per cent of the base costs.

How this global success fee was actually calculated depended on each case and firms had their own policy on this. Some firms undertook the risk assessment on a case-by-case basis, while others looked at a cross-section of similar cases and considered the probability of success in that way. Generally, the success fee had to be reasonable. It was also possible, and indeed popular, to have staged success fees, starting low and increasing as the case progressed, or starting high and decreasing if admissions of liability were made. As the 1 April 2013 changes are not retrospective in relation to CFAs with a success fee entered into before that date, it is important that the legal representative understands, at least for the next year or two, what the court takes into account when assessing the success fee for those cases. The court looks at matters as they appeared to the legal representative at the time that the CFA was entered into when coming to its decision and exercising its discretion. The following considerations have been taken into account by the court and as you can see they are not entirely consistent

- Where a success fee was fixed at 100 per cent it is unrealistic to suppose that a competent firm of legal representatives would invest so much in such a speculative claim.

- Success fees can be 100 per cent at the outset of a retainer when in a position of relevant ignorance of the prospects of success.

- Success fees can be staged so that it is ultimately 100 per cent if the claim proceeds to 28 days after service of the defence and beyond.

Position from 1 April 2013

The way in which the discretionary success fee is calculated for all matters remains unchanged. However, as far as the success fee is concerned in **personal injury** matters, there is a cap on recovery of that success fee from the client as this cannot represent more than 25 per cent (inclusive of VAT) of the client's damages, excluding the future loss element, whether the matter settles before trial or goes to trial.

3.3.5.2.2 *Fixed success fees both pre and post April 2013*

Pre April 2013, there were some personal injury cases where there were fixed success fees awarded (and recoverable from the opponent), for example in certain road traffic accident claims where proceedings were not issued and the value of the claim was £10,000 or less. This does not however continue post April 2013.

The low-value personal injury claims in road traffic accidents and low-value personal injury employers' and public liability claims do not have any fixed success fees but do have a sliding scale of fixed costs according to damages recovered once these cases have exited the low-value protocol process and entered the litigation forum. Whilst these cases remain within the online protocol system, there are, however, no fixed success fees.

3.3.5.3 The regulation of CFAs

3.3.5.3.1 *What governs CFAs?*

Position until 1 April 2013

There were three sources of authority by which CFAs were to be regulated:

- the Courts and Legal Services Act 1990, ss. 58 and 58A;
- the Conditional Fee Agreements Order 2000; and
- the SRA Code of Conduct 2011.

Position from 1 April 2013

There are similarly three sources of authority for the new regime:

- the Courts and Legal Services Act 1990, ss. 58 and 58A as amended by s. 44 LASPO 2012;
- the Conditional Fee Agreements Order 2013 ('the CFA Order') which revokes the Conditional Fee Agreements Order 2000; and
- the SRA Code of Conduct 2011.

3.3.5.3.2 *What does the legal representative need to discuss when advising his client on entering into a CFA post 1 April 2013?*

There are a number of mandatory requirements that must be brought to the client's attention and these are as follows:

- The CFA must be in writing.
- It must not relate to proceedings that cannot be the subject of an enforceable CFA (that is, criminal—excluding some environmental matters—and family proceedings).
- The success fee is not recoverable from the opponent under any circumstances.
- The maximum amount of the success fee must be expressly stated to the client, and must not exceed 100 per cent of the base costs for all claims with a cap on the amount of success fee recoverable for personal injury and clinical negligence cases of no more than 25 per cent of the damages awarded (excluding future losses) net of any sums recoverable by the Compensation Recovery Unit (see Chapter 7 at paragraph 7.6.3.1.1).
- You must explain to your client when he may be liable for his own and his opponent's costs.
- You must explain the client's entitlement to an assessment of costs when you intend to seek payment of costs from your client.
- You must disclose to your client whether you have any interest in any funding policy.

 Practical Considerations

Practically, it is advisable to consider matters from your client's perspective: a client receiving a model Law Society CFA with a success fee agreement is likely to be very much at a loss if he is expected to read and understand all of this material on his own. Additionally, he needs to know that this is still a legally binding contract, and that it represents the retainer between himself and the firm.

The requirements noted earlier make no mention of explaining to the client the detail of the success fee calculations. Essentially, you should explain the terms of the CFA with a success fee to your client in detail, probably at a meeting, and back up important aspects in writing. The aspects that you may wish to discuss are likely to include what happens on termination of the agreement, and why the success fee has been set at a certain level.

3.3.5.4 What happens if you fail to adhere to these requirements?

If you fail to adhere to the requirements set out previously, the result of which is to have an adverse effect on the client, or you fail to make appropriate enquiries of your client as to other existing methods of funding such as BTE before entering into a CFA, the CFA is very likely to be held unenforceable. What this means is that you may be deemed to have had an unenforceable contract with your client and therefore to have no legal basis upon which to charge for the work done. This would, effectively, prevent you from recovering your legal costs from either your client or his opponent.

If, however, you fail solely to comply with Chapter 1 of the Code, it is unlikely that this would make the CFA invalid. Any breach in this particular situation will not prevent you from recovering, if your client wins, any disbursements. It is only the legal costs and success fee that may remain irrecoverable.

3.3.6 'AFTER THE EVENT' (ATE) INSURANCE

3.3.6.1 What is ATE insurance?

ATE insurance has traditionally worked in one of two ways within the realms of litigation. Its most popular use has been to supplement a CFA either with a success fee or a discounted CFA. It was usually purchased to provide insurance to cover the case in which the client lost and was ordered to pay some or all of his opponent's legal costs and disbursements. It can also be purchased to cover payment of his own disbursements and also can include cover for any shortfall of the costs recovery order against a losing opponent (the premiums for each level of cover can be significantly different). With the 1 April 2013 changes to the way in which CFAs with a success fee operate (as discussed earlier) it is thought unlikely that this will continue, primarily due to the forecast downturn in firms offering such agreements to their clients. The second way in which it was used was as a stand-alone insurance policy without a CFA, whereby the client was seeking funding from a reputable insurer against his own and his opponent's legal costs and disbursements. This is very likely to continue to be the case.

In either of these scenarios, ATE insurance is only available after the dispute has arisen and should only be obtained if there is no other insurance or funding option available to the client. ATE insurance will, however, never cover the payment of a court order or judgment in respect of damages.

3.3.6.2 The premium

As with all insurance policies, the client is responsible for payment of the premium, and the level of the premium is usually based on the strength of the case and the level of cover required. In the ATE market for personal injury claims, the premium is not too onerous, usually totalling less than £500 for the basic cover in non-complex fast track cases. However, in commercial cases, it is not uncommon for premiums to be as much as 20–30 per cent of the amount of cover required. For example, if the client seeks cover in respect of an adverse costs order only, and his legal representative believes that the opponent's likely legal costs and disbursements are in the region of £20,000, then the premium will be approximately £4,000–£6,000. Insurance providers will generally fix the premium of ATE insurance in commercial matters on a case-by-case basis.

As you can see, premiums can be expensive, but some insurers will allow the staged payment of premiums. The usual stages that underwriters consider for triggering payment of these staged premiums is pre issue of proceedings, after completion of many of the standard directions during the litigation (see Chapter 12 on case management for details of these important steps in the action), pre trial and post trial. With each stage comes a greater premium. Other insurers may agree that part or all of the overall premium be paid at the conclusion of proceedings. If the premium or any part thereof is payable by your client, you may need to consider with your client whether he should take out a loan to pay for the premium.

Professional Conduct

Legal representatives must exercise care when discussing with the client which ATE policy and insurer should be used, because they do not want to be found to have been in breach of Principles 4 and 7 and Outcomes 6.1 and 6.2 of the Code. The legal representative should therefore expressly give no guarantees that the means of funding adopted will be the most appropriate and inform the client of any constraints. In practice, there are now many specialist ATE brokers who, for a small fee, will locate a selection of policies for the client's needs, and the client can then choose. However, there is a cost implication, because the application forms are detailed and require the legal representative to give a full review of the case and his views on the prospects of success. If the prospects of a case are estimated to be lower than 60 per cent, it is unlikely that an insurer will underwrite the policy, unless in exchange for an extremely high premium.

3.3.6.3 The recoverability of the premium

Up until 1 April 2013, the premium, in principle, in respect of ATE cover was recoverable from the opponent where a costs order was made in favour of the client (Access to Justice Act 1999, s. 29), although it must have been reasonably incurred and reasonable and proportionate in amount.

From 1 April 2013, s. 46 of LASPO 2012 now provides that the ATE premium is no longer recoverable from the opponent and must be borne by the client in the event of a win, save for in the following types of cases:

- defamation, publication, and privacy cases—deferred for the foreseeable future;

- mesothelioma cases—under review by the Lord's Chancellor's department; and

- clinical negligence cases where the value of the claim is in excess of £1,000 and the premium relates solely to the cost of medical experts' reports on liability and causation.

The same transitional arrangements apply to ATE policies taken out before 1 April 2013 as they do for CFAs with success fees: these continue to be recoverable from the opponent provided they are reasonable in amount and the decision to purchase the ATE was a reasonable decision based on the risk factors in the case.

Before 1 April 2013, the issues surrounding the assessment of the insurance premium were often tied in with the issue of its recoverability: whether the premium was reasonable and whether it should, in fact, have been taken out in the first place. It is still important to understand potential difficulties in this area, as it will take time for pre 1 April 2013 cases with ATE premiums to come to some form of finality either by settlement or trial, and in these cases it is likely that the opponent will challenge the level of premium. For example, in *Kris Motor Spares Ltd v Fox Williams LLP* [2010] EWHC 1008 (QB), on an appeal, the costs judge emphasized that when it comes to a party challenging the amount of the premium, the paying party should adduce evidence of the level that they believe is appropriate and must do so promptly. There is no question of reversing the burden of proof, even where, as in this case, the premium was expensive (£95,000 to obtain cover of £130,000!).

The post 2013 regime inevitably leaves potential claimants and legal practitioners in a more disadvantageous position where CFAs with success fees and ATE premiums are concerned: claimants are much more likely to have to look to their damages to pay the success fee if successful and legal representatives risk losing clients, if CFAs with success fees are not offered, and if offered and the action won, they simply agree to forgo the success fee as a matter of discretion to retain the client, resulting in a much lower level of fee income.

However, the 1 April 2013 changes have not left claimants and their legal advisers completely without access to justice and a 'fair deal'.

3.3.7 **AN INCREASE IN DAMAGES AWARDED**

To assist claimants meeting the additional costs and risks of litigation arising from these changes, the post 2013 regime provides for a 10 per cent increase in the award of general damages for all non-pecuniary loss claims, i.e. all personal injury cases (notably those were the types of cases most affected by the 1 April 2013 amendments) where damages for pain and suffering or loss of amenity, physical inconvenience, discomfort, and mental distress are claimed. This increase in general damages is limited to these types of claims only and will apply to all judgments given after 1 April 2013. Any CFA with a success fee/ ATE premium secured before that date will not attract the 10 per cent increase but will, as indicated earlier, benefit from the recoverability of the success fee and premium from the opponent if the client is successful and secures a costs order in his favour.

3.3.8 **DAMAGE BASED AGREEMENTS (DBAs)**

3.3.8.1 What are DBAs?

DBAs are another type of 'no win no fee' agreement, also referred to as a type of contingency fee arrangement, which allow legal representatives to claim fees from the damages their clients recover in successful proceedings. Recovering a contingency fee is consequently dependent on the success of the claim and the recovery of damages from the opponent. Therefore, if the case is lost, then nothing is recovered.

Traditionally these types of fee arrangements were unavailable in civil court proceedings, until s. 45 of LASPO 2012, which came into force on 1 April 2013, amended s. 58AA of the Courts and Legal Services Act 1990 (CLSA 1990) permitting the use of DBAs without limiting this to employment matters (as was the case). Further, The Damage Based Agreements Regulations 2013 ('the DBA Regulations') now prescribe the requirements with which DBA must comply in order to be enforceable under the CLSA 1990.

3.3.8.2 How do they operate?

The DBA Regulations state that the damages a legal representative can claim under a DBA should be capped as follows:

• to no more than 25 per cent cap on the *sum recovered* in personal injury cases, excluding damages for future care and loss;

• to no more than 50 per cent cap on the *sum recovered* in all non-personal injury cases, excluding employment tribunal cases.

VAT and counsel's fees are to be included in the fee caps, but disbursements such as court fees and experts' reports are not. It should also be noted here that DBAs are not available for an appeal, as these are expressly excluded.

The *sum recovered* element, however, impacts on the circumstances in which legal representatives will be paid their fees. If a claimant client does not 'recover' damages and costs awarded against his opponent, the legal representative will not be paid. As a result, at the outset of the retainer, and, as has always been the case with CFAs, in deciding whether to offer the client a DBA, the legal representatives will need to assess accurately whether the opponent will have the means of satisfying a judgment, and how difficult it will be to enforce that judgment.

3.3.8.3 The requirements of DBAs

As with CFAs, the DBA is a legally binding document which must specify the following in writing:

• the claim or proceedings (or parts of them) to which the agreement relates, including whether the costs of any enforcement proceedings should fall within the DBA (or should be paid for by the client separately);

- the circumstances in which the legal representative's payment, expenses, and costs, or part of them, are payable;
- the reason for setting the amount of the payment at the level agreed; and
- what disbursements are likely and their approximate amount inclusive of VAT.

There is no other guidance in the DBA Regulations on what should be included in a DBA, but Lord Jackson has suggested that there is a minimum of six matters that should be provided for:

1. a definition of 'success';
2. how to calculate the legal representative's reward;
3. who pays the disbursements;
4. who is responsible for adverse costs, the representative or the client;
5. how to resolve settlement disputes between the client and the legal representative;
6. when the legal representative and the client respectively can terminate the DBA.

The Online Resource Centre will contain the new standard form of DBA, but it is still awaited (even three years after the changes were implemented!) from the Law Society at the time of writing. The Ministry of Justice continues to consider representations received on a number of issues of implementation (mainly concerning the use of hybrid or quasi DBAs) with a view to then undertaking a consultation. It is not currently known when further guidance will be provided.

online resource centre

3.3.8.4 Uncertainties in the DBA Regulations

It is interesting to note that within the DBA Regulations, there are no firm provisions (just previous suggestions from Lord Jackson) for a number of important matters which are likely to cause satellite litigation in the future. The 'rushing through' of the DBA Regulations in April 2013 meant that there are still a number of unclear pathways ahead. It is hoped that at some point in the near future these will become clarified. They are as follows:

- the circumstances in which a DBA can be terminated and the consequences of such termination on both the client and the legal representative;
- whether the ATE premium is included or excluded from the cap—the authors' view is that it is likely to be treated as an expense outside the cap;
- what information is to be provided to the client before the DBA is entered into.

3.3.8.5 How does a DBA work in practice?

Should your client succeed, recover damages, and secure a costs order in his favour, he should be able to claim his costs plus disbursements from the losing party. As with CFAs, the indemnity principle (see Chapter 4, paragraph 4.3.1 for a definition) will apply so that your client will not be able to recover, by way of costs, more than the total amount payable by him to his legal representative under the DBA.

In practice, therefore, the successful client's legal representative would keep the base costs recovered from the opponent, and set them off against the DBA fee. The client would then be responsible for any shortfall between the costs recovered and the DBA fee (that is, the successful claimant would pay his own lawyer from the damages recovered).

 Example

The claimant's legal representative and the claimant enter into a 50 per cent DBA in a commercial case. The claimant recovers £500,000 in damages and £50,000 in costs from the defendant, being £550,000 in total.

> The claimant's legal representative can recover a maximum DBA total fee of £250,000 (being 50 per cent of damages). The £50,000 in costs recovered from the losing party is paid to the claimant's legal representative as part of the £250,000 due. The claimant pays his legal representative the £200,000 difference from the recovered damages. This leaves the claimant with a net recovery of £300,000.
>
> The legal representative *may not* recover the full £250,000 DBA fee in addition to the £50,000 in recovered costs.

If the case is lost, then there is no 'sum recovered' and the client has no liability to pay his legal representative's legal costs or percentage cap. Disbursements, however, are required to be paid by the client.

3.3.8.6 Can defendants use DBAs?

It is still not clear from the DBA Regulations whether DBAs are available to defendants. However, the DBA Regulations define 'payment' as 'a part of the sum recovered in respect of the claim or damages awarded that the client agrees to pay the representative' excluding expenses. This suggests that if a defendant were to assert a counterclaim, then arguably a DBA could be agreed as a percentage of the potential damages recovered under that counterclaim, but if a defendant has no counterclaim, then a DBA is simply not an option for him. Therefore, a defendant would probably need to consider entering into a CFA or another method of funding described in this chapter.

3.3.8.7 Are DBAs a viable funding option?

Legal representatives considering whether to take on a DBA-based claim will have to consider the following issues:

- **Assessment of the merits of a claim.** Legal representatives will need to assess the strengths and weaknesses of a case, the potential level of damages, whether the opponent is likely to be able to pay any damages and costs awarded against it, and the timing of possible recovery. They will then need to decide whether those factors make it prudent and economic for the firm to take on the case and its associated risks. Pre-action analysis of facts and law should be used to help the firm assess what level of DBA fee it would be prepared to act on, if any.

- **Cash flow.** Taking on one or more cases under a DBA may have a significant impact on cash flow, as the firm will not be paid the contingency fees until the outcome of the case is known and the judgment paid, which could be a considerable time after the initial instructions are received. Further, the firm may never be paid those fees if the client loses the case or if damages are not recovered.

- **Counsel's fees.** For cases that require the involvement of barristers, an agreement as to whether the barrister shares part of the DBA fee will have to be reached with the law firm. As general disbursements are not to be included in the DBA fee caps but specifically counsel's fees are, then counsel's fees could be funded by the client (in the same way as many clients find disbursements in CFA cases), or they might be paid by the law firm subject to cash flow (and the level of recovery for the law firm under the DBA fee would need to reflect this extra cost).

- **Client relations.** Clients may be more demanding of their legal representative's time. In a DBA relationship with no element of hourly billing (see Chapter 4, paragraph 4.4.2), clients might feel more confident about making contact with their legal representatives, knowing that they are not being charged for each minute of their lawyer's time. Legal representatives will have to handle this issue with care so as to maintain high professional standards, but also efficiency.

Professional Conduct

Law firms using DBAs could stand to make significant profits, particularly on cases that settle early where the amount of work needed to secure the DBA fee is minimal. There is a danger that legal representatives could cherry-pick cases which have the potential to settle early, electing to run those on a DBA, whilst conducting cases which might go to trial and entail more risk on a discounted CFA. Legal representatives will need to ensure that they are not gaining a financial advantage at their client's expense in advising the use of one fee structure over another, or alternatively, in offering a DBA the client must be expressly advised that this may mean that they will pay more in legal fees if the case settles early or does not involve the hours of legal work that amount to the percentage of the damages recoverable under the DBA. For example, in a personal injury claim that is valued at £100,000, the legal costs under the DBA would be capped at £25,000 plus experts' fees. However, if settlement concluded the claim early, the pre-issue legal costs, if the client were to have paid privately, would probably not have exceeded £10,000 plus experts' fees. The client must be given the option of choosing and their decision is very likely to be based on their own personal cash flow. DBAs have the potential to create satellite litigation, involving aggrieved clients who feel their legal representatives have been negligent or have exerted undue influence in suggesting a DBA, where either a CFA or hourly billing would have been better.

3.3.8.8 What the legal representative must tell the client

As can be seen, there is no requirement in the DBA Regulations to provide specific information to the client or to advise the client to obtain independent advice (as recommended by Jackson LJ) before entering into a DBA. However, the Code will help legal practitioners here, and there are a number of relevant mandatory Outcomes (1.1, 1.6, and 1.13) and Indicative Behaviours (1.14–1.17).

All of these are subject to SRA Principle 4 to act in the best interests of each client.

It is not clear if the Code imposes an obligation to advise clients of a funding option even if a legal practitioner does not intend to offer it. In these circumstances, it may be best to explain all of the different means of funding that are potentially relevant and the rationale for your firm's approach to which funding options to offer, and to explain that others may take a different approach. You should also consider explaining the potential conflicts as described earlier between a legal representative and client if a DBA is used (for example, between the legal representative's interest in an early settlement and the possibility that the client's best interest will be in continuing with the claim).

3.3.9 LITIGATION FUNDING

3.3.9.1 What is litigation funding?

Litigation funding, previously known as third-party funding, essentially involves the provision of funds by individuals or companies who have no other connection with the litigation (and who are not practising lawyers). This type of funding was originally labelled 'champertous', meaning that an independent body, which was financing an action on behalf of another, may be able to apply pressure in the litigation, ultimately distorting the concept of justice. This could be done by exerting influence over the decision to accept or reject offers or over general strategy.

However, with the demise of many forms of funding over the years, litigation funding is now a legal and viable form of funding in civil litigation matters. The litigation funder might fund some or all of the client's legal representative's fees, his disbursements and barrister's fees, and the cost of the ATE premium to cover the risk of having to pay the opponent's costs. It is not usually intended to cover the actual costs of the opponent, as ATE is designed for that purpose.

Professional Conduct

As you can see, there is an overlap with ATE, as ATE can be purchased to cover some or all of the earlier stated costs. As a result, it may not be in the best interests of the client (Principle 4, Outcomes 1.2, 1.6, 1.7.1.12, and IB 1.17) to ask the litigation funder to pay these costs. It may be cheaper for the client to fund some or all of these costs himself, knowing that he will get his money back from an ATE insurance policy if he loses. If litigation funding is employed, then the legal representative will also need to ensure that his own retainer does not conflict with the litigation funder's agreement and that a confidentiality clause is in place.

3.3.9.2 How is litigation funding regulated?

Despite the fact that there is still no statutory regulation of these types of funding agreements, a voluntary code of conduct for litigation funders has been established and sets out the standards of practice and behaviour for funders. The code primarily addresses four main areas. The funder:

- must have adequate financial resources to cover his funding liability for 36 months;
- must have at least £2 million of capital and a mandatory annual audit;
- can only withdraw from a case in three specific circumstances; and
- is restricted from trying to control the litigation by the funding agreement.

A funder may provide the full legal costs of the proceedings, may partly fund the proceedings, or may fund only the disbursements. Protection from adverse costs orders is often, but not always, provided and, in some circumstances, the funder may provide no direct funding at all, but instead agree to cover a party's potential exposure to adverse costs. In return, the funder would expect to make a financial profit for its outlay. This profit is usually calculated at 15–45 per cent of the damages recovered.

The 'penalty' to the funder if the funded party loses is that he does not recoup his outlay and the court has a discretion to order that the funder—effectively, a non-party to the litigation—be ordered to pay the costs of the successful opponent, rather than the funded party. The court derives its authority from s. 51(1) and (3) of the Senior Courts Act 1981. The discretion is only exercised in exceptional circumstances.

Practical Considerations

Because litigation funding is now a real alternative to CFAs and probably DBAs in the litigation market, when discussing funding options with your client, you will need to raise the possibility of this type of funding. A competent legal representative should also consider seeking costs against a non-party, especially in situations in which an unsuccessful opponent does not 'look good for the money'. Equally, a person considering supporting the litigation of another will require careful advice to avoid making himself a potential target for a costs application and to ensure he complies with the Code of Conduct for litigation funders.

3.3.9.3 Types of case suitable for litigation funding

Litigation funding is primarily used for commercial cases of large value. It is not generally thought appropriate for personal injury or non-monetary relief claims. As with DBAs, litigation funders are unlikely to be interested in defendant claims unless there is a sizeable and realistic counterclaim having taken into account the likelihood of success of the claimant's claim.

If your client's claim is suitable, then the legal representative will need to investigate the prospects of the claim and, if better than 60 per cent, approach either a broker or a funder directly on a confidential basis to ascertain a quote for the funding. The Association of Litigation Funders currently has eight funder members.

3.4 WHAT DO YOU TELL YOUR OPPONENT ABOUT FUNDING?

3.4.1 CFAs AND ATE

Until 1 April 2013, ATE insurance, either on its own or coupled with a CFA with or without a success fee, was very likely to increase your client's opponent's costs if your client was successful. Therefore, notice had to be given to the opponent of both the CFA with the success fee and/or any ATE insurance, in order to warn him of this cost implication. This had to be done both pre action in accordance with section IV paragraph 9.3 of the Practice Direction on Pre-Action Conduct (as it was known at that time), and once litigation had commenced where a notice of funding (N251) must be filed and served on issue of proceedings if funding is already in place (or with the acknowledgement of service or the defence if no acknowledgement has been filed), or within seven days of entering into the funding if after the issue of proceedings.

The consequence of not giving notice was that the party in receipt of the funding was generally unlikely to recover the success fee and/or premium for the time period over which the funding was not declared.

If you review the notice of funding (N251, available amongst the court forms presented on the Online Resource Centre), you will see that it only concerns the disclosure of a CFA with a success fee and ATE, and requires details only of the date of the CFA and the claim to which it relates, along with the name of the ATE insurer, the date of the policy, the policy number, and the claim to which it relates. Similar notification is required for a publicly funded client.

Therefore, if your client enters into any type of CFA without a success fee and does not take out ATE, then there is no requirement to give any notice to your opponent.

As of 1 April 2013, as the success fee and ATE premium are not recoverable from the opponent, there is now no CPR requirement to inform your opponent of either.

3.4.2 DBAs AND LITIGATION FUNDING

DBAs and litigation funding do not impose an additional burden on the opponent. Consequently, there is no statutory or CPR requirement to formally notify your opponent.

However, it is often tactically conducive to settlement and the smooth running of the case to let your opponent know by letter how your client's case is funded: if your opponent is informed that your client has funding either by way of a CFA, DBA, or a litigation funder, then this will alert them to the fact that the legal representative must genuinely believe the client's case has better than reasonable prospects of success.

3.4.3 BTE, UNION, ASSOCIATION, AND LEGAL AID

As regards BTE and union-backed cases, the funding pre-dated the dispute and does not therefore impose an additional liability to the opponent. However, it is best practice to inform your opponent of the funding arrangement.

In relation to legal aid, it is mandatory to inform the opponent that your client is legally aided. This is primarily because a legally aided opponent cannot be ordered to pay an opponent's costs. This is crucial for your client to know if they ever face this situation as an opponent to a legally aided case, as it will inevitably affect how the case is conducted on a proportionate, commercial, and financial basis.

3.5 **MISCELLANEOUS POINTS**

3.5.1 **BARRISTERS AND CFAs WITH SUCCESS FEES AND DBAs**

Despite the 1 April 2013 changes to the recoverability of the success fee from the opponent, it is thought that it will be possible, though obviously less commonplace, to invite any barrister (known as counsel) instructed in an action in which the legal representative has a CFA with a success fee or a DBA with his client to enter into a similar CFA with a success fee or DBA with the legal representative.

It has to be appreciated, however, that the barrister is being asked to share the risk of the action in the same way as the client's legal representative, but that the barrister is probably taking on a greater risk, because it is the riskier cases that go all the way to trial. However, barristers who are asked to give early advice may be more likely to agree to a similar funding arrangement with the client.

It should also be noted here that there is no requirement for the disclosure of a CFA with a success fee or a DBA made between the legal representative and counsel.

3.5.2 **COLLECTIVE CONDITIONAL FEE AGREEMENTS (CCFAs) AND COLLECTIVE DBAs**

CCFAs are based on exactly the same principle as CFAs, both with and without success fees, and are used by legal representatives who act for clients who are routinely involved in litigation, such as trade unions and other associations or corporations. Instead of entering into a separate CFA with each new matter for the client, there will be one CCFA, which does not specify each individual matter, but instead provides for fees to be paid on a common basis in relation to a type of claim: for example, a tripping claim or a road traffic accident. Accompanying a CCFA with a success fee will be a risk assessment document in respect of each individual claim. The 1 April 2013 changes in relation to the inability to recover the success fee from the opponent also apply here to CCFAs. In practice, however, many CCFAs, even before this new regime came into force, were without success fees, which removed the requirement to comply with the disclosure of the funding arrangements. Post 1 April 2013 these CCFAs do not need to be formally notified to the opponent.

It is not thought that DBAs are suitable for operation on a collective basis and no mention has been made of this in the DBA Regulations.

KEY POINTS SUMMARY

- Before bringing a claim, consider ADR or, if available, whether the dispute might be resolved by a trade body or another means.

- If litigation is the only feasible option, undertake a risk assessment whether acting on behalf of the claimant or defendant. This risk assessment will include consideration of the likely costs recovered (by the firm or the client) and those unlikely to be recovered.

- On the basis of the value and risk assessment, consider what method of funding is suitable or available to your client, giving your client the advice they need to make a sound judgment of choice (where a choice is available).

- Discuss whether the client needs or wants insurance to bring or defend the claim and the timing of both.

- Consider whether insurance is available and, if so, at what cost.

- Review with the client what court fees or expert fees will be payable and when.

- Keep in mind your professional conduct obligations in relation to client care and information on costs.

- Maintain a detailed written account of the costs advice and information that you give to your client, and review it periodically.

SELF-TEST QUESTIONS

1. What is the difference between a CFA with a success fee and a DBA?

2. Why are DBAs not suitable for many defendant claims?

3. What are the sanctions if you fail to provide costs information to your client in accordance with Chapter 1 of the SRA Code of Conduct 2011?

online resource centre

Suggested answers to these self-test questions can be accessed in the Student Resources section of the Online Resource Centre.

TABLE 3.1 COMPARISON OF FUNDING OPTIONS

Funding option	Summary	Comparison
BTE	Legal expenses insurance is usually attached to home and motor insurance policies and can provide full or partial cover.	Sometimes the terms exclude certain types of civil claims and the cover is often restricted. Even if there is a limit on the cover it is usually beneficial to make use of the BTE and then move on to another form of funding such as a CFA, ATE, or private funds.
Private funds	Funds provided from client's own cash flow or capital.	Commercial clients are usually better placed to use this option. Many clients begin paying privately where there is no BTE or union funding in place and then move to one of the other options, such as CFA, ATE, or DBA if appropriate, or vice versa. This is probably the only funding option that does not require at least a 60% chance of winning as the client carries all the risk.
Union and Association Funding	Cover provided by virtue of the client's membership.	Once claim has been accepted cover is usually provided for the entirety of the claim, rendering it a very attractive funding option for the client. There is usually no need to look to any other type of funding to support the client in the litigation.
Conditional Fee Agreements	Client does not pay any legal costs until the point of winning, which is usually the recovery of damages at which point the legal representative's costs become payable. Costs orders against the opponent are usually secured in these circumstances in respect of the legal costs and disbursements but the client remains responsible for payment of the success fee.	CFAs are not an overly attractive funding option for the client in lower value cases due to the non-recovery of the success fee. This method is used where the client has no other financial means of paying his legal costs. Generally the success fee is paid to the legal representative, to all intents and purposes, from the damages recovered, which can often significantly reduce the compensation to the client. Even if this is the only option open to the client, many clients will think hard as to whether the pursuance of the claim is financially viable. For this reason CFAs are losing their appeal. They can be used alongside ATE and run consecutively with BTE and private funds.

(contd.)

Funding option	Summary	Comparison
ATE	Insurance that is purchased after the dispute has arisen to protect the client against an adverse costs order and/or to fund the litigation and disbursements. The premium is not recoverable from the opponent in the event that the client is successful in his claim.	A popular choice in some forms of litigation but not in others where the premium is high. In those cases the client will think hard about whether to purchase it due to the non-recoverability of the premium. ATE is often used alongside privately funded, CFA-, DBA-, and litigation-funded matters.
DBAS	A contingent arrangement whereby the client does not pay for legal costs until the point of success. In the absence of a costs order in favour of the client, at that point the legal representative is contractually entitled to take payment of his fees (usually capped) from the actual damages recovered by the client.	These have had little presence in civil litigation but it is thought that claims will need to be of a high value for a legal representative to offer this form of funding to a client. These can be used with ATE and run consecutively with privately paying matters or where BTE has expired. They are thought to be an alternative to CFAs. Legal representatives are wary of the new DBAs and they are rare in practice. Even if they become more popular they are thought to only be available to the high-value claimant market.
Litigation funding	The provision of funding by third parties who are not connected to the dispute.	This is realistically only intended for high-value commercial cases, which are a small percentage of claims. ATE can be used concurrently to support the client, with BTE and private funding being used consecutively.

4 THE NATURE, EXTENT, AND RECOVERY OF LEGAL COSTS

Relevant parts of the CPR and its PDs: 1, 3, 27, 35, 36, 44, 45, 46, and 48

4.1 INTRODUCTION

The term 'legal costs', for the purposes of litigation, is intended to cover the amount of time that a legal representative spends on a matter. These are otherwise known as 'profit costs'. The term 'disbursements' covers counsel's fees, court fees, ATE premiums (although these have their own rules in relation to recoverability, as has been seen in Chapter 3 at paragraph 3.3.6), expenses, and payments to other third parties, such as experts, incurred from the outset of the retainer until it is terminated or concluded. For the sake of clarity, the term 'costs' is intended to cover both legal costs and disbursements.

The client has a contractual obligation to pay for all of his costs incurred in bringing or defending a claim subject to the type of funding arrangement into which he may have entered with his legal representative, as set out in Chapter 3, paragraph 3.3. These costs are known as 'solicitor and client costs' and are discussed in Chapter 6, paragraph 6.2.2.3. However, the client may be able to recover a proportion of those costs from his opponent either by agreement or by an order of the court. Once the client has established an entitlement to the recovery of his costs, the parties will endeavour to agree the amount. If they cannot agree, then the court will assess those costs. The procedures for assessing costs are not detailed in this chapter but are discussed in Chapter 20 on 'Assessment of Costs Proceedings'.

The way in which the court will deal with the recovery of costs is primarily based on the 'overriding objective' contained in CPR 1, the aim of which is to deal with cases justly. The overriding objective was discussed at some length in Chapter 2. However, three of the methods that the court is specifically encouraged to use to meet that objective have an obvious bearing on costs and are worth looking at again.

To deal with a case justly, the court must, so far as is practicable:

• ensure that the parties are on an equal footing;

• save expense; and

• deal with the case in ways that are proportionate to the amount of money involved and to the parties' financial positions.

Therefore, as a starting point, it should be borne in mind that whoever pays the costs at the end of the day, those costs should be kept, overall, within sensible proportions, having regard to the case in question.

Against the background of the overriding objective, this chapter will focus on the control and recovery of costs including:

• the discretionary nature of costs awards;

• the general principle that the loser pays;

• how the court controls costs incurred;

• the basis upon which costs orders are made;

• the aspects of a legal representative's work that are recoverable and how they are formulated; and

• the different types of costs order.

4.2 THE GENERAL PRINCIPLES OF COSTS IN LITIGATION

The two fundamental principles that underpinned costs within the litigation framework until 1 April 2013 were:

• the payment of costs by one party to another is at the discretion of the court; and

• a general rule has emerged that the loser should pay the winner's costs.

However, a new principle was introduced from 1 April 2013, solely in relation to personal injury claims, which is that of Qualified One Way Costs Shifting. This seeks to refine these general principles. Qualified One Way Costs Shifting is considered in paragraph 4.2.3.

4.2.1 THE DISCRETIONARY NATURE OF COSTS

The court's discretion in the award of costs is founded on s. 51 of the Senior Courts Act 1981 and CPR 44.2, and is wide-reaching. The court is required to take into account all of the circumstances of the case, particularly regarding the following (CPR 44.2(4)):

• the conduct of all the parties;

• whether a party has succeeded on part of its case, even if that party has not been wholly successful; and

- any admissible offer to settle made by a party which is drawn to the court's attention and which is not an offer to which costs consequences under Part 36 apply.

CPR 44.2(5) further suggests what a party's conduct may include:

- conduct before as well as during the proceedings and in particular the extent to which the parties followed the Practice Direction on Pre-Action Conduct and Protocols or any relevant pre-action Protocol;
- whether it was reasonable for a party to raise, pursue, or contest a particular allegation or issue;
- the manner in which a party has pursued or defended its case or a particular allegation or issue; and
- whether a claimant who has succeeded in the claim in whole or in part exaggerated its claim.

As can be seen, it is the parties' conduct in virtually every aspect of litigation that is under scrutiny by the courts in the exercise of its discretion. This conduct issue should be highlighted to the client at the outset, and wherever it may need reiterating within a costs review during the action, in order that he understands how the recovery of his costs could be affected by his behaviour both before and during proceedings.

There is, however, one situation in which the court has no discretion in whether to make an award of costs between parties: that is, where a valid CPR 36 offer has been accepted (see Chapter 15, paragraphs 15.7.1 and 15.8.1).

4.2.2 THE LOSER PAYS THE WINNER'S COSTS

This second general principle is only a starting point and the courts frequently depart from it when considering costs at the end of a hearing, sometimes ordering only a partial costs recovery or no costs recovery at all. The main reason why the court may not order the loser to pay the winner's costs is, again, due to the conduct of one or both parties. CPR 44.2 and 44.4 require the court to take into account the conduct of the parties to the litigation both pre and post issue.

There is a plethora of cases demonstrating how the court may exercise its discretion on costs and costs recovery both before and after the 1 April 2013 costs reforms, which you will find throughout this manual. Instances in which the court frequently departs from these general rules, as stated previously, and makes a different costs order, whether claimant or defendant could be any one of the following:

- failure to comply with a pre-action Protocol;
- failure to negotiate;
- refusal to enter into an ADR process, particularly mediation;
- rejection of a without prejudice or Part 36 Offer;
- exaggeration of a successful party's claim;
- failure to succeed on the whole claim.

It is worth noting that these situations do not represent an exhaustive list of the occasions on which the court will exercise its discretion, but illustrate how wide the court's discretion can be.

4.2.3 QUALIFIED ONE WAY COSTS SHIFTING (QOCS)

From 1 April 2013, in personal injury cases, including clinical negligence, a claimant will in general no longer have to pay the defendant's costs if the claim fails but the defendant will continue to have to pay the claimant's costs if the claim succeeds. This can tentatively reduce the necessity for the claimant to purchase ATE (to protect against an adverse costs order) as this is effectively eliminated by these changes effected by Part 2 LASPO 2012 and CPR 44.13–44.17 and PD 44 Section II.

QOCS applies to all claimants in personal injury and clinical negligence actions no matter when the accident occurred (save for applications for pre-action disclosure made under s. 33 of the Senior Courts Act 1981 or s. 52 of the County Courts Act 1984; and where the claimant has entered into a pre-commencement funding arrangement as defined in CPR 48.2, such as a CFA with a success fee, as discussed in Chapter 3 at paragraph 3.3.5), whatever their means, but there are exceptions to this new rule, as follows:

1. where the claim is found to be fundamentally dishonest (fraudulent);
2. where the claim is for the financial benefit of another (intended to catch property damage insurers or credit hire providers);
3. where the claim has been struck out, where it discloses no reasonable cause of action, or where it is otherwise an abuse of the court's process.

In all these cases, it is very likely that the claimant will be required to pay the defendant's costs, either on the standard or the indemnity basis. However, as a proviso to this, it should be noted that CPR 44.14–44.16 permits orders for costs against the claimants in categories 1–3 to be enforced (either with or without the permission of the court), but only up to the level of the damages and interest recovered by that claimant. Therefore, if the claimant did not recover any damages, then that claimant will not be ordered to pay the defendant's costs under the QOCS rules.

However, the QOCS rules do not preclude a successful claimant being deprived of all or part of his costs or being ordered to pay all or some of the defendant's costs in other circumstances: a claimant can lose the QOCS protection where the defendant has made a successful Part 36 offer. (See Chapter 15 for full details of Part 36 offers.) What this means is that the claimant will be potentially back on risk for costs if he fails to beat the defendant's Part 36 offer at trial, but again only up to the amount of the claimant's damages and interest award. As seen in Chapter 3 at paragraph 3.3.6, if ATE is taken out in respect of this risk, then the claimant will be insured against payment of those costs, but he will have to meet the payment of the premium himself. This is therefore one of the reasons claimants still purchase ATE even in light of the QOCS rules.

 Practical Considerations

When advising a client on the recovery of costs in litigation, whether claiming or defending, it is best to reinforce with him that the primary obligation for payment of his own legal costs rests with him, but that the court has a discretion to order that some—but, most probably, not all—of those costs be paid for by his opponent in certain circumstances. It is better for the client to see the recovery of legal costs as a 'bonus' rather than 'the norm', because judges have such a wide discretion in the award of legal costs that it is becoming increasingly difficult to predict when and how much will be recovered. Clients should also be made aware that their conduct both before and during the litigation may also be called into question and, if thought not to be in accordance with their duty to the court, then they may in fact be punished by costs orders against them or be at risk of falling into one of the excluded QOCS cases.

4.2.4 THE LEGALLY AIDED LITIGANT

Despite the fact that legal aid is restricted in civil matters, in cases in which it has been awarded and the legally aided litigant is unsuccessful in the litigation, what happens to the legal costs of the winning party?

The Civil Legal Aid (Costs) Regulations 2013 and LASPO 2012, s. 26, state that a legally aided litigant is generally protected against adverse costs orders. This is known as 'costs protection', but only extends to the ambit of the Legal Aid certificate and to the duration of the proceedings in which the litigant was legally aided. Therefore, if your client is successful against a legally aided opponent with full costs protection, he will rarely recover any of his legal costs.

A legally aided litigant can lose his costs protection in the following circumstances:

- when, on the report of his instructing solicitor informing the Legal Aid Agency (LAA) of a change in the merits of his case or his income, the certificate is withdrawn, leaving the remainder of the action without funding and consequently the litigant unprotected; or

- where the opponent of a legally aided litigant contacts the LAA, making representations about the conduct and/or merits of the legally aided party to the extent that the certificate is withdrawn or partially withdrawn.

 Practical Considerations

It is therefore very important that your client is made aware as soon as an opponent is in receipt of a Legal Aid certificate that he is very unlikely to secure any costs recovery in respect of that part of the proceedings in the event of a successful outcome to the dispute, whether at trial or otherwise. This may affect your client's decision to pursue the litigation or to accept (or reject) offers.

4.3 THE BASIS ON WHICH COSTS ARE AWARDED

In paragraph 4.2, we have looked at the basic principles and how the court decides who is to pay the costs of an action. Underlying those principles are two further considerations that the court and the parties have to bear in mind when deciding how much the winning party is entitled to recover.

4.3.1 THE INDEMNITY PRINCIPLE

The indemnity principle is a long-standing principle that the winning party cannot recover more from his opponent than he has paid to his legal representative in the course of the litigation. To this end, if a client care retainer letter is not sent to the client, it could be argued that, in the absence of a formal contract, the client has no liability to pay his legal representative's costs and therefore the losing party has no liability to pay the winning party's costs.

 Example

You act for a client in a privately funded personal injury matter and send a client care letter. You make a successful application to the court for an interim payment. The court also awards you your costs. When the court is assessing those costs at the end of the hearing, the amount that you are seeking to recover cannot exceed the amount of costs that you have incurred on behalf of your client in respect of the application. Consequently, if the total cost of making the application was £750, you are limited to recovering that amount from your opponent.

There are, however, four notable exceptions to the indemnity principle, as follows:

• CFAs had the potential to breach the indemnity principle on the basis that the purpose of the agreement was that the client paid the legal representative only nominal legal fees (see Chapter 3, paragraph 3.3.5, for more on the nominal amount that the client may have to pay if he loses) should he have lost the case. However, this potential trouble spot was catered for by s. 31 of the Access to Justice Act 1999, which permitted the winning CFA with success fee client to recover his base legal costs plus a success fee up until 1 April 2013 if the CFA was in the prescribed form, and thereafter to recover just the base legal costs from 1 April 2013.

• In-house legal representatives are presumed to cost the same as instructing an independent firm to act, although, in practice, this may not be the case. Nevertheless, the case of *Re Eastwood* [1975] 1 Ch 112 established this pragmatic approach and it has remained ever since.

• A legally aided party's legal representative is only entitled to prescribed rates, although he is entitled to a full recovery of costs from a losing opponent.

• Pro bono representation, whilst free of charge to the client, can, in certain circumstances, be paid for by the unsuccessful opponent in accordance with s. 194 of the Legal Services Act 2007.

Interestingly, the indemnity principle does apply to DBAs so that a party will not be able to recover, by way of costs, more than the total amount payable by that party under the DBA. Using the example in Chapter 3, paragraph 3.3.8.5, if the claimant recovers £500,000 in damages, the claimant's legal representative cannot recover more than the maximum DBA total fee of £250,000 (being 50 per cent of damages in that example).

4.3.2 THE TWO BASES OF ASSESSMENT

The two bases of assessment are known as the 'standard basis' and the 'indemnity basis', and the court has the discretion to award costs using either one.

4.3.2.1 The standard basis

If the court awards costs to be assessed on the standard basis, CPR 44.3(2) states that only costs that are proportionate are to be allowed, but that if there is any doubt, then the doubt will be resolved in favour of the paying party. The key point here is that the costs must be reasonably incurred, reasonable in amount, and proportionate. (A discussion on proportionality merits its own stand-alone section and this is dealt with in paragraph 4.3.2.4.)

4.3.2.2 The indemnity basis

If the court awards costs on the indemnity basis, CPR 44.3(3) provides that if there is any doubt as to whether a cost has been incurred reasonably or is reasonable in amount, then the doubt is resolved in favour of the receiving party. The key point here is that proportionality is not taken into account under the strict interpretation of the CPR.

The word 'indemnity' is used here again, but it takes on a different meaning when used in assessing costs.

The 'indemnity principle' and 'indemnity costs' are two separate issues that those new to practice often find confusing: the former is the global background against which costs are assessed, as described previously; the latter is a formula that the court will use to calculate costs.

The same fundamental rule applies to costs assessed on the standard and indemnity bases: in each case, they must be reasonably incurred and reasonable in amount. Costs are usually awarded on the standard basis unless the court feels that there has been some culpable behaviour, in which case, indemnity costs may be awarded.

Practical Considerations

Such instances of situations in which an indemnity costs order may be made include pursuing an unjustified claim, rejecting a CPR 36 offer (that is subsequently beaten), an abuse of court process, dishonesty, or repeated flouting of court orders. A party who is faced with an intransigent or obstructive opponent can increase his chances of securing a costs recovery order on the indemnity basis if, before proceeding with any application or step (that the party now has to take because of the opponent's intransigence or obstructive behaviour), a letter is written to that opponent, warning him that an application for costs on the indemnity basis will be sought.

In light of the comments on applications for costs on the indemnity basis, it is worthy of note that the case of *Hobson v West London Law Solicitors* [2013] EWHC 4425 QB commented that when the court is left to consider whether indemnity costs should be awarded, the parties must act in a proportionate manner in pursuing that application.

4.3.2.3 What does the court take into account when deciding the amount of costs on either basis?

In deciding what costs have been reasonably incurred, are reasonable in amount, and are proportionate for a standard basis assessment, and what costs have been unreasonably incurred or are unreasonable in amount for an indemnity basis assessment, the court, in accordance with CPR 44.4(3), will take into account the following (subject to the indemnity principle):

- the conduct of the parties at all times, including in particular (i) conduct before as well as during the proceedings and (ii) the efforts made, if any, before and during the proceedings in order to try to resolve the dispute;
- the amount or value of any money or property involved;
- the importance of the matter to the parties;
- the particular complexity of the matter, or the difficulty or novelty of the questions that it raised;
- the skill, effort, specialized knowledge, and responsibility involved;
- the time spent on the case;
- the place where and the circumstances in which the work or any part of it was done; and
- the receiving party's last approved or agreed budget.

4.3.2.4 Proportionality in relation to costs

As mentioned in paragraph 4.3.2.1, costs on the standard basis must be proportionate as well as reasonable.

Prior to 1 April 2013, if the costs were held to be proportionate, the court would consider whether it was reasonable to incur each item. If the costs were held not be proportionate then the court would first consider whether an item was necessarily incurred and, if so, a reasonable amount was then normally allowed. In deciding what was 'necessary', the conduct of the parties was highly relevant.

However, since 1 April 2013, the position is now as follows: the mere fact that costs may have been necessarily incurred does not make them proportionate. CPR 44.3 has also now been amended to include a definition of 'proportionate costs' as follows: the costs incurred should bear a reasonable relationship to:

- the sums in issue in the proceedings;
- the value of any non-monetary relief in issues in the proceedings;

- the complexity of the litigation;
- any additional work generated by the conduct of the paying party; and
- any wider factors involved in the proceedings, such as reputation or public importance.

This definition is contained in CPR 44.3(5) and does not apply to claims commenced before 1 April 2013. These post April 2013 amendments are fundamental, as they dispense with the 'necessity argument' as an argument in support of costs being proportionate. What this essentially means is that disproportionate costs will not now be allowed even if they were necessarily incurred.

It is therefore the authors' view that if a client wishes to pursue his case at a disproportionate cost, he can do so, but most probably this will be largely at his own expense. Wealthy litigants who, however, seek to put their opponent to excessive and disproportionate costs by tactical manoeuvres may face an indemnity costs order against them.

4.4 HOW LEGAL COSTS AND DISBURSEMENTS ARE FORMULATED

Now that we have looked at the fundamental costs provisions, we need to ascertain exactly what can be charged for and ultimately recovered from the opponent if a favourable costs order is made.

4.4.1 WHAT WORK CAN BE INCLUDED?

A legal representative's work is calculated and ultimately assessed by reference to time spent on a variety of tasks, including various attendances either by telephone or at face-to-face meetings with clients, opponents, counsel, experts, the court, and others. Time spent considering and preparing documentation, including statements of case, letters, reports, advices, schedules, and perusing original documentation, is also allowable. Much of a legal representative's work is taken up with these items of work in the run-up to an interim hearing or trial, and added to this will be time spent at the hearing. The total of all the work done on an hourly rate is known as the 'base costs' to which, if your client is funded by way of a CFA, will be added the success fee, as discussed is Chapter 3 at paragraph 3.3.5.

At paragraph 4.1, we discussed disbursements: these are to be added to the overall statement of costs or bill to be presented to the opponent at the conclusion of a successful action or application.

 Practical Considerations

It is crucially important to understand the importance of accurate time recording by legal practitioners in a dispute resolution department, both in respect of being able to bill a client on an interim basis, usually monthly, and in relation to being able to provide a costs estimate or costs budget to the court as well as to the client. Time recording is done electronically and allows a fee earner, at any time, to ascertain and control the level of costs being incurred. This will assist with the compliance of your professional conduct rules in Chapter 1 of the Code, particularly in relation to updating your client on the costs being incurred.

4.4.2 HOURLY RATES

Once you have identified what items of work have been done and what disbursements have been incurred, you will need to consider what hourly rate will be applied to the hours spent in undertaking those tasks. These are considered periodically by the Civil Justice Council Costs Committee (CJCCC), although the Master of the Rolls has confirmed that the 2010 Guideline Hourly Rates will continue to apply for the forseeable future. See Table 4.1 for the rates in force.

You can see that there are zonal rates in England and Wales that include groups of towns and cities: National 1 and National 2. These involve two bands covering the whole country,

TABLE 4.1 CURRENT GUIDELINE HOURLY RATES (£)

	Band A	Band B	Band C	Band D
London 1	409	296	226	138
London 2	317	242	196	126
London 3	229–267	172–229	165	121
National 1	217	192	161	118
National 2	201	177	146	111

except London, with a further three bands for the City of London, Central London, and Outer London. The rates for London 3, Bands A and B are presented as ranges following the format of *The Guide to the Summary Assessment of Costs*. These ranges go some way towards reflecting the wide range of work types transacted in these areas.

In addition, there are four levels of fee earner within these bands:

- Grade A—solicitors and Fellows of CILEx with over eight years' post-qualification experience (PQE), including at least eight years' litigation experience;

- Grade B—solicitors and legal executives with over four years' PQE, including at least four years' litigation experience, and suitably qualified and regulated costs lawyers;

- Grade C—other solicitors, legal executives, and fee earners of equivalent experience to include suitably qualified and regulated costs lawyers;

- Grade D—trainee solicitors, paralegals, and fee earners of equivalent experience.

It is further recognized that, in certain complex, major litigation, the appropriate rate may exceed the guideline—sometimes by a significant margin. It is within the court's inherent discretion whether it is prepared to allow a greater hourly rate. This often arises when a party instructs a legal representative from outside his locality, in which case charging rates are much higher.

 Practical Considerations

The client needs to be aware that the figure to which he agrees in his retainer with his legal representative at the outset of the case (and any subsequent increase, decrease, or change in fee earner as the matter moves along) may be higher or lower than these guideline hourly rates. If it is the case that the client care letter denotes a higher hourly rate than the guideline figure, unless the court can be persuaded, it is likely that the Senior Courts Costs Office (SCCO) guideline figure will be adhered to. If the retainer letter figure is lower than the guideline figure, then, because of the indemnity principle, the client will be stuck with a costs recovery based on the lower figure in his client care letter.

4.4.3 WORK DONE BY COUNSEL

Work undertaken by counsel, including advocacy, drafting or amending documentation, and written, telephone, or conference advices, can be recovered against an opponent.

However, it is essential that the legal representative negotiates counsel's fee (known as a 'fee note') with counsel's clerk in advance of incurring the fee—particularly if it will have to be justified in detailed assessment proceedings. Counsel also operates on an hourly rate basis, denoted by experience and seniority.

4.4.4 EXPERTS' FEES

It is important that the terms of engagement with the expert are agreed in writing before any work is undertaken. CPR 35.4(2) states that any party seeking permission to adduce expert evidence must provide a costs estimate of that evidence to the court.

4.5 **THE DIFFERENT TYPES OF COSTS ORDER MADE BY THE COURT**

As the litigation of a case progresses, the court can make a variety of costs orders at interim hearings and at trial. At Table 4.2 at the end of this chapter, we list some frequently made costs orders that can be made both at interim hearings and at trial. At interim hearings (see Chapters 13–14), once the district judge or master has made his decision, he will then decide the costs order of the application or case management conference (but not the whole action). Most of the costs orders listed in Table 4.2 are also available to the trial judge after handing down his judgment at the final hearing.

4.6 **THE COURT'S POWERS TO CONTROL COSTS RECOVERED BY ONE PARTY AGAINST ANOTHER**

The courts are constantly looking at ways of reducing the cost of litigation and making it less unpredictable. In addition to the court's discretion in the award of costs, the court has developed a number of alternative costs orders and approaches that can be employed, usually in multi-track cases in which matters are particularly complicated.

CPR 44.2(6) permits the court to make the following orders of costs recovery:

(a) *a proportion of another party's costs;*

(b) *a stated amount in respect of another party's costs;*

(c) *costs from or until a certain date only;*

(d) *costs incurred before proceedings have begun;*

(e) *costs relating to particular steps taken in the proceedings;*

(f) *costs relating only to a distinct part of proceedings; and*

(g) *interest on costs from or until a certain date, including a date before judgment.*

In the next section we focus on two conventional approaches of cost capping and percentage-based or issues-based costs orders and the new costs management powers of the court.

4.6.1 **COST CAPPING**

'Cost capping' refers to the situation when the court places a limit on the amount that a party can recover from its opponent. It can do this prospectively or retrospectively, although the latter is rare. The court derives its general powers under s. 51 of the Senior Courts Act 1981 and the newly revamped CPR 3, 3.19–21 and also Section II at PD 3F.

The process of cost capping involves making an application to the court under CPR 23 (although oral applications can be made), usually at an early stage in multi-track actions, such as early directions or a subsequent early case management conference (CMC).

The evidence in support of the application usually takes the form of a witness statement detailing whether the costs capping order is in respect of the whole or part of the litigation and why the costs should be capped. It is usual to suggest here that, without cost capping, costs will be unreasonably or disproportionately incurred. A costs budget in the form of Precedent H is also usually required in relation to costs already incurred as well as those to be incurred.

The court will exercise its inherent discretion as to whether to cap a party's cost in accordance with the overriding objective and CPR 3.19(5) and (6). Case law that pre-dated the 1 April 2013 suggested that there had to be a significant and real risk that disproportionate and unreasonable costs would be incurred, and that the conventional case management powers would not prevent that. Post 1 April 2013, there have been a number of cases where the court has refused to make a cost capping order even where there has been a real risk of disproportionality and has chosen instead to order costs management to deal with the potential issue of disproportionate costs.

If a costs cap is ordered, the court will have regard to CPR 3.19 and the circumstances to be taken into account, as well as to a party's right to continue his proceedings under Art. 6 of the European Convention on Human Rights. Once a cost-capping order is made, as with any other type of costs order, the party is not limited to what he spends on litigation, but simply to what he can recover from the other party if he wins and obtains a costs order in his favour.

4.6.2 PERCENTAGE-BASED AND ISSUES-BASED COSTS ORDERS

Percentage-based and issues-based orders are considered where there are a number of issues in the case upon which the judge at trial has to make a ruling. Often, there will be a clear and significant cost attached to either proving or disproving the issue. In the circumstances in which both parties are successful on some, but not all, of the issues, instead of awarding all of the costs of the action to the ultimately successful party, the court will award costs of proving the issues and disproving other issues to the respective parties. This is done by either making a party pay a percentage of its or its opponent's costs, or allowing costs incurred on the issues proved or disproved.

 Practical Considerations

In practice, the courts favour making percentage-based costs orders rather than issues-based costs orders because, once the trial judge has made the order (having had the advantage of hearing all of the issues in the case in detail), it is then for the costs judge to decipher the issues before deciding whether individual items are attributable to certain issues that have been allowed or disallowed. As cases progress from 1 April 2013, it will be interesting to see how frequently the courts continue to use these types of costs orders in multi-track matters in light of the new mandatory costs budget requirements.

4.6.3 COSTS BUDGETING

4.6.3.1 The pre-1 April 2013 position

Parties in either a fast-track or multi-track case provided costs estimates to the court when filing their Allocation Questionnaires (now known as Directions Questionnaires) and, at a later stage of the litigation, when filing their Pre-trial Checklists. Additionally, in multi-track cases, at case management conferences (CMCs) there was also a requirement to file costs estimates. These costs estimates were not considered by the court until after judgment or settlement unless the parties could not agree on the level of costs to be paid by one party to another during what is known as Detailed Assessment Proceedings (see Chapter 20 on 'Assessment of Costs Proceedings'). There was no required format or template for the costs estimates, although they were often based on the N260 as a starting point. A copy can be found on the Online Resource Centre.

 online resource centre

4.6.3.2 Post-1 April 2013

The position since 1 April 2013 for all multi-track cases commenced after 1 April 2013 in the Queen's Bench or Chancery Division of the High Court and the County Court, excluding:

- the Admiralty and Commercial Courts,
- litigants in person, and

• any Part 7 claim valued at over £10 million, notwithstanding the fact that the court should retain a discretion to apply or not apply costs management both above and below the threshold

is that both parties must file and exchange costs budgets seven days before the first case management conference (CPR 3.13), unless the court orders otherwise under CPR 26.3(1). These are then considered by the court during the litigation. The aim is to give the court control over costs and to try and ensure that the parties are on an equal footing (see CPR 3.12–3.18 and PD 3E). This essentially means that all parties need to provide a detailed analysis of their likely costs in a prescribed costs form known as Precedent H to include the new Precedent Q form for each phase of the proceedings. This form enables the parties to set out what they believe will be their costs for bringing or defending a claim to a conclusion up to and including trial. This includes the fees of the parties' legal representatives (including counsel), court fees, medical records fees, and experts' fees. This new form can be found on the Online Resource Centre and has its own prescribed statement of truth: 'This budget is a fair and accurate statement of incurred and estimated costs which it would be reasonable and proportionate for my client to incur in this litigation.'

online
resource
centre

In practice the court now has cost management powers which it exercises throughout the litigation (rather than at the conclusion) either on paper, by telephone, or at costs management conferences which can be heard at the same time as CMCs. At these conferences, if a party objects to another party's budget, the court can now intervene and either approve the budget or order a revision by making a costs management order (CMO). If at any stage any party's budget exceeds the agreed or approved budget, the onus is on that party to notify the opponent and the court seeking further approval or a revised CMO. A failure to do so is likely to limit the recovery of costs to the agreed/approved budget unless there is good reason to depart from the approved budget. If there is not, there will be a loss to the party who exceeded the budget and failed to update their opponent and the court.

 Practical Considerations

What is often overlooked in practice is that once costs budgets have been filed, the making of a CMO, i.e. approving or not approving a party's budget, is discretionary (CPR 3.15). Therefore, it is not in every case that the filing of costs budgets will result in a budget being fixed by the court under a CMO, although the court is likely to pay close regard to the budgets provided when deciding what case management decisions are to be made. It is inevitable that case management and costs management are inextricably linked and consequently, your reading of Chapter 12 on Case Management will inform your understanding of the reasons costs budgeting is likely to form a core part of the strategy for tackling disproportionate costs and active case management.

It will therefore come as no surprise that since April 2013 there has been a plethora of case law on costs budgets, particularly in relation to the courts' approach to exceeded budgets and budgets that were not filed on time or at all. Such decisions are appearing on a monthly basis and serve as a warning to legal practitioners to note the CPR requirements on costs budgets and to take proactive steps and apply to the court in advance of a deadline or the upper limit of a budget to seek the court's approval for late service or a revised budget. Failure to do so will leave those defaulters in the hands of CPR 3.9 seeking relief from sanctions.

4.6.3.3 Effect on litigation practice and detailed assessment of costs

Chapter 20 deals with the assessment of costs after judgment, but it is worth noting here the implications of these costs budgets in relation to the detailed assessment of costs. In the authors' view, costs budgets will provide much less scope to challenge costs in detailed assessment proceedings if those costs fell within the agreed or approved budgets. Whilst there is still little guidance, if parties were routinely allowed to exceed the approved budget at a detailed assessment without very good reason, then the budgeting process would become a costly and pointless exercise. However, CPR 3.18 assists, and states that where a CMO is made (but remember that CMOs are not always made), the court will have regard to the successful party's last approved or agreed budget and should not depart from that budget without good reason where costs are being assessed on the standard basis only. The reality is likely to be that the paying parties will struggle to reduce bills by negotiation if they do indeed fall within the budget. As such, there is a real risk that some parties will submit at best comfortable budgets and at worst exaggerated budgets.

During the litigation, there is likely to be a greater need to fully consider and if necessary challenge the opponent's costs budget because failure to do so may tie the other party's hands on a detailed assessment. Similarly, legal representatives and their clients will need to keep a close track of budgets throughout the case to avoid unrecoverable costs outside an unapproved budget. Judges are also more likely to consider the new proportionality test at cost management conferences when approving budgets.

On a positive note, there is clearly good opportunity for both parties to have a far greater input and understanding of the total likely costs and to accurately see the full implications of litigation at a much earlier stage. This greater transparency to clients must be beneficial, although of course there is an increased cost element in preparing the budgets and dealing with cost management.

There is also a potential tactical advantage that the parties can take from understanding how their opponent intends to conduct the litigation because the parties will gain a clearer idea from Precedent H of the steps the opponent has taken or intends to take as regards witnesses and experts and how they intend to use counsel. This is likely to influence the thinking of the tactically astute party both in the overall approach to litigation and what representations it makes to the court in trying to restrict or expand what work can be carried out.

4.7 **FIXED COSTS**

Not all costs will be assessed by the court; in some circumstances costs are 'fixed'. The CPR deal with many kinds of fixed costs in CPR 45. In this section, we explain four of the most common types of fixed costs.

4.7.1 **FIXED RECOVERABLE COSTS IN ROAD TRAFFIC ACCIDENT (RTA) CLAIMS**

CPR 45.9–45.15 and PD Section II set out the fixed recoverable costs regime for road traffic claims that settle in a total sum of up to £10,000 before the issue of proceedings. These fixed costs do not apply to cases where the new Low Value RTA Pre-Action Protocol applies and consequently there will be few cases in which these will arise.

The costs that are recoverable are limited to:

- fixed costs relating to the agreed damages—that is, £800 plus 20 per cent of the damages up to £5,000, plus 15 per cent of the damages between £5,000 and £10,000, and a 12.5 per cent London weighting;

- VAT; and

- disbursements from a specified list in CPR 45.12.

Example

You practise in Exeter and have negotiated a settlement during the Personal Injury (PI) Protocol phase of your client's PI claim arising out of a road traffic accident earlier in the year. During your handling of the claim, you obtained your client's doctor (GP) and hospital notes, and instructed a consultant orthopaedic surgeon to prepare a report, which was disclosed to the defendant. You also obtained a copy of the police accident report book, on receipt of which you instructed an enquiry agent to locate witnesses, but none were found. Damages have been agreed at £8,000 pre issue.

Your fixed costs are as follows:

- £800; plus

- £1,000 (being 20 per cent of £5,000); plus

- £450 (being 15 per cent of £3,000); plus

- VAT on £2,250; plus

- recovery of the GP and hospital note fee, the fee for the medical report, and that for the police accident report book.

Unfortunately, you are unlikely to recover the enquiry agent's fee, because it does not fall within any of the disbursements in CPR 45.12.

4.7.2 **LOW-VALUE PERSONAL INJURY CLAIMS IN RTAs AND LOW-VALUE PERSONAL INJURY, EMPLOYERS' AND PUBLIC LIABILITY CLAIMS**

These Low Value Pre-Action Protocols stipulate the requirements for the low-value claims of up to £25,000 that can be dealt with. The whole process is undertaken online and is described as proceeding through three stages or until settlement is no longer possible, and then it reverts to the court system. There are Protocols for each of these types of case. (See Chapter 8 on Protocols and Chapter 9, paragraph 9.2.7 for further detail.)

The fixed costs for each of these three protocol claims are set out in CPR 45 Section III, where at CPR 45.18 fixed costs throughout each of the three stages are set out in Table 6 in relation to RTA protocol claims which settle within the protocol itself. Similarly, for EL and PL protocol cases, the fixed costs are set out in Table 6A. There are also stipulations regarding the costs of disbursements and provision for the cost of additional advice on the value of a claim.

If any of these protocol claims are incapable of settlement, then, as previously stated, the parties are at liberty to step out of the Protocol and issue proceedings through the courts in the normal way. However, there are fixed costs entitlements (except where it is a EL/PL disease case) in respect of these litigation costs, described as 'fixed recoverable costs'. These are not to be confused with those costs at CPR 45.9–15 in Section II also described as 'fixed recoverable costs' set out in paragraph 4.7.1.

CPR 45 Section IIIA deals with these fixed recoverable costs. Similarly, they are subdivided at CPR 45.29A–L into Table 6B for RTA claims, Table 6C for EL claims, and Table 6D for PL claims. Provision is also helpfully made in respect of defendants' costs in those cases where the fixed costs regime would otherwise apply (including those cases where a defendant successfully counterclaims—see Chapters 10 and 11 for further details of counterclaims) and the costs recoverable by both parties in related interim applications (see Chapters 13 and 14 for further details on interim applications).

We should also highlight here that these protocol fixed costs cases do not escape the operation of CPR 36 offers to settle with corresponding costs penalties. Chapter 15 details the complex requirements of Part 36 offers, but with the complete overhaul of Part 36 in April 2015, there are now specific provisions for the costs consequences of Section IIIA low-value RTA, public liability (PL), and employers' liability (EL) claims that have stepped out of the Protocol. There is also a new Section II within Part 36 that deals solely with RTA, EL, and PL protocol offers to settle.

4.7.3 FAST-TRACK FIXED COSTS

CPR 45.37–45.40 and PD 45 Section VI deal with fast-track trial costs.

It is only the costs of the fast-track trial that are fixed; the costs of the rest of the matter from date of instruction are not, unless your client's claim falls within those fixed costs in paragraphs 4.7.1 or 4.7.2.

These trial costs that the court may award are based on the value of the claim, although the court does have the power to award more or less than the fixed amounts. A common example of this is where your client asks you to attend the trial with him, in addition to your trial advocate. This is often for comfort or a 'belt and braces' approach. CPR 45.39 indicates that the additional fee of £345 will only be recoverable by your client if it was 'necessary' for you to attend to assist your trial advocate.

4.7.4 FIXED COSTS ON A SPECIFIED DESIGNATED MONEY CLAIM

Fixed costs can be recovered in an action in which a defendant to a claim for a specified sum of money admits the whole sum claimed, and pays it on receipt of the claim form and particulars of claim. Details of the fixed costs allowed can be found in CPR 45.1 and a further discussion on this is in Chapter 10, paragraph 10.5.1.

4.8 WASTED COSTS ORDERS

Wasted costs orders are governed by s. 51(6) of the Senior Courts Act 1981, as substituted by s. 4 of the Courts and Legal Services Act 1990 and CPR 46.8 and PD 46.8.

These are costs orders whereby the court has held that the conduct of a legal representative has been shown to have been improper, unreasonable, or negligent. The result of this is that the legal representative is ordered to pay either his own client's costs by way of an indemnity, where those costs have been disallowed as against the other party, or to pay the costs of his opponent.

PD 46.8 sets out the three factors to be considered by the court in hearing such an application as follows:

1. The legal representative must have acted improperly, unreasonably, or negligently.

2. His conduct must have caused a party to incur unnecessary costs.

3. It must be just, in all of the circumstances, to make the order.

The court's discretion to make a wasted costs order follows a two-stage formula:

- whether, on the evidence of the applicant alone, a wasted costs order is likely; and

- whether such a costs order is justified, notwithstanding the cost involved.

The respondent adviser to the application is given the opportunity to object to the application, but the burden rests with the applicant, although there is no burden on the respondent to excuse himself.

As for the timing of the application, wasted costs orders are usually dealt with at the end of the trial when the judge is hearing cost applications. The reason for this is that the conduct can be scrutinized in the context of the whole proceedings and the issue of proportionality can also be considered.

Wasted costs orders are only designed to apply to a small number of cases, which according to case law defines improper, unreasonable, and negligent conduct as being a breach of professional duty, vexatious, and incompetent, respectively.

In so far as the test for 'unnecessary' is concerned, the way in which the court will deal with this is by looking to the 'but for' test—that is, 'but for' the conduct of the legal representative, would the costs, on a balance of probability, have been incurred?

Practical Considerations

It is not always clear when to proceed with a wasted costs order. Conduct that might be considered appropriate for wasted costs orders probably includes failing to attend a court appointment, breaching court orders, negligently misstating a case, continuing with an action after it has become hopeless, and where a real loss has been suffered as a result of the legal representative's conduct. This is not a complete list of the occasions on which the court might consider a wasted costs order.

Professional Conduct

Where a wasted costs order is made and the client is not present in court to hear the order, the party's legal representative must notify the client in writing of the costs order no later than seven days after the legal representative receives notice of the order (CPR 44.8). If the legal representative fails to do so, he will be in breach of Principles 1, 4, and 5 and Outcome 1.13.

KEY POINTS SUMMARY

- Bear in mind the overriding objective, reasonableness, and proportionality.

- Costs orders are discretionary but the principle 'the winner is awarded his costs against the loser' is the starting point against which the discretion can be exercised. This has further been amended in personal injury cases with qualified one way costs shifting.

- Remember the wide variety of costs orders that can be made, both at an interim stage and the final stage of an action, and advise your client accordingly.

- Understand the difference between 'standard' and 'indemnity' costs.

- Note the far-reaching changes to the current costs regime implemented in April 2013 and beyond, particularly in relation to proportionality of costs, QOCS, and costs budgeting.

SELF-TEST QUESTIONS

1. What basis of costs is the usual basis upon which costs are awarded?

2. Is proportionality taken into account when assessing costs on the indemnity basis?

3. What are the general principles in costs in litigation and how have these been amended?

4. What is the likely consequence if a party exceeds his agreed or approved costs budget?

online
resource
centre

Suggested answers to these self-test questions can be accessed in the Student Resources section of the Online Resource Centre.

TABLE 4.2 THE DIFFERENT TYPES OF COSTS ORDER MADE BY THE COURT

Costs in any event	These can be made at trial (and are often known as costs of proceedings) or at interim hearings. It means that whatever other costs orders are made at trial or other interim hearings, a party in receipt of this costs order has an absolute entitlement to the costs of that particular application or hearing.
Costs in the case/application	These are usually made at interim hearings, particularly CMCs and pre-trial reviews. A party in receipt of this costs order will only get his costs of the application or hearing if he gets a cost order in his favour at trial.
Costs reserved	Here the court postpones making a decision on costs, usually until trial or another substantive hearing. If it does not make a later costs order regarding the reserved costs then the costs will be costs in the case.
Claimant's/defendant's costs in the case/application	This is often used where one party has been successful at an interim hearing but the court is not minded to give that party a costs in any event order but neither is it minded to make a costs in the case order. When the court makes such an order it has the effect of allowing the party who was successful on application a costs in any event order only if he secures a costs of proceedings order at trial. If he does not obtain a costs of proceedings order at trial then each party bears their own costs of the application to which this order relates.
Costs thrown away	Where a judgment or order is set aside, or the whole or part of any proceedings are adjourned, the party in whose favour the costs order is made is entitled to costs he has incurred as a consequence.
Costs of and caused by (an amendment)	This is the usual order the court makes in respect of an application to amend a statement of case. The order requires the party making the amendment to pay the other party's costs of preparing for and attending the hearing and any consequential amendments to his own statement of case.
Costs here and below	This order is often made on appeal and allows the party who is successful on the appeal to recover his costs of the appeal and the lower court.
No order as to costs/each party to bear their own costs	Each party is to bear its own costs of the part of the proceedings to which the order relates, whatever costs order the court makes at trial.

5 ALTERNATIVE DISPUTE RESOLUTION

Relevant parts of the CPR and its PDs: 1, 7, 24, 26, and 44

5.1 INTRODUCTION

Alternative dispute resolution has been available in this country for many years, and has now become an important and necessary consideration as an alternative to litigation. The court now has a duty, as part of its active management of cases, to further the overriding objective, which includes, under CPR 1.4(2)(e), encouraging ADR as a method of dispute resolution.

This chapter will deal with the methods by which the Civil Procedure Rules (CPR) encourage parties to settle their disputes at an early stage and, ultimately, without proceeding to trial. It will also look at the methods of dispute resolution that may be available, including a more detailed look at the most common of them. This chapter covers:

- the different types of ADR;
- the integration of ADR into the CPR;
- the philosophy of ADR; and
- a detailed look at mediation.

5.2 A DEFINITION OF ALTERNATIVE DISPUTE RESOLUTION (ADR)

There is no single overarching definition of ADR, but it has been said that a starting premise must be that it is a voluntary process and must therefore be consented to by the parties to a dispute. However, the Glossary to the CPR defines ADR simply as a 'collective description of methods of resolving disputes otherwise than through the normal trial process'. These descriptions are of limited help, because it appears that they exclude negotiations and any type of process which is not voluntary.

For the purposes of this manual, we seek to include the most prevalent ADR processes. All of these are looked at in this chapter.

5.3 THE DIFFERENT TYPES OF ADR

5.3.1 NEGOTIATIONS, OR ROUND TABLE DISCUSSIONS

Whether you negotiate over the telephone or arrange a meeting to sit around a table to try to resolve a dispute, this can be done at any time, but should always be conducted on a 'without prejudice' basis. The legal representative for each party usually carries out telephone negotiations. 'Round table' meetings more commonly involve each party attending with his legal representative and, possibly, counsel. Breaks can be taken during the negotiation to give each party the opportunity to have confidential discussions with its legal team.

This forum gives the client the opportunity to have his case aired, and to appreciate the strengths and weakness of his opponent's case. It is usually—but not always—the first step taken in trying to resolve a dispute before proceeding with one of the other alternatives listed here.

This is a non-adjudicative form of dispute resolution.

5.3.2 MEDIATION

The process of mediation is confidential and conducted without prejudice to impending or continuing litigation between parties. It may take place at any time before or during litigation and can normally be set up at very short notice, although, like other forms of negotiation, the timing may be critical. The process is also non-binding until a final written agreement has been signed by the parties. The parties can walk away from it at any time before a settlement is concluded, although the court may, to a degree, investigate their behaviour during any mediation, as well as their attitude towards it.

The parties appoint a neutral intermediary who endeavours to facilitate a settlement. The mediator does not act as judge or arbitrator, nor does he rule on the merits and neither will he suggest or impose the settlement terms. Rather, by shuttling between the parties, exploring their positions, and bringing them together as and when appropriate, the mediator helps the parties to find common ground. As the settlement emerges from consensus, one of the key advantages is that the parties then 'own' the settlement and do not see it as having been forced upon them by a court or third party.

It is often capable of achieving commercially sensible solutions, which can leave both parties satisfied—not something that a court decision following great expenditure and a 'gloves off' approach can often achieve. The solution may also be in the form of relief that the court itself had no power to order. If successful, it will probably be a great deal cheaper than a trial. Even if unsuccessful, both parties are likely to benefit by knowing more about the strengths and weaknesses of each other's position, and this may promote settlement at a later date.

There is no formal regulation of mediation as yet in this country, but the Civil Mediation Council exists to drive mediation forward in the UK in terms of accreditation of mediators. The EU Mediation Directive has, however, defined five key provisions relating to mediation in cross-border disputes for civil and commercial matters. It is the authors' view that mediation in the UK complies with the Directive.

This is a non-adjudicative form of dispute resolution.

5.3.3 CONCILIATION

As with mediation, conciliation is based on a neutral intermediary liaising with the parties, but usually the conciliator will be more proactive and may suggest his own solutions. This method of dispute resolution is common in employment disputes, often through the Advisory, Conciliation and Arbitration Service (ACAS).

This is a non-adjudicative form of dispute resolution.

5.3.4 THE EXECUTIVE TRIBUNAL

The 'executive table' is usually used to resolve commercial disputes. A panel is formed from senior representatives of the parties who have not themselves been involved in the dispute. The representatives sit together with a neutral adviser. The process is similar to a mini-trial, although, in reality, it is not a trial at all. The parties present their cases to the executives, who then have an opportunity to evaluate the respective claims. Rather than making a determination, however, the panel members then retire and endeavour to negotiate a settlement on a commercial basis. If the executives struggle to come to an agreement, the independent adviser issues a non-binding advisory opinion.

This is a non-adjudicative form of dispute resolution.

5.3.5 EARLY NEUTRAL EVALUATION (ENE)

Under early neutral evaluation (ENE), a third party—usually an independent legal representative or a judge as permitted by CPR 3.1—considers the issues and advises on the likely outcome. If a judge is chosen to provide the evaluation, he will not determine the action if it goes ahead. Having the view of an independent arbiter, respected by both parties, may then act as a spur to settlement—or at least enable the parties to re-evaluate their cases or appreciate the critical issues and the likely outcome if they do not settle.

This is a non-adjudicative form of dispute resolution.

5.3.6 JUDICIAL OR EXPERT DETERMINATION

If pursuing judicial or expert determination, the parties jointly instruct and make written submissions to a senior judge (often one who has retired) or Queen's Counsel (QC), who then makes a written appraisal. The parties are required to agree the form and extent of the instruction in advance, and whether the appraisal is to be binding or not. It is extremely important that the client understands the nature and extent of the instruction, especially if it is to be binding, because this will ultimately determine the case. These decisions cannot generally be appealed, but can be challenged on limited grounds—usually where the expert has materially departed from his instructions. Legal representatives must therefore exercise great care when drafting the instructions or 'mandate' to the expert determiner.

In practice, expert determination can be on a preliminary issue, such as liability, leaving the parties to negotiate or mediate the quantum part of the claim.

This is a form of adjudicative dispute resolution.

5.3.7 ARBITRATION

Arbitration features heavily in many industries, including the construction and football arenas, and appears commonly as the dispute resolution clause in many national and international commercial agreements. The 1996 Arbitration Act governs current arbitration practice in this country, and introduces mandatory and non-mandatory provisions.

The arbitrator is usually a solicitor, barrister, architect, or quantity surveyor, who conducts the arbitration on a private basis according to a timetable set by him in discussion with the parties, with a view to coming to a final and binding decision known as a 'final award'. The process involves meetings between the arbitrator and the parties, as well as the presentation of statements of case, written submissions, and documentary evidence.

Once the award has been made, the arbitrator does not release it until he has been paid by the parties. The award can be enforced in the High Court if not paid, or set aside by a High Court judge on the application of the disgruntled party to a specialist division of the High Court.

The main features of arbitration are that it is expensive, as is litigation, because you must use an expert arbitrator, and it can be fairly long-running as a dispute resolution process. However, your client may have no option but to arbitrate if there is a valid arbitration clause in the contract and, if this is the case, litigation cannot be considered (unless both parties agree). The common practical effect of this is that if a party attempts to litigate a matter where there is a valid contractual arbitration clause, then the opponent can usually apply to the High Court under s. 9 of the Arbitration Act 1996 to stay proceedings whilst the arbitration continues.

This is a form of adjudicative dispute resolution.

5.3.8 ADJUDICATION

If adjudication is pursued, either by virtue of a contractual term, agreement between parties, or pursuant to the Housing Grants, Construction and Regeneration Act 1996, as amended by the Local Democracy, Economic Development and Construction Act 2009, a party serves on his opponent a 'notice of intention to proceed to adjudication' and nominates an adjudicator (usually a surveyor, architect, engineer, solicitor, or barrister). The adjudicator will issue directions on paper as to when full written submissions are to be made to him. These submissions are known as the 'referral notice' on the part of the party who commences and the 'response to referral' on the part of the defending party. The adjudicator may require a site inspection or a directions hearing. There are strict time limits imposed under the 1996 Act (as amended), which regulates the principles of adjudication.

The most important features of adjudication are that:

- the contract must be a 'construction' contract;
- there must be a dispute to refer, not only a difference—that is, a dispute can arise only once the subject matter of a claim, issue, or other matter has been brought to the attention of the opposing party, and that party has had an opportunity to consider, admit, modify, or reject it;
- the adjudicator must come to his written decision within 28 days of the service of the referral notice (subject to a short extension if agreed);
- the adjudicator has limited jurisdiction on costs, dependent on whether the parties have agreed to confer jurisdiction on the adjudicator to award costs, therefore each party must bear its own costs, no matter who is successful; and

- the adjudicator's decision is binding unless and until it is appealed to the High Court. As such, the losing party must comply with the decision until such time as it may be appealed. If he does not, then an application for a CPR 24 summary judgment can be made.

This process is frequently used in construction and engineering disputes both between contracting parties and professional advisers, such as architects and engineers. There are exclusions as to the type of contract to which this process can apply—notably, domestic building matters and food processing plants, to name but a few.

This is a form of adjudicative dispute resolution.

Table 5.1 at the end of this chapter offers a summary of some of the advantages and disadvantages of the different types of ADR process to help you to identify which method is most appropriate for your client. The summary is not, however, exhaustive.

The most commonly used process as an alternative to litigation in England and Wales for general civil disputes is *mediation*, and, for this reason, much of this chapter will focus on mediation as a form of dispute resolution.

5.4 **THE BENEFITS OF ADR**

Litigation conducted in an adversarial and combative manner can prove time-consuming and expensive. The process can last many months, or even years, and because the parties are vying to 'win', litigation can end up driving them further apart. The parties become focused on seizing the tactical initiative and undermining each other's case in whatever way they can. In this way, the parties can sometimes forget, if they were in a commercial relationship, why they were in business together in the first place.

Whilst the media hype concerning ADR can sometimes give the mistaken impression that ADR is a panacea, it is true that ADR does have a number of major attractions.

- ADR (save for arbitration)—and mediation in particular—is relatively inexpensive by comparison with litigation.

- Most forms of ADR, in terms of the final meeting or hearing, rarely take more than a day or two, although complex arbitrations can be lengthy.

- Because non-adjudicative ADR is not based on 'winners' and 'losers', it tends to encourage the parties to talk more freely. The intention is to provide the parties with a neutral, non-threatening, and totally confidential environment in which they can explore their respective cases, as well as their business relationship.

- ADR, save for arbitration and adjudication, is more flexible than litigation. The basis of any settlement arrived at is not limited by the legal remedies available from the courts; rather, settlements can be used to regulate the parties' relationship in the future. For example, a party who has suffered loss arising from a breach of contract may be prepared to forgo the normal legal remedy of damages in return for more preferential trading terms going forward. This may be particularly important if the defendant does not actually have the means in the immediate future to meet an expensive damages claim, in which case a victory at trial is likely to be a pyrrhic one.

- Many forms of ADR (again save for arbitration and adjudication)—notably mediations—are conducted in total confidence and on a 'without prejudice' basis. Therefore, the content of the settlement discussions cannot (although there are exceptions) be disclosed to a court or to other third parties. This contrasts with the open arena in which litigation is conducted and the media publicity that is often attendant.

- Many forms of ADR (save for arbitration and adjudication) are only possible if both parties agree and, unless the parties choose otherwise, settlements cannot be imposed on them.

Only once a settlement is reached does it become binding. Before that time, the parties can withdraw or revert to litigation. In litigation, the parties are bound by the rulings of the court, however unfair they consider them to be.

- The whole purpose of ADR is to promote early settlement. Even if it does not achieve this aim, it will often provide the parties with a better understanding of the psychology of their opponent and the issues that they see as important. This knowledge may prove useful in any subsequent settlement negotiations.

The key words are therefore: speed, flexibility, cost, consensus, confidentiality, and settlement.

5.5 THE ENCOURAGEMENT OF ADR

Having established that ADR is a 'good thing'—that is, a useful tool in the armoury of dispute resolution—how are the parties and their legal representatives being encouraged to use it? There is provision and scope for ADR during the Pre-Action Protocol period, and the CPR also give guidance and direction on the use of ADR within proceedings. HM Courts and Tribunals Service has also made strides to help mediation as a form of ADR become more accessible to parties. Commercially ADR is becoming more intrinsic in 'business to consumer' disputes both within the UK and the EU.

5.5.1 ADR AND THE PROTOCOLS

A standardized approach has been undertaken for all Pre-Action Protocols, including the Practice Direction on Pre-Action Conduct and Protocols. They all embody similar paragraphs requiring the parties to consider whether ADR is appropriate and, if so, in what form, warning that the court may, at a subsequent hearing, require evidence that ADR was considered pre issue. Each Protocol and the Practice Direction on Pre-Action Conduct and Protocols summarizes the appropriate ADR methods, which are commonly discussion and negotiation, and mediation.

 Practical Considerations

Best practice suggests that a degree of discussion with your opponent should be attempted in advance of any type of ADR. This could take the form of a 'without prejudice' chat or negotiations with your opponent's legal representative over the telephone, or a face-to-face discussion and a Part 36 offer.

5.5.2 ADR AND THE CPR

Judicial encouragement of ADR is now prevalent in the CPR. Proceedings can be stayed if the parties wish to attempt ADR and/or the court considers ADR to be appropriate. The CPR encourage the use of ADR in the following ways and at the following prescribed stages of litigation—but remember that the Court Guides for High Court matters also deal with the divisional courts' requirements for ADR.

5.5.2.1 Staying proceedings for ADR after filing Directions Questionnaires

In all Part 7 claims (for a definition of a Part 7 claim see Chapter 9, paragraph 9.3), after the defendant has served its defence, a court officer will provisionally track the claim and then serve a Notice of Proposed Allocation. This Notice, amongst other things, requires the parties to complete a Directions Questionnaire (DQ) in either form N180, for cases in the small claims track, or form N181 for cases in the fast track and multi-track (for the detailed rules, see CPR 26.3 and Chapter 12). The DQ asks the parties specifically about settlement and whether they would like a one-month stay (or such a period as the court deems appropriate) in which to attempt to settle the case by ADR or other means (CPR 26.4(1)).

If all of the parties request a stay, or the court, of its own initiative, considers that such a stay would be appropriate, the court will direct that the proceedings be stayed for at least a month (CPR 26.4(2)). Judicial comments published to date indicate that if one of the parties requests a stay in order to attempt ADR and the party opposing a stay cannot show good reasons why ADR is unlikely to work, the court is likely to order a stay.

Where a stay is ordered, the onus is then on the claimant to notify the court if a settlement is reached. If no notification is given by the end of the period of the stay, the court will go on to make such directions as to the management of the case as it considers appropriate.

5.5.2.2 Case management conferences (CMCs) and pre-trial requirements

Even if ADR is not attempted at the DQ stage of the proceedings, the door remains open to a reference to ADR, and possibly a stay of the litigation for that purpose, throughout the litigation process.

Intrinsic to current-day litigation is the concept of 'case management'. It therefore seems likely that the courts will ask parties attending case management conferences (CMCs) whether they have attempted ADR and to justify their position if not.

The point of raising ADR on all of those occasions is to ensure that alternatives to litigation receive proper consideration. It will no longer be sufficient to tick the box in the DQ, indicating that ADR has been considered or rejected as unsuitable. On occasions such as the first CMC and the pre-trial hearing, you should be prepared to explain, in some detail, why your client does not consider ADR to be appropriate or, possibly, why it was tried and failed (without exceeding the realms of confidentiality).

 Practical Considerations

Best practice would suggest that in cases involving many parties, in which the availability of individuals attending an ADR process final meeting or hearing is difficult to coordinate, the court is generally agreeable to granting stays for ADR for periods of three to six months.

 Practical Considerations

ADR in practice is more overarching than the Protocols and CPR actually suggest, because ADR can effectively take place at any time. It is not limited to the Protocol phase, or to points in an action dictated by CMCs or pre-trial matters. Mediation, for example, can take place during lengthy trials. The key point here is that, as a legal representative, you should be constantly considering when and how and what form of ADR can be used to avoid trial and/or judgment.

5.5.3 ADR AND HM COURTS AND TRIBUNALS SERVICE

A number of County Court hearing centres in England and Wales have piloted and set up voluntary mediation schemes for fast, and multi-track cases, but not all hearing centres offer these schemes.

The way in which these schemes operate in fast and multi-track cases is that, on the filing of a defence to a two-party action, the court writes to the parties asking if they will agree to submit to a fixed three- or four-hour mediation for a fast- or multi-track case at court, usually to take place outside court hours and therefore between 4 p.m. and 8 p.m. for a fixed fee per party.

If both parties agree, the court allows the mediation to take place in the court building, with both parties attending, along with an accredited mediator. The process is wholly independent from the court and, if settlement is reached, a consent order is drawn up there and then, and placed with the court file to be sealed, and the action comes to an end.

If settlement is not reached, the court file is returned to the court for consideration by the district judge.

However, in all small claims, on the filing of the DQ (here in form N180) where the parties have both indicated a desire to attempt mediation in claims of less than £10,000, the court will ask the parties if they are willing to participate in a telephone mediation for up to one hour at a time to suit the parties and the appointed mediator. Should settlement ensue, a consent order is drawn up the following day, signed by the parties and submitted to the court to bring the action to an end. Should settlement not occur, then the mediator will inform the court and the matter will be listed for a final hearing to be adjudged either orally or on paper. See Chapter 9, paragraph 9.2.1.2 for further details.

5.5.4 ADR AND COST CONSEQUENCES

A party who refuses to enter into an ADR process may well be penalized in costs if the matter proceeds to trial and they are successful. They may not secure a costs order in their favour. In deciding the level of costs to award at trial, the court must have regard to 'the efforts made, if any, before and during the proceedings in order to try and resolve the dispute' (CPR 44.4(3)(a)(ii)).

There have been many costs awards made based on a party's refusal to mediate and what is to be taken into account by the court. The most prominent of these was *Dunnett v Railtrack* [2002] 2 All ER 850, which was the first case in the courts to seriously penalize a successful party for refusing to mediate appropriately, and *Halsey v Milton Keynes NHS Trust* [2004] EWCA Civ 576, which still provides the most comprehensive guidelines on what the court will take into account when assessing whether a party was justified in refusing to mediate.

The court will consider in such circumstances:

- the nature of the dispute;
- the merits of the case;
- the extent to which other settlement methods were attempted;
- whether the cost of ADR would be disproportionately high;
- whether any delay in setting up the ADR would have been prejudicial; and
- whether ADR had reasonable prospects of success.

Over the years since *Halsey*, the courts have made some important extensions as follows:
- The Court of Appeal extended the *Halsey* principle to cover a failure to engage with mediation at all. It held in *PGF II v OMFS Company 1 Ltd* [2013] EWCA Civ 1288 that, as a general rule, a failure to respond at all to an invitation to participate in ADR is in itself unreasonable, regardless of whether there was a good reason for refusing ADR. This case therefore sends a clear message: reject mediation if inappropriate, but engage with the idea. Simply not responding to an invitation to mediate, as in this case, puts the successful 'refusing' party at risk of not recovering a proportion of his costs.

- The High Court in *Reid v Buckinghamshire Healthcare NHS Trust* [2015] EWHC B21 (Costs) (28 October 2015) held that the costs sanctions which may follow when a party unreasonably refuses to mediate can apply equally where the party refusing to mediate is the losing party. In this case the losing party was ordered to pay the winning party's costs on the indemnity basis as the penalty.

- In the case of *Northrop Grumman Mission Systems Europe Ltd v BAE Systems (Al Diriyah C4i) Ltd* [2014] EWHC 2955, despite BAE's contention that they had an extremely strong case, their refusal to mediate was still held to be unreasonable because they ignored the positive effect that a mediator can bring to the resolution of the dispute. Well-trained mediators can use their evaluation skills to find solutions that had not been previously considered and that are not able to be ordered by the court. In essence what the court has indicated is that the mediator can bring a different perspective to dispute resolution and to ignore that is tantamount to acting unreasonably in the circumstances. It is still unlikely however, that such a party would be ordered to pay his opponent's costs, as that penalty is still regarded as draconian. The imposition of an adverse costs order on a successful party who either refused or ignored an invitation to mediate is still inherently at the discretion of the court.

Practical Considerations

Best practice would suggest that it is a question of knowing the strengths and weaknesses of your client's case, and balancing those with proportionality in terms of time and costs. It is not simply a matter of railroading your client's case to trial if it is strong, but nor is it necessary to agree to an ADR process where it is clearly inappropriate. Examples of the former would be if, rather than risk trial, you were to consider an application for summary judgment or a strike-out at an early stage (where your opponent's case is weak or misconceived); an example of the latter would be if you were to evaluate your client's conduct against the Halsey guidelines: perhaps where mediation is sought within weeks of the trial date, or negotiations had been suggested and refused, or the client feels it has a particularly strong case. In these instances, cases that predated *Northrop* had suggested that a refusal to mediate could be reasonable. But the situations where this is likely to be the case are ever decreasing. In any event, it is apparent that, as a matter of course, all members of the legal profession should now routinely consider with their clients whether their disputes are suitable for ADR and ensure their clients understand what the court may consider as a reasonable or unreasonable refusal to mediate. In view of the extent of the cost consequences, it is advisable that this is evidenced in writing.

Costs

There should be clear documentary evidence (attendance note or letter) on your file of the occasions on which you considered ADR with your client and your opponent. The suggestion of ADR can be a very useful and valuable weapon to use to attempt to defeat an application for costs, even if that party has lost the litigation.

5.5.5 THE MEDIATION HANDBOOK

In the quest to continue educating legal representatives and clients alike on the benefits of ADR, The Mediation Handbook has been described as a 'neutral, authoritative manual', which aims to provide a practical guide to using mediation for both legal representatives and clients, as well as guidance for identifying cases that may be suitable for mediation. It includes:

- an insight into the role of the mediator;
- sample mediation documents; and
- a list of Civil Mediation Council (CMC) accredited mediation providers.

The Mediation Handbook is frequently referred to in judgments by the courts when they consider contentions that a party has unreasonably refused to mediate. It is therefore suggested that legal practitioners should familiarize themselves with its contents.

5.5.6 LEGISLATION AND ADR

The ADR Directive requires British businesses to ensure that ADR is available for any contractual dispute between a consumer and a business. In addition, the ODR Regulation provides for the establishment of an online dispute resolution (ODR) platform to assist consumers in resolving disputes with retailers in relation to contracts for the sale of goods and services within the EU.

5.6 IS ADR ALWAYS SUITABLE IN DISPUTE RESOLUTION?

ADR may not be appropriate to resolve every dispute. Consider the following:

- A client's commercial objectives may be best achieved by embarking on litigation. The commencement of proceedings may exert more pressure, at least initially, than a suggestion that the parties attempt ADR.

- The litigation may be necessary because the prime remedy needed is an emergency injunction, which can only be obtained from the courts, or because the parties are looking for a definitive court ruling on a particular issue in order to establish a binding precedent (public interest).

- There may be little point in delaying litigation if the opposing side is not yet ready to talk settlement in realistic terms, for example, where there is no final prognosis available in a personal injury case.

- Your client's case may be strong enough to justify an application for summary judgment. In those circumstances, pursuing the litigation by way of an interim application route may well result in a quicker conclusion or settlement than a reference to ADR.

Even if ADR is considered appropriate, there may be a particular type of ADR that is best suited to a client's case or in which the client may achieve a tactical advantage. Likewise, the timing of a reference to ADR may itself be a delicate matter. Whilst there is now a duty imposed on all parties to a dispute to consider ADR pre-issue, sometimes, ADR will be most effective after litigation has progressed to a point at which the issues have been crystallized in the statements of case. These can be difficult decisions that need to be taken on a case-by-case basis. All legal representatives need to be trained to assist clients in making the right decision in line with their personal and commercial objectives.

5.7 PREPARATION FOR ADR GENERALLY

As is apparent from this chapter, from the outset of any dispute, the parties should now actively consider whether ADR is likely to be of benefit and, if so, how the process is to be handled. This is an exercise that is likely to involve the client and legal representative collaborating closely, since the issues are likely to be commercial, or personal, as well as legal. Even if a client is intractably opposed to ADR, it can no longer bury its head in the sand and ignore it: if it cannot justify its opposition, it may well find itself penalized in costs, as suggested earlier.

So what issues need to be considered at the outset?

1. A realistic appraisal of the case is essential, because ADR is likely to be ineffective if the key issues have not been identified and evaluated. As part of this process, the legal representative and client need to consider any commercial and/or personal objectives and whether they might be better achieved by ADR or litigation. The likely costs, timescale, and pressure points may all have a bearing here.

2. Careful consideration needs to be given to any settlement discussions to date, the likely readiness of the opposing side to negotiate realistically, and the timing of any attempt at ADR. Reconsider the points made in paragraph 5.6: if ADR is a possibility, the merits of the different types of ADR should be considered. (Table 5.1 at the end of this chapter may assist.)

3. If some form of intermediary, mediator, expert, or judge is needed, the identity of that person should be discussed. Does the intermediary require expert knowledge of a particular field to grasp the issues, or would a generalist be better suited? Does the legal representative already know a suitably qualified individual, or would it be better to

approach one of the leading ADR bodies or courts? Can agreement be reached with the opposition regarding the appointment of the intermediary?

4. The selection of the ADR team to represent a client and/or prepare submissions for the client also requires careful planning. Usually, it will be the client and the legal representative in attendance, but consideration should be given to whether an expert, counsel, or witnesses may be required. (These would only ever be necessary to clarify issues.)

5. Finally, the negotiation strategy needs to be thought through in advance and parties who have not experienced ADR before should be informed about the process, so that they are not caught unawares. Clearly, your strategy and tactics may vary once the process gets underway and depending on how it develops, so it is important to remain flexible and open minded.

5.8 MEDIATION AS A FORM OF ALTERNATIVE DISPUTE RESOLUTION

Mediation is becoming more predominant in dispute resolution both within our own jurisdiction and in Europe. The Mediation Directive, in this regard, applies to European cross-border disputes (rather than disputes arising within any one member state such as the UK) and was implemented by May 2011. Many of its regulations are similar in essence to mediation practice in this country.

The remainder of this chapter will concentrate on aspects of mediation in practice within the UK that are important to bear in mind when conducting a piece of litigation and when advising a client.

5.8.1 THE INTERPLAY OF MEDIATION AND LITIGATION

Mediation is a flexible process and can therefore be used at any time: before proceedings are issued, during proceedings, even during a lengthy trial. However, whilst the ethos of the CPR was to encourage the use of ADR and mediation in particular, some thought is required as to the exact timing of the mediation.

It may be the case that there are glaring evidential gaps in relation to liability, causation, and quantum, such as experts' reports to help to assess responsibility and value. Without such a report, it would be pointless to try to compromise any of those issues, because agreement could only ever be 'subject to' its findings. The main focus of mediation is to resolve disputes more quickly and cheaply than litigation. This may not be the case if mediation is entered into too early.

5.8.2 THE COST OF MEDIATION

One of the advantages of mediation is that there will be cost savings if resolution is reached. There will also be time savings to the client, whether it is a personal or commercial matter. The cost and time savings will be greater the sooner mediation is entered into (subject to it being an appropriate time to mediate), compared to proceeding through to trial.

However, there is still a cost implication to the client in entering into mediation and, depending on the value of the claim, it could even be seen as disproportionate to mediate. Nevertheless, even if this is the case, it will be wholly disproportionate to litigate. The client must therefore not be misled on the benefits of mediation and, whilst it is considerably cheaper and quicker than litigation, the costs of the mediator are borne jointly and severally between the parties. A party's legal representative's time, the preparation, and any expenses must be met by that party (subject to any agreement reached during the mediation itself).

Mediators are usually either solicitors or barristers, or other professionals, such as architects, surveyors, and engineers, who have been specially trained by accredited bodies such as the Centre for Dispute Resolution (CEDR)—http://www.cedr.com—and the ADR Group (ADRg)—http://www.adrgroup.co.uk. These accredited bodies can be contacted to find a suitable mediator or, alternatively, individuals can be approached directly. The Civil Mediation Council has set up an online Mediation Directory, which allows users to search for civil mediator providers by county at http://www.civilmediation.justice.gov.uk/.

The mediator's fees are usually based on a fixed fee for a day or half a day and are dependent on experience. The piloted schemes mentioned in paragraph 5.5.3 are subject to a nominal fixed fee payable by the parties to the court, although each party is still bound by its retainer with its own legal representative in respect of the preparation for, and attendance at, the mediation.

5.8.3 HOW DO YOU 'SELL' MEDIATION TO YOUR CLIENT?

The following are some of the major selling points of mediation of which the client should perhaps be made aware at a meeting when the ADR options are being discussed.

- It has been said that mediation leads to a sudden outbreak of common sense, because the aim of mediation is to solve problems, not to find fault—that is, what the client actually wants and can live with, as opposed to what the issues are in the case.

- Mediation provides the forum to 'get things off your chest'. Sitting down face to face with the opponent and telling them what has happened, and the effect that the wrongdoing or breach has had, goes a long way to diffusing the situation and sets the stage for the real work of reaching a settlement.

- Mediation also provides the equivalent for the client of a day in court. Whilst it is an informal and private process with an impartial third party present, the client feels that, within the four walls, he is telling the world that he has been wronged. The presence of the mediator seems to fulfil the client's emotional need in this regard.

- It gives the client the chance to see his case unfold before the mediator and his opponent, and to acknowledge the strengths and weaknesses of both parties' cases. It also gives the client an opportunity to see his legal representative in action, because it is usually the legal representative who conducts the opening statement on behalf of the client. The client has a chance to see his case being presented and feels as though something is finally happening.

- Mediation gives each party an opportunity to hear its opponent's case, facts, and issues. The key point here is that all of the parties hear the same information even if they perceive it differently. It is then the mediator's job to define and clarify certain facts and issues.

- Mediation has a way of unearthing the real issues in a case. Sometimes, this requires some digging around by the mediator to get to the root of the problem, because it has been masked by ancillary ones.

5.8.4 WHAT DOES THE CLIENT NEED TO KNOW ABOUT MEDIATION?

The client needs to know full details of the mediation process, including preparation and procedure, how long is required, and what it can achieve in terms of time and cost savings. The length of the mediation will determine the cost, and therefore thought should be given to whether a full day is, in fact, necessary, or whether a shorter period—for example, five hours—would suffice. However long the mediation day is anticipated to last, it is always worthwhile blocking out time in your own and your client's diaries in case it should overrun. It would undermine the process if progress were to be made towards settlement during the mediation day, but the parties have to leave for other commitments.

It is often appropriate, when discussing mediation with the client, to provide details of the costs incurred to the date of the prospective mediation and an estimate of costs to trial. The client may already have had this costs information if the claim is a multi-track case, as it is likely that a costs budget has been or will need to be prepared in any event, as examined in Chapter 4 at paragraph 4.6.3. It would also be advisable to undertake a risk analysis on the prospects of success and proportionality.

It is, however, very important—especially for those who are new to the mediation process—that the client understands what he will achieve. The client should not be led to have enhanced expectations about a 'victory' at the hands of his opponent. Mediation is not about 'point scoring'; rather, it is about getting on with life and business, and laying the dispute to rest.

As such, it is the legal representative's job to manage those expectations. Mediation is about compromise and it is very unlikely that as matters settle at mediation, either party will be elated with the outcome. It is, however, still a preferable process than proceeding to trial, at which a third party, the judge, decides the case for the parties, and at which there is always a 'winner' and 'loser' on the issues in the case.

5.8.5 PREPARATION FOR THE MEDIATION DAY

5.8.5.1 The appointment of the mediator

The parties may be able to agree on a known individual to act as mediator. Alternatively, they may approach one of the recognized mediation bodies to obtain a list of possible candidates to act as mediator, as set out in paragraph 5.8.2. Consideration should be given to whether the mediator needs specialist skills and whether a legal or other professional is required. Sometimes, the appointment of joint mediators may be appropriate. The urgency of the mediation may, of course, determine which mediators are available. Curricula vitae (CVs) are usually requested, along with dates of availability.

online resource centre

Once the parties have agreed on the identity of the mediator, he is informed and contacts both parties simultaneously to confirm his appointment. Most mediators or mediation bodies will require the parties to enter into a mediation agreement. Each party enters into the agreement with the mediator in advance of the mediation day, although it is common that these are left for signing on the morning of the mediation. The agreement will usually cover some basic ground rules, which predominantly include confidentiality and fees. A sample mediation agreement can be seen on the Online Resource Centre.

5.8.5.2 Procedural steps

5.8.5.2.1 *The mediator's requirements*

On the agreed appointment of the mediator, the mediator will write to the parties simultaneously, confirming his understanding as to who they and their legal representatives are, when and where the mediation is to take place, the anticipated duration of the process, and his specific requirements as to documentation. It is very important that a person with authority to settle from each party is present at the mediation. It is frustrating if that person has only a limited authority, although having a client representative at the end of the telephone is a better alternative.

5.8.5.2.2 *The position statement*

The mediator will usually require a position statement as part of the specific documentation from each party. These will be copied to the opposite party and the mediator seven days before the mediation (although this time limit varies in practice). The parties need to consider who will be responsible for the preparation of these submissions and, frequently, this is a role assigned to the legal representative. Generally, mediators will want submissions kept fairly short, giving only a summary of the case and each party's stance in relation to the issues.

 Practical Considerations

The parties should try to agree a core bundle of documents to send to the mediator along with the position statements, because this limits the amount of reading time. The preparation of the core bundle will usually fall to the party who would be the claimant in any litigation.

5.8.5.2.3 *Preliminary discussions with the mediator*

Before the day of the mediation, the mediator may wish to discuss with the parties or their lawyers any difficulties that he has with his understanding of the case, the manner in which the initial presentation of their cases is to be made, and possibly details of any previous failed settlement attempts. These discussions are confidential to each party.

It also gives the mediator a chance to get to know the legal representatives or client ahead of the day, and this will ultimately save time and money. These discussions are usually done over the telephone, but are not always necessary.

5.8.6 **THE MEDIATION DAY(S)**

The following describes the likely procedure during a mediation day. However, it is import-ant to remember that each mediation day is different and that the discretion lies with the mediator as to how it is conducted. For example, if the relationship between the parties was particularly acrimonious, the mediator may decide to dispense with the opening joint session or to curtail it significantly.

5.8.6.1 The initial joint meeting

The mediation may take place at a neutral venue or at one of the party's legal representa-tive's offices. Once the mediator is ready, the parties will be called into a room, where the mediator will outline the mediation process and establish the ground rules. It is at this stage that the parties or their legal representatives will normally be asked to make short opening statements of their cases. In essence, this will amount to a short summary of the written submissions, again with a view to clarifying the issues in the case. An opening joint session can be seen on the Online Resource Centre video clips.

online resource centre

5.8.6.1.1 *Private 'caucuses' or 'sessions'*

Once the submissions are complete, the mediator may choose to keep the parties together or to invite them into separate rooms, where they can speak privately. These private meetings are called 'caucuses' and nothing said in caucus can be revealed to the other side without the permission of the party in caucus. The caucuses are useful means of exploring the busi-ness relationship between the parties, of finding out where they are coming from, flushing out the issues that each side sees as key, and perhaps looking at why previous settlements have failed.

The mediator may well engage in 'shuttle diplomacy', moving between rooms in a series of private sessions, looking for common ground or areas in which the parties feel able to make movement.

5.8.6.1.2 *Joint meetings*

The mediator will not simply wish to act as messenger for the parties. At times during the process, the parties may be brought together for joint meetings so that they can negotiate directly or tackle issues that are proving to be a stumbling block. Likewise, the mediator may wish to meet with the legal representative or the experts separately, or to meet with the parties in the absence of their lawyers. The process is voluntary, however, and the mediator cannot compel a party to do anything with which he does not feel comfortable.

5.8.6.1.3 *The settlement*

If the mediation results in a settlement, the mediator will normally be keen to have the terms written up into a formal agreement there and then. This may be a task delegated to the parties' legal representatives or it may be something that the mediator takes on. It is normally desirable to record the agreement in writing as soon as terms are agreed and whilst there is still an impetus to settle. Once the settlement has been written up and the parties have signed up to it, it becomes binding and can be enforced in the usual way through the courts as examined in the Onlinel Chapter 'Enforcement of Judgments'. A closing settle-ment meeting can be seen on the Online Resource Centre video clips.

online resource centre

KEY POINTS SUMMARY

- Consider ADR seriously—if it is not to be tried, have a good reason why not and, even if it gets rejected early on, do not be afraid to reconsider later.

- Change your mindset—aim for resolution, not a judicial determination.

- Understand the different types of ADR and which one may be best suited to the client's case.

- The CPR expect parties to engage with ADR and there can be cost penalties for an unreasonable refusal to consider ADR.

- Consider when is best to mediate. It will be different in every case.

- Make sure that your client understands what he can expect from mediation and curtail those enhanced expectations.

- Be prepared for mediation in terms of written submissions and documents. Whilst mediation is a flexible process, there is no excuse for sloppy or inaccurate presentation.

- If settlement is achieved, ensure that the agreement or order drafted is legally binding and enforceable.

SELF-TEST QUESTIONS

1. What type of ADR process is voluntary but imposes a decision on the parties?

2. How can mediation in low-value cases be used effectively and proportionately?

online
resource
centre

Suggested answers to these self-test questions can be found in the Student Resources section of the Online Resource Centre.

TABLE 5.1 A COMPARISON OF ADR PROCESSES

Type of ADR process	Positive features	Negative features	Common use in
Negotiation/round table discussions	Voluntary, without prejudice, flexible, legal representation not essential, arranged at short notice, and inexpensive.	Inequality of parties and parties often become entrenched in their own positions.	All types of disputes at any stage.
Mediation	Voluntary, confidential, non-binding, proactive intervention of neutral third party, ascertains what your opponent really wants, free to leave at any time, can be arranged quickly, and cheaper than proceeding to trial.	Both parties must be willing to make it work and there is still a cost implication to the parties.	All types of disputes (save for test cases) at any stage even during trial. Can also be used either consecutively or concurrently with adjudication if appropriate.
Conciliation	Voluntary, without prejudice, proactive intervention of independent third party, gain a better understanding of opponent's dispute.	Usually no formal written submissions required and this can sometimes hamper the process by clouding issues.	Usually a precondition in many contracts to arbitration or litigation and is common in employment matters.

(contd.)

Type of ADR process	Positive features	Negative features	Common use in
Executive Tribunal	Voluntary and can be quick and effective. Very low cost implication.	The opinion does not have to be followed and the executives can remain entrenched in their respective positions.	Commercial matters with reasonably sized commercial entities.
ENE	Voluntary and non-binding, usually occurs early on in a dispute, focuses on central issues and relevant law only.	If a judge is wanted it may take time to arrange. Still, a cost implication as submissions and documentation needs to be prepared.	Larger technical building and engineering or commercial cases.
Expert Determination	Binding but voluntary process. Decision can be obtained quickly and written submissions are not onerous.	Decision cannot be enforced as a court judgment. A fresh action in contract would have to be raised. Selection of agreed expert and the limits of his instruction can be problematic.	In ongoing contract where there is an ongoing business relationship to preserve, mostly used in cases with technical issues.
Arbitration	Specialist arbiter to hear the case, private, can prohibit litigation, finality of award provides commercial certainty.	Expensive and time-consuming (similar to litigation) but award if unpaid can be easily enforced through the courts.	Construction and engineering claims.
Adjudication	Quick, choice of specialist adjudicator, adjudicator has no jurisdiction to award costs (less risk in a difficult case), retains a business relationship or ongoing contract thereby reducing disruption, private.	Adjudicator has no jurisdiction to award cost (limits recovery), no automatic right to interest, only binding until appealed, to enforce the decision you must issue fresh proceedings and apply for P24 Summary Judgment, costs implication on enforcement.	Construction and engineering claims, and some professional negligence claims. Can also be used either consecutively or concurrently with litigation if appropriate.

6 THE FIRST CLIENT MEETING AND INITIAL CONSIDERATIONS

Relevant parts of the CPR and its PDs: 7, 19, and 21

6.1 INTRODUCTION

As a legal representative new to practice, you will be expected initially to assist in clients' cases and ultimately to handle your own files. New cases for existing and new clients are usually fielded through an existing fee earner in the practice or through the firm's receptionist to the litigation (otherwise known as 'dispute resolution') department, where cases are allocated to the various fee earners. In smaller firms, this may mean only one or two fee earners.

In every new matter for every client, your professional conduct duties, particularly client care issues, should be at the forefront of your mind as a legal representative before you proceed to undertake any work for the client. These can be addressed to some degree in advance of the first attendance on the client.

The first meeting that you have with a new client is likely to take some time and there will usually be a number of action points that arise as a result of the meeting.

LITIGATION TRAIN: THE FIRST CLIENT INTERVIEW AND INITIAL CONSIDERATIONS

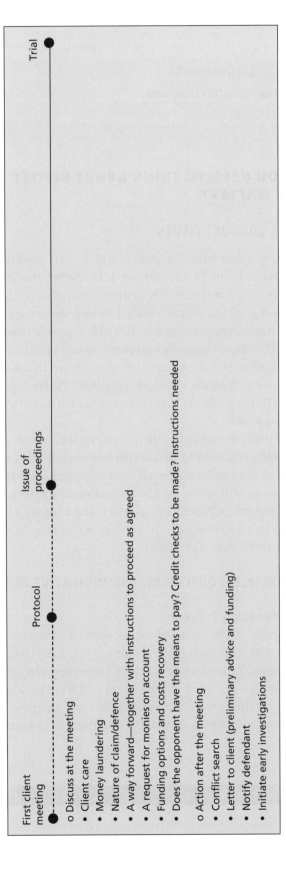

All of these aspects require you, as the legal representative, to spend time with, and incur a cost to, the client.

This chapter will focus on:

- professional conduct issues;
- client care;
- money laundering requirements;
- the first meeting with the client; and
- initial investigations.

6.2 WHAT DO YOU NEED TO THINK ABOUT BEFORE DEALING WITH EVERY NEW MATTER?

6.2.1 PROFESSIONAL CONDUCT ISSUES

As you are already aware from Chapters 1 and 3, your professional conduct duties, as a whole, are contained in the SRA Handbook 2011. We felt that it would be beneficial, however, if these were looked at specifically in the context of working in a litigation department so that you have a complete picture of what to look for as a legal representative and what to consider when acting in new matters. You will, however, need to consult the full text of the Code in the Handbook, partly because here we set out only those issues that will appear frequently in litigation, but also because we are not permitted, for copyright reasons, to replicate the Code in our manual. When we examined the Principles, Outcomes, and Indicative Behaviours (IBs) in Chapters 1 and 3, we considered how they are applied in practice on costs and funding issues.

Remember, at the beginning of every new matter for a client, and throughout the matter until its conclusion, you need to ensure that you comply with the relevant Principles and Outcomes and can refer to the suggested, or other appropriate, IBs.

In this section, we will reflect on the ten mandatory Principles again and will look at Chapter 1 on client care, Chapter 3 on conflict, and Chapter 4 on confidentiality and disclosure. These rules are looked at in the context of this chapter and the commencement of your relationship with your client only.

6.2.2 RELEVANT PRINCIPLES, OUTCOMES, AND INDICATIVE BEHAVIOURS

6.2.2.1 The ten mandatory Principles

You should consider, with these Principles in mind, whether you are the correct level of fee earner to deal with each matter, whether you have the appropriate expertise, and whether you can do the best for your client. Legal practitioners are now being measured on the level of service provided to each client and what may be good for one client may not be good for another. To accommodate this, the Principles, corresponding Outcomes, and IBs have been drafted broadly, leaving it to those in practice to 'tailor make' them for each client.

 Practical Considerations

If you feel that you are out of your depth in handling any client matter, discuss this with your supervising partner and the client. It is essential that your client knows your status and experience as a legal representative when you become involved in his case. (We discuss this in more detail in paragraph 6.3 as part of your client relations.)

6.2.2.2 Client Care—Chapter 1

There are a number of client care issues that need to be addressed either before you have that first meeting with your client or at the meeting itself. These arise out of Chapter 1 of the Code. There are in total 16 Outcomes and 28 IBs, and we recommend that you read them. The IBs are helpfully divided into sub-headings for dealing with client matters, fee arrangements, complaints handling, and accepting and refusing instructions. You may find it useful to have a 'client care checklist' based on the points raised in this section.

Chapter 1, particularly Outcomes 1.1–1.5 and IBs 1.1–1.12, identifies specifically what aspects of your client relations you must consider at the outset of your retainer. We have already identified and discussed those relevant to costs and funding, and as with those aspects, client care must also be explained to your client both right at the start and as the matter progresses. It is best practice both to discuss these with your client and to give this information in writing.

These important aspects are as follows:

- providing a proper standard of service;
- taking into account the individual needs and circumstances of each client;
- providing all relevant information to enable clients to make informed decisions about the services they require;
- explaining how these will be delivered.

An example of 'providing all relevant information' could be ensuring that you explain procedurally what will or may happen as the dispute unfolds. This could include highlighting the different stages of a potential litigation in terms of pre-action protocol right through to trial, discussing ADR alternatives, and placing any information given in the context of costs and time frame. The client can then decide, armed with this information, the nature and extent of the services he requires from your practice.

 Practical Considerations

When explaining general client care obligations to your client, you should stress that the relationship between the client and yourself as a legal practitioner is a two-way process. You should therefore highlight to your client that he has to make a time commitment to his own case. It is important to control his expectations early on and to ensure that he appreciates that, with his cooperation, you will endeavour to do your best for him.

6.2.2.3 Information about the Costs—Chapter 1

This has been discussed at length in Chapter 3 of the manual at paragraph 3.2.2. However, in addition, it is best practice also to explain to your client the distinction between 'solicitor and client costs'—that is, the sum that the client must pay to his own legal representative—and 'costs between the parties' (otherwise known as '*inter partes* costs')—that is, costs that may be awarded, at the discretion of the court, between the parties once litigation has commenced. This distinction is important, because, as can be seen from Chapter 4, paragraph 4.3, the amount that a client is able to recover from his opponent, should he receive a favourable costs order, is very likely to be less than the client is liable to pay his own legal representative—subject of course to the type of funding arrangements the client has. The client will therefore usually be left with 'irrecoverable costs' from litigation. The client must fully understand his liability for those.

6.2.2.4 Complaints Handling—Chapter 1

This is self-contained in Outcomes 1.9–1.11 and IBs 1.22–1.24. These professional conduct duties primarily focus on ensuring that:

- the client is aware of the complaints handing procedure within the firm;

- if a client is not happy with the service they have received, they know how to make a complaint;
- all complaints are dealt with promptly and fairly.

 Practical Considerations

It is a bizarre concept that, when establishing your client retainer and setting out the terms for a successful and fruitful relationship, you are obliged to raise the issue of complaints. This must not be overlooked, no matter how awkward you feel about discussing this aspect.

Legal representatives should also be aware of the Provision of Services Regulations 2009, which impose requirements to give information to your client on additional client care issues. These concern the Legal Ombudsman (LEO). The LEO was established by the Office for Legal Complaints (OLC) under the Legal Services Act 2007, provides a free complaints resolution service to clients, and can deal with complaints about many categories of lawyers, including barristers and solicitors.

6.2.2.5 Conflict of interest?—Chapter 3

The main Outcomes here are 3.4 and 3.5: as a legal representative, you are prohibited from acting where a conflict of interest arises between:

- you and your current clients (own interest conflict); and/or
- two or more current clients (client conflict).

You can therefore never act where there is a conflict, or a significant risk of conflict, between yourself and your client.

If there is a conflict, or a significant risk of conflict, between two or more current clients, you must not act for one or both of them unless the matter falls within the scope of the limited exceptions set out in Outcomes 3.6 or 3.7. In deciding whether to act in these limited circumstances, the overriding consideration will be the best interest of each client and whether the benefits to the clients of acting for all or both outweigh the risk.

The relevant IBs are 3.2–3.4.

 Example

You are instructed by a husband and wife driver and passenger, respectively, of a vehicle involved in a road traffic accident (RTA). Both are existing clients, as your private client department dealt with their wills. They want to sue the motorcyclist for damages for the personal injuries they each sustained. The motorcyclist, however, alleges that the husband was either wholly or partly to blame for the collision.

The potential conflict exists at the outset of the retainer, even before the allegation against the driver has been made, because there is clearly a risk that the innocent passenger may have a claim in negligence against the husband driver.

 Professional Conduct

If you were faced with this example, then, during your first contact with the clients—whether by telephone or face to face—you would need to explain this potential conflict to them. You are likely to be in breach of Principles 2, 3, 4, and 5, with the relevant Outcomes being 1.1, 1.2, and 3.5. It is unlikely that either Outcome 3.6 or 3.7 would assist, as your acting for both clients would not outweigh the risk as the wife could ultimately seek damages against her husband. In these circumstances, as they are both existing clients, you must advise that they both seek separate independent legal advice elsewhere. The relevant IB is 1.7 and, in any event, IB 3.2 provides guidance that you should decline to act in this particular situation.

6.2.2.6 Confidentiality and Disclosure—Chapter 4

The relevant Outcomes here are 4.1–4.4. You are under a duty to maintain the confidentiality of your client's affairs at all times unless your client (or former client) agrees to the disclosure of confidential information or it is permitted by law. Further, you are also under a duty to make your client aware of material information within your knowledge. However, your duty goes further than this, because you are not permitted to act if, by acting, you are putting confidentiality at risk at some point in the future.

Again, there are exceptions to this contained in the Outcomes. The relevant IBs are 4.2–4.5. Perhaps the key point to make here is that the duty of confidentiality will always override the duty of disclosure.

 Professional Conduct

In the example cited, it would be very difficult to continue to act for both clients, because, in any event, you would be unable to comply with your duty of confidentiality, given that one client is a potential defendant to a personal injury claim. It is likely that you would be in receipt of material information that would be in either client's adverse interest, such as witness statements and experts' reports. The relevant Principles here would be Principles 2 and 3, with the relevant Outcomes being 4.2 and 4.3. The relevant IBs are 4.2 and 4.5.

6.2.3 MONEY LAUNDERING REGULATIONS

We thought it appropriate to discuss briefly here how you deal practically with your obligations under the Money Laundering Regulations 2007, as a legal representative in a litigation department. We do not intend to set out your money laundering obligations in detail. A link to further advice from the Law Society can be found on the Online Resource Centre.

 online resource centre

When you enter practice, your firm will be required to provide staff with appropriate training on their legal obligations, and information on how to recognize and deal with money laundering and terrorist financing risks (reg. 21). Further, the Code also requires firms to train staff to a level that is appropriate to their work and level of responsibility, and legal representatives are required, as part of induction requirements, to receive money laundering training.

Money laundering within the litigation and dispute resolution framework is not as prevalent as in other areas of practice, because litigation can probably be classed as fairly low risk. However, you are still required to identify your client's name and address, usually by a passport or driver's licence and a utility bill for an individual. For a company, you will need to consider the appropriate individual identification requirements for the company directors and, where the company is limited, undertake a company search. You are required to report any reasonable suspicions to your money laundering reporting officer.

The Money Laundering Regulations 2007 brought additional burdens to legal representatives in the identification of beneficial owners of client trusts, companies, and partnerships (reg. 5), the customer due diligence measures (reg. 7) to be applied to high-risk (reg. 14) and low-risk (reg. 13) situations, and revised administrative and training requirements.

6.3 WHAT DO YOU NEED TO DO BEFORE COMMENCING A NEW MATTER?

Based in part on the theoretical considerations in paragraph 6.2, there are some essential tasks that you must undertake before you take substantive instructions from your client, whether a new or an existing client. These items will be mirrored in each new matter that arises, but as you undertake repeat work for an existing client, you will get to know your client and some of these items will become easier to deal with.

6.3.1 **SEND A CLIENT CARE LETTER**

The nature and content of Chapter 1 of the Code discussed in paragraph 6.2.2, are contained in what is known as a 'client care letter', 'retainer letter' or Terms of Engagement. Attached to this letter are the firm's standard terms and conditions of acting, such as when bills will be rendered, interest provisions for late payments, VAT, storage of client files and documents, dispute resolution and jurisdiction clauses, etc.

The client care letter, along with the standard terms and conditions, must be sent out to the client before he has his first meeting with you, and before you commence work on his behalf. Usually the legal representative will speak with the client over the telephone to ascertain the general background to the dispute and either offer a free, time-limited meeting or a fixed-fee meeting. As the client care letter and standard terms and conditions are sent out in advance of the first meeting, you will not be able to set out—other than to highlight in a general way—the client's objectives for that particular matter, what the main issues are, the options available, or what steps should be taken, nor be able to give an estimate or fixed-fee indication of the costs of the matter. These will have to be set out in a subsequent letter after the first interview.

Client care obligations have become more onerous with the implementation of the Consumer Contracts Regulations 2013 ('the Regulations'). The Regulations give any individual or individuals, who are clients, the right to cancel the contract (being the client care letter and standard terms and conditions) without giving any reason in situations where the legal representative contracts with the individual client away from the office. The Notice to Cancel is usually referred to in the client care letter and set out in full in the standard terms and conditions.

The consequences of not complying with these Regulations are very serious; it is a criminal offence to do work for an individual if the necessary notices and procedures have not been given or followed. Further, the contract is treated as unenforceable. This effectively means that the legal representative cannot be paid.

The burden of proof is on the legal representative to establish compliance. A number of examples are set out below:

 Example 1

- The legal representative sees an individual in the office. He hands out the client care letter and the standard terms and conditions of the firm.
- The individual reads and signs them in the office.
- No cancellation period applies and work can be commenced immediately.

 Example 2a

- The legal representative sees an individual in the office who takes the client care letter and the standard terms and conditions of the firm away with him to consider.
- The individual then signs and returns them to the firm.
- Cancellation period applies and work cannot be commenced until the expiry of the 14-day cancellation period.

 Example 2b

- The legal representative sees an individual in the office who takes the client care letter and the standard terms and conditions of the firm away with him to consider.

- The individual then brings them back to the office and signs them there (and does not just hand them in signed).
- No cancellation period applies and work can be commenced immediately.

 Example 3a

- The legal representative attends the individual's home/hospital/other location away from the office where he gives the individual the client care letter and the standard terms and conditions of the firm.
- The individual reads, signs, and returns them to the legal representative away from the office or returns them by post or email.
- Cancellation period applies and work cannot be commenced until the expiry of the 14-day cancellation period.

 Example 3b

- The legal representative attends the individual's home/hospital/other location away from the office where he gives the individual the client care letter and the standard terms and conditions of the firm.
- The individual then brings them to the office and signs them (and does not just hand them in signed).
- No cancellation period applies and work can be commenced immediately.

 Example 4a

- The legal representative talks to the individual initially on the telephone and then sends out the client care letter and the standard terms and conditions of the firm by email or post.
- The individual signs and returns them by email or post.
- Cancellation period applies and work cannot be commenced until the expiry of the 14-day cancellation period.

 Example 4b

- The legal representative talks to the individual initially on the telephone and then sends out the client care letter and the standard terms and conditions of the firm by email or post.
- The individual then brings them to the office and signs them (and does not just hand them in signed).
- No cancellation period applies and work can be commenced immediately.

It is hugely important to remember that if the legal representative does not give notice and follow these procedures, then no work can be undertaken during the 14-day cancellation period. If work is undertaken during that period, it is a criminal offence and the firm does not get paid.

The Regulations only apply to clients who are individuals. If a firm acts for a corporate or business entity such as a limited company/LLP/PLC/partnership/sole trader in their business capacity, they fall outside the Regulations. No cancellation rights or periods apply and consequently there are no cancellation notices required.

It is also worth noting that emailing the client care letter with the standard terms and conditions to the individual is only permitted if the individual expressly agrees to receive them by email.

Practical Considerations

In practice legal representatives can bypass the burden of the Regulations as follows: they notify the individual that because they have cancellation rights, unless he agrees, the legal representative cannot start work. The individual is invited to indicate in writing that he expressly agrees that the legal representative can begin work. If the individual does agree, then the legal representative must inform the individual that if he does in fact proceed to give notice to cancel within 14 days, the firm is at liberty to charge for the work done to the date of cancellation. The legal representative then hands/sends to the individual the client care letter and standard terms and conditions of the firm, which include a written provision that, if he signs, he agrees for work to be commenced straight away.

6.3.2 REQUEST MONIES ON ACCOUNT

As can be seen from Chapter 3, paragraphs 3.2 and 3.3, the question of how a client is to proceed with or defend a claim needs to be identified right at the beginning of the retainer. However, you are not usually able to help your client to decide how he is able to fund matters until you have attended on him and taken detailed instructions at a first meeting. This first meeting needs to be paid for by the client, unless your firm offers free first interviews or is under a general retainer with a trade union, insurance company, or other association.

It is therefore good practice to explain why and how a first meeting, the time needed to review any documentation, and any early work to be undertaken need to be paid for and to ask your client to provide monies on account to cover these. The amount will depend on the type of matter and your hourly rate.

It is good practice to ask for the monies in the form of a cheque, banker's draft, or an account transfer to the client account for money laundering reasons. For every new matter that you have for a client, your accounts department, on your instruction, will need to open an account for the client and matter. The account will have a client account and an office account.

The monies on account are client monies. Once you receive the monies, you should ask your accounts department to place it in the client account. The monies stay there until you render a bill to your client. The monies will then be transferred across to the solicitor's account for that matter and any balance due can be requested from the client. If there is a surplus in the client account, that can remain there until the next bill is rendered.

If monies are to be taken from the client account purely to pay a disbursement (without an interim bill being rendered at the same time), the monies can be used directly from the client account to pay that disbursement.

If disbursements are paid out of the office account (in advance of receiving monies from your client), the appropriate amount in the client account becomes office money and should be transferred to the office account within 14 days. This would only happen where monies on account were received from the client in respect of disbursements and costs (called 'mixed monies'). These must be placed in the client account, then transferred across to the office account.

6.3.3 COMPLY WITH MONEY LAUNDERING REQUIREMENTS

The identification documents for an individual highlighted in paragraph 6.2.3 are usually dealt with by your firm's receptionist, who will copy them when the client attends the office. Sometimes, the client will bring them with him to your first meeting. If your client is a limited company, then a company search can be done online with Companies House for a nominal fee. In either case, you will need to examine the identification documents to ascertain whether you are satisfied that your money laundering obligations have been complied with. Consequently, it is not enough merely to undertake a company search against your limited company client. Once the identity of the directors has been ascertained, passports and utility bills are required for those directors. If another company holds shares in your client company or the shareholders differ from the directors, then if their shareholding exceeds 25 per cent, further investigations are necessary of those shareholders before you can conclude your money laundering obligations.

 Practical Considerations

A common problem arises when you have made a request for the identification documents and they are not forthcoming. The work that your client has instructed you to do may be urgent, such as making an application to set aside default judgment, or going on record as acting and attending a hearing on his behalf. Best practice and compliance with the Money Laundering Regulations 2007 suggest that you are not permitted to act further until you have received such documentation. You may feel that this puts you in difficulties with your professional conduct duties of acting in your client's best interest. However, this frequently occurs in practice and a nominal amount of work can be done whilst the documentation is awaited—but, at some early point, you will need to inform your client that you will be unable to do any further work until the documentation is received.

It is therefore essential that the question of identification is dealt with when you first speak to your client over the telephone.

6.3.4 UNDERTAKE A CONFLICT SEARCH

Your secretary or accounts department will usually undertake a conflict search. Alternatively, larger firms' case management systems have a conflict check provision. Most firms have detailed file opening forms to be completed by the fee earner. On this form, you will need to state the identity of your client's opponent. A check will be carried out to see if anyone in the firm:

- is acting, or has acted, for that opponent, or
- whether another member of the litigation department is acting against the same opponent.

In the latter case, a conflict may not be so obvious, but if it exists, you will need to ascertain whether the exception to the conflict rule (Outcome 3.5) applies, i.e. whether the clients have a substantially common interest or are competing for the same objective and consent to your firm continuing to represent both. If any of these circumstances exist, then you will need to consider whether you can, in fact, act for either client in respect of that particular matter. You may need to discuss this with the fee earner who is acting or has acted for the opponent or the other competing client, as well as with your supervising fee earner and the firm's compliance officer, in accordance with the firm's conflict policy.

6.3.5 ASK FOR ANY RELEVANT DOCUMENTATION

In order to enable you to be of more assistance to your client at the first substantive meeting (and ultimately to save time and cost to your client), it is sensible, when arranging the first meeting, to ask for any paperwork that he has in relation to the case itself and in relation to the potential funding of the case, such as insurance policies (see Chapter 3, paragraph 3.3).

For example, if your client has a breach of contract action, contractual documentation should be provided in advance of the first meeting or telephone call to allow you to consider what the relevant terms of the contract are, such as provisions for interest, exclusions, and dispute resolution and jurisdiction clauses. If your client has been injured, any existing insurance policies should be supplied to ascertain whether he has any legal expenses cover for any part of his claim, as identified in Chapter 3 at paragraph 3.3.1.

With such documentation available to you before you take substantive instructions, you have the opportunity to form preliminary views, devise a list of questions, and consider funding options.

6.3.6 **PRE-INTERVIEW QUESTIONNAIRES**

Some firms—particularly smaller firms or firms that undertake a lot of personal injury work—send out client questionnaires before the first meeting with the client. These are pro forma questionnaires and are designed to act as an aide-memoire and checklist, particularly for professional conduct, client care, and money laundering requirements.

There are advantages and disadvantages to using these questionnaires. As a legal representative, you will need to recognize your firm's policy on this.

6.4 **THE FIRST CLIENT MEETING**

Preparation is the key to a good client meeting and we would suggest that you allocate enough time to prepare fully before attending your client. This will include a review of all of the information that you have received and a double check on your professional conduct (especially costs), client care, and money laundering duties. It may also be helpful to prepare your own agenda to form the basic structure for the meeting.

In practice, meetings can be challenging for the legal representative who is new to practice—especially if you are to conduct the meeting on your own. In the early part of your legal career, it is more likely that you will sit in on meetings with other, more experienced, fee earners.

Often, in repeat business with existing commercial clients, there will be no face-to-face meeting, but only an email or telephone call to provide new instructions. However you receive those first substantive instructions, you must still have regard for paragraphs 6.2 and 6.3.

The following sets out some suggestions as to what should and may happen at a first meeting with your client.

6.4.1 **CLIENT ETIQUETTE AND PRELIMINARY MATTERS**

Client interviewing is a skill that you will develop as you become more confident and experienced in your legal career. If you are having a face-to-face meeting with your client, ensure that you know the date, time, and place of the meeting, because these can take place in the office or at another venue. Wherever the location, of course, you must always be on time.

There are the usual pleasantries in the first few minutes of a client meeting, such as enquiring as to the client's well-being and journey (if he has travelled), offering refreshments, and generally making the client feel at ease. If the meeting is to take place at your offices, either book a conference room or, if the meeting is in your room, make an attempt to tidy and remove from sight any confidential information, and do notify your secretary that you do not want any interruptions.

You may need to deal with any outstanding professional conduct and client care issues, but these can be done either at the outset or the conclusion of the meeting.

6.4.2 **THE FORMAT OF THE MEETING**

Whether the meeting is undertaken by telephone or in person, there are six main tasks for you to perform during the attendance.

6.4.2.1 Identify what your client wants you to do for him

You need to identify what your client's objectives are, but, at the same time, ensure that your client does not have any enhanced expectations. Your client needs to know the implications of embarking on steps that could involve him in litigation or another form of dispute resolution and all of the financial risks that go with that, but he must be realistic as to the likely cost and the prospects of success.

Your client's goal may be straightforward: for example, in a breach of contract case, this may simply be recovery of losses, or in a personal injury matter, it may be compensation. Your client may, in fact, want something different: for example, in a breach of contract case, it may be rectification of reputation damaged by the breach, or in a personal injury matter, it may be an apology and assurance that the defective piece of equipment has been repaired so as to avoid damage to others.

6.4.2.2 Take full details of your client's version of events

Without wishing to oversimplify any case, there will nearly always be two differing accounts of how the accident happened, how the contract was breached, or why someone was negligent. Your client will need to recount to you his version of events in his own words and it is important that you allow him to do this. Please see the Andrew Pike case study on the Online Resource Centre for an example of an initial attendance note.

online resource centre

 Practical Considerations

You will spend some time writing this down as your client speaks and therefore do not be afraid to ask your client to clarify anything for you. As your client recounts the facts, you may wish to ask questions—but remember that clients are not always clear on what is relevant to their case, so do not be too keen to interrupt, because they are unlikely to be satisfied that what they have to say on a particular point is not important until they have been given the opportunity to tell you. There is a balance to be struck, because some clients will talk continuously if you allow them to.

This attendance note will, in effect, form your client's proof of evidence and later be used to prepare the particulars of claim (or defence) if proceedings are issued. Examples of these documents can be seen in Chapter 11 and in the Appendices at the end of the manual. It may also be useful at this point to ask for any additional documentation in relation to your client's case. For example, if your client has been injured in an RTA, it may be helpful if he draws a sketch plan of the site of the accident, and the direction and position of the vehicles.

6.4.2.3 Explain some basic legal principles

The key to helping your client to resolve his dispute is to identify from the outset the relevant legal issues. Most cases are based on actions in contract and/or tort. Every case is made up of legal components, and your client will need to have a basic understanding of these components and how they fit into pursuing or defending his claim.

Any legal action must have a cause of action and can theoretically be divided up into three legal parts, known as 'liability', 'causation', and 'quantum'. Some, or all, of these may be in dispute in a case. For example, if your client were to have a contractual dispute, he would need to prove that there was a contract (cause of action) that the opponent had breached (liability), that the breach caused the losses (causation), and the nature and extent of those losses (quantum). These legal components are discussed in more detail in Chapter 7, paragraph 7.5.

These three legal components are looked at in light of the underlying principle that the claimant has to prove his case against the defendant on a balance of probabilities by way of either original and/or documentary evidence, and lay witness or expert evidence. (See Chapter 17, paragraph 17.2, for a fuller discussion on burdens of proof and evidence.) Most disputes will include the preparation and service of at least one type of evidence on your opponent for use at trial.

In essence, you will need to explain to your client in basic terms, avoiding too much technical legal language, that he may have three hurdles to overcome if he is to be successful in his case—namely, who was responsible, who caused the losses, and what those losses were—and that he will have to prove his case on the basis of what was more likely than not to have occurred. It will also be usual for you to undertake some kind of risk assessment when discussing these fundamentals of his case. (See paragraph 6.4.3.6 for an outline of how you should approach a risk assessment.)

6.4.2.4 Discuss how his dispute can be resolved

Remember that your client may never have been involved in any type of dispute and its resolution before. If he has, then some of the following suggestions may already be familiar to him.

You will need to explain to him briefly and in simple terms the ethos of dispute resolution, as highlighted in Chapter 2—particularly in relation to the overriding objective, and the principles of proportionality and reasonableness in terms of costs.

He needs to be clear that litigation is a last resort and that his problem may be better resolved by one of the alternatives to litigation. Alternative dispute resolution (ADR) is discussed in detail in Chapter 5, and most commonly includes negotiation and mediation. You should, however, point out to him what he can expect from litigation, if that is the way that his matter is to ultimately proceed, and discuss the necessity and purpose of the Protocol phase (see Chapter 8, paragraph 8.3), as well as outline how a case gets to trial.

ADR considerations

When discussing the possible ADR options, it is important to highlight to your client not only the benefits of ADR, but also the potential costs consequences of failing to consider ADR—most notably, costs sanctions if he should win.

Tied in with this, as with paragraph 6.4.2.3, is your risk assessment, and this is discussed in paragraph 6.4.3.6.

6.4.2.5 Answer difficult questions

First and foremost, if you are unsure of the correct answer to a client's question, then always inform your client that you will need to check the position—perhaps by undertaking some research or by speaking to a more experienced fee earner—and that you will then get back to him, either in writing or by telephone.

During a first meeting with a client, there will always be a number of questions that he will ask. Most of them can be easily dealt with: for example, 'What can I recover?' However, there are questions that clients usually always ask and which are very difficult to answer with any degree of certainty at this early stage. These include:

- **'Have I got a good case?'** The best that you can do is answer the question based on the information that you have at that particular time, and consider making the advice provisional on further investigations and therefore preliminary.

- **'How much will I get?'** You are unlikely to be able to put a precise figure on this, although at a later stage, after further investigations and the collating and exchange of evidence, you will be able to give a bracketed figure.

- **'How long will it take?'** Again, the answer to this question will very much depend on the conduct of the opponent and to which method of dispute resolution your client agrees. A bracketed time period can probably be identified.

- **'How much will it cost?'** The costs question is the only question here that must be addressed with some degree of accuracy, as discussed in paragraph 6.2.2 (see also Chapter 3, paragraph 3.2).

6.4.2.6 Summarize and explain what happens next

Towards the end of the meeting, once both you and your client have discussed the case as described previously, it is good practice to summarize your client's case, the options available to him, and how you can help him. This will enable you to ensure that you have all of the correct material facts and to reassure your client that you fully understand the main issues.

In order for your client to feel that his meeting has been worthwhile, you will need to set out what you will both do following the meeting. All of this should, of course, be followed up by a letter, but it is important that your client feels satisfied that something is being done when he leaves. The problem or dispute still belongs to the client, but a client can feel that he is sharing the burden by feeling satisfied with your understanding and your suggestions as to a way forward. At the end of each meeting with the client, or in a letter following the meeting, the client should be told when he will hear from you again. Good file management practices dictate that you diarize your file to the date upon which you intend to contact the client further. In the interests of good client relations, you must then do so, because he will be expecting to hear from you. Even if there is nothing to report, contact should be made and an explanation for any delay that has occurred provided.

6.4.3 **SPECIFIC CONSIDERATIONS ON FIRST TAKING INSTRUCTIONS**

Each case that you take on, or in which you assist, will differ to some degree from the last. However, there are certain aspects that can fundamentally shape a case that should also be considered at the first meeting in addition to the six tasks set out previously. In many cases, these will not feature heavily, but in others they may require some detailed consideration, research, or even counsel's advice.

As you start your legal career, it may be helpful to prepare a checklist of these points to which you can refer mentally during the meeting. This may remind you to consider and act upon them, or to consider and dismiss them.

6.4.3.1 Limitation and jurisdiction

Both limitation and jurisdiction are dealt with in some detail in Chapter 7, paragraphs 7.4 and 7.2. It is essential, however, in every case and for whichever party you act, that you consider whether there is a limitation issue looming and, if so, what can be done about it to protect your client's interests.

Similarly, if an accident happened abroad, or a contractual dispute involves foreign parties and issues, you will need to turn your mind to any jurisdictional issues.

6.4.3.2 Funding

Unless you are acting frequently for an existing client, you will need to discuss the variety of funding options at the first meeting (see Chapter 3). Remember to make a detailed note of what was discussed and how this is to be followed up.

6.4.3.3 Who is your client?

A legal representative is entitled to act for any person able to instruct him to bring or defend proceedings. There are a variety of different litigants and you will need to ensure, whether you act for the claimant or the defendant, that you know whether your client is one of the following:

- an individual over the age of 18;
- a child or a protected party (CPR 21.1);
- a limited and public limited company, including a limited liability partnership;
- a partnership or sole trader (CPR 7.2A and PD 7.5A–5C);
- the estate of a deceased person (CPR 19.8);
- another incorporated or unincorporated association, including a trade union, a building society, a charity, a local government body, or a club; or
- a trust or trustee (CPR 19.7A).

There are a number of reasons why you need to know who your client is at this early stage, as follows:

- You will need to consider whether the person from whom you are taking instructions has the authority and capacity to give those instructions. There is a detailed discussion on capacity for children and protected parties in Chapter 7, paragraph 7.3.2, and in Chapter 9, paragraph 9.5.
- The identity of your client is necessary to enable you to identify your client properly for the purposes of money laundering compliance.
- If proceedings do eventually ensue, you will need to know how to describe the parties on the claim form (see Chapter 9, paragraph 9.6 and Table 9.2).

- You will need to serve those proceedings and there are different rules for service on all of the different types of legal entity listed here. (This is dealt with in Chapter 9, paragraph 9.7 and Table 9.3.)

For a fuller discussion on legal entities, see Chapter 7, paragraph 7.3.

6.4.3.4 Who do you sue?

In most cases, this will be fairly straightforward. However, in some instances, this may require a little more thought, as follows:

- **Retailer or manufacturer?** For example, if your client purchased a defective portable gas stove, there may be three causes of action to consider: a claim in negligence against any person who puts defective goods in circulation; a consumer claim under the Consumer Protection Act 1987 against a producer of defective goods; or a claim in contract against the seller by the buyer. Under the last two options, there are some strict limitations, so it is as well to know which is your best cause of action and against which defendant, although, wherever possible, proceedings may be taken against both. Clear client instructions will help you to decide which is the most appropriate course of action.

- **Employer and employee?** Where your client was injured by the negligent act of an employee, then the employer will be vicariously liable for the acts of that employee—but only if the employee was acting in the course of his employment. What is deemed to be 'in the course of employment' has, over the years, been extended to include employees not following instructions and even deliberate acts of negligence, but each case will have to be looked at individually (see Chapter 7, paragraph 7.5.1.2).

- **Agent or principal?** This dilemma will feature in commercial cases usually involving contracts. It is best illustrated by way of an example.

 Example

A carpet cleaning company (the principal) appoints a sole trader (the agent) to secure carpet-cleaning contracts for commercial premises. The business relationship is formalized by an agency agreement. The carpet-cleaning services are performed, but damage several carpets at your client's office. The correct opponent in this case would be the carpet company, by virtue of the agency agreement, because the agent concluded the contract on behalf of the principal and not himself. It is essential that the agent acted within his actual or ostensible authority. If he did not, then unless the principal ratified the actions of the agent, the action will lie against the agent if it was clear to the contracting party that the agent was acting for himself.

- **Motorist and insurer?** If your client was injured in an RTA by the negligent driver of an insured vehicle, whilst your client has no common law right to sue the insurer, the insurer has a right to conduct the claim on behalf of the defendant driver. This is usually by way of an express term contained in the contract of insurance entitling the insurer to 'step into the shoes' of the person that it is insuring and to bring or defend an action in the name of the insured—a principle that is known as 'subrogation'. In certain circumstances, it is also possible for a claimant to sue the insurer under the provisions of the European Communities (Rights against Insurers) Regulations 2002, SI 2002/3061 (see Chapter 9, paragraph 9.6.5.1).

 Example

Roger Smith was driving his BMW 3 series and was stationary at a set of traffic lights. A Mondeo, being driven by Peter Anderson, collided with the rear of Roger Smith's car. The car was not owned by Peter, but by his father Simon Anderson, who was fully comprehensively insured with Peter as a named driver with Albatross Insurance Company. Albatross Insurance is entitled to conduct the defence of the claim on behalf of Simon Anderson, but if proceedings are issued, then Roger will need to issue them against Peter Anderson, because he was the negligent driver.

6.4.3.5 Is the opponent worth suing?

At this first client meeting, it is essential that you discuss with your client, once you have identified who the opponent is, whether that opponent is financially capable of satisfying any judgment or order (including costs) made in your favour.

In commercial cases, there are certain limited methods of trying to ascertain the solvency of your client's opponent, which include a bankruptcy search at the Insolvency Register or winding-up search at the Royal Courts of Justice, a company search, a credit search, a Land Registry search, a search of the Register of Judgments, Orders and Fines, or instructing a private investigator to gain a picture of the opponent's ability to pay. Often, your client will have some general information on his opponent from industry rumour. It is important that the question of whether the defendant has the money to satisfy a judgment is kept under review throughout the action.

In personal injury cases, most opponents are insured and so the concern over the opponent's ability to pay is not so troublesome—but see paragraph 6.4.3.7 for the uninsured position in road traffic cases.

 Professional Conduct

If you do not discuss with your client at the outset of the matter the financial viability and ability of his opponent to pay, and you go on to secure successfully a consent order or judgment in your client's favour, only to find that the opponent is insolvent or does not have the ability to pay, then you are likely to be in breach of your professional conduct obligations to your client under Principles 4 and 5 and Outcomes 1.2, 1.4, 1.5, and 1.12. The relevant IB is 1.13. Your client will have incurred time and, probably, significant expense in pursuing his claim, only to be left with the outstanding debt and additional further costs. Further, depending on the type of funding arrangement you have with your client, notably a DBA, the legal practice will suffer financially, as the basis for the recovery of legal costs is calculated on the actual recovery of damages from the opponent. Should the opponent ultimately be unable to pay damages or costs, then the practice earns no legal fees for the work undertaken in that case.

6.4.3.6 Risk assessment

A risk assessment needs to be undertaken periodically throughout a client's case and the first one will be done either at the first meeting or in the follow-up letter of advice.

In order to undertake a thorough risk assessment, you will need to consider and weigh up:

- the substantive legal argument;
- the strength of the three component parts of liability, causation, and quantum, and how you will prove or defend each part evidentially;
- the prospects of success;
- the prospect of losing;
- the cost of proceeding; and
- the likelihood of costs recovery.

Conducting a risk assessment will usually entail a full file review.

Let us consider an example of an RTA in which your client was injured. Acting for the claimant, you will need to include the following in your risk assessment:

1. The cause of the action and who is the opponent—that is, you must acknowledge that this is a negligence action against another road user.

2. What, as a matter of law, your client must establish—that is, that there was a duty of care owed to him, that this was breached by the other driver's negligent driving, that the negligent driving caused the losses, and that the losses were of a specific nature and amount.

3. What facts your client will have to establish—that is, that your client was another road user, details of the other driver's negligent driving, that, by colliding with the claimant, he suffered losses, and the details of those losses.

4. What evidence your client will need to establish these material facts—that is, your client's own evidence in a witness statement (and perhaps other independent witnesses) attesting to his presence on the road, the other driver's negligent driving, the fact of the collision, and the fact that he suffered losses. The losses will need to be proven by documentary and expert evidence.

5. What the strengths and weaknesses of your client's case are—which will depend on any additional information or facts, and these are different in every case. For example, in relation to the liability argument, who was responsible for the accident? If the other driver received a conviction as a result of his driving in relation to the accident and that conviction is relevant to the issues (of liability and quantum) in the case, then this conviction may be used to support your client's case (s. 11 of the Civil Evidence Act 1972 permits you to make use of the conviction by stating it in your particulars of claim). However, in the absence of a relevant conviction, if the opponent had independent witness evidence to support his case, then this would be potentially damaging to your client's case.

6. What the likely value of this case is and the cost of pursuing it—as a legal representative new to legal practice, you will need assistance in both these. Ascertaining these figures requires litigation experience. In respect of the value of the case, you will need to consult practitioner texts such as *Kemp and Kemp on Damages*, *Current Law*, and the *Judicial College Guidelines*, or you may even seek counsel's advice. A more senior fee earner will help you to consider the total costing of the matter.

 Practical Considerations

The value of your client's case and its likely costs are difficult figures to assess, but doing so will get easier with experience. If you do find yourself at a meeting with a client on your own at the outset of your legal practice, always inform your client that your views are subject to review by a more senior fee earner and are, as such, preliminary. It may well be the case that, due to the lack of information and evidence, your views would be preliminary in any event at that stage. Do not forget that, in the more complex cases, it may be prudent to seek counsel's advice on any aspect of the substantive case. The dangers of giving robust advice on the merits of a claim without conducting a thorough investigation can be seen from the case of *Levicom International Holdings BV v Linklaters (a firm)* [2010] EWCA Civ 494, where the Court of Appeal held that Linklaters had been negligent when they initially advised the claimant (without all the requisite information available to them) that their chances of success 'were not less than 70 per cent'. Based on that advice, the claimant rejected the defendant's offer and commenced arbitration proceedings. Later, counsel's advice on behalf of the claimant was much less positive and a less valuable settlement was concluded.

In commercial cases, in addition to the risk assessment, you should also consider the commerciality of pursuing the claim or defence on behalf of your client. Commercial clients often settle cases purely for commercial reasons (cash flow or preservation of a business relationship), but there are also those commercial clients who choose to pursue matters on a point of principle (such as business reputation, industry hierarchy, or just plain stubbornness).

6.4.3.7 The Motor Insurers' Bureau' (MIB)

This section is particular to RTAs in which your client has been injured in a collision with either an uninsured or untraced driver. The MIB is an independent body voluntarily set up and financed by motor insurance companies to deal with claims in which injuries were caused by drivers who have no, or no relevant, insurance or in hit-and-run cases.

The MIB has made two main agreements with the government, which can be viewed online at http://www.mib.org.uk. If you are ever consulted by a client in one of these two situations, then it is advisable that you read the agreements in full, because they both contain quite a list of formalities with which you must comply.

The claim will otherwise proceed in line with any other RTA personal injury matters with the usual conduct and procedural requirements.

6.4.3.8 The Criminal Injuries Compensation Authority (CICA)

The CICA is a statutory body that administers the Criminal Injuries Compensation Scheme (CICS). The Scheme provides compensation payments to victims of violence, such as assault or rape, and covers both physical and psychological injuries valued at a minimum of £1,000. This process is most commonly used where the offender is penniless or not known, and is therefore an alternative to litigation.

Unlike the CPR, the CICS covers injuries sustained in Scotland, but the limitation period for all injuries wherever they were sustained is two years from the date of the incident. The process is by way of an application form to the CICA.

The Scheme will assess the injuries in a similar manner to that used by the courts when assessing damages for personal injuries, but there are some important differences.

If you are ever consulted by a client injured as a result of a criminal offence, you should obtain full details of the Scheme, including the application form and various guides, from http://www.cica.gov.uk. The CICA will obtain medical records and request that the applicant be medically examined.

6.5 ACTION BY YOU AFTER THE FIRST INTERVIEW

There will usually be a number of action points for you to follow up after the first meeting if the case is to be taken forward. Legal representatives should be proactive in their approach to litigation, although what exactly will need to be done will very much depend on the type of case. The following are some basic suggestions of what you might need to do, but remember—whatever the action or steps in a case that you take on behalf of your client, you must have his express instructions to do so.

6.5.1 WRITE TO THE CLIENT

A legal representative should always confirm in writing to his client what was discussed at the meeting. This will usually span the following:

- **The funding arrangements.** If a CFA, after the event (ATE) insurance, or a DBA is to be entered into, the copies of the agreement and/or broker forms (to secure a quote for the insurance) should be included and explained in the letter. A further meeting may be necessary to go through these documents with your client before signing him up, in order to comply with best practice and your professional conduct rules (under Chapter 1 of the Code). If the client is to pay privately and/or is only funding disbursements, then you will require further monies on account to cover the work that you are about to do.

- **The return of the signed client care letter (if the client is a corporate entity) and any outstanding money laundering identification documents.**

- **The nature of the client's problem, the advice given (including any risk assessment), and the client's instructions.** Often, at first meetings, clients do not usually give initial instructions on the advice given at the meeting, because they need time to think about it. If this is the case, then the letter will be requesting instructions, usually regarding investigations and moving the claim forward.

- **Costs information.** In most standard client care letters there is a section for detailed calculations for costs estimates for both litigation and ADR options. This must be completed at the time the client care letter is sent. If it is not appropriate to complete this detailed estimate, due to lack of information or the fact that the client has instructed you to undertake a very limited amount of work, then it may be appropriate to place a cap on legal costs and disbursements to be incurred. This can be reviewed when the cap has been met and a full costs estimate or a further costs cap given at that later stage. Alternatively, as mentioned in Chapter 3 at paragraph 3.2.3, a fixed fee for a defined phase of the claim can also be given. In any event, costs information needs to be addressed with the client in this letter to the client to comply with Chapter 1 of the Code.

- **A request for documentation from your client, such as original documents and photographs.** It is also advisable to remind your client to preserve any relevant documentation as evidence to prove part of his claim: for example, return taxi fares to hospital for out-patient appointments in a personal injury claim, or photographs of renovations in a building dispute. Additionally, your client will need to appreciate the nature of the exchange of information and documentation in the Protocol phase and in litigation itself, and that even documents that harm his case may need to be disclosed. This may have been touched on at the first meeting, but is more likely to be dealt with at subsequent early meetings and correspondence in the run-up to, and the duration of, the Protocol. (For details of your client's disclosure duty, see Chapter 8, paragraphs 8.4 and 8.8, and Chapter 16, paragraph 16.4.)

- **Details of when you will next contact your client and what you are doing until you next do so.**

 Practical Considerations

Your client will believe that he is singularly the most important client that you have and, to maintain good client relations, you should provide your client with a time frame within which you will work and report back to him. Even if there is nothing with which to update your client, you should tell him just that. Your client wants to know what you are doing and, if paying privately, how you are spending his money.

6.5.2 DRAFT YOUR CLIENT'S STATEMENT OR PROOF OF EVIDENCE

After you have seen your client, the notes of what your client said in the interview can be formulated into the basis of a statement. This should be done as early as possible, especially in personal injury cases. It is even common practice to send the first draft with the letter of advice (see paragraph 6.5.1), and to ask for it to be signed and returned. In commercial cases, this is not usually done at this early stage, although a detailed proof of evidence is prepared from which a statement can be formulated later.

6.5.3 NOTIFY YOUR OPPONENT

In most cases, it will be sensible either to call or to write to your opponent or their legal representative (if they have appointed one) to inform them that you have been instructed by your client and that all further correspondence should be directed to you.

This contact also gives you the opportunity to inform your opponent that you intend to comply with Protocol and provides the forum to discuss how you are to proceed in this regard. (See Chapter 8, paragraph 8.2, for a full review of Protocols.)

In some cases, it is appropriate to ask your opponent whether they intend to dispute your client's claim, because this may save a great deal of time and money in the furtherance of the claim by undertaking the investigations detailed in the next section.

6.5.4 **INITIATE EARLY INVESTIGATIONS**

At this early stage, but subject to funding arrangements being in place, there will usually be a variety of investigations that can be carried out to enable you to give firmer views on how successful you think your client will be. Some of the information necessary for you to give a firmer view on success will come from your client—particularly in commercial cases, in which the client will be in possession of contractual documentation. If not, then your opponent will be, and the securing of such documentation is usually completed through the 'full and frank' exchange of documentation in the Protocol phase (see Chapter 8, paragraph 8.4).

These early investigations can serve a dual purpose, because they can also provide the type of evidence that your client will need to prove his claim at trial. Remember (see paragraph 6.4.2.3): your client's claim has three legal components—that is, liability, causation, and quantum—all of which must be proved if your client is the claimant, or disproved if your client is the defendant (unless, of course, your opponent has admitted them).

Before undertaking any investigations, you will need to outline to your client the nature of the investigation and the approximate cost, and receive his express instructions to proceed.

 Practical Considerations

You will need to discuss with your client which investigations are appropriate for his case. If he has a case that is difficult on liability, then it may be more proportionate and reasonable for you to advise that only the liability investigations be done, and the results considered and assessed by you, before proceeding with the causation and quantum investigations. Some investigations, however, provide evidence for more than one of the component parts: for example, a medical report can provide evidence that the type of injury sustained was caused by the negligent act, as well as document the nature and extent of that injury to enable you to assess its value later.

6.5.4.1 Liability investigations
Liability investigations will differ slightly, depending on the type of case that you are preparing.

6.5.4.1.1 *A personal injury matter*
These early investigations are likely to include:

- interviewing witnesses to the accident and preparing draft witness statements (see Chapter 17, paragraph 17.4);
- obtaining a copy of the police accident report book (or an extract if there is a pending prosecution), which should contain any statement taken from the parties, measurements, a sketch plan, and photographs of the site of the road accident;
- attending any proceedings relating to any prosecution;
- obtaining a certificate of conviction if the other driver was convicted as a result of the collision and the conviction is relevant to the issues of the case;
- attending any inquest in a fatal accident case should someone involved have been killed, at which the coroner will try to decide—based on post-mortem evidence, and that of witnesses and police officers (which evidence may be useful for any civil case)—whether the death was accidental or whether there are grounds for a criminal prosecution;

- requesting a copy of the accident report book from your client's employer and a copy of the report of the Health and Safety Executive (HSE) on the incident, as well as the employer's general Health and Safety guidance and information;
- attending the scene of the accident yourself to inspect the area and take photographs; and
- considering steps that may be needed to preserve evidence.

6.5.4.1.2 *Commercial cases*
These early investigations are likely to include:

- identifying potential parties and causes of action—remembering that commercial cases often have a number of likely parties and/or causes of action, depending on the nature of the dispute (for example, in a building case, if your client instructed an architect and a structural engineer to design and build a commercial warehouse that turned out to be structurally dangerous and therefore unfit for purpose, the cause of action may lie against one or both of the professional parties);
- obtaining copies of all of the relevant contracts and any revisions to those contracts;
- verifying the insurance position of the potential opponents;
- seeking to preserve for inspection any original evidence, such as a defective machine or piece of equipment (for example, a faulty alarm box, which led to the failure of a sensor, which, in turn, led to water-damaged stock);
- seeking to identify and preserve the relevant electronic documents and ascertain where they are stored;
- requisitioning reports or letters written by third parties (for example, an open letter written by the manufacturer of an inadequate part of a gearbox that was supplied through a chain of contracts to your client, stating that the part manufactured has limitations of use); and
- considering the type of expert that you need and finding one (for example, if your client purchased an unsatisfactory precision piece of engineering for steel cutting, you would need to locate the appropriate type of engineer to prepare a report).

6.5.4.2 Quantum investigations
Again, the nature of quantum investigations will vary.

6.5.4.2.1 *A personal injury matter*
In a personal injury matter, you will need to:

- obtain your client's hospital, GP, and X-ray notes;
- obtain curricula vitae (CVs) from appropriate experts; and
- write to your client's employer for information on loss of earnings and employment details.

6.5.4.2.2 *A commercial matter*
In a commercial matter, you will need to:

- obtain letters or quotations for the replacement cost of goods damaged;
- write to third parties for information (for example, if your client is pursuing a claim alleging that an ex-employee poached customers in breach of a confidentiality and restrictive covenant clause in the contract of employment, enquiries could be made with those customers regarding the liability issue of poaching and how much business was lost); and
- consider instructing an accountant or another appropriate expert to quantify your client's business losses.

Once in possession of all relevant information, you will then be able to discuss with your client the implications of the information that you have secured, with a view to moving into the Protocol phase.

KEY POINTS SUMMARY

- Not just with every new client, but with every new matter, you will need to go through your professional conduct obligations, including client care and money laundering, as well as undertaking a conflict search and considering how your client is going to fund the claim.

- Conflicts can arise as litigation progresses, so be alert to the possibility.

- The impressions gained by a client at a first meeting are very important. The key words are: professionalism; competency; empathy; confidence; honesty; and reliability.

- Follow up preliminary views at a first meeting with your further views after you have received further information or undertaken research.

- Keep your client updated with what you are doing.

- Never act without instructions.

Case Study *Andrew James Pike v Deep Builders Ltd*

Consider the materials available on the Online Resource Centre in relation to this chapter and answer the following questions.

Question 1

Read the attendance note on Andrew Pike. Consider the viability of Andrew Pike's claim at this stage, based on the information contained in the attendance note.

Question 2

Using the partially completed letter on the Online Resource Centre, complete the letter of advice to your client in light of the issues raised in the attendance note.

---

online resource centre

Any documents referred to in these case study questions can be found on the Online Resource Centre—simply click on 'Case study documentation' to access the documents that you need for Chapter 6 and to be reminded of the questions. Suggested answers to these case study questions can be accessed on the Online Resource Centre when released to you by your lecturer.

7   PRE-ACTION SUBSTANTIVE MATTERS

Relevant parts of the CPR and its PDs: 2, 3, 7, 17, 19, 21, 25, 29, and 40

LITIGATION TRAIN: PRE-ACTION SUBSTANTIVE MATTERS

First client meeting

o Discuss at the meeting
- Client care
- Money laundering
- Nature of claim/defence
- A way forward—together with instructions to proceed as agreed
- Request monies on account
- Funding options and costs recovery
- Does the opponent have the means to pay credit checks? Instructions needed

o Action after the meeting
- Conflict search
- Letter to client (preliminary advice and funding)
- Notify defendant
- Initiate early investigations

o Consider the following matters
- Jurisdiction
- In which court should the potential action proceed?
- Does my client/opponent have legal capacity?
- Limitation
- Issues on liability, causation and quantum
- What is my client seeking to recover?

Pre-Action or Protocol phase

Issue of proceedings

Trial

7.1 INTRODUCTION

A student's or a practitioner's role in the dispute resolution (or litigation) department is to assist in the procedural and theoretical aspects of a client's case. These latter aspects can include consideration of matters that can determine where an action proceeds and whether it is capable of proceeding.

The contents of this chapter are purposely substantive in nature and may be considered by you, to varying degrees, either before you see your client on a new matter, at the first meeting, or, more commonly, after you have received detailed instructions and are able to reflect on the overall issues in the case.

In practice, it is crucial that you allow them to become part of your 'checklist' of items that may or may not feature in your client's case. It is also self-evident that the decision 'where to claim' should also consider the costs of the claim in a particular jurisdiction, the conduct of the claim in a jurisdiction, and the outcome and enforcement of a claim in a jurisdiction.

The following matters may be considered:

- the location of witnesses;
- the location of documents and other evidence. Consider the provisions for enforcing production of documents in the intended jurisdiction;
- whether an injunction or other pre-emptive remedy should be sought in the action;
- the length of time a claim may take to proceed in the intended jurisdiction and the consequences of any delay for your client;
- whether the availability or non-availability of public funding in the intended jurisdiction is an issue;
- the cost provisions in the intended jurisdiction and how they are applied;
- the enforcement provisions of judgments in the intended jurisdiction and how effective they are and whether a foreign judgment would be readily enforceable in that jurisdiction;
- the remedies available in the intended jurisdiction.

This chapter will consider:

- jurisdiction and governing law;
- the capacity to sue or be sued;
- limitation;
- the legal components of an action; and
- remedies.

7.2 JURISDICTION AND GOVERNING LAW

7.2.1 IN WHICH COUNTRY SHOULD PROCEEDINGS BE COMMENCED?

7.2.1.1 Jurisdiction

It is important to be sure, firstly, that the courts in England and Wales have jurisdiction to hear a potential action, and secondly, that the courts in England and Wales are the appropriate place in which to hear the dispute. In any action in which the client or opponent is based abroad, or in which the cause of action arose outside of that jurisdiction, questions of jurisdiction must be considered.

EU Regulation 1215/2012 came into force on 10 January 2015 and in effect recast the Brussels Regulation. The Brussels Regulation 44/2001 continues to apply to cases commenced before 10 January 2015. This chapter concentrates on pre-action substantive matters for new cases and thus will apply only the new rules. Any practitioner with a case that may have issues of jurisdiction will need to study the regulations in detail to ensure the correct rules are identified. Essentially under the new rules Art. 25 gives jurisdiction to the courts of the member state chosen by the parties. There is no requirement that either party is domiciled within the EU for Art. 25 to apply—so even where the parties are not EU members any clause that states that they have chosen the jurisdiction of the courts of a member state will be effective. However, the detail of these rules needs to be studied as there are exceptions— certain land disputes, for example—and there are special rules relating to employment, consumer contracts, and insurance. Where parties have agreed to the non-exclusive juris- diction of another member state court, that will not necessarily prevent the English court from taking jurisdiction over the dispute. If another member state court has already issued the proceedings, however, the English court must stay its proceedings under Art. 29. This is known as the 'first seized' rule (i.e. where proceedings were commenced first).

Further, under Art. 31(2) any other member state court must stay its proceedings if a court in another member state court commenced proceedings first. Under Art. 7(1) of the new regulations, in matters relating to a contract, a person domiciled in a member state may alternatively be sued in the courts of the place of intended performance of the contract. Where the new regulation does not apply (for example where the defendant is not domi- ciled in a member state and the competing jurisdiction is outside the EU) the English court will apply common law rules to determine whether or not to exercise jurisdiction. The common law rules consider such matters as whether the defendant is properly served with the proceedings. If the defendant in this situation has a company registered office or other address in England and Wales, or is an individual resident, or a temporary resident, then proceedings may be served on that defendant regardless of whether the claim has any other connection with the jurisdiction.

7.2.1.2 Contractual disputes

In addition to the considerations in paragraph 7.2.1.1, in breach of contract actions, it will be important to ensure that there are no provisions in the agreement that provide that the parties must arbitrate rather than litigate. Where this is the case, the parties will not be permitted to litigate unless by mutual consent. Parties will be bound by a valid arbitra- tion clause in their agreement. The agreement will usually cover both the 'seat' for the arbitration (that is, where it should take place) and the governing law. These could be either national (that is, specifying that the arbitration should take place in England and Wales, and be subject to the laws of England and Wales) or international clauses. The new EU jurisdiction rules (see paragraph 7.2.1.1) do not include arbitration matters but do include Art. 12, which states that there is an absolute exclusion of arbitration from its scope. This means that any member state court can examine the validity of an arbitration clause and refer matters to arbitration.

Often, in commercial agreements, there will be staged alternative dispute resolution (ADR) clauses under which the parties have agreed to try a form (or forms) of ADR, usually culminating in arbitration. These clauses are enforceable, subject to the usual arguments of incorporation and reasonableness, and often include (depending on the nature of the agree- ment) suggested ADR methods, such as conciliation, followed by mediation, then adjudica- tion, and, finally, arbitration. (See Chapter 5, paragraph 5.3, for a brief discussion on the variety of ADR processes.)

 Practical Considerations

Although a detailed study of the statutes and regulations concerning proceedings outside the jurisdiction of the court is beyond the scope of this manual, there are some basic guiding principles that can be used to alert the new legal representative to the need to consider 'jurisdiction' in more detail and to ask the assistance of a supervising partner, as follows:

- Is there a binding agreement that contains a jurisdiction clause to be applied?

- Is there a 'governing law' clause in the agreement?

- Does a party reside or have its business outside the jurisdiction?

- Was the agreement concluded outside the jurisdiction?

- Determine the costs of both your enquiries and the costs of service outside the jurisdiction, and obtain your client's instructions to incur those costs.

- Have you advised your client of the additional time that it may take to issue or serve outside the jurisdiction of England and Wales?

- If your opponent is a limited company registered abroad, does it have a UK division registered in the UK or a UK trading site?

- Might determination of the action outside the jurisdiction be preferable in terms of convenience, cost, or justice?

- Have you checked the provision for the enforcement of any judgment that may be obtained in the proceedings?

7.2.2 IN WHICH COURT SHOULD PROCEEDINGS BE COMMENCED?

The High Court and the County Court have concurrent jurisdiction over most claims. Where there is concurrent jurisdiction between the High Court and the County Court, a claimant generally has freedom to choose in which court to issue his proceedings. However, this general freedom must also take account of those parts of the Civil Procedure Rules (CPR) that exercise restrictions on parties.

In some circumstances, including the following, it can be seen that the complete 'freedom' (of which court to choose) provided by statute is restricted in practice by the CPR.

- CPR Practice Direction (PD) 7A.2.1 (amended) states that all claims for money may only be issued in the High Court where the sum claimed exceeds £100,000 (except in a personal injury case, £50,000).

- PD 7A.2.2 states that a claim for personal injuries may not be issued in the High Court unless the value of the claim is £50,000 or more. In determining the value of the claim, interest, costs, a reduction for contributory negligence against the claimant, the value of any counterclaim or set-off, and the recoupment of benefits under the Social Security (Recovery of Benefits) Act 1997 are all to be disregarded in accordance with Art. 9 of the High Court and County Courts Jurisdiction Order 1991, SI 1991/724 (which cross-references CPR 16.3(6)).

- PD 7A.2.3 states that a claim must be issued in the High Court or in the County Court where a statute requires it.

- Although PD 7A.2.1 permits a specified sum claim with a value exceeding £100,000 to be issued in the High Court, PD 29.2.2 restricts a claimant's right to *continue* proceedings issued in the High Court if the claim has a value of £100,000 or less. Unless one of the exceptions set out in that paragraph applies, the claim will usually be transferred to the County Court. These exceptions include that:

  - the claim is one that, by statute, should be heard in the High Court;

  - the claim falls within a specialist list, as defined by CPR 2.3(2)—these include claims that would be heard in the Commercial Court, the Mercantile Courts, the Patents Courts, or the Technology and Construction Court (TCC);

- the claim is one relating to professional negligence, fraud or undue influence, defamation, malicious prosecution or false imprisonment, claims against the police, claims under the Fatal Accidents Act 1976, or contentious probate claims;

- there is an anomaly in the value of claims that may be brought in the High Court. Clinical negligence claims may only be brought in the High Court if their value is over £100,000 (whereas for personal injury claims—which exclude clinical negligence claims—the limit is £50,000) (Art 2 High Courts and County Courts (Jurisdiction) (Amendment) Order 2009 and Order 2014 at Article 2(7).

It is clear that any practitioner wishing to issue a claim in the High Court will need to justify doing so using one or more of the above provisions.

 Practical Considerations

The decision, 'in which court to issue proceedings?' should never be taken without care or consideration, because the penalties for issuing in the wrong court can be severe. In the worst-case scenario, the wrong decision could result in an action for professional negligence. In most situations, when a genuine mistake has been made and a claim has been commenced in the wrong court, the court will either take the initiative to transfer the action or will do so upon the application of a party. The court will usually effect the transfer, but may impose cost penalties on the claimant representing the costs of the transfer. These penalties can include a continuing penalty as to costs, although the court has the power to reduce the whole costs of the claim by up to 25 per cent (Senior Courts Act 1981, s. 51(8) and (9)). Equally, in cases in which the claimant knew, or ought to have known, that the claim was being commenced in the wrong court, the court has the power to strike out the claim (County Courts Act 1984, ss. 40(1)(b) and 42(1)(b); CPR 3.4).

 Professional Conduct

In any situation in which a mistake has been made, the Code, Principles 2, 4, 5, and 6 need to be upheld. Informing the client as soon as it is known that a mistake has been made would indicate that these Principles are being upheld. Further action may also be required, which could include further advice in the light of the mistake.

7.2.2.1 Rome II

EC Regulation 864/2007 contains the law relating to non-contractual obligations (known as 'Rome II'). This contains provisions that apply to tortious claims in European Union member states. Its application will have most impact in general litigation, in personal injury claims in which a party has been injured abroad, and in product liability cases. Its provisions will affect questions of liability (and grounds for exemption from liability), and the existence, nature, and assessment of damages in such cases.

The practical significance of the provisions is that a court will now have to hear evidence and consider how damages are assessed in the jurisdiction in which the accident or the harmful physical impact occurred.

The full scope of Rome II is outside the remit of this book, but it is noted for completeness and so that practitioners can be aware that further knowledge should be sought in such cases.

7.3 LEGAL CAPACITIES

7.3.1 INDIVIDUALS OVER THE AGE OF 18 AND MENTAL CAPACITY

A person who is over the age of 18 or who is not a patient under the Mental Health Act 1983, and has capacity under the Mental Capacity Act 2005, has the capacity to sue and be sued in his own name. If a person is not over 18 or does not have the requisite mental capacity defined under the Mental Capacity Act 2005, then they are a 'protected party' and they cannot litigate in their own name (subject to CPR 21.2(3)). Issuing a claim by a person who, in fact, does not have the mental capacity to give proper instruction to understand and to conduct litigation can have serious consequences. This was very clearly illustrated in the case *Joanne Dunhill (by her litigation friend Paul Tasker) v Shaun Bergin* [2012] EWCA Civ 397, where the court was considering, on appeal, whether to set aside a settlement on the grounds that the claimant did not have the requisite mental capacity. The Court of Appeal concluded that the correct question was not whether the claimant had proper capacity to approve the settlement agreement, but whether she had the mental capacity to litigate at all.

7.3.2 CHILDREN AND PROTECTED PARTIES (CPR 21)

CPR 21 governs the provisions that apply when acting for or against a child or a protected party. CPR 21.1(2) defines a 'child' as 'a person under 18' and a 'protected party' as 'a party, or an intended party, who lacks capacity to conduct the proceedings'—that is, a person who, by reason of mental disorder within the meaning of the Mental Health Act 1983, is incapable of managing and administering his property and affairs. CPR 21.2.1 provides that a protected party must have a litigation friend to conduct proceedings. A child will usually also conduct litigation through a litigation friend, though in respect of children the court does have the power to permit the child to conduct the litigation—CPR 2.2(3). The court will not generally exercise this power—one of the key reasons for this being that a child does not have contractual capacity (for example to pay his legal representative's fees!)

7.3.3 COMPANIES

Companies are legal 'persons' and therefore can sue or be sued in their own name. A company is one registered under the Companies Acts. When suing or being sued, it must do so in the full, registered, company name. If the company is in liquidation, then that fact must be added to the name—that is, '(in liquidation)'. A company that is not required to use 'limited' or 'plc' (or the Welsh equivalents) in its name should be referred to by its name, followed by an appropriate description.

7.3.4 LIMITED LIABILITY PARTNERSHIPS (LLPs)

Limited liability partnerships (LLPs) were created by the Limited Liability Partnerships Act 2000 (LLPA). Like a company, an LLP is a legal person separate from its members and, like a company, it must sue or be sued in its own name, which must be the registered name. Many legal practices now operate as LLPs, so are now incorporated rather than partnerships. Litigators need to take care when issuing proceedings against such bodies and ensure that any proceedings are issued correctly. The case of *Insight Group v Kingston Smith* [2012] EWHC 3644 (QB) gives some guidance on the issues arising.

7.3.5 PARTNERSHIPS

Partnerships are not legal entities, and the liability of partners is generally joint and several (Partnership Act 1890, ss. 9 and 12). Partners may sue or be sued in their individual names. Alternatively, partners carrying on business within the jurisdiction may sue or be sued in the name of the firm and the words '(a firm)' added to the case title. A party suing or being sued by partners in the name of the firm may serve notice on the firm, requiring all of the partners who were partners at the time that the cause of action arose to disclose their names and addresses. Failure to disclose is likely to result in an order for disclosure, with an order that the action be stayed (or the firm be debarred from defending) if disclosure is not made.

7.3.6 SOLE TRADERS

A sole trader may be sued, but may not sue in his trading name. A claimant sole trader should sue in his own name, adding the words 'trading as' (or 't/a') and the trading name. A defendant sole trader whose real name is not known may be sued in the business name, followed by the words '(a trading name)'.

7.3.7 ASSOCIATIONS

These may include trade unions and employers' associations, building societies, charities, local and central government bodies or departments, and other public bodies. All of these may be sued or sue in their name. Clubs, however, may not; these may sue or be sued in the names of the members of the club, or representative proceedings may be brought. An incorporated club may sue or be sued in its own name.

7.3.8 TRUSTS AND TRUSTEES

A claim by or against a trust is brought by or against all of its trustees. The beneficiaries of the trust need not be parties to the action (CPR 19.7A), but any judgment or order made in the action will bind the beneficiaries unless the court orders otherwise.

7.3.9 ESTATES OF DECEASED PERSONS (CPR 19.8)

Under the Law Reform (Miscellaneous Provisions) Act 1934, s. 1(1), most causes of action subsisting against or vested in an individual survive his or her death. If a party to a claim dies (or is adjudged bankrupt), the court has the power, under CPR 19.5(3), to add or substitute as a party in the action the person to whom the interest or liability of the deceased or bankrupt party has passed.

7.3.9.1 Where the death of the party is before the claim is issued
The claim must be brought or defended by the personal representatives of the deceased person. If the claim is made against a deceased defendant before there has been a grant of probate or letters of administration, the claim form cannot be served until the court (usually upon the application of the claimant before the expiry of the time limit for service of the claim form) has appointed a person to represent the deceased defendant.

7.3.9.2 Where the death of the party is after the claim has been commenced
The surviving party in the action needs to make an application to the court either to substitute the deceased party for the personal representatives of the estate of the deceased party, or, if no personal representatives have been appointed, to direct a person to represent the estate of the deceased party or to order the action to proceed without the deceased party being represented.

Where an action is continued by or against a deceased person, the court has power to order that any interested parties should be served with notice of the action (CPR 19.8A) and, in so doing, that person will be bound by any judgment or order made in the action. If the person so served files an acknowledgement of service, they will become a party to the claim.

These provisions must be distinguished from the restricted circumstances in which a party may voluntarily assign its interest (or liability) in the action to another. Such assignments are, however, outside the scope of this book.

7.4 LIMITATION

7.4.1 THE PURPOSE OF LIMITATION PERIODS

The primary purpose of limitation is to protect a defendant from the potential injustice of having to face a claim that has gone stale and for which reliable, or any, evidence may be difficult to obtain. It also provides an end to the time during which a person has an 'expectation' or concern that an action may be brought against him.

7.4.2 HOW IS 'LIMITATION' APPLIED TO ACTIONS?

7.4.2.1 From the claimant's perspective

Satellite litigation may arise on issues arising to clarify whether a limitation period has expired or not, or from applications in which the claimant seeks to proceed with the action and seeks the court's discretion to permit the action to continue.

Periods of limitation may vary in different jurisdictions; the periods of limitation within the jurisdiction may also vary, depending on the type of claim. The issue of the claim form stops the 'limitation clock' ticking and where the limitation period is nearing its end for the action, there will be a need to issue as a matter of urgency to avoid the claim becoming statute-barred.

 Practical Considerations

Where protective proceedings have to be issued to avoid an action becoming statute-barred, it must be remembered that further investigation can take place before service of the claim form—but care must be taken to serve within the lifespan of the claim form issued. Any application to extend the life of the claim form must be made 'within the period specified by CPR Rule 7.5'—that is, before the expiry of the time for service. Only in exceptional cases can the life of the claim form be extended after the end of the period specified by CPR 7.5 (CPR 7.6(3)—see Chapter 9, paragraph 9.7.1.5).

7.4.2.2 From the defendant's perspective

Limitation is a procedural defence, but it must be specifically stated in the defence itself. It will not arise and apply to the claimant's action automatically. The consequence, therefore, of the expiry of the limitation period for an action is that the defendant, in most cases, acquires an unassailable defence provided he has pleaded it in his defence.

7.4.3 LIMITATION PERIODS

Most limitation periods are laid down in the Limitation Act 1980 (LA 1980), as amended. Some procedural rules impose time limits that act rather like limitation periods.

A claim that is outside the provisions of the LA 1980 is not subject to a strict period of limitation. It may, however, be subject to a time limit by analogy to the Act, or it may be subject to the defences of laches and acquiescence.

The main limitation periods are as outlined in Table 7.1.

TABLE 7.1 LIMITATION PERIODS

Class of claim	Limitation period
Fraudulent breach of trust	None (LA 1980, s. 21(1))
Recovery of land	12 years (LA 1980, s. 15(1))
Recovery of money secured by mortgage	12 years (LA 1980, s. 20(1))
Speciality	12 years (LA 1980, s. 8(1))
Recovery of money due under statute	6 years (LA 1980, s. 9(1))
Enforcement of a judgment	6 years (LA 1980, s. 24(1))
Contract	6 years (LA 1980, s. 5)
Recovery of trust property and breach of trust	6 years (LA 1980, s. 21(3))
Recovery of arrears of rent	6 years (LA 1980, s. 19)
Tort (except those listed below)	6 years (LA 1980, s. 2)
Note: This includes claims under s. 2(1) of the Misrepresentation Act 1967	
Defective Premises Act 1972 (DPA 1972) claims	6 years (DPA 1972, s. 1(5))
Personal injury claims	3 years (LA 1980, s. 11(4))
Fatal Accident Act 1976 claims	3 years (LA 1980, s. 12(2))
Claims under the Consumer Protection Act 1987	3 years (LA 1980, s. 11A)
Carriage by Air Act 1961 (CAA 1961) claims	2 years (CAA 1961, Sched. 1)
Claims for personal injury or damage to vessel, cargo, or property at sea	2 years (Merchant Shipping Act 1995, s. 190(3) and Sched. 6)
Disqualification of company directors	2 years (Company Directors Disqualification Act 1986, s. 7(2))
Contribution under the Civil Liability (Contribution) Act 1978	2 years (LA 1980, s. 10(1))
Contributions under the Maritime Conventions Act 1911	1 year (Merchant Shipping Act 1995, s. 190(4))
Carriage of Goods by Road Act 1965 (CGRA 1965) claims	1 year (CGRA 1965, Art. 32(1))
Defamation and malicious falsehood	1 year (LA 1980, s. 4A)
Applications for judicial review	3 months (CPR 54.5)
Unfair dismissal under the Employment Rights Act 1996 (ERA 1996)	3 months (ERA 1996, s. 111(2))
Applications for new business tenancies under the Landlord and Tenant Act 1954 (LTA 1954)	Not less than 2 months nor more than 4 months (LTA 1954, s. 29(3))
Actions for an account	Period applicable to claim on which account is based (LA 1980, s. 23)

7.4.4 WHICH LIMITATION PERIOD APPLIES TO AN ACTION?

It is sometimes difficult to determine into which category a particular case may fall. It is possible that the nature of the claim itself may affect the application of a limitation period. If the action arises from fraudulent behaviour, the court will consider whether it was the fraudulent behaviour of a party or of another. Where the fraud is that of a person who is not a party, then the defendant will normally be able to rely on a limitation period applying. But if the fraudulent behaviour is that of a party, then it is more likely that the court will determine that no limitation period applies. Claims that are a mixture of tort and contract can also cause difficulties.

A full examination of the more complex issues arising from limitation is outside the scope of this manual, but any legal representative acting in an action in which 'limitation' is raised will need to examine the law applying in detail (see *Blackstone's Civil Practice* in this regard).

The court has a discretion to dis-apply the limitation period in personal injury actions under s. 33 of the LA 1980. In these circumstances, the court will decide whether it would be equitable and whether it would be prejudicial to the defendant, taking into account all of the circumstances of the case. There may be good reasons not to rely on what appears to be a limitation defence, where a fair trial can still take place despite the delay. Two recent cases have considered the application of s. 33 LA—in *Kara Rayner v Wolferstans (A firm), Medway NHS Foundation Trust* [2015] EWHC 2957 (QB), the judge allowed the claimant to proceed with her personal injury claim seven years after the statutory period of limitation had expired where the judge found that the claimant had been prejudiced by delays not of her making. This case is a clear example of the court assisting a 'deserving' claimant. In *Collins v Secretary of State for Business Innovation & Skills* [2013] the court would not exercise its discretion, as it decided that the evidence was sketchy and unreliable, and there would be real prejudice to the defendant if the limitation period was dis-applied.

7.4.5 FOREIGN LIMITATION PERIODS

Where the rules of private international law provide that the law of any other country is to be taken into account in any claim in England or Wales, the law of that other country relating to limitation must be applied under the Foreign Limitation Periods Act 1984.

7.4.6 WHEN DOES THE 'CLOCK' BEGIN TO RUN ON LIMITATION PERIODS?

There are a number of important features that you will need to consider when dealing with a case with an actual or potential limitation problem. These are addressed in this section, and will be followed by a summary of the practicalities of dealing with cases that are near to the expiry of their limitation period.

7.4.6.1 The time runs from the accrual of the cause of action

Time begins to run from the earliest time at which an action may be brought—that is, time runs from the point at which facts exist establishing all of the essential elements of the cause of action.

A distinction is drawn between mere procedural requirements and substantive elements. This can sometimes be a difficult distinction to draw. The difference between the accrual of a cause of action in contract and tort can be problematic, because for contract, there is no need for damages to have been caused before a claimant is able to sue in contract—the cause of action accrues on the date of the breach and the six-year limitation period runs from this date. For an action brought in tort—for example, in negligence—the limitation period runs from the date on which the damage is suffered (because the 'loss' is an essential component of the tort of negligence). For such actions, therefore, the cause of action accrues when the alleged act of negligence causes loss. Damage may be caused much later than the date of the breach.

In *Haward v Fawcett* [2006] UKHL 9, the House of Lords considered the three-year limitation period prescribed by LA 1980, s. 14A, and the extent of knowledge required by the claimant to start the period running. LA 1980, s. 11 (4)(b) deals with the date at which the claimant is deemed to have knowledge of a loss. The case *Hoey v Sir Robert Lloyd & Co Ltd & Others* (2011) EWCA Civ 1060 considered the principles that should be applied to consider when the claimant 'had knowledge'—he would need to have knowledge of his injury, but also that it was linked to the negligent acts of the defendant.

It concluded that, for time to start to run, the claimant must have knowledge of the 'factual essence of the act or omission' that caused the loss. It was not necessary for the claimant to know the precise details of the alleged negligence, or for him to identify conclusively that the defendant's acts or omissions were the cause of his loss. It was sufficient that the claimant had enough information to make it reasonable for him to commence investigations into the potential claim against the defendant and s. 14A gives the claimant three years in which to complete those investigations. This section of the LA was strictly applied in the case *Boycott v Perrins Guy Williams* [2011] All ER (D) 113 (Oct).

Practical Considerations

Although the case of *Fawcett* restates (and clarifies) established principles and gives excellent guidance to a practitioner towards an understanding of the provisions of LA 1980, s. 14A, it also gives a clear warning to practitioners that claimants should be advised of the potential difficulties that may arise if investigations are delayed, even in a situation in which the claimant is not certain that the potential defendant caused the loss.

7.4.6.2 Potential parties to an action must exist

There must be a party capable of suing and a party capable of being sued. For example, a company may have been removed from the Register of Companies in the intervening period between the accrual of the cause of action and the issue of proceedings. However, in these circumstances, a company may be restored to the Register for the purposes of making or defending a claim, but the limitation period will run from the date of breach (or whatever the cause of action) and not the date of registration.

7.4.6.3 Persons under disabilities

Where the claimant is a person under a disability, being either a child or a protected party (see paragraphs 7.3.1 and 7.3.2), the limitation period does not start to run until:

- if a child, from the date of the child's 18th birthday;

- if a protected party, if they were of unsound mind at the time of the cause of action (or the unsound mind was caused by the cause of action), from the date on which they are no longer of unsound mind (whenever that may be medically certified). If the person was of sound mind at the time of the cause of action, the limitation period will continue to run.

7.4.6.4 Fraud, concealment, and mistake

In claims based on fraud, the limitation period does not begin to run until the claimant discovers (or could, with reasonable diligence, have discovered) the fraud. The limitation period will also not run whilst the defendant deliberately conceals a relevant fact. Where the claim is for relief from the consequences of a mistake, time does not run until the mistake is discovered, or could have been discovered with reasonable diligence.

7.4.6.5 Latent damage

The Latent Damage Act 1986 created greater fairness in situations in which the limitation period may expire before a party is even aware that a claim exists. In claims in tort (other than for personal injuries), the Latent Damage Act 1986 provides new sections (inserted into the LA 1980, ss. 14A and 14B). The provisions added to the LA 1980 by the 1986 Act provide two periods of limitation: one that is six years from accrual (the usual period for claims in tort), and another that is three years from the 'starting date'—that is, the earliest date at which the claimant knew that the relevant damage was sufficiently serious to justify proceedings, enabling a claim to subsist, and when it could be attributed to the act of negligence and the identity of the defendant.

To prevent defendants being potentially 'at risk' of a claim indefinitely, s. 14B of the LA 1980 provides a long-stop period for bringing proceedings of 15 years from the act or omission alleged to constitute the negligence causing the claimant's damage.

7.4.6.6 The discretionary extension of limitation periods

Discretionary provisions to extend the statutory limitation period apply in:

- judicial review proceedings (the three-month time limit can be extended if good reasons are shown);

- defamation claims (the one-year limitation period can be extended if it can be shown, on a balance of prejudice between the claimant and the defendant, to be equitable to allow the limitation period to be extended); and

- personal injury claims, in which a wide discretion is provided in s. 33 of the LA 1980 to extend the limitation period. See also paragraph 7.4.4.

7.4.6.7 Practical pointers when calculating the limitation period

As stated, time 'runs' from the day following the day of accrual of the action. Parts of a day are ignored. Time 'ends' when the claimant delivers his request for the issue of a claim form, accompanied by the claim form and fee, to the court office. The court will not issue a case until all of the necessary documents for issue, and the appropriate fee, have been lodged at court. If the court office is closed on the final day of the limitation period, the action will still be 'in time' if all of the documents and the fee are lodged on the next court business day. If documents and the fee are sent to the court by post, receipt of the documents and fee will be date stamped on receipt and the action will still be 'in time' even if the court does not issue on the day on which it receives the documents. Clearly, in any case in which the limitation period is about to end, it is crucial for the practitioner to ensure that the court receives the documents and fee on time. This is a situation in which the practitioner would make a personal attendance at court to issue the proceedings.

7.4.7 HOW DO THE PROVISIONS OF AMENDMENT AND SUBSTITUTION AFFECT THE LIMITATION RULES?

Amendment and substitution are governed by CPR 17.4 and 19.5. These provisions of the CPR are, to a degree, overlapping, in that they both deal with amendments to a statement of case after the expiry of the relevant limitation period. CPR 17.4 deals with applications to allow an amendment to include a new cause of action, or to allow an amendment of the name of a party where there has been a mistake in the name given to a party. CPR 19.5 deals with the provisions applying to add or substitute parties after the expiry of the limitation period.

There is a clear overlap in the provisions and both need to be examined where a new party is to be added after the expiry of the limitation period. Confusion has arisen whether the mistake in naming the wrong party is one concerning the actual identity of the party, rather than a mistake in the name given to the party. In general, the cases seeking to clarify this have upheld the view that a mistake as to name is within the provisions, but not a mistake as to the identity of a party.

7.4.8 LIMITATION PERIODS APPLYING WHERE THE CLAIM SEEKS A CONTRIBUTION FROM AN ADDITIONAL PARTY

A claim for a contribution under the Civil Liability (Contribution) Act 1978 must be brought within two years from the date on which the person seeking a contribution is 'held liable ... by a judgment' (LA 1980, s. 10).

The provision was not clear whether the time ran from the date of judgment or the date on which damages are assessed, and these may often be at different times. In *Aer Lingus v Gildacroft Ltd & Sentinel Lifts Ltd* [2006] EWCA Civ 4, the Court of Appeal clarified that the time runs from the date of assessment of the damages.

 Practical Considerations

Limitation is one of a series of 'key dates' that should be logged with any new instructions. On receiving any new instructions, the expiry of the relevant limitation period should always be checked and noted.

Equally, in new instructions from a defendant to proceedings, the relevant limitation period should always be checked and noted, because a defendant who takes a step in the action beyond filing his acknowledgement of service and raising limitation in his defence will be unable to raise the issue later in the action.

7.5 THE LEGAL COMPONENTS OF AN ACTION

In Chapter 6, we looked at the concept of an action having three legal components: liability, causation, and quantum. Here, we aim to focus on these in more detail.

 Practical Considerations

Whilst we have divided the legal components into three parts, not every claim will have an issue on all three parts. Part of your role as a legal representative is to ensure that your client understands, in very basic terms, why he has a good, or not so good, case. This will inevitably require an explanation from you on the prospects of success in relation to the claim. To help you to provide this advice, we consider that breaking the case down into legal components will allow you to see the case as a whole and advise the client accordingly.

7.5.1 LIABILITY

Liability is the first hurdle that your client will have to get over—unless, of course, the opponent has admitted liability. You will first have to ask yourself, and your client, who was responsible for the breach of contract or accident. In most cases, this will be fairly self-evident. In those cases in which it is not, the most common liability issues that you will come across as a legal representative are as follows.

7.5.1.1 Joint and several liability
Where two or more persons are liable to another, they may be either jointly liable, severally liable, or jointly *and* severally liable. A contract that provides that more than one person will be liable will usually set out the parties' liability. If the contract fails to state the nature of the parties' liability, then determining that liability will be a matter of construction.

7.5.1.1.1 *Joint liability*
Where parties are jointly liable, then either is liable up to the full amount.

7.5.1.1.2 *Several liability*
Where liability is several, then the parties are liable only for their respective shares.

7.5.1.1.3 *Joint and several liability*
Joint and several liability is a mixture of both of these. The person to whom the parties owe the joint and several liability may elect to pursue the whole claim against either one of those liable (as in joint liability), but as between those liable, the liability is several and thus any party pursued by the recipient of the liability may seek a contribution from his co-obligors in the share of each of their liability (several liability).

7.5.1.1.4 *Who should the claimant sue?*
For joint debts, the general rule is that all of the joint debtors should be made parties to the action. Where the claimant fails to do this, the defendant may make an application for his joint debtor to be added to the action as an additional party. The claimant then has the option of joining in that additional party as a defendant to his action.

For joint and several liability debts, the claimant can choose whether to sue one or more of those who are jointly and severally liable.

7.5.1.2 Vicarious liability

'Vicarious liability' is an employer's liability for the acts of its employees. In common law, an employer is vicariously liable for the tortious acts of its employees if they are carried out 'in the course of employment'. This has, in recent times, had a wide definition, but will not extend to employees acting 'on a frolic of their own'. The court will look at, amongst other factors, the relationship between the employer and the third party, and whether the act of the employee was in sufficiently close connection to his employment. The connection between the tortious person's actions and 'course of employment' has been subject to recent review by the courts (*Catholic Child Welfare Society v Various Claimants (1) and the Institute of Christian Brothers (2)* [2012] UKSC 56), and the concept of vicarious liability has widened and can, on the facts of a case, include actions that may not be considered to be 'in the course of employment' and to other persons akin to an employee though not an employee. A detailed look at these points is outside the scope of this manual, but practitioners should be aware of this and when an issue arises in practice be prepared to undertake research to check the position and advise accordingly.

 Practical Considerations

When considering who is responsible for the wrong done to your client, you will need to turn your mind to whether the person who carried out the breach is the person with legal liability or, indeed, whether there is an additional person or entity that may also be to blame. Be aware that you may need to make some enquiries before you secure a definitive answer.

7.5.2 CAUSATION

Causation is very often either overlooked or simply assumed to be unproblematic in the success of a case. This is a misconception, because causational factors can condemn a case to complete or partial failure.

We have found it helpful to divide causation into two categories: liability causation and quantum causation.

By 'liability causation', we mean whether the negligent acts caused the accident or breach. In many cases, this will be uncomplicated, but you should ask yourself the question in any event.

 Example

Did the negligent driving of the opponent (such as driving through a red light or driving too fast) cause the collision in which your client was injured, or was it the opponent's defective vehicle that caused the accident (the fact that the brake pads were worn and the tread was bare on the front two tyres), or both? It is important that you consider this, because it will affect what you say to your opponent, and how you state your client's claim in the letter of claim and in any proceedings that may result. Remember that only facts in issue can be dealt with at trial.

By 'quantum causation', we mean whether the breach caused the loss. At first glance, this may seem unlikely to feature in many cases, but consider the following example.

Example

Did your client's former solicitor's failure to issue proceedings for breach of contract within the limitation period cause the loss that your client is seeking (by depriving him of the opportunity to pursue a claim through the courts), or was his case so poor on liability (your client failed to perform his part of the contract) that it would have failed in any event?

7.5.3 QUANTUM

In paragraph 7.6.3, we look at the different types of damages that your client can recover in a civil claim. Here, we will seek to remind you of the theoretical basics that you would have come across in your academic studies in contract and tort.

The general principles that we would like to remind you of are as follows.

- In contract cases, the damages must not be too remote from the breach. What this means is that the losses must have flowed naturally from the breach or have been in the reasonable contemplation of the parties at the time that the contract was made as being the probable result of the breach.

 Practical Considerations

In practice, you are likely to come across this in commercial contract cases, in which you will need to consider whether the losses were consequential losses. Many contracts have incorporated into them purported valid exclusion clauses in this regard, excluding any consequential losses. In these cases, you will need to examine the clause carefully (considering whether the clause is, in fact, incorporated into the contract and reasonable) and discuss with your client the circumstances surrounding the making of the contract, as well as the true nature of the losses that occurred and whether they would really fall into the category of consequential losses.

- In cases in tort, the damages must also not be too remote and this is, in part, based on the damages being a reasonably foreseeable consequence of the tort.
- In both contract and tort cases, the claimant has a duty to mitigate his loss. If he fails to do so, then his damages claim may be reduced. The duty only arises at the time of the breach of contract or commission of the tort.

 Example

In a personal injury case, the claimant may fail to attend physiotherapy sessions, consequently prolonging his rehabilitation period. In a breach of contract case, the claimant may fail to secure a replacement machine (for the defective machine supplied by the defendant) and so allow a significant loss of production claim to accrue.

 Practical Considerations

If the defendant wishes to make an allegation that the claimant has failed to take all reasonable steps to mitigate his loss, then he should raise this initially in his response to the letter of claim, then state it in his defence. The burden of proof in this circumstance will lie with the defendant.

7.6 **REMEDIES**

7.6.1 **THE PURPOSE OF A REMEDY**

There are several remedies that may be sought in a civil action. The aim of any action will be to:

- establish, or seek to change, a legal status;
- determine legal rights and duties;
- rectify an infringement or denial of legal rights; and
- seek a declaration of the state between the parties with no further remedy.

In all of these cases, the courts seek to create justice between the parties. The decision, or order, of the court will be based on the law, the evidence, the cogency of the evidence, and the rules of the court.

The remedy that the court decides is called a 'judgment', or an 'order'. In Chapter 9 it will be seen that, in the drafting of a claim form, the remedy that the claimant seeks must be set out. This does not, however, restrict the court in the making of a remedy that it sees to be just and appropriate, although remedies can only be granted in accordance with principles of law. The court does not have an inherent jurisdiction to make any order that appears to be just (but compare this with the outcomes available in ADR when the parties may agree terms that may be far more flexible, pragmatic, or commercial).

Any action commenced in the courts must have a viable cause of action to succeed. The basic outline of the cause of action will be set out in the particulars of claim (the claim will be expanded upon in the witness statements), and to succeed, it must include all of the elements that the action needs. For example, for negligence, there must be a duty of care, a breach of that duty, and, for this part of the allegation, the claimant will need to list all of the aspects of the defendant's conduct that the claimant says fell below the appropriate standard of care. There must be consequential loss or damage, and the claimant must provide details as to how the defendant's conduct caused, or materially contributed towards, his injury (causation) and provide details of the loss or injury (loss).

7.6.2 **WHAT REMEDIES ARE AVAILABLE?**

The principal remedies available in civil proceedings are:

- legal remedies—usually damages, these are legal rights to which the person seeking them is entitled as of right on sufficient proof of the infringement; and
- equitable remedies—usually injunctions or specific performance, the court may award these at its discretion when a legal remedy would be inadequate or is unavailable. Such discretion to award an equitable remedy is exercised by the court in accordance with established principles.

7.6.3 **DAMAGES (INCLUDING THE CRU AT 7.6.3.1.1)**

Damages are a monetary payment for an infringement of a legal right. The amount to be paid reflects the sum required to compensate for the loss caused by the defendant's breach or wrongdoing (compensatory damages).

Where the damages arise from a breach of contract, the contract may provide how the damages are to be calculated. Where the infringement of a legal right has caused no loss, the damages may be only nominal.

Damages are categorized in a number of ways: tort and contract; specified and unspecified sums. The most common judgment given is for a sum of money; the money due will either be a debt or damages. Interest may be awarded on a money judgment, but this relief is ancillary to the principal remedy, rather than an independent remedy. Damages in contract aim to put the claimant in the position in which he would have been had the contract been performed satisfactorily. Damages in tort aim to put the claimant in the position in which he would have been but for the commission of the tort. Contributory negligence (that is, when the claimant has contributed to the harm caused to him) will reduce the damages awarded by an appropriate percentage of up to 100 per cent (under the Law Reform (Contributory Negligence) Act 1945).

7.6.3.1 Personal injury damages

Although personal injury damages are tortious cases, the basis for assessment of damages for personal injury cases is a specific field of 'damage assessment'.

Personal injury damages are divided into two categories:

- special damages—all of which are past quantifiable damages that arose from the commission of the tort up to the date of trial; and

- general damages—that is, all other damages, the sum of which is assessed by the court based on the evidence adduced.

The eleventh edition of the Judicial College Guidelines contains details for the assessment of damages. This is updated every two years. As a result this percentage uplift should be applied when considering the value of a client's potential claim by reference to case law. The publication also gives further guidance on minor injuries, chronic pain, death, repetitive strain injury cases, and sexual abuse cases. It is a very useful guide for all legal practitioners undertaking personal injury work.

7.6.3.1.1 *Personal injury damages—the Compensation Recovery Unit (CRU)*

The CRU is a department of the Department for Work and Pensions (DWP). It seeks to recover state benefits that a claimant has received as a result of their injury or disease where the claimant is receiving damages for loss from a defendant or insurer. The aim of the scheme is to ensure that a claimant is not, in effect, compensated twice.

The elements of the scheme are contained in the Social Security (Recovery of Benefits) Act 1997, the Social Security Act 1998, and the Social Security (Recovery of Benefits) Regulations 1997 (SI 1997/2205).

The aims are as follows:

- to ensure that a person does not receive compensation in respect of the same injury or disease twice;

- to ensure that a defendant (or compensator) cannot make a compensation payment (unless it is an 'exempt' payment) to a claimant without first applying to the CRU for a Certificate, and, when making any payment to the claimant, must pay to the DWP an amount equal to the total amount of the recoverable benefits on the Certificate;

- in some circumstances the defendant (or compensator) may deduct some, or all, of the amount he pays to the DWP from the compensation award to the claimant (this is known as 'off-setting');

- the defendant (or compensator) is responsible for payment of all relevant benefits paid to the claimant;

- the period in respect of which listed benefits can be recovered starts on the day following an accident or injury (or when benefits are first claimed as a consequence of the accident or injury) and ends on: (i) the day on which a compensation payment is made in final discharge of the claim, (ii) the date on which an agreement is made between the compensator and the claimant under which an earlier compensation payment is treated as having been made in final discharge of any claim, or (iii) the date five years after the relevant period begins—which comes first (the 'relevant period').

A useful summary of the scheme appears on the DWP's website at www.dwp.gov.uk/cru.

Most social security benefits are paid for three main reasons and cover:

1. loss of earnings if a person is rendered incapable of work;

2. the cost of care arising from a condition; and

3. loss of mobility arising from a condition.

Benefits falling within each category can be deducted from specific heads of damage in the claimant's action against the defendant. Thus, there are certain benefits that can be deducted from damages paid to a claimant by the defendant in respect of loss of earnings (during the relevant period). Loss of earnings does not include compensation awards in respect of future loss of earnings or a 'Smith and Manchester' (handicap on the open labour market) award, loss of congenial employment, or loss of pension rights. Claims in respect of the cost of care will not include damages paid for the cost of future care of the claimant, the loss of ability to undertake DIY tasks, loss of housekeeping capacity, for special diets, or for aids or equipment. Claims in respect of loss of mobility will similarly not apply to the element of damages that deals with the claimant's future costs.

No benefits can be deducted from damages in respect of pain, suffering, or loss of amenity, loss of expectation of life and bereavement, loss of society, loss of leisure, loss of specific enjoyment, loss or deprivation of privacy, loss of marriage prospects, or breakdown of marriage.

A full list of the benefits that fall within the remit of the CRU rules for loss of earnings, the cost of care, or loss of mobility can be found on the DWP website.

Where the defendant has obtained a Certificate of Deduction of Benefits, either the claimant or the defendant can ask the CRU to review the Certificate. Requests for a review must be in writing (there is no particular form), giving reasons why it is alleged that the Certificate is wrong. If a party still asserts that the reviewed Certificate is wrong, they may appeal the CRU Certificate. An appeal must be made within one month of: (i) the date on which the compensator makes the full payment of recoverable benefits to the DWP, (ii) the date on which a decision is given by the CRU on an application for a review of the Certificate, (iii) the date when it is agreed that previous interim payment(s) should be treated as a final discharge of the claim, or (iv) the date when it is agreed that an offer is accepted.

Late appeals can be considered where there are special circumstances to justify a late appeal, but this is subject to a 'longstop' of 13 months after the date that the right to appeal arose.

7.6.3.1.2 *Personal injury damages—the recovery of NHS charges*

The CRU is also responsible for collecting from a defendant or insurer the cost of any NHS treatment that a claimant has received following an accident. The sums that may be recovered are set by the government (DWP department) and are revised from time to time by way of an annual amendment to the Personal Injuries (NHS Charges) (Amounts) Amendment Regulations.

7.6.3.2 Contract damages

The aim of damages in contract is to put the claimant in the position in which he would have been but for the breach. The assessment of this principle is made on two different bases:

- to restore the claimant to the position in which he would have been had the contract been properly performed (loss of bargain); or

- to compensate the claimant for expenditure rendered futile by the breach.

When the sum due is known (for example, for the supply of goods that have not been paid for), this would be a 'specified' claim. In contract, however, there may be other losses that are unspecified, which, on the basis of evidence before it, are assessed by the court. These may include damages for loss of profit, distress, or inconvenience. These may relate to 'expectation' loss, 'reliance' loss, or 'restitution'. Where a claim constitutes a claim for a specified sum and unspecified sums, it is called an 'unspecified sum claim'.

7.6.3.3 Nominal damages

Nominal damages may be awarded where there has been an infringement of a legal right, but where there have been no losses arising from the infringement. If actual damage to the claimant is an essential element of a cause of action (for example, for actions in negligence), then a failure to prove any damage will result in the action being dismissed.

7.6.3.4 Aggravated damages

Aggravated damages are defined in the CPR Glossary as 'additional damages', which the court may award as compensation for the defendant's objectionable behaviour. They are intended to compensate for 'injured feelings' (meaning that a company, which has no feelings, may not be awarded aggravated damages). An award is most often made when the defendant's behaviour was designed to injure the claimant's pride or dignity.

The court may increase the sum because of the way in which the defendant may have behaved and because of the additional hurt caused by the objectionable way in which the defendant caused the loss (aggravated damages).

Any claim for aggravated damages must be specifically stated.

7.6.3.5 Exemplary damages

In exceptional circumstances, the court may award enhanced damages as a penalty. These damages are distinct from aggravated damages, but they may be awarded alongside aggravated damages. These damages are defined in the CPR Glossary as 'Damages which go beyond compensating for actual loss and are awarded to show the court's disapproval of the defendant's behaviour'.

Again, as with a claim for aggravated damages, any claim for exemplary damages must be specifically sought in the claim. They will only be made in exceptional circumstances, which include:

- oppressive, arbitrary, or unconstitutional behaviour by government servants;
- where the conduct of the defendant, as well as being objectionable, was designed to make a profit in excess of the compensatory damages that are payable; and
- where exemplary damages are expressly provided by statute.

7.6.3.6 Provisional damages

Provisional damages may be awarded in cases where the claimant *may suffer* a change in his condition, that change being a risk that the injuries he suffered may change in the way identified. For example, the injury may cause an early onset of arthritis, arthritis not yet being a part of the claimant's injury. Section 32A of the Senior Courts Act 1981 provides that an award for provisional damages may be made when conditions are satisfied—the claimant has suffered injury—and there is a chance or risk of developing a serious disease or deterioration in his condition—the court will exercise its discretion when and if to make such an award. The requirements for an award of provisional damages in a personal injury claim were considered and restated (the case did not change the application of s. 32A) in *Chewings v Williams & Abertawe Bro Morgannwyg University NHS Trust* [2009] EWHC 2490 (QB). The 'risk' (of change or deterioration) must be measurable, not merely fanciful.

7.6.4 **THE DELIVERY UP OF GOODS**

A final judgment ordering the delivery up of goods may take one of three forms permitted by the Torts (Interference with Goods) Act 1977, s. 33(2):

- an order for the delivery of the goods and payment of any consequential damages—a discretionary remedy that will generally often only be made when the goods in question are unique or exceptional;

- an order for the delivery up of the goods, but giving the defendant the option of paying a set value for the goods, together with any assessed consequential damages, if any (but any payment of the set value by the defendant extinguishes the claimant's title to the goods); and

- a judgment for damages and not for the return of the goods (but, again, any payment of the set value by the defendant extinguishes the claimant's title to the goods).

7.6.5 **INJUNCTIONS**

An injunction may be either mandatory (that is, requiring some act to be done) or prohibitory (that is, requiring some conduct to stop or prohibiting threatened conduct). Any injunction is an equitable, and therefore discretionary, remedy and cannot be obtained 'as of right'. The court may award damages in place of an injunction, and will always do so if damages are a suitable and adequate remedy. See also the Additional Chapter 'Injunctions and other Equitable Remedies' on the Online Resource Centre, and Chapter 14, paragraph 14.7.

7.6.6 **SPECIFIC PERFORMANCE**

An order for specific performance is an equitable remedy and requires the performance of the obligations of a party. Again, it will be awarded if damages would not be an adequate remedy and the principles of equity are met. Specific performance is sought most often in claims related to land, but it can also be ordered in relation to goods that are rare or unique. Specific performance and damages may be awarded.

7.6.7 **RECTIFICATION**

Rectification to reflect the parties' true position is also a discretionary remedy. It is not the bargain that is rectified, but the written record of the bargain. An order for rectification is retrospective and the agreement is seen to be in the form rectified from the date on which it was originally made.

7.6.8 **ACCOUNTS**

A party alleging that an account is inaccurate must give notice of the objections of the account in his claim. The objections must give full particulars and specify the ground on which it is alleged that the account is inaccurate. Accounts are a common remedy between principal and agent, between partners, and in claims involving jointly owned property.

7.6.9 **DECLARATIONS**

The power to make a final binding declaration is contained in CPR 40.20 and the power to make interim declarations in CPR 25.1(b). The court will consider the justice to both parties in making a declaration and whether the declaration will serve a useful purpose. A declaration may make findings of fact, as well as of legal rights.

7.6.10 RESTITUTION

Claims for restitution can be made in law and in equity, and are based on the principles of unjust enrichment. Restitution deals with the principle of unjust enrichment at another's expense (in contrast to contract, in which the underlying principle is agreement and compensation is for breach of the agreement).

Restitution is used to restore the claimant to his previous position by making good the loss that he has suffered. The claim is for repayment of benefit received by the defendant, not for loss suffered by the claimant. Such a claim can arise when the damages are less than the benefit received by the defendant. The most common claims in restitution are for payment of money had and received, which covers both money paid under a mistake and money paid where there has been a total failure of consideration.

Restitution is viewed as separate and distinct from the laws of contract and tort, although it is, to a large extent, based on remedies and obligations found in contract and tort. The law of restitution does not depend on the existence of a breach of contract, but it may be an alternative action. Enrichment may be either positive (that is, the receipt of money or goods) or negative (that is, the saving of a necessary expenditure).

The remedy to which the claimant is entitled under the law of restitution is generally a personal remedy, which requires the defendant to pay to the claimant the value of the enrichment that the defendant has obtained at the claimant's expense. Alternatively, a claimant may be able to:

- seek a proprietary remedy, such as a declaration that the defendant holds an identifiable asset on trust for the claimant;

- assert a lien over an asset; or

- assert that he should be subrogated to the rights of a third party over the property of the defendant.

The courts have recognized a number of circumstances in which the law of restitution may be utilized—for example, an action for money had and received, or an action for money paid, services rendered, rescission, an account of profits, subrogation, and tracing.

A defendant may seek to defend a claim for restitution where he can show that the benefit was received by him as a valid gift, or as part of a valid agreement, or an equitable or statutory obligation owed by the claimant to the defendant. He may also seek to defend such a claim against him if he can show 'a change of position' as a result of the benefit alleged: for example, if he has donated the money to charity and he is neither a wrongdoer, nor has he acted in bad faith. There are other defences, and a practitioner acting for a client making or defending an action in restitution will need to study this area of law in detail.

7.7 YOUR CLIENT'S DISCLOSURE OBLIGATIONS

Full particulars of the disclosure obligations of a party to litigation are contained in Chapter 16, but these obligations are onerous and a client should be made aware of the need to preserve documentary (or real, or electronic) evidence, whether these documents (or things) might assist in any future action or may assist his opponent. For this reason, 'disclosure' and the client's obligations in this respect can be considered to be a pre-action substantive matter.

KEY POINTS SUMMARY

- Identify the type of action that you have, and consider jurisdictional and limitation issues at the outset.

- If acting for a child, diarize any imminent 18th birthday to enable you to deal with the consequential procedural matters.

- Break your case down into the three legal components to help you in risk assessment and evidential issues.

Case Study *Andrew James Pike v Deep Builders Ltd*

In the Andrew Pike case study, based on the information contained on the Online Resource Centre (the client's attendance note) consider the following questions.

Question 1

When does the limitation period expire?

Question 2

In which court and area should you issue proceedings, and why?

Question 3

What remedy is Mr Pike seeking? Provide details for your answer.

online resource centre

Any documents referred to in these case study questions can be found on the Online Resource Centre (Lecturer Resources)—if released to you simply click on 'Case study documentation' to access the documents that you need for Chapter 7 and to be reminded of the questions. Suggested answers to these case study questions can also be accessed on the Online Resource Centre when released to you by your lecturer.

8 PRE-ACTION PROTOCOLS

> Relevant parts of the CPR and its PDs: 3, 25, 31, 35, 36, and 44

8.1 INTRODUCTION

In this chapter, we will look at Protocol practice in general, the aims of Protocol, the content of two Protocols (the Personal Injury Protocol and the Construction and Engineering Protocol), and the Practice Direction on Pre-Action Conduct and Protocols (PDPACP). Clearly, for any action covered by a Protocol, it would be essential to look at that Protocol in detail. The aim in looking at two Protocols is to give a flavour of Protocols in practice. Because Protocols are all in a similar (but not the same) format, a closer look at two diverse ones will help the understanding of others. We will also consider the consequences of non-compliance with Protocol or the PDPACP, and the occasions on which it may be appropriate to issue proceedings without complying with Protocol practice. We also look at some pre-action applications that may be made under the CPR.

LITIGATION TRAIN: PRE-ACTION PROTOCOL AND PROTOCOL PRACTICE

First client meeting

Pre-action or Protocol phase

Issue of proceedings

Trial

General steps to note

• Letter of Claim or Letter before Claim (for debt or general contract claim). Copy documents to accompany

• Acknowledgement from defendant

• Response from defendant

• Exchange of information and documentation

• Consideration of expert evidence

• Potential meeting of parties

• Negotiations—including P36 offers

• ADR process

Note: In the context of this chapter, all references to the 'claimant' or the 'defendant' mean 'potential claimant' or 'potential defendant', because proceedings have not yet been started.

8.2 WHAT ARE 'PRE-ACTION PROTOCOLS'?

The word 'protocol' or 'Protocol' in terms of litigation is both legal jargon and a document containing specific guidance for the conduct of pre-action work for cases falling within the ambit of the specific Protocol. Legal professionals will refer to the term 'protocol' to mean work undertaken before any proceedings have been commenced, but also to mean *a* 'Protocol'—comprising specific guidance on pre-action work to be undertaken.

All the Pre-Action Protocols and the PDPACP seek to encourage a pattern of behaviour between litigants before proceedings are commenced. In many cases where this work is undertaken a settlement may be achieved and litigation is not commenced at all—'seeking settlement' (where it can be achieved with appropriate pre-action work) is a key aim of protocol practice. Work conducted in this pre-action stage under the guidance of the Protocols and the PDPACP also encourages and enables parties to enter into a form of ADR to seek a settlement. In cases where settlement is not achieved at this stage and proceedings are, by then, ultimately issued, the Protocols in place and the PDPACP aim to ensure that cases are well prepared for management by the court in litigation. It should be noted that there is an emphasis that all pre-action work (seeking to further the aims of Protocol) should also be proportionate.

8.2.1 THE CASE-SPECIFIC PROTOCOLS

It is important to remember that the Protocols do not have the same status as the Civil Procedure Rules (CPR). The Protocols have been designed to give guidance for steps to be taken before litigation in specific types of cases. There is not a specific Protocol for every type of case: so far, they have been promulgated for:

- clinical disputes;
- personal injury claims;
- defamation;
- construction and engineering disputes;
- professional negligence;
- judicial review;
- housing disrepair;
- possession claims based on rent arrears;
- disease and illness;
- possession claims based on mortgage or home purchase plan arrears in respect of residential property;
- the Practice Direction on Pre-Action Conduct and Protocols (PDPACP);
- dilapidations; and
- low-value personal injury claims in road traffic accidents and employers' liability and public liability claims. (**Note:** these procedures provide a claims procedure for cases that fall within the claims process. Such claims are handled by the Claims Portal.) (For further detail on this procedure see Chapter 9, paragraph 9.2.8.)

The more general guidance contained in the PDPACP probably indicates that there will be fewer case-specific Protocols in the future, although a specific debt action protocol is being considered (at the moment pre-action guidance for debt matters is contained within s. 6 of the PDPACP. Amendments are also expected to the Construction and Engineering Protocol and the Housing and Dilapidations Protocol during the course of this year. It may be worth noting, although outside the scope of this manual, that the Technology and Construction Court (TCC) has adopted an e-disclosure Protocol indicating that the Ministry of Justice may be inclined to approve protocols dealing with certain aspects of procedure in litigation, as well as those which give guidance for general pre-action work.

8.2.2 THE PDPACP

A party, which includes additional parties to an action arising under CPR 20 (and the parties' legal representatives), needs to consider the impact of the Practice Direction on Pre-Action Conduct and Protocols (the PDPACP). This replaced the PDPAC on 6 April 2015.

The PDPACP (and all the case specific Protocols) expect parties to exchange information and make appropriate (and proportionate) attempts to resolve the dispute without issuing proceedings. In complying with objectives of the PDPACP (and other Protocols) in seeking to identify the issues, narrow the issues, and seek to resolve legal, factual, or expert issues, the parties are expected to take such steps as are proportionate (to the dispute). Protocol practice must not be used to obtain an unfair advantage over another party.

Such steps to achieve these objectives may include:

- Seeking to understand the position of the parties.
- Making decisions how to proceed.
- Attempting to identify and settle the issues without issuing proceedings.
- Considering ADR (to assist with settlement or the identifying or narrowing of issues).
- Taking steps that support the efficient management of subsequent proceedings if litigation is commenced.
- Taking steps to reduce costs.

(PDPACP paragraph 3).

Supporting these objectives may include taking the following steps in the pre-action phase of a dispute:

- By the parties setting down, in writing, the concise details of their claim. These exchanges will be carried out in an order and timescale that the PDPACP suggests (though there is nothing to stop the parties agreeing other sensible, efficient, proportionate timescales for this exchange of information). These steps will include the Letter of Claim and the Letter of Response.
- Disclosing key documents relevant to the issues in dispute.
- Taking steps to obtain relevant and necessary expert evidence.
- Seeking to agree a form of ADR process and embarking on the process.

8.2.3 RECOVERING PRE-ACTION COSTS INCURRED

When the parties have complied with the aims and objectives of protocol practice but a claim has been subsequently issued the parties may recover costs reasonably incurred in complying with the relevant Protocol, but only to the extent that such costs are proportionate (PDPACP paragraph 5). The extent of recovery of those costs will be discretionary and in accordance with costs recovery principles (see Chapter 4).

If a case settles as a result of protocol (and proceedings have not therefore been issued), the court will not have jurisdiction over costs and the parties should seek to deal with costs in any settlement agreement. If the parties have agreed who is to be liable for costs but have not agreed the sum of those costs they may commence 'costs only' proceedings under CPR Part 8.

If a prospective claimant decides not to pursue their claim as a result of the steps taken in complying with protocol, then the costs incurred by the prospective defendant in responding and itself complying with protocol will not, generally, be recoverable. However, if a claim has been issued, but then stayed to enable the parties to engage in protocol procedures (for example, when an action has been issued for protective reasons, for example the period of limitation for the claim was near its end), the defendant may be entitled to recover its costs if the claimant subsequently discontinues the claim.

8.2.4 WHAT ABOUT DEBT ACTION WORK?

There has been discussion and consultation about a specific Protocol for debt action work. A Debt PAP has been re-drafted and is (at the time of writing) subject to consultation. This consultation closed on 11 January 2016. It is expected that further announcement will be made during the latter part of this year. At the present time guidance for this work is contained within s. 6 of the PDPACP.

Debt collection is one area of litigation where there is often justification for less pre-action investigative work and for the prospective claimant to be able to seek debt recovery quickly. In these circumstances it may be more appropriate to give the prospective defendant less time to respond to the Letter of Claim.

The debt action letter before claim is a concise letter requesting payment and usually includes only the following details:

- the identity of the claimant and defendant;
- a copy of the invoice or contract;
- details of the amount sought;
- a statement confirming that an amount is owing;
- an indication of when the amount should have been paid;
- a request for payment by a certain date (usually seven days);
- particulars of how the payment is to be made;
- a warning of costs and interest penalties if payment is not received;
- the basis upon which you are claiming interest (usually contractual or by statute); and
- your contact details.

If no payment is made, it is, however, good practice to attempt to contact the debtor by telephone—but if this fails, then you are entitled to commence proceedings immediately without any sanction from the court.

 Professional Conduct

Many clients in commercial work—particularly debt collection work—want to take immediate action and issue proceedings without compliance with Protocol behaviour or writing a letter of claim or letter before claim. This is usually because of their wish to safeguard, as far as they can, their cash flow position and often because they may have been seeking to recover the debt themselves for some time before consulting a legal practitioner and therefore feel that the debtor has 'had enough time'. However, as his legal representative, under the Code Principle 4 you are obliged to act in your client's best interest. This would include advising him to comply with the spirit of Protocol and best practice. You will need to explain to your client the potential consequences of failing to comply (as detailed in paragraph 8.6). If he continues to choose not to comply, then you must ensure that you have a detailed note on your file and a letter to your client pointing out those consequences of non-compliance. You are entitled to continue to act, however.

The litigation train in this chapter sets out a flowchart of matters to consider and the path to follow in the pre-action stage of an action.

8.3 **THE AIM OF THE PROTOCOLS OR PROTOCOL PRACTICE**

The broad objectives of the Protocols are:

- To encourage the exchange of early and full information about a prospective claim in order that the parties may understand the position or claim of their opponent.
- To enable parties to avoid litigation by agreeing a settlement of a claim before the commencement of proceedings.
- To support the efficient management of proceedings where litigation cannot be avoided.

In the same way that costs penalties may follow for a litigant who unreasonably refuses to participate in a form of ADR or who refuses a reasonable pre-action offer, costs penalties may also follow for litigants who unreasonably do not comply with Protocol (see Chapter 4, paragraph 4.2.2 for further examples).

The concept of Protocol practice is relevant to a range of initiatives for good litigation and pre-litigation practice—especially:

- the predictability of the time needed for steps that should reasonably be taken pre-proceedings; and
- a standardization of relevant information, including documents to be disclosed.

8.4 **WHAT ARE THE COMMON FEATURES OF THE PROTOCOL PHASE?**

There is a pattern to all of the Protocols in place. Each contains:

- a template for the recommended contents of a letter of claim, so that appropriate enquiries can be commenced upon receipt;
- guidelines for the contents of a letter of response. See Chapter 10 paragraph 10.3.2 for guidance on the content of a letter of response;
- guidelines for parties to provide pre-action information to each other, using standard forms and questionnaires;
- guidelines for parties to give pre-action disclosure;
- guidelines to encourage parties to instruct a single, agreed, expert—instead of each party having its own expert witness;
- guidelines to encourage the parties to try to settle their dispute without resorting to litigation—for example, by mediation, or another form of ADR; and
- a suggested bar on starting proceedings until a certain period has elapsed from the sending of the initial letter of claim.

8.5 **HOW DOES THE COURT ENCOURAGE COMPLIANCE WITH PROTOCOL PRACTICE?**

The need to undertake pre-action work within the spirit of the Protocols cannot be over-emphasized.

A party who unreasonably fails to comply with the aims of protocol practice is likely to face penalties and or sanctions by the court in any subsequent litigation. The court will consider imposing such sanctions or penalties when:

- It makes the case management directions order (see Chapter 12).
- It makes decisions on costs or interest on sums due.

In deciding the amount of costs, pre-action conduct is one of the factors that the court will consider (CPR 44.4(3)(a)(i)).

The sanctions or penalties the court may impose include:

- Making an order that the parties are relieved of the obligation to comply, or further comply, with protocol.
- Staying the action while particular steps are undertaken.
- Applying sanctions.

(PDPACP paragraph 15).

The sanctions that may be imposed for non-compliance with protocol include:

- Making an order that the party at fault pays part, or all, of the costs of the other party or parties.
- Making an order that the party at fault pays those costs on an indemnity basis (CPR 44.3(3) and see Chapter 4).
- If the party at fault is the claimant who has been awarded a sum of money, depriving the claimant of interest on that sum for a specified period or reducing the rate of interest on that sum that would otherwise have been awarded.
- If the party at fault is the defendant, and the claimant has been awarded a sum of money, awarding interest on that sum for a specified period at a higher rate (up to 10 per cent above base rate) than would otherwise have been awarded.

(PDPACP paragraph 16).

The courts will be robust in seeking an explanation of a party's pre-action conduct if it has failed to meet the aims and objectives of protocol. The case of *Webb Resolutions Ltd v Waller Needham & Green (a firm)* [2012] EWHC 3529 (Ch) is a reminder that the court will be robust in seeking to impose a sanction where it believes that a party has not complied with the letter or spirit of protocol unless there was good reason not to do so. However, the court has also made it clear that compliance with protocol should be 'proportionate' and 'appropriate'. The court will take a pragmatic view when considering an action by a litigant asking the court to impose sanctions or penalties for an opponent's non-compliance. In *Higginson Securities (Developments) Ltd & Another v Hodson* [2012] EWHC 1052 the court held that a failure to comply with an advised step in the pre-action phase was 'justified' and imposed no penalty for the failure. This case also highlighted the need for parties to incur costs in the pre-action stage 'proportionately' (to the complexities of the case and the amount of money that is at stake). See *Sainsbury's Supermarkets Ltd v Condek Holdings Ltd and Others* [2014] EWHC 2016 (TCC) In this case the claimant took no steps to comply with protocol. After the claims were struck out, the court ordered the claimant to pay part of the defendant's costs in the indemnity basis. Again, look at the case of *CIP v Galliford Try* (unreported, 3 June 2014) (TCC), in which the claimant was awarded its pre-action costs in relation to a defence pleaded by the defendant but abandoned shortly before the hearing. However, the court refused to award these costs on the indemnity basis as there had been some compliance with protocol by the defendant.

 Practical Considerations

The following are useful guidelines to ensure that Protocol practice is followed.

- Always engage with the opposing party at the earliest opportunity.
- Always write a full letter of claim and give a reasonable time in which the potential defendant can respond (other than debt collection work where the 'short form' letter before claim should be used).

- If proceedings have to be issued before Protocol steps (for example, because of the limitation period), always give a clear indication of the reasons for issuing at this stage and suggest that directions are sought to provide a stay for Protocol practice to run its course, or give full reasons why the Protocol cannot be followed.

- Protocols are not inflexible, and where it is not possible to adhere to the 'letter' of a Protocol, it should be possible nonetheless to adhere to its 'spirit'. For example, where time limits can justifiably and reasonably be varied, they should be varied to take account of the particular characteristics of the dispute.

- Reasonable early exchange of documents is essential, as is the move towards attempting to use agreed experts. Consider exchanging experts' reports early or seeking to engage an agreed expert.

- Take care not to overstate the case or to fail to mention issues that were known at the time, but which 'tactically' have not been mentioned at an early stage.

- If an opponent is failing to engage with Protocol, make this clear as soon as possible, in open correspondence. Where necessary (or at every occasion on which there has been non-compliance), state that a claim for costs or indemnity costs will be sought in any subsequent action for the non-compliance (see Chapter 4, paragraph 4.3 for a definition of indemnity costs).

- Do not reject the opponent's proposals without giving your considered (and reasonable) reasons.

- Remember that Protocol does *not* mean that you have to bend and concur with every request made. Protocol is essentially an exchange of letters, detail of the claim, and a settlement meeting. Once those obligations are concluded, you are at liberty to refuse to continue corresponding with the opponent until proceedings have been issued.

- Undertake a full 'stocktake' when Protocol has been exhausted and before issuing proceedings.

8.6 WHEN WOULD IT BE APPROPRIATE TO ISSUE PROCEEDINGS WITHOUT REFERENCE TO PROTOCOL PRACTICE?

There are essentially three situations in which it may be appropriate to take steps in the action without the cooperative communication with the opponent anticipated in any Protocol practice or when proceedings should be issued without reference to Protocol, as follows.

8.6.1 WHEN THE END OF THE LIMITATION PERIOD FOR THE ACTION IS CLOSE

When the end of the limitation period for the action is close, the claimant should issue 'protective' proceedings to avoid the action becoming statute-barred. To comply with Protocol practice and the overriding objective, the claimant should inform the defendant of the reason for his early issue. The claimant then needs either to:

- serve the proceedings and suggest to the opponent that the court be asked to grant a stay of the action for Protocol practice to be observed; or

- diarize the time by which the claim form must be served (within four months after issue—or six months after issue if the defendant resides outside the jurisdiction of the court) and suggest that the parties continue to conduct their exchanges in accordance with Protocol practice in the intervening time and before serving the claim form. (See also Chapter 7, paragraph 7.4.)

8.6.2 WHEN AN INTERIM REMEDY IS REQUIRED TO PROTECT OR PRESERVE EVIDENCE OR THE ASSETS OF THE PROPOSED DEFENDANT

When an interim remedy is required for the protection or preservation of evidence, or of the assets of the proposed defendant, once the interim application has been heard, the claimant should consider seeking directions to enable Protocol practice to be engaged with and conducted. An interim application that could be required before engaging in Protocol might be that for a search order or freezing injunction. (See also Chapter 14, paragraph 14.7.)

8.6.3 **WHEN THE PROPOSED DEFENDANT MAY ATTEMPT TO ISSUE PROCEEDINGS OUTSIDE THE JURISDICTION OF THE COURT TO AVOID THE COURTS OF ENGLAND AND WALES ASSUMING JURISDICTION OF THE ACTION**

Some actions may have a choice of jurisdiction and if it is felt that a party may issue proceedings to avoid the jurisdiction of the courts of England and Wales, it may be reasonable and justifiable to issue proceedings quickly. Again, once the proceedings have been issued, the claimant should seek directions of the court to consider how best to incorporate Protocol practice.

8.7 PRE-ACTION DISCLOSURE APPLICATIONS

An application for pre-action disclosure is a step that can be taken pre action—in the Protocol phase of an action—but making such an application is not part of Protocol. Where the circumstances for seeking pre-action disclosure are met under the provisions of CPR 31.16, such an application is one made under the CPR, not Protocol, even though the intended purpose of the application may be to seek pre-action disclosure of documents that Protocol suggests should be exchanged. It is one of the instances in which a party can seek an order of the court for compliance with a pre-action step.

An application for pre-action disclosure is sometimes necessary to investigate a potential claim fully, and if the documents needed are not forthcoming from the opponent, an application for pre-action disclosure may be required.

A court order (for pre-action disclosure) can only be made in limited circumstances—usually where:

- the respondent is likely to be a party to the proceedings;
- the applicant is likely to be a party to the proceedings;
- the documents, or classes of document, requested would be disclosed under standard disclosure rules; and
- disclosure now would fairly assist in disposing of the claim without the need to issue proceedings and save costs.

(For more details on applications for pre-action disclosure, see Chapter 14, paragraph 14.6)

An order made will specify the documents, or classes of document, which must be disclosed. The respondent must specify any documents that he no longer has or which he claims the right or duty to withhold from inspection.

Orders can be made against a person who is a non-party, but only where the document sought will support the applicant's case (or adversely affect the other party's case) and disclosure is necessary to dispose of the claim fairly or save costs. (For further details, see Chapter 14, paragraph 14.6)

Both potential parties to a claim should fully identify if there are any other potential parties, and their names, addresses, and details of insurers (if known). A delay in notifying such information could lead to a delay in progress and such delay could be construed as a failure to abide by the Protocol practice.

8.8 PRE-ACTION APPLICATIONS TO INSPECT PROPERTY

These applications are also contained within the CPR, not the Protocols, although the application is made in the Protocol phase. Again the intended purpose of the application may be to seek a party's compliance with something that clearly falls within the aims of Protocol—but, as with applications for pre-action disclosure, when the application can meet the criteria set out in the CPR for the application it will be an application under the CPR, not Protocol. In these situations the court will also have the power to enforce compliance.

CPR 25.5 deals with the ability to inspect property before the commencement of proceedings against a potential party to the action or against a non-party. This may be required when dealing with an accident at work claim. If the injury was caused by machinery, it may be prudent to inspect this machine before it is altered, adjusted, repaired, or removed. To obtain such an order, it must be shown that the property:

• is, or may become, the subject matter of the proceedings; or

• is relevant to the issues that will arise in relation to those proceedings.

 Practical Considerations

The template letter of claim supplied in the Protocol does not include a request that evidence should be preserved intact. This may be due to CPR 25.5, but it may be worth considering including this request in either the letter of claim or in the first letter to the proposed defendant.

8.9 PART 36 OFFERS TO SETTLE

An offer can be made before proceedings are commenced and, provided that it is not withdrawn, it will have the same impact and cost consequences as a Part 36 offer made after the issue of proceedings if rejected. (For further detail on offers to settle, see Chapter 15.)

8.10 THE PERSONAL INJURY (PI) PROTOCOL

In this section, we will take a closer look at the Protocol that is in place for PI cases. The aim, as with all Protocols, is to encourage better and more standardized pre-action work.

8.10.1 FOR WHICH CASES IS THE PI PROTOCOL DESIGNED?

The PI Protocol is primarily designed for personal injury claims which are likely to be allocated to the fast track (at the moment PI cases with a value between £1,000 and £25,000). However the government is committed to increasing the small claims limit for PI claims to £5,000, thereby reducing the number of lower value PI claims being allocated to the fast track. Students should look out for this amendment with the bi-annual CPR updates issued by the MoJ and to the entirety of those claims: not only to the personal injury element of a claim which also includes, for instance, property damage. It is not intended to apply to claims which proceed under:

• The Pre-Action Protocol for Low Value Personal Injury Claims in road traffic accidents (claims which exit this procedure prior to Stage 2 will proceed under this Protocol in accordance with paragraph 1.3). (For further detail of this claims procedure, see Chapter 9, paragraph 9.2.7).

• The Pre-Action Protocol for Low Value Personal Injury (Employer's Liability and Public Liability) Claims (claims which exit this procedure prior to Stage 2 will proceed under this Protocol in accordance with paragraph 1.3);

• The Pre-Action Protocol for the Resolution of Clinical Disputes; and,

• The Pre-Action Protocol for Disease and Illness Claims.

Although the PI Protocol is designed for fast-track cases, paragraph 1.1.2 states that if at any stage the claimant values the claim at more than the upper limit of the fast track, the claimant should notify the defendant as soon as possible. However, the 'cards on the table' approach advocated by this Protocol is equally appropriate to higher value claims. The spirit, if not the letter of the Protocol, should still be followed for claims which could potentially be allocated to the multi-track.

Annex A of the protocol includes an illustrative flowchart of the likely progression of a claim under this Protocol.

 Practical Considerations

It is essential to come to a conclusion as soon as possible about to which track a potential case would be likely to be allocated. The court makes a final determination of 'which track' a case will be allocated to, but legal representatives should undertake all of the relevant Protocol steps before such an allocation is made. It is therefore important to know where the case may fall, because a failure to abide by the Protocol in a case in the fast track may have significant cost consequences for you or your client. Even for a case falling within the multi-track, you will have to justify any steps taken that diverge from Protocol.

8.10.2 WHAT PRE-ACTION STEPS ARE RECOMMENDED BY THE PI PROTOCOL?

8.10.2.1 Early contact

The claimant is encouraged to contact the prospective defendant as soon as practicable to advise that investigations are underway, giving as much detail as possible at that stage. It may be some weeks before the claimant is in a position to prepare a full letter of claim (see paragraph 8.10.2.2), but any early contact apart from putting the prospective defendant on notice may enable useful questions to be asked about the selection of experts, the availability of documents, or the intention to abide by the Protocol. Such a letter could also usefully make enquiries about the prospective defendant's views on seeking to mediate or resolve the potential dispute by way of another form of ADR. The letter should say how long it is likely to be before a formal letter of claim might be sent.

An early letter of this kind will not start the timetable of time limits proposed in the Protocol.

8.10.2.2 The letter of claim

The time limits of Protocol-compliant steps are started once the formal letter of claim is sent to the proposed defendant.

The letter should contain the information described on the template at Annex B1:

- a clear summary of the facts on which the claim is based;
- an indication of the nature of all injuries that have been sustained;
- an indication of the way the injuries sustained impact on the claimant's day-to-day life;
- an indication of other financial losses, with an indication of the heads of damage unless this is impracticable;
- a request to identify the name of the proposed defendant's insurers;
- the documents that the prospective claimant proposes to disclose (if any) and seeks from the prospective defendant; and
- the date on which the letter must be acknowledged (under the Protocol, this is within 21 days).

The letter needs to be phrased in such a way that the defendant (possibly an individual) can easily understand it. It also needs to stress the requirement that this should be passed to the defendant's insurer (if there is one) immediately. If the details of the insurer are known, then a copy should be sent to the insurer at the same time. The letter should also state when a reply is expected—usually within 21 days. It should state clearly on the letter that it is the letter of claim for the proposed action.

The PI Protocol has a template letter of claim annexed to it as Appendix B1.

 online resource centre

Practical Considerations

Although the PI Protocol has a template letter of claim, it should not be thought that the letter of claim should contain only those matters set out in the template. Each particular case will be different, and there will be other matters that can usefully, and effectively, be raised and added to the template letter. It is therefore useful to see the template letter as a template for the bare minimum that the letter should contain. For example, where no earlier attempt has been made to agree a medical expert, the letter of claim could include proposals to set in motion the process for agreeing a medical expert. The letter of claim could also set out any proposed alterations to the Protocol timetable, as well as the reasons for the suggested alterations. Similarly, if earlier correspondence had not made any reference to the claimant's willingness to embark on a form of ADR, this could be a useful time to do this and, at the same time, to set out the suggested ADR timescale.

8.10.2.3 Details of any Conditional Fee Agreement (CFA), After the Event Insurance (ATE), or Damages Based Agreement (DBA)

If the claimant has a post April 2013 CFA, or ATE insurance, or a DBA there is no impact on the defendant as the success fee and ATE premium are not recoverable from the opponent. There is therefore no CPR requirement to inform your opponent of these funding arrangements. However, it may be tactically conducive to settlement and the smooth running of the case to let your opponent know how your client's case is funded: if your opponent is informed that your client has funding either by way of a CFA, DBA, or a litigation funder then this will alert them to the fact that the legal representative must genuinely believe the client's case has better than reasonable prospects of success.

8.10.2.4 Sufficient detail of the value of the claim

The priority at the letter of claim stage is for the claimant to provide sufficient information for the defendant to assess liability *and* sufficient information for the defendant to assess the likely value of the claim.

8.10.2.5 Rehabilitation

There is a duty on both the claimant and defendant to consider, at a very early stage, any reasonable needs on behalf of the claimant for rehabilitation and/or medical treatment.

The Protocol reads:

> The claimant or the defendant or both shall consider as early as possible whether the claimant has reasonable needs that could be met by early rehabilitation treatment or other measures.

The parties should therefore consider at an early stage (even before liability is resolved) how those needs might be met. The provision of any report obtained for the purposes of assessment of provision of a party's rehabilitation needs shall not be used in any litigation arising out of the accident, the subject of the claim, save by consent.

The Rehabilitation Code 2015 applies regardless of the severity of the claimant's injury (though the Code recognizes the differences in practice in the handling of a low-value claim and a claim of more serious or catastrophic injuries. For the latter the Serious Injury Guide came into effect on 12 October 2015). Both parties and the insurer have duties to consider rehabilitation (and the insurer will pay the costs of any rehabilitation report). (For further detail of the Code, see Chapter 18, paragraph 18.8.3.) Consideration of rehabilitation options should be an ongoing process throughout Protocol.

8.10.2.6 The defendant's response

Note: There is further detail of the defendant's pre-action responses in Chapter 10, paragraph 10.3.

The defendant (or his insurer) needs to reply by acknowledging the letter within the time limit (for example, 21 days). If there is no response within the 21 days, then proceedings can be started. It can be sensible to try to make direct contact with the defendant (or his insurer) to find out the reason for any delay. This may not be caused by the defendant (or his insurer) trying to avoid the issue; it is more likely to be the tardy process of the letter of claim being passed from the defendant to his broker, then to the insurer, and ultimately being allocated to a case handler, which can often take more than 21 days.

Once a response has been made, the defendant (or his insurer) has three months in which to investigate the claim. The reply must deal with liability, either admitting or denying it. If the defendant wants to admit the claim, then the defendant is bound by any admission (up to £25,000). If the defendant denies the claim, then his reasons for denial must be given.

8.10.2.7 The early disclosure of documents

Disclosure of the defendant's documents can clarify the issues that are in dispute. The claimant can send a list requesting documents that are considered relevant, and which are believed to be in the defendant's possession and should be disclosed. Where there is a denial of liability, the reply should include a list of all documents material to the issues and likely to be ordered to be disclosed by court.

If the defendant admits liability, but alleges contributory negligence, the defendant should disclose the documents that are relevant to his allegations.

Annex C of the PI Protocol sets out tables of the expected documents for disclosure in different PI actions.

8.10.2.8 The selection of experts

Whilst the use of experts in the Protocol phase is not governed by the CPR (Part 35, in particular), it is still intended that an agreed expert is used by the parties either pre or post the issue of proceedings. (For further details on joint experts, see Chapter 18, paragraph 18.8.)

However, the treatment of joint experts during the Protocol stage is fundamentally different from the treatment of experts during the course of litigation. This is because the PI Protocol suggests that the expert is jointly selected by the agreement of both parties, although there is nothing stopping the parties from agreeing to the joint instruction of a medical expert pursuant to CPR 35.

Joint selection under the Protocol, however, is effected by the claimant or defendant (usually the claimant) putting forward a list of suggested joint experts. If, within 14 days, no objections are raised by the opponent, then one of the mutually acceptable experts can be approached to examine the claimant medically and he will be an 'agreed' expert. The claimant will pay the fee in its entirety.

Once a jointly selected report has been prepared, it is only sent to the claimant. If the claimant decides to rely on the report, then he must disclose it to the defendant. Both parties can ask the expert written questions on relevant issues, such questions usually being copied to the opponent. Answers to the questions will be sent to both parties.

If a defendant has agreed to the joint expert, but then wishes to instruct his own expert witness in any subsequent proceedings, he is not entitled to rely on such a report unless:

- the claimant agrees that he may do so; or
- the court so directs; or
- the claimant's expert's report has been amended and the claimant is not prepared to disclose the original report.

Under the Protocol, however, if the parties cannot agree on the identity of a jointly selected expert, then the parties may instruct experts of their own choice. If proceedings are subsequently issued, the court will decide whether either party has acted unreasonably and, if so, the court will consider whether any expert evidence is required (and, if so, in what fields and how many), and will consider whether costs penalties should be imposed.

The key features, therefore, of joint selection are that there is likely to be a letter agreed by the parties instructing the medical expert to prepare a report, but that the report belongs to the claimant and is paid for by the claimant. It is therefore the claimant's decision whether he wishes to rely on it and subsequently to disclose it to the defendant. The agreement by the defendant to agree a particular medical expert gives him no entitlement to see the report unless the claimant discloses it. Any report prepared by a joint expert selected in the Protocol phase is therefore not a joint report for the purposes of CPR 35.

Annex D of the PI Protocol contains a template letter of instruction to a medical expert.

8.10.2.9 ADR

There are no rules regarding which methods of ADR to adopt. Discussion and negotiation are usually considered first, then perhaps early neutral evaluation (ENE) and mediation. However, with any of these options, it will not be easy to proceed fully before receiving expert evidence—especially the medical report—because full awareness of the injuries is needed to assist in quantifying the claim (see further Chapter 5, paragraphs 5.6 and 5.7).

8.10.2.10 If settlement fails, what next?

If the PI Protocol fails to secure settlement, then the claimant can proceed to issue his claim, although, in practice, the parties usually reflect on what has been achieved during the Protocol phase rather than rush to issue. This may involve seeking counsel's opinion.

8.10.2.11 If an admission is made

If protocol procedures secure an admission of liability from the prospective defendant the prospective claimant should send the prospective defendant:

- Any medical reports obtained in the Protocol stage on which the prospective claimant wishes to rely;

- A schedule of any past and future expenses and losses which are claimed (even if the schedule is provisional). The schedule should contain as much detail as reasonably practicable and should identify these losses that are ongoing. If the schedule is likely to be updated before the settlement is concluded it should say so.

The prospective claimant should delay issuing proceedings for 21 days from disclosure of the above information (unless to do so would make the claim statute barred) to enable the parties to consider whether the claim is capable of settlement. (Paragraph 8).

8.10.2.12 Stocktake

Where the protocol procedures have not resolved the dispute between the parties, each party should undertake a review of its positions and the strengths and weaknesses of its case. The parties should then consider together the evidence and the arguments in order to see whether litigation can be avoided, or, if that is not possible, for the issues to be narrowed before proceedings are issued. Where the prospective defendant is insured and the pre-action steps have been taken by the insurer, the insurer would normally be expected to nominate solicitors to act in the proceedings and to accept service of the claim form and other documents (this is not mandatory). (Paragraph 11.1).

8.11 THE CONSTRUCTION AND ENGINEERING PROTOCOL

8.11.1 GENERAL OBSERVATIONS

The Construction and Engineering Protocol is one of the shorter Protocols. As a legal representative, you should be aware that this Protocol applies to all construction and engineering disputes, including professional negligence claims against architects, engineers, and quantity surveyors. The Professional Negligence Protocol would therefore be inappropriate to use in such negligence cases for these professions. This is the only Protocol that provides that the parties should meet before any proceedings are issued, so to that extent it differs from the others (see paragraph 8.13.4).

As with all Protocols, it expressly states in its introduction its aims and objectives. It also specifically highlights how the court should deal with compliance with this Protocol and suggests that 'it will be concerned with substantial compliance and not minor departures' in so far as sanctions are concerned. This Protocol also indicates that the overriding objective applies to the pre-action period, but that whilst the Protocol should be entered into in 'good faith' and not to secure a 'tactical advantage', with building cases generating a plethora of documentation, it will not be necessary for the parties to collate and disclose 'all supporting details and evidence that may be ultimately required for litigation'.

8.11.2 THE LETTER OF CLAIM

Like the majority of the Protocols, the commencement of the Protocol is signified by a letter of claim containing enough basic information to enable the defendant to investigate the claim further. The Protocol suggests that the following information should be included:

- the parties' full names and addresses;
- a clear summary of the facts upon which each claim is made;
- the principal contractual or statutory provisions relied on;
- the nature of the relief sought—in building cases, this may be damages (for which calculations must be provided), an extension of time, or even specific performance;
- details of why the claimant believes that the defendant has wrongly rejected his claim (if the parties had been in prior correspondence); and
- the name of any expert instructed by the claimant and the issues to which that evidence will be directed.

 Practical Considerations

The upfront costs of litigation, when adhering to the Protocol, can often involve costly experts right from the very start. Consequently, the whole exercise can become very expensive. Moving towards the use of a joint expert in these kinds of dispute is likely to be more cost-efficient, as well as proportionate, for both parties.

8.11.3 THE DEFENDANT'S RESPONSE

The defendant has 14 days in which to acknowledge the letter of claim and has a total of 28 days from the date on which he received the letter of claim in which to send a full response to the claimant.

The response will indicate the following:

- which are agreed and which are not agreed facts, with reasons;
- claims that are accepted or rejected, with reasons;
- if any claims are accepted, either in whole or in part, whether the relief claimed is accepted or rejected—again, with reasons;
- details of any allegation of contributory negligence on the part of the claimant;
- details of any proposed counterclaim (on a similar basis as that which is required by a letter of claim); and
- the name of any expert instructed by the defendant and the issues to which that evidence will be directed.

If the defendant either fails to acknowledge within the 14 days or to provide a full response within the 28-day period (or any other period agreed up to a maximum of three months), then the claimant is able to commence proceedings without fear of sanctions. Clearly, if a counterclaim has been raised, then the claimant will be required to respond to that within the same time limit and to the same degree of detail as the defendant's response.

online
resource
centre

Practical Considerations

There is still a great deal of reluctance in practice about this Protocol, with the result that you may have to bring this to the attention of your opponent. With these types of case generating a lot of paperwork, there is also a reluctance to photocopy files on large projects. Remember, copying charges can be mutually requested from the opponent, but be mindful of becoming embroiled in protracted discussions regarding who should pay for the copies. Realistically, there is a practical limit to what the opponent will supply you with in terms of documents that should accompany a letter of claim or response.

8.11.4 **THE PRE-ACTION MEETING**

The pre-action meeting is the main feature of this particular Protocol and can often incur the greatest expense. However, the Protocol requires that, within a time period of a further 28 days after receipt of the defendant's response (or after the claimant's response to a counterclaim), the parties are to meet.

Practical Considerations

Construction and engineering disputes often involve many parties. In order to meet the strict timetable of the Protocol, the parties may, for example, need to fix a date for an all-parties meeting in advance of the final exchanges of correspondence on the issues to ensure availability and that the meeting takes place within 28 days of the end of that exchange. In practice, it may take more than 28 days for the meeting to take place, but as long as the parties are cooperating and acting reasonably, it is unlikely that either party will be penalized.

It is envisaged that more than one meeting may be necessary, as the purpose of the meeting is to narrow issues and identify how the issues can best be resolved. Obviously, ADR is strongly suggested in the Protocol, but it is acknowledged that if the parties see litigation as the only way forward, then the Protocol contains provisions for the parties to agree:

- whether expert evidence is required, on what issues, and whether this should be joint;
- the extent of disclosure; and
- the conduct of any potential litigation, having regard to minimizing delay and cost.

It is also worth noting that the Protocol permits any party who attended the pre-action meeting to disclose the following facts to the court if proceedings ultimately ensue:

- where and when the meeting took place;
- who attended, who did not and why, and any agreement reached; and
- whether ADR was discussed.

This is notwithstanding the fact that the court recognizes that these pre-action meetings are without prejudice.

Practical Considerations

As a legal representative, you will need to be careful in disclosing the facts of the meeting to the court. Legal representatives may be expected to supply information to the court that meets these requirements whilst at the same time protecting the 'without prejudice' status of the meeting.

8.12 THE LOW-VALUE RTA, EMPLOYERS' LIABILITY, AND PUBLIC LIABILITY CLAIMS PROCEDURE

This claims procedure is designed to be outside the court processes and may apply to low-value personal injury claims in road traffic accidents and employers' liability, and public liability claims with a value up to £25,000. For details of this procedure, see Chapter 9, paragraph 9.2.8.

KEY POINTS SUMMARY

- Be familiar with which Protocols apply to which types of case, and understand how to comply reasonably and proportionately with the guidance for best practice in the pre-action work for that type of case.

- Be familiar with the guidance laid down in the Practice Direction on Pre-Action Conduct (PDPACP), because this guidance applies both to cases that have a specific Protocol and those that do not.

- Do not be afraid to request amendments to any of the Protocols to suit your case. As long as you act reasonably and within the spirit of the Protocol generally, you cannot be criticized.

- Ensure that your client understands what the Protocol phase is all about and that he understands the possible consequences of failing to abide by Protocol or within the spirit of Protocol.

- Understand the interplay of the CPR in some pre-action applications that can be made in the Protocol (pre-action) phase.

Case Study *Bollingtons Ltd v Mrs Elizabeth Lynch t/a The Honest Lawyer*

Consider the following questions.

Question 1

What information would go in your letter before claim to Mrs Lynch?

Question 2

What points would you cover in your first letter to your new client Bollingtons Ltd? Consider which matters it would be advisable to reiterate, advise on, request from, or send to the client. Please ensure that you are certain who the client is. Consider whether you should justify and explain the steps that you have taken, and what professional conduct points could arise at this stage in this case study.

Case Study *Andrew James Pike v Deep Builders Ltd*

Consider the following questions.

Question 1

Does the PI Protocol apply in this case? If it does, explain why. If it does not, also explain why and suggest which other Protocol might apply.

Question 2

Consider the Template Letter of Claim in Annex A of the PI Protocol as it appears on the Online Resource Centre. What amendments, by way of either additions or deletions, would you make to this letter to ensure that the letter was PI Protocol compliant?

Question 3

If, by way of example only, Andrew Pike's claim was valued at less than £25,000, which Protocol or pre-action process may apply? Give reasons for your answer.

online resource centre

Any documents referred to in these case study questions can be found on the Online Resource Centre—simply click on 'Case study documentation' to access the documents that you need for Chapter 8 and to be reminded of the questions. Suggested answers to these case study questions can also be accessed on the Online Resource Centre when released to you by your lecturer.

9 STARTING YOUR COURT ACTION AND SERVING IT ON THE DEFENDANT

Relevant court forms relating to this chapter:

- N1 Claim Form
- N208 Part 8 Claim Form

LITIGATION TRAIN: STARTING YOUR CLAIM AND SERVING IT ON THE DEFENDANT

- Forms EL1, ELD1, PL1, RTA1, and RTA3 all referred to as the CNF (Claim Notification Form) if the claim is under the low-value RTA procedure

---

Relevant parts of the CPR and its PDs: 1, 6, 7, 27, 28, and 29

9.1 INTRODUCTION

No resolution has been found to your client's dispute. If Protocol has been undertaken this will be despite all of the steps taken in line with Protocol guidance and perhaps an early (but failed) attempt to settle with alternative dispute resolution (ADR). Perhaps it is because your client is faced with an intransigent opponent. If your client wishes to proceed to seek justice, litigation is now your last option.

Clearly, when we consider the emphasis that there is for pre-action preparation of a case to create every possible chance for a resolution to be found before issuing a claim, it will be clear that it is only those more difficult, less black-and-white cases that *will* proceed to litigation. Obviously, there will be those cases that proceed because the opponent has no intention of cooperating in finding a settlement or because he does not have the funds to settle. But, in general, the cases that proceed to litigation will be those in which both parties feel they have a good case—to win or to defend.

 Practical Considerations

This very generalized overview of the nature of the cases that do proceed to litigation is worth bearing in mind. It is rare that a party will want to proceed to litigation and face the heavy burden and uncertainty of it without feeling, in his own mind, that he has a good case. As the legal representative for such a client, you need to manage his expectations very carefully. A client may have a very firm conviction that he has a good case or that he has the moral high ground, but this does not necessarily mean that there is a good case in law. It is these 'certain' clients who nonetheless have a difficult case to prove who are perhaps the most difficult to manage. It is also these clients who will look to complain if things do not go as they expected, so all advice and risk assessment analysis needs to be carefully explained, and supported with a file note and correspondence. There is a balance to be struck between positive support and risk assessment: you may be doubtful, but do not overlook the fact that your client may win.

This chapter will deal with the procedural steps, considerations, and issues that need to be considered when commencing proceedings. It will include:

- the 'tracks' created by the CPR—the 'small claims track', the 'fast track', and the 'multi-track';
- the documents needed to issue proceedings;
- parties and joinder; and
- service provisions.

The initial stages of an action (issue, service of the claim form and service of the particulars of claim) are largely within the control of the claimant—the claimant will decide, within the time limits he has, when to serve and will choose a method of service available to him. However, once a defence has been filed, the court's proactive case management processes will begin. In effect the court will 'take over' the management of the case. But that is the continuing story (see Chapter 12); for now, we are assuming that the decision to commence proceedings has been taken by your client *and* that you have your client's instructions to proceed. This chapter will tell you how you will take the necessary steps towards the process of litigation.

9.2 **THE TRACKS**

The CPR have divided litigation into three different 'tracks'. The aim of these divisions is to ensure that the overriding objective of litigation is maintained—that is, to ensure that litigation is conducted justly (which includes at a proportionate cost), fairly, efficiently, proportionately, and in compliance with the rules. The court will allocate a case to a track but legal representatives are able to determine which track a client's case is likely to be allocated to, as the division between the tracks is largely according to value. The legal representative may also seek to influence, by representations made to the opponent and to the court (usually when completing the Directions Questionnaire (DQ) for the case), to which track the case is allocated (see Chapter 12, paragraph 12.6.3). Cases will be *tried* by the courts also according to value and complexity. In this way, court resources will be allocated to those cases that, in terms of value or importance, justify the time employed on them and also in a way that ensures that judges hear cases that they have the experience to hear or that justify his time (bearing in mind his experience and seniority) in hearing them.

An awareness of the likely track allocation is important because it will bring with it an appreciation of the likely management decisions the court will make for the case. For example, for a case likely to be allocated to the small claims track, the legal representative will be aware that only very limited costs for legal representation are recoverable. He will clearly need to take this into account when advising his client so that the client is also aware of this. Equally, if the claim is likely to be allocated to the fast track, the client needs to be made aware of the likely timescale of such an action and of the tight control that the judge will exercise to manage the case, to ensure that it can be concluded within 30 weeks of allocation to the fast track and a one-day trial time. To ensure this, the time and resources that the court will allocate to a fast-track case may appear, to the client, to be very restricting. The client needs to understand the reasons.

Multi-track cases encompass, by value, a huge range of cases (of a value of £25,000 upwards) and although a case may be allocated to the multi-track, if it is at the lower end of the spectrum by value, it may be necessary to discuss with clients the likelihood or merits of attempting to agree a fast-track regime for the case. It may also be necessary to advise the client that such a case (at the lower end of the spectrum in terms of value in this track), although allocated to the multi-track, is likely to be tried by a circuit judge or district judge, and will be restricted in terms of the resources and time that the court will allocate to it, so that the time spent on the case is proportionate to the value claimed.

The following represents a brief overview of the tracks. Further details of the court's case management powers that start when the case is allocated to track can be found in Chapter 12.

9.2.1 **THE SMALL CLAIMS TRACK**

CPR 27 governs the procedure of cases in the small claims track. The notes that follow are an overview of the main characteristics of cases in this track. A legal representative involved in a small claims track case will need to study the provisions in CPR 27.

9.2.1.1 What cases are likely to be allocated to the small claims track?

Cases that have an upper limit value of £10,000 will be those allocated to the small claims track, except in the following cases:

- personal injury cases, in which the upper financial limit in this track is £1,000 in value of damages for pain, suffering, and loss of amenity; (note: this limit is expected to rise, probably during 2016);

- claims by a residential tenant against his landlord for repairs or other work to the premises, with an upper limit of £1,000 in value of those repairs and an upper limit of damages;
- cases involving claims against landlords for harassment or unlawful eviction; and
- disputes involving an allegation of dishonesty that is disputed will not usually be suitable for the small claims track.

Once the court office has determined that a case is suitable for the small claims track it will send Form N149A to the parties, who will then be required to complete the DQ Form N180 (Form N181 will be used for cases allocated to the other tracks).

 Practical Considerations

In cases that fall below the financial limits of the small claims track by an admission of part of the claim by the defendant, the claimant should consider making an application for judgment on the admission under CPR 14.1(4) in order to recover costs, because these may amount to more than will be permitted in the small claims track. CPR 46.11 states that a case that has been in another track before transfer to the small claims track will have those costs provisions applying in its previous track. This provision will not apply, however, in the circumstances of a part admission, because the case will not have been 'previously allocated'.

9.2.1.2 What are the main features of cases in the small claims track?

The main characteristics of small claims track cases are as follows:

- Hearings will be less formal. The court has the power (under CPR 27.8) to conduct the hearing in a way that it considers is fair. Evidence will often not be taken on oath and the court may limit cross-examination. The judge may act as 'advocate' and may ask questions of witnesses, and he may limit or exclude cross-examination. The hearing will be tape-recorded and a party may obtain a transcript upon payment of the fee. CPR 27.10 permits the court, at the request of the parties, to hear the case without the parties being present—that is, as a 'paper' hearing.
- Lay representation is permitted and it is common for parties to represent themselves. Lay representatives or lawyers may represent companies.
- Costs are restricted and, in general, will be fixed costs, any court fees paid, and the reasonable expenses of the successful party in attending the hearing, including a sum, not exceeding £95, for lost earnings or loss of leave. The total fees of any experts permitted will be restricted to £750. The court may also award such other costs as it thinks reasonable if it thinks that a party has behaved unreasonably.

 Costs

Although the court has a wide discretion to award costs in the small claims track, it will rarely do so outside the fixed costs listed. The power to award additional costs in the face of 'unreasonable behaviour' could include making a wholly false claim, paying the whole sum just before the hearing, or deliberate delay. Where the party seeking these discretionary costs is legally represented and the party against whom these costs are sought is not, the court will look very carefully before making any additional discretionary order for costs. Clients instructing a lawyer to represent them in cases in this track need to be aware of this even in the face of what appears to be 'unreasonable behaviour'.

- Some procedural rules do not apply—these include CPR 25 (except those parts relating to interim injunctions) and CPR 31 (disclosure and inspection in this track is governed more informally). Appendix A of Practice Direction (PD) 27 sets out the documents that will normally be required. CPR 32, 33, 35, 36, 39, and 18 also do not apply to this track. These, in general, deal with evidence, offers to settle, and requests for further information.

• The path a small claims track case will take from issue of the case to its final hearing is short-circuited and the district judge may well set a final hearing date when the case is allocated to this track and a directions order for the case is made. The hearing itself will usually be before a district judge or deputy district judge. All small claims will automatically be referred to mediation where both parties have consented to mediation on their DQs. The action will be automatically stayed if the parties have been referred to mediation with liberty to apply for the purposes of carrying into effect the settlement agreement, if one is achieved at the mediation, unless the parties have agreed that the claim is to be dismissed or discontinued. For small claims where the parties have not consented to enter mediation or the mediation has failed, the court will decide whether the claim will be determined at a hearing or as a paper hearing. A paper hearing will save the time and cost of a hearing. Judges have the power to order a hearing where they think it appropriate to hold a hearing, but paper hearings are likely to be granted in the vast majority of cases in this track.

9.2.1.3 Can small claims track judgments be set aside or appealed?

9.2.1.3.1 *Setting aside*

A party in a small claims track case who was neither present nor represented at the hearing, and who had not given notice to the court and the other party that he would not be attending under the provisions of CPR 27.9(1), may apply to have any decision made at the hearing set aside and the claim reheard. To do this, the party will need to make his application to set aside not more than 14 days after the order has been served on him (CPR 27.11(2)) and he will need to establish that:

• he had a good reason for not attending or not being represented, or that he had not given notice to the court to proceed in his absence; and

• he has a reasonable prospect of success.

Therefore, a party, no matter how good his case, will have no right to have the order set aside if he was deliberately absent from the hearing. If the court does make an order to set aside, it may continue to rehear the case immediately after its decision on the application to set aside or it may list an alternative date and give such further directions as it sees fit.

Any other party who is 'unhappy' with the judgment of a small claims track hearing will need to consider whether he has grounds to appeal.

9.2.1.3.2 *Appealing*

The provisions for appeal in the small claims track are similar to those in the fast track and multi-track, but simplified. Any appeal can only be with the permission of the court that decided the case or the appellate court.

9.2.2 A 'EUROPE-WIDE' SMALL CLAIMS PROCEDURE

This procedure enables a simplified procedure for cross-border civil and commercial debt collection and small claims procedures. These are known as the European Order for Payment (EOP) and the European Small Claims Procedure (ESCP). They are both paper-based processes, using the standard forms and procedures set out in CPR 78.

9.2.2.1 The European payment order procedure (EPOP)

The EPOP was adopted under EC Regulation 1896/2006. The purpose of the EPOP is to speed up and reduce the cost of debt collection in cross-border uncontested money claims. This is achieved essentially by creating a payment procedure between member states that obviates the requirement for prior recognition of the resultant payment order by member states before enforcement.

The procedure serves as an option to claimants. In the UK, should a claimant not wish to proceed with EPOP, he is free to proceed with his own debt collection under the CPR.

9.2.2.2 The European Small Claims Procedure (ESCP)

The ESCP was adopted under EC Regulation 861/2007. The purpose of the ESCP is to simplify and speed up small claims litigation in cross-border cases, with the ultimate aim of reducing costs. As with the EOP, this is achieved by means of a procedure that eliminates the need for the issue of further proceedings to recognize and enforce the eventual judgment.

Again, as with the EOP, it is an optional process for claimants to take. It can, however, only be used where the value of the claim does not exceed €2,000.

9.2.3 THE FAST TRACK

CPR 28 governs the procedure of cases in the fast track. The notes that follow are an overview of the main characteristics of cases in this track. A practitioner involved in a fast-track case will need to study the provisions in CPR 28. The stages of a fast-track action will also be considered in greater detail later in the manual.

9.2.3.1 What cases are likely to be in the fast track?

Cases in this track will be those cases that:

- have a monetary value of between £10,000 (£1,000 in the personal injury, landlord and tenant, and other claims detailed in paragraph 9.2.1.1) and £25,000;

- have no monetary value (these could include a claim for an injunction, specific performance, or a declaration), which the court considers suitable for this track (and which do not require the more complex treatment that may be given in the multi-track);

- any other case, irrespective of its monetary value, which the court considers is suited to this track; and

- cases that the parties elect to be in this track (and where the court agrees that it is appropriate to manage the case in this track).

9.2.3.2 What are the main features of cases in the fast track?

The main characteristics of fast-track cases are as follows:

- There will be tight court control with strict time limits. When a case is allocated to the fast track, the court will set a programme for the case that enables the trial to take place within 30 weeks of allocation. The trial 'window' (a period of time—usually three weeks—within which the trial date will ultimately be set) will be set at allocation.

- Costs will be strongly linked to 'proportionality'. Increasingly, the CPR are looking to impose (and increase the scope of) fixed costs in this track. The fast track provides a 'no frills' procedure for medium-sized cases that do not justify detailed or extensive preparation. In effect, there will no more than seven months available in which to make the case ready for trial.

Once a case is issued and the court office indicates that it is likely to be allocated to the fast track, it will issue a notice of intended allocation in Form N149B(FT). On receipt of this the parties will need to consider the following procedure and standard directions:

- Accept allocation to this track and download and complete the DQ. In the fast track the DQ will be in form N181. Parties must send a copy of the completed form to the court and all parties. Parties are under an obligation to consult with each other when completing their DQ. In considering and completing the DQ, parties may have regard to the standard directions set out in CPR 28. Parties are encouraged to agree directions, and where these agreed directions enable the case to proceed within fast-track principles, the court is likely to make the directions orders requested.

- The court will restrict expert evidence, and if expert evidence is permitted, the emphasis will be on joint experts and written, but not oral, evidence from the expert(s) at the trial. Any party seeking expert evidence will need to provide justification for it and provide an estimate of the likely cost. Cost capping is likely to be applied to any expert evidence in this track.

- Evidence of fact will also be restricted so as to enable the case to be heard within the short trial time of one day for cases in this track. A witness's statement will invariably be ordered to stand as his evidence-in-chief.

- Requests for further information (usually to clarify another party's case) will be controlled and time limits imposed to respond will be tight—usually within 14 days of the order.

- The filing of pre-trial checklists will be standard. As a further incentive to settle, the hearing fee paid on the filing of pre-trial checklists will be refunded if a settlement is reached at least 14 days before the trial date.

- Trial timetables will often be set. Simple trial timetables will set a limit for the time that each party will have in which to submit its evidence and give its closing submissions. More complex trial timetables will set the time allowed and the order of each stage of the trial—the whole providing for a five-hour trial period, to include judgment and summary assessment of costs.

- Trial bundles will be standard and a direction may be made for a case summary to be lodged.

- The parties will submit costs schedules before the trial and the judge will be expected to deal with costs at the end of the trial by way of summary assessment. The court's power to award costs in fast-track trials is limited by CPR 28.2(5), which sets fixed amounts for the costs of the trial depending on the amount recovered.

- Trials will be heard by circuit judges or district judges.

 Costs

The emphasis for fast-track trials is to provide an efficient, speedy resolution to disputes that have not been settled by other means. Costs are restricted and clients need to be kept fully informed of the amount of time that their legal representative can justifiably spend on the case. Where a client has not been kept fully informed of this and a high legal bill is incurred, even where the client may have won the action, the courts are unlikely either to impose a full costs recovery order against the losing party, and in circumstances in which the legal representative cannot show that the client has been kept fully informed of what is a 'reasonable level of time spent', the courts are unlikely to allow those costs to be recovered from the client either.

9.2.3.3 Can fast-track judgments be set aside or appealed?
The provisions for setting aside default judgments in the fast track are those set out in CPR 12 and 13, and these are dealt with in Chapter 14, paragraph 14.2. Appeals procedure against judgments is contained within CPR 52 and is dealt with in Chapter 19, paragraph 19.7.3.

9.2.4 THE MULTI-TRACK

CPR 29 governs the procedure of cases in this track. The notes that follow are an overview of the main characteristics of cases in this track. A legal representative involved in a multi-track case will need to study the provisions in CPR 29. The stages of a multi-track action will also be considered in greater detail in the relevant sections of this manual.

9.2.4.1 What cases are likely to be in the multi-track?
Cases in the multi-track will be those cases that:

- have a value over £25,000;

- have a value of less than £25,000, but in which the trial will last for more than one day; and

- are complex or important cases of any, or no, value, where it is appropriate for them to be dealt with in this track.

Cases in the multi-track may be issued in the County Court or the High Court (or District Registry of the High Court), but note CPR 7A 2.1 and 2.2 (see paragraph 9.3.3).

The financial value of cases in the multi-track will not be the only criterion to be applied when considering its suitability for this track, and CPR 26.8 sets out additional criteria that will be applied to the allocation of cases to this track. These include:

- the nature of the remedy sought;
- the likely complexity of the facts, law, or evidence;
- the number of parties or likely parties;
- the value of any counterclaim or other CPR Part 20 claim (additional claim) and the complexity of any matters relating to it;
- the amount of oral evidence that may be required;
- the importance of the claim to persons who may not be parties to the proceedings; and
- the views expressed by the parties (although the court is not bound by these views).

The court has the power to take any other factors into account when considering whether to allocate a case to this track. Cases within the financial criteria of the track may still find that they are transferred for trial to the equivalent of a fast-track judge, because the case does not require the experience of judges hearing the multi-track trials. In general, cases with a value of £100,000 or less will be transferred to the County Court hearing centre for trial.

Cases that are likely to stay and be **tried** in the High Court or a district registry in this track will be:

- cases of a high financial value (exceeding £100,000);
- cases involving issues of public importance;
- test cases;
- clinical negligence cases; and
- cases in which there is a right to trial by jury, including deceit cases.

9.2.4.2 What are the main features of cases in the multi-track?

The main features of cases in the multi-track include the following:

- Once a case has been identified by the court office as one suitable for the multi-track it will issue a notice of intended allocation to the parties in form N149C (MT). As with the fast-track cases, the parties will be expected to download and complete the DQ in form N181. Again, parties should consult with one another as to the directions they seek, using a menu approach to the directions they seek and by reference to the standard and model directions suitable for cases in the multi-track directions that are available online. Cases in this track at the lower end of the spectrum in terms of value are likely to have directions orders that are similar to those in the fast track. As with all the tracks judicial case management is tight, but in this track, the courts will employ a greater range of management decisions, because the value of cases in this track is so broad. The case management decisions in this track will be designed to reflect this range. The more complex cases may have several CMCs and a pre-trial hearing. The lower-value, simpler cases will have directions applied to them that are the same as, or not very dissimilar to, fast-track directions. Directions that are tailored to the requirements of each case are more likely to be made in this track if it is proportionate to do so.
- Statements of case are still intended not to be technical. Simplicity and clear English is the key with all documents drafted for trials under the CPR, and the multi-track is not excluded from these aims.

- There will be a focus on precise issues. As with all tracks, the courts will expect parties to narrow the issues in dispute.

- Stays for the purpose of ADR will be encouraged. In this track, the procedural judge, who will have experience of these cases, may use CMCs as mediation-style hearings to promote settlement, and will attempt to restrict and identify the issues to be tried.

- If a multi-track case is being dealt with in the Commercial Court or the Technology and Construction Court a judge will be assigned to that case, and he will handle all CMCs and pre-trial reviews. The High Court also encourages this and judges can reserve future CMCs or pre-trial reviews, or hearings, for a case to themselves. As with any CMC in this track or the fast track, it should be a legal representative (or counsel) who has knowledge of the case who attends and, when attending, he should ensure, as far as possible, that he has authority to act on the matters likely to arise at the CMC. Where the person attending does not have this knowledge and authority, and this causes an adjournment of the hearing, the courts will be more ready to impose a wasted costs order in this track.

- The court will exercise greater flexibility with expert evidence in this track and will more commonly allow parties to have their own experts or experts in more than one field. However, the principles of the overriding objective will still apply—notably, that of proportionality.

- Case summaries and skeleton arguments are commonly ordered in the directions in this track for CMCs, and interim and final hearings.

9.2.4.3 Can multi-track judgments be set aside or appealed?

The provisions for setting aside judgments in the multi-track are those set out in CPR 12 and 13, and these are dealt with in Chapter 14, paragraph 14.2, for default judgments. Appeals against judgments procedure is contained within CPR 52 and is dealt with in Chapter 19, paragraph 19.7.3.

9.2.5 ISSUING A CLAIM IN THE COUNTY COURT

There is a single County Court. Cases in the County Court will be issued either in:

1. The County Court Money Claims Centre (CCMCC), unless special procedures are provided in the Rules or PDs (see PD 2C and PD 7A.4A.l). All County Court money claims under CPR 7 should be issued in the CCMCC.

   Once claims have been issued, they are likely to be managed in the CCMCC until a hearing is required. Proceedings will then be sent to an appropriate County Court hearing centre. There is a discretion for a court officer to send the case to a preferred hearing centre, the defendant's home court, or such other court as may be appropriate at any time if he considers the claim should be referred to a judge for directions (CPR 26.2A).

   Or

2. A County Court hearing centre unless any rule, PD or amendment provides otherwise (PD 2C.2). These include:

   a. Probate claims.

   b. TCC claims.

   c. Intellectual property claims.

   d. Proceedings under Parts 1 to 11 of the Insolvency Act 1986.

      i. Proceedings under s. 67(1) and (2) of the Race Relations Act 1976.

   e. Proceedings under the Companies Acts or the Limited Liability Partnerships Act 2000 in respect of which the County Court has jurisdiction.

(PD 2C.3.1(3) and 3.3)

Also, claims of a debtor or hirer for an order under s. 129 of the Consumer Credit Act 2006 (known as a 'time order') must be made at the County Court hearing centre where the claimant debtor or hirer resides or carries on business (PD 7B.4.3).

A full list of all of the County Court hearing centres in England and Wales can be found on the HM Courts and Tribunals Service website under 'Court Finder'.

Or

3. Certain claims may be started at any County Court hearing centre. These include:

- Certain Consumer Credit Act 2006 claims.
- Possession claims.
- Accelerated possession claims.
- Landlord and tenant claims.
- Applications for certain types of injunctions.

(PD 2C.4)

Or

4. Part 8 claims which may be started at any County Court hearing centre unless a rule, practice direction or enactment provides otherwise. However, when a claim is given a hearing date, the court may direct that the claim be transferred to another County Court hearing centre, if appropriate (PD 2C.6).

9.2.6 ISSUING A CLAIM IN THE HIGH COURT

The High Court has three divisions:

- Chancery Division.
- Queen's Bench Division.
- Family Division.

And within the Chancery Division and the Queen's Bench Division there are 'specialist courts'. Cases in the Family Division are not within the scope of this manual.

The Chancery Division typically deals with claims involving:

- Equity.
- Trusts.
- Commercial fraud.
- Tax.
- Intellectual property.
- Land.
- Business disputes.
- Contentious probate.
- Regulatory work.
- Bankruptcy.
- Professional negligence.

Some claims must be brought in the Chancery Division and these are listed in the Chancery Guide at paragraph 18.1. There are some County Court hearing centres that can handle Chancery Division matters and some claims in Chancery may be issued in the County Court in those hearing centres (PD 7 A.2.5).

The Queen's Bench Division typically deals with claims for:

- Defamation.
- Breach of contract.
- Negligence.
- Personal injury.
- Land possession claims.
- Non-payment of debts.

Some claims must be brought in the Queen's Bench Division and these are listed in the Queen's Bench Guide at paragraph 1.5.5. Certain cases may also be brought in one of the specialist courts of the Chancery Division or the Queen's Bench Division but these are also outside the scope of this manual.

Cases brought within the High Court may be brought in the High Court in London or one of the District Registries (see Chapter 7 paragraph 7.2).

9.2.7 LORD JUSTICE BRIGGS INTERIM REPORT JANUARY 2016

It is worth noting the topics raised by LJ Briggs in his review of the future of the civil courts structure published on 12 January 2016. This included the recommendation that an Online Court should be created for claims up to £25,000 (intended to enable litigants in person to pursue claims). Legal representatives should be alert to changes in this field. LJ Briggs also recommended a review of the financial limits of claims issued in the County Court and the High Court. Again legal representatives should be alert to the announcement of possible changes.

9.2.8 THE CLAIMS PROCESS FOR LOW-VALUE ROAD TRAFFIC CLAIMS, EMPLOYERS' LIABILITY CLAIMS, PUBLIC LIABILITY CLAIMS, AND DISEASE AND EMPLOYERS' LIABILITY CLAIMS

This claims process is contained within the Pre-Action Protocol for low-value personal injury (employer's liability and public liability) includes claims for personal injury in:

- road traffic accident claims (injury arising out of the use of a vehicle);
- employers' liability (EL) claims; and
- public liability (PL) claims.

with a value up to £25,000. Cases in this portal are handled by Claims Portal Limited. The claims process for cases in this portal is intended to speed up matters where liability (but not quantum) is admitted and that are relatively straightforward up to this value. 'Straightforward' in this context would not include, for example, claims in which contributory negligence is alleged or those in which issues of causation are raised. It is thought that many of the higher-value claims within the bracket up to £25,000 will exit this procedure into litigation on grounds of complexity.

9.2.8.1 Low-value RTA claims procedure

A brief resume of this procedure is detailed here:

- This procedure came into force on 30 April 2010 and was extended to also include EL and Pl claims in July 2013.
- It applies in those cases with a value of damages between £1,000 and 25,000 (in RTA actions with the claim for personal injuries of at least £1,000, excluding vehicle damage). The following claims are excluded from the procedure: Motor Insurers, Bureau claims, deceased party (claimant or defendant) claims, claims where the claimant is bankrupt, claims where the defendant is insolvent and there is no identifiable insurer, or claims where the claimant or the defendant is a protected party or a vulnerable adult. In respect of disease or personal

injury claims, claims where there is more than one defendant are also excluded, as are claims where the accident or alleged breach of duty occurred outside England and Wales, and claims involving clinical negligence and any mesothelioma claim.

9.2.8.1.1 *The most relevant sections from the Protocol*

These are:

1.1 Admission of liability' means that the defendant admits that:

    (a) the breach of duty has occurred;

    (b) the defendant thereby caused some loss to the claimant, the nature and extent of which is not admitted; and

    (c) the defendant has no accrued defence to the claim under the Limitation Act 1980.

If causation is an issue, the claim should exit the Portal:

(1) Employer liability claim' means a claim by an employee against their employer for damages arising from:

    (a) a bodily injury sustained by the employee in the course of employment; or

    (b) a disease that the claimant is alleged to have contracted as a consequence of the employer's breach of statutory or common law duties of care in the course of the employee's employment, other than a physical or psychological injury caused by an accident or other single event.

Disease claims (within the value) are therefore likely to start in the Portal, but most will probably exit if causation is not admitted.

Most EL claims are likely to exit the Portal for a number of reasons:

    (a) lack of information to investigate;

    (b) time taken to investigate—there is often more complexity for EL claims;

    (c) the difficulty of obtaining a report from the policyholder and documents within the Portal time periods.

PL claim means a claim for damages for personal injury arising out of a negligent breach of a statutory or common law duty of care made against:

    (a) a person other than the claimant's employer; or

    (b) the claimant's employer in respect of matters arising other than in the course of the claimant's employment; but

    (c) does not include a claim for damages arising from a disease that the claimant is alleged to have contracted as a consequence of breach of statutory or common law duties of care, other than a physical or psychological injury caused by an accident or other single event.

Again, most PL claims are likely to exit the Portal for a number of reasons:

    (a) the lack of time to investigate for the defendant and obtain an accident report. The insurer also needs time to obtain the records from the policyholder;

    (b) the complexity of the claim—often more information is required from the claimant before an admission can be made;

    (c) most insurers will not admit causation readily and without seeing the GP/hospital records.

9.2.8.1.2 *Commencement procedure—Stage 1*

The standard forms used in the process set out by this Protocol are available from Her Majesty's Courts and Tribunal Service (HMCTS) website at www.justice.gov.uk/forms/hmcts.

- Depending on the claim being made (whether an RTA, PL, or EL claim), Forms RTA1, EL1, ELD1, or PL1 will be used; these are called a Claims Notification Form (CNF) (See Appendix 11.). Before commencing a claim in the Portal legal representatives are required to undertake 'previous claims' checks on potential claimants and to confirm to the defendant that this has been done.

- The procedure is dealt with online and the CNF form is completed and submitted online.

- The CNF is also submitted electronically to the insurer and by first-class post to the defendant. The insurer must acknowledge receipt of the CNF the next day, but has 15 days to respond in full.

- If the claim is admitted, costs of £200 are payable for Stage 1 of an RTA claim (£300 for an EL or PL claim) within ten days.

9.2.8.1.3 *The procedure in cases where the CNF procedure does not settle the action*
The case re-enters pre-action Protocol if:

- the insurer had failed to respond to the CNF;

- liability has been admitted but subject to an allegation of contributory negligence (in an RTA claim, other than on the issue of the wearing—or not—of a seat belt);

- liability is denied;

- it is alleged that the CNF is incomplete;

- it is alleged that the claim is overvalued;

- if the fixed costs on an admission have not been paid within ten days.

9.2.8.1.4 *CNF procedure—Stage 2*
This will occur when liability has been admitted on the CNF and fixed costs paid. In this situation:

- The claimant completes the Medical Report Form EPL3 and sends it to an appropriate expert who completes the form, dealing with injury (diagnosis), opinion, and prognosis. The expert also deals with any seat belt issues if raised.

- A medical report in soft tissue injury claims brought under the RTA PAP may be sought from a not for profit company, MedCo Registration Solutions (MedCo). Medico-legal experts and medical reporting organizations (MROs) will need to be registered with MedCo in order to provide medico-legal reports for RTA soft tissue injury claims. Users will be able to use the MedCo Portal to search for individual experts or MROs and they will receive a number of randomly generated results from which to choose, to prevent the potential for conflicts of interest between those commissioning and those providing medico-legal reports. There is an accreditation requirement for medico-legal experts and MROs (this is intended to improve the quality of medical evidence and reports). The claimant confirms the content of the Medical Report Form.

- The claimant's legal representative completes the Settlement Pack Form (EPL4)—this will include the agreed Medical Report Form and sets out calculations and a settlement figure the claimant feels is justified.

- The insurer has 15 days in which to accept or make a counter-offer. If a counter-offer is made, the claimant has 20 days within which to consider it.

- If the action is concluded, the agreed sum is paid plus an additional sum of £300 (for an RTA claim), and £600 (for EL or PL claims) costs for this stage (note: the relevant Stage 1 fixed costs will already have been paid for Stage 1).

9.2.8.1.5 *CNF procedure—Stage 3*
This stage will be implemented where there has been a settlement on liability but not on quantum. In this situation:

- The claimant's legal representative sends the insurer a Court Proceedings Pack (Form EPL6).
- Proceedings are commenced by a modified Part 8 procedure.
- The final assessment hearing can be a paper or oral hearing.
- The fixed costs for this stage are £250 (if a 'paper' hearing) plus an additional £250 advocate's fee (if the matter is listed for a hearing) (this fixed cost is the same for all claims in the Protocol). Please see the Online Resource Centre for examples of sample documents and correspondence of a claim in the Portal. These documents provide an example of a completed CNF (PL1) and the accompanying correspondence. Note that in this example the defendant is acting in person and failed to respond to the claim within the time limits. As a consequence of this, the matter reverted to the Personal Injury Protocol and may ultimately result in litigation. You will see in the letters the degree of explanation given in the correspondence to a defendant acting in person.

9.3 THE DOCUMENTS NEEDED TO COMMENCE AN ACTION

The most common way in which to start civil proceedings is by issuing a claim form (Form N1), although there are still several different ways in which an action may be commenced depending on the type of action, as follows:

1. A claim form under CPR Part 7—Form N1—is the standard (and by far the most common) method under the CPR. There are specialist versions of Form N1 for use in Admiralty claims and in the Commercial Court in the Queen's Bench Division of the High Court.

2. A claim form under CPR Part 8—Form N208—can be used in proceedings in which there are no substantial factual disputes (for example, in a claim by or against a child or patient that has been settled before the commencement of proceedings and the sole purpose of which is to seek approval of the court to the settlement), or where a Practice Direction directs the use of a Part 8 claim form (for example, in actions seeking a company director's disqualification). (See paragraph 9.3.6 for further discussion on the Part 8 procedure.)

3. A CPR Part 20 claim form—Form N211—can be used for additional claims and other subsidiary claims.

4. An arbitration claim form—Form N8—is available for use in applications under the Arbitration Act 1996.

5. Special claim forms—Forms N5, N5A, and N5B—are available for starting a claim in possession cases and for actions seeking relief from forfeiture.

6. A specialist claim form—Form N2—is available for use in probate proceedings.

7. A 'petition', rather than a claim form, is used in family proceedings, the winding up of a company, or administration proceedings and bankruptcy actions.

8. An originating application form can be used in actions under the Insolvency Act 1986.

9. An interpleader notice is to be used in some County Court interpleader proceedings.

10. 'Informal' applications may be available under a specific statutory authority (for example, an application under the Deeds of Arrangements Act 1914, s. 7).

Although each of these forms of initiating proceedings is quite common, a legal representative new in the litigation department is unlikely to have much experience of many different methods of initiating proceedings outside the use of Form N1 procedure. However, one of the other proceedings that may more commonly be used is the Part 8 proceeding. We will therefore look at the Form N1 procedure in some detail for Part 7 claims and highlight the main features of Form N208 for a Part 8 procedure.

9.3.1 THE CLAIM FORM N1 FOR PART 7 PROCEDURE

Unless, under the CPR, another method of commencing proceedings is required or permitted, an action will be commenced using the claim form in Form N1. The definition of 'starting proceedings' is when the court issues, at the request of the claimant, a claim form prepared by, or on behalf of, the claimant. Issuing a claim involves the court sealing the claim form with its official seal. This is important because it:

- *stops* time running for limitation purposes (it is 'issue', not service, that is the relevant date for limitation purposes); and

- *starts* time running for service.

CPR 7 and 16.2 govern the claim form requirements. The front page of the claim form is essentially an administrative document. It assists the court office to see 'at a glance' for which court the claim is intended, the names of the parties, the nature of the action (for example, contract or tort), the value of the action (which will determine the court fees that will be payable to issue the claim), the addresses of all of the parties to be served, and the fee paid. The fees payable can be found in the Civil Proceedings Fees and Family Proceedings Order (Amendment) Order 2015. See paragraph 9.2.5 in respect of designated money claims which will all be issued out of the CCMCC.

See the Online Resource Centre for a completed and annotated Form N1.

> ### ✓ Practical Considerations
>
> It is always worth remembering these basic facts about the front page of the claim form. Those new to litigation commonly and consistently tend to put far too much detail on the front page of the claim form—especially at the section headed 'Brief details of claim'. The judges who will be managing the case and hearing the trial of the action will rarely, if ever, read the front page of the claim form. The detail of the claim should be reserved for the particulars of claim.

9.3.2 WHAT INFORMATION SHOULD BE INCLUDED ON FORM N1?

CPR 16.2 states that the claim form must include all of the following.

1. It must set out the names and addresses of the respective parties, including the parties' titles and postcodes. (The postcode can be obtained from Royal Mail, online at http://www.royalmail.com.)

2. It must concisely state the nature of the claim, and whether the Practice Direction on Pre-Action Conduct and Protocols (PDPACP) has been complied with.

3. Where possible, it must state the value of the claim (CPR 16.3) by stating that the claimant expects to recover:

   - not more than £10,000 (but note the exceptions to this—in a claim for personal injuries or in a claim by a tenant against his landlord for repairs where the figure is stated as 'not more than £1,000'—see paragraph 9.2.1), which will indicate a case that is likely to be allocated to the small claims track; or

   - more than £10,000 (or £1,000), but not more than £25,000, which will indicate a case that is likely to be allocated to the fast track;

   - more than £25,000, which will indicate a case that is likely to be allocated to the multi-track; or

   - the claimant cannot say how much is likely to be recovered.

   If the claim is to be issued in the High Court, it must include one of the following statements:

- the claimant expects to recover more than £100,000; or
- some other enactment (giving details) provides that the claim may be commenced in the High Court.

If the claim is for personal injuries, that the claimant expects to recover £50,000 or more.

The statement of value on the claim form does not limit the court to award a judgment in that sum. The statement of value determines the court fee that will be payable on the issue of the claim form (Civil Proceedings and Family Proceedings Fees (Amendment) Order 2015).

In computing the value to place on the claim form, the following are disregarded:

- interest (for unspecified sum claims);
- costs;
- any potential finding of contributory negligence (unless admitted);
- any potential counterclaim or set-off (unless admitted); and
- any amounts to be recovered from state benefits under the Compensation Recovery Rules contained under the Social Security (Recovery of Benefits) Act 1997, s. 6.

If the claim is for a sum set out in a foreign currency, then the claim form must specify the sterling equivalent and the source of the conversion rate used.

4. On the back page of the claim form, the claimant has the option of stating his case in full in accordance with the drafting requirements for the particulars of claim (see Chapter 11, paragraph 11.4) if there is room to do so. Where the particulars of claim are included in this section, the claim form is called an 'indorsed' claim form. In these circumstances, the statement of truth must also be completed. If, as is often the case, there is insufficient room to set out the claimant's case fully, the claim form will merely indicate whether the particulars of claim are 'attached' or 'to follow'. The options available for the claimant are:

- to serve the indorsed claim form, together with the documents detailed in paragraph 9.3.5;
- to serve the 'unindorsed' claim form—in which case, the particulars of claim must be served within 14 days of service of the claim form (see paragraph 9.3.5); or
- to serve the unindorsed claim form with the accompanying particulars of claim, together with the other documents set out in paragraph 9.3.5.

The claimant will also need to indicate whether a Human Rights Act 1998 issue is being raised in the claim on this reverse side of the claim form (and, if so, the human rights issue being raised must be specifically stated in the particulars of claim).

 online resource centre

9.3.3 IN WHICH COURT SHOULD THE CLAIMANT CHOOSE TO ISSUE?

There is an apparent 'conflict' between the law and the CPR in the choice of court. The provisions relating to jurisdiction need to be considered when completing the claim form. As stated in Chapter 7, the High Court and County Court have, in general, jurisdiction for all cases, whatever the value in contract and tort. Under the law, therefore, a party may issue his claim in the High Court or the County Court. However, the CPR provide that a case should not be issued out of the High Court unless the value exceeds £100,000 (PD 7A.2.1), and if the claim is for personal injuries, should not issue out of the High Court unless the value of the damages claimed exceeds £50,000 (PD 7A.2.2). (See also Chapter 7, paragraph 7.2.2.)

TABLE 9.1 TYPES OF CLAIM

Type of claim	Jurisdiction
A money claim	May be commenced in the High Court only if the claimant expects to recover more than £100,000 (PD 7A.2.1).
A money claim issued in the High Court (Royal Courts of Justice)	May be commenced in the High Court, but the claim will usually be transferred to the County Court if the claim is worth less than £100,000, unless one of the exceptions stated in PD 29.2.2 applies.
A claim for personal injuries	May be commenced in the High Court only if the value of the claim is £50,000 or more (PD 7A.2.2).

 Practical Considerations

As long as you can justify your decision (in terms of the overriding objective) to issue in the chosen court, the court will not penalize you. The prime point to note is to act reasonably.

9.3.3.1 Summary

For the practitioner undertaking less specialist litigation, the important rules can be summarized as in Table 9.1.

 Practical Considerations

If a claim is issued in the High Court when it should have been issued in the County Court, the court will often exercise its powers of management contained in CPR Part 3 and, specifically, the powers for transfer contained within CPR Part 30. The powers under these provisions include a power to rectify such an error (and order a transfer), as well as a power to strike out. A practitioner cannot be certain which of these powers the court will decide to exercise. The court will consider whether the error was deliberate or a bona fide mistake. It is important that the court is informed if an error is noted as soon as practicable. Care must always be exercised when deciding in which court to issue, because the consequences could be significant. If a mistake is made very close to the end of the limitation period, an order to strike out the claim issued in error could be a grave mistake. Even if the order to strike out were well within the limitation period, the issue fees would have to be paid again. If an order to transfer is made that rectifies the error, then the party at fault will usually be ordered to pay the costs involved in the transfer.

It should be noted that the court officials who deal with issue will generally accept the papers for issue even if they believe that the case has been issued in the wrong court, because these court officials have no power to make judicial decisions.

 Professional Conduct

Where a mistake has been made by a legal representative, it should be noted that certain professional conduct Principles may apply and require the legal representative to inform the client of the mistake. The Code Principles 2, 4, 5, and 6 need to be upheld. Informing the client as soon as it is known that a mistake has been made would indicate that these Principles are being upheld. Further action may also be required which could include further advice in the light of the mistake.

Also consider CPR 44.2: where a costs order has been made against a legally represented party, that legal representative must inform the client of this within seven days of receipt of the order. Consider also CPR 48.7.5 in a situation in which the court considers making a 'wasted costs order' and the information that should be given to the client concerning this.

9.3.4 DOES INTEREST NEED TO BE SPECIFIED ON THE CLAIM FORM?

In specified sum claims, only the sum of interest accrued needs to be stated on the claim form, but the sum of interest will not be part of the 'value' of the case for tracking purposes.

9.3.5 WHAT OTHER DOCUMENTS ARE NEEDED TO START THE ACTION?

Although the claim can be issued by sending (or taking) to the court the completed Form N1, the court will not issue the claim until the following steps are taken and the further documents are lodged:

- the court fee—the fee to be paid will vary according to the sum claimed. The level of fees to be paid can be found in SI 2014/874 (L. 17)—Civil Proceedings Fees (Amendment) Order 2014. The fee to issue proceedings for the recovery of money is approximately 5 per cent of the value of the claim for all claims over £10,000. The fees for claims of less than £10,000, which represent over 90 per cent of all money claims, were not subject to the fee rises introduced in March 2015 and largely remain at pre-2015 levels. There is a maximum fee to issue proceedings of £10,000 but with a discount of 10 per cent being applied to these fees where the claim is initiated electronically using the Secure Data Transfer facility or Money Claims Online;

- sufficient copies of the claim form for service on each of the defendants, together with a copy for the court file. Where there is more than one defendant, each copy of the claim form will have the relevant address of the defendant (including his postcode) on the front of the form in the bottom left-hand box. The address needs to be an appropriate address for service on that defendant (see the service provisions in paragraph 9.7); and

- where there is a party acting through a litigation friend, the litigation friend's certificate of suitability (Form N235).

Once the relevant documents have been received, the court issues the claim by sealing the claim form and enters details of the claim in the court 'issue book'. It enters a claim number against these details in the issue book and stamps the number on each claim form. The court will then send a notice of issue to the claimant. Form N205A will be used for a specified sum claim, Form N205B will be used for a non-specified sum claim, and Form N205C will be used in a non-monetary claim.

The court may then effect service of the claim form on the defendant(s) or return the documents to the claimant for service (see paragraph 9.7.2).

The claimant has the option of filing with these documents the particulars of claim, in which case, the response pack (Form N9) will be included in the documents served on the defendant. The court will supply Form N9 for this purpose. If the claim form is served on the defendant(s) without the particulars of claim, the defendant need take no action in response and the response pack (Form N9) is not served until the particulars of claim are served.

The claimant must serve the particulars of claim within 14 days of service of the claim form. Service of the particulars of claim must be accompanied by the response pack (and if it is not, there has not been effective service).

Once he has been served with the particulars of claim and response pack, the defendant must now take steps to respond to the action (see Chapters 10 and 11 for detail of the particulars of claim and see the court forms available on the Online Resource Centre).

online
resource
centre

9.3.6 THE FORM N208 PART 8 PROCEDURE

Part 8 procedure is intended for cases in which the nature of the relief or remedy sought, or the lack of factual dispute, makes using standard Part 7 Form N1 procedure unnecessarily cumbersome: for example, Part 8 will be used if a case concerning a child litigant is 'settled' in the

Protocol phase of the action. Such a settlement will not give a sufficient discharge to the paying party unless the court has approved the settlement. To do this, an application will be made in Part 8 proceedings using Form N208. Similarly, a CPR 8 application may commonly be made when your client is seeking a declaration, for example, that a contractual term is incorporated into an agreement. Part 8 proceedings are also used in 'costs only' applications and in the new low-value personal injury cases arising out of road traffic accidents (see paragraph 9.2.8).

Part 8 procedure differs from Part 7 in that the witness evidence upon which the claimant wishes to rely must be served with the claim form and 'particulars' (which may be a summary of the witness statement). This procedure does not require the formal particulars of claim. The defendant does not need to file a formal defence, but the defendant will need to file their witness evidence with their acknowledgment of service. A failure to file witness evidence will mean that the non-serving party will be unable to make representations at any hearing unless the court grants permission to do so. DQs are not required (because all Part 8 claims are 'treated' as allocated to the multi-track). Costs budgets are only likely to be required if the case would otherwise be a Part 7 multi-track case or if the court requests costs budgets. Judgment in default is not available.

Though seemingly much simplified, Part 8 procedure cannot be used as a means of avoiding Part 7 Form N1 procedure and can be used only when:

- the claimant seeks the court's decision on a question that is unlikely to involve a substantial dispute of fact; or
- when a Practice Direction, or rule, requires that Part 8 procedure be used and the ruling or Practice Direction has modified or disapplied parts of the procedure for the action to enable this procedure to be used. Sections A, B, and C of the CPR PD 8 set out general provisions about claims and applications to which Part 8 applies.

9.3.6.1 What forms are needed for a Part 8 application?

Form N208 must be used for Part 8 claims and applications. Form N208 must state on it:

- that Part 8 applies;
- the question that the claimant wants the court to decide, or the remedy sought and the legal basis for the claim to that remedy;
- details of the claim if being made under an enactment; and
- the capacity of the representative if the claim is being made in a representative capacity.

Any evidence supporting the claim must be served with Form N208 and this must contain a statement of truth. Additionally, the service requirements are the same as those set out for Part 7 claims—except in the situations in which a defendant is not being named in the Part 8 claim and permission has been granted to issue without naming a defendant.

9.3.6.2 Responding in Part 8 claims

CPR 8.3 sets out the procedure for responding to a Part 8 claim. The defendant must acknowledge service in Form N210. If he objects to the use of the Part 8 procedure, he needs to set down his reasons. If a defendant wishes to rely on written evidence, he must file this with his Form N210. If the defendant fails to return Form N210, he may attend the hearing of the claim, but may not take part in it unless the court gives permission.

9.3.6.3 The hearing of Part 8 claims

Any evidence at the hearing is usually written evidence that has been served as set out in paragraphs 9.3.6.1 and 9.3.6.2. The court has power to permit oral evidence, but it will be rare that this will be required (because when it is, the Part 8 procedure is probably not appropriate for the claim).

9.4 CAN MORE THAN ONE CLAIM, OR MORE THAN ONE PARTY, BE INCLUDED IN ONE CLAIM?

9.4.1 JOINDER

CPR 7.3 reflects the statutory requirement of s. 49(2) of the Senior Courts Act 1981 that 'as far as possible, all matters in dispute between the parties are completely and finally determined, and all multiplicity of legal proceedings with respect to any of those matters is avoided'.

Generally, it is for the claimant to decide which causes of action he wishes to pursue against which parties. Where he has more than one claim against the same party, he has the right to issue separate claims for each (and to pay separate fees in respect of the issue of each). However, CPR 7.3 permits more than one cause of action to be claimed on one claim form and therefore, in terms of economy and the provisions of s. 49(2) of the Senior Courts Act 1981, he would be best advised to issue all claims that he has against the defendant in the one action unless it would be inconvenient to do so.

Where there is more than one defendant, the claimant will usually issue against all defendants that he alleges are liable to him in the claim in the one action. His decision to do this will depend on a number of factors, including the nature of the liability of the defendants (whether they are jointly liable, or severally liable, or jointly and severally liable—see Chapter 7, paragraph 7.5.1), and whether all of his potential defendants are worth suing and his claim can be more easily satisfied against one. CPR 19.1 provides that 'any number of claimants or defendants may be joined as parties to a claim'. No guidance is given about which claims it might be considered convenient to dispose of in the same action. The court will take into account the overriding objective—in particular the objectives of saving expense, and ensuring that cases are dealt with justly, expeditiously, and fairly. Thus, in general, claims involving common questions of law or fact between different parties, or different causes of action involving the same parties, should be dealt with in the same proceedings.

Where there are joint claimants, they must have the same legal representative (and have no conflicting interests between them). Co-defendants may choose whom they wish to represent them.

Even though a party may issue a multiple of claims in the one action, and/or multiple parties may be joined in the action, the court has a discretionary power in CPR 3.1(2)(i) to order separate trials and it will do so if, in separating the claims or the parties, the cases will proceed more efficiently.

Further, parts of CPR 19 need to be considered if it seems convenient to allow 'representative' actions. These provisions allow a single action to proceed that would bind all parties into an identified group. CPR 19.7 also deals with situations in which the persons that may be the subject of the action are unascertained or as yet unknown—this may apply in actions in an estate of a deceased person and persons unknown or not yet born, who may have an interest in the estate.

CPR 19.4 also contains the rules that relate to a person who wishes to intervene in an action and be added as a party. This may arise when the party who wishes to 'intervene' would be affected by any judgment that may be made in the action.

9.5 PROCEEDINGS BY AND AGAINST CHILDREN OR PROTECTED PARTIES

9.5.1 HOW DOES A CHILD OR PROTECTED PARTY EITHER MAKE OR DEFEND A CLAIM AGAINST HIM?

With the exception set out in CPR 21.2(3), a child or a protected party must sue and be sued by a litigation friend. Under the provisions of CPR 21.2(3), the court may grant permission for a child to conduct proceedings without a litigation friend. In practice, this is only likely to arise if the child is very close to becoming of age, and can show that he has the skill, knowledge, and understanding to conduct those proceedings. Any defendant faced with an application by a child to conduct proceedings himself will wish to be assured that any costs payable are secured in some way.

9.5.2 WHO MAY BE A LITIGATION FRIEND?

A child's litigation friend is normally a relative with no interest in the litigation adverse to that of the child. A protected party's litigation friend is usually a deputy appointed by the Court of Protection.

Unless the court appoints a litigation friend, the person who is to act as the litigation friend must follow the procedure set out in CPR 21.5. These provisions include:

- filing an official copy of his authority to act if his authority to act has been given under Part VII of the Mental Health Act 1983; or

- filing a certificate of suitability, which certifies that the person seeking to be the litigation friend satisfies the conditions set out in CPR 21.4(3); and

- serving the certificate of suitability on each party and filing a certificate of service when the certificate of suitability has been served.

The court may appoint the litigation friend upon the application of the person wishing to be the litigation friend or upon the application of a party. The claimant will need to make the application if the defendant in his action requires a litigation friend and no appointment has been made.

9.5.3 WHEN DOES THE APPOINTMENT OF A LITIGATION FRIEND TERMINATE?

When a child (who is not otherwise a protected party) attains the age of 18, the litigation friend's appointment will cease automatically and the litigation friend has no further authority. When a protected party ceases to be such, the appointment of his litigation friend continues until it is ended by a court order—the application to do this may be made by the former protected party, the litigation friend, or a party.

Once the appointment of the litigation friend has terminated, the new party (being the former child who is now of age or a former protected party) must:

- serve notice on the other parties, stating that the appointment of his litigation friend has ceased;

- state his address for service; and

- state whether he intends to carry on the proceedings.

He must do so within 28 days of the date on which the appointment of his litigation friend ceased. If he fails to do this, then the court, or another party, may seek to strike out his claim or defence.

On his appointment as litigation friend, the litigation friend undertakes to pay any costs that the child or protected party may be ordered to pay in relation to the proceedings (subject to any right that he may have to be repaid from the assets of the child or protected party) (CPR 21.4(3)(c)). The liability for the costs continues until either the former child or protected party has served his notice, or when the litigation friend serves notice that his appointment has ceased.

 Practical Considerations

Once a child attains the age of 18 or a former protected party is no longer a protected party, then he becomes a new client for the purposes of client care and any CFA entered into with the litigation friend. The new client must then receive the standard retainer and client care correspondence that all new clients receive. If a funding arrangement is to be entered into with the new client, then notice of this must be given to the court and the other parties to the action in the normal way.

9.5.4 WHAT IS THE POSITION WITH REGARD TO EXPENSES INCURRED BY THE LITIGATION FRIEND IN CONDUCTING THE ACTION?

A litigation friend is entitled to recover money paid and expenses incurred from any monies secured by the action provided that they have been reasonably incurred and are reasonable in amount (CPR 21.12(1)). The criteria that the court will use to determine the reasonableness of their expenses are those set out in CPR 44.5(3). The litigation friend may not receive more than 25 per cent (of the sum awarded) if the claim is concluded by settlement or judgment in a sum not exceeding £5,000, unless the court directs otherwise.

9.5.5 SERVICE WHERE A PARTY IS A CHILD

Service of proceedings where that party is a child must be in accordance with CPR 6.13 (for service of the claim form) and CPR 6.25 (for service of an application for an order appointing a litigation friend and service of documents other than the claim form).

9.6 HOW ARE THE PARTIES IN AN ACTION DESCRIBED?

9.6.1 THEIR TITLES

The words that should be used to describe the parties in an action are set out in CPR PD 16.2.6.

- Under the CPR, the party who makes a claim is known as 'the Claimant'.
- The party against whom proceedings are brought is 'the Defendant' (CPR 2.3(1)).
- Parties to applications are referred to as 'Applicant' and 'Respondent' (CPR 23.1).
- Parties to petitions are referred to as 'Petitioner' and 'Respondent'.

Parties to Part 20 counterclaims and other additional claims are known by their names in the main statement of case (if they were a party), but if they have been brought in under CPR 20, they are known as 'third party' or 'fourth party', etc.

Table 9.2 details the description to be given to parties in an action depending on their form of 'identity'.

For further clarification of the identity of a party, see Chapter 7, paragraph 7.3.

9.6.2 WHAT HAPPENS IF A MISTAKE IS MADE IN THE NAME GIVEN TO A PARTY?

The court may substitute a new party for an existing party. Remedying the name of a party may even occur after the limitation period has expired, but this is limited to situations in which the mistake is in the name, not the identity of the party (CPR 19.5, and see Chapter 7, paragraph 7.3). The provisions for substitution of a party to rectify such a mistake apply when the mistake was genuine. In situations in which there has been a mistake as to the identity of the person, the proper course of action will be to reissue proceedings.

9.6.3 WHAT HAPPENS IF A PARTY DIES?

Under the Law Reform (Miscellaneous Provisions) Act 1934, s. 1(1), most causes of action subsisting against or vested in an individual survive his or her death. If a party to a claim dies (or is adjudged bankrupt), the court has the power under CPR 19.5(3) to add or substitute as a party in the action the person to whom the deceased (or bankrupt party's) interest or liability has passed.

TABLE 9.2 PARTIES AND THEIR DESCRIPTIONS IN STATEMENTS OF CASE

Class of party	Form of description
An individual	The full name if known and the title by which he or she is known
A child, or a protected party within the Mental Health Act 1983	The child's (or protected party's) full name followed by the full name of the litigation friend, that is, Jane Bloggs (a child by Joe Bloggs her litigation friend or if a protected party: by Joe Bloggs her litigation friend)
A child conducting the proceedings himself (where the court has permitted this under CPR 21.2(3))	Master Thomas Green
A child once he has adopted the proceedings on attaining 18 years of age	Miss Hilary Green (formerly a child but now of full age)
An individual who is trading under another name	Joe Bloggs t/a Blogg's Store
An individual who is suing or being sued in a representative capacity	Joe Bloggs as the representative of Jane Bloggs (deceased)
An individual who is being sued in the name of a club or other unincorporated organization	Joe Bloggs, suing/being sued on behalf of the Brown-town Tennis Club
A firm (other than an LLP)	Bloggs and Co (a firm) or the full name of each partner
A corporation (other than a company)	The full name of the corporation
A company	The full name of the company with an indication of its legal form (that is, Ltd, LLP, plc) and if registered outside the jurisdiction, the place of registration

Further details of the effect that the death of a party may have either before proceedings are commenced or during proceedings are set out in Chapter 7, paragraph 7.3.9.

9.6.4 CAN A CLAIM BE MADE AGAINST A PERSON WHO IS NOT KNOWN?

There are limited circumstances in which a claimant can avoid the requirements set out in PD 7A.4.1, which provides that the claim form should include the full name of each party. When a claimant does not know the identity of the defendant, but can identify him by a description that is sufficiently clear to determine who would be within that description, then he may seek permission to commence the claim by the description of the defendant (as yet unknown). This is useful in some intellectual property claims and is outside the scope of this book.

9.6.5 PARTIES IN CLAIMS FOR LOSS AND DAMAGE ARISING FROM A ROAD TRAFFIC ACCIDENT (RTA)

In an RTA claim, the usual procedure will be for the claimant to issue proceedings against the person(s) whom he alleges owed the claimant a duty of care and who has breached that duty of care, as a result of which breach the claimant has suffered loss. These are the normal provisions for a claim in tort. However, there are further provisions that may need to be considered concerning a claim arising from an RTA, as follows.

9.6.5.1 A claim against the insurer of a vehicle

Under the European Communities (Rights against Insurers) Regulations 2002, SI 2002/3061, a claimant who is resident in the European Economic Area (EEA)—that is, any member state of the European Union, but also Iceland, Liechtenstein, Norway, and Switzerland—bringing proceedings in tort arising out of an RTA may issue proceedings against the insurer of the vehicle alleged to be responsible for the accident. This right is in addition to the right to issue proceedings against the driver of the vehicle. In most circumstances, the claim will be made against the driver, not the insurer, but it will be the insurer who will meet any judgment in the claim. The judgment may be enforced directly against the insurer, provided that notice has been given to the insurer either before or within seven days of proceedings being commenced (Road Traffic Act 1988, s. 152).

 Practical Considerations

The notice under s. 152 of the Road Traffic Act 1988 is a vital part of any claims arising from an RTA and should form part of the aide-memoire or list of 'key dates' that will be created for any new claim of this nature. The letter of claim written in the Protocol phase of such an action is not sufficient notice by itself unless the notice specifies that it is 'notice under the provisions of s. 152 of the Road Traffic Act', and the letter of claim is written directly to the insurers and not simply 'handed to the insurers' by the insured. If notice has not been given and the insurer takes the point—that it has not been served—the claimant is left with no alternative but to discontinue the defective claim and issue fresh proceedings, giving proper notice under s. 152.

9.7 SERVICE OF THE PROCEEDINGS

9.7.1 WHAT (AND WHEN) IS 'SERVICE'?

9.7.1.1 What is 'service' of the claim form?

'Service' involves formally notifying the defendant(s) of the action against them. It is worth noting here to avoid confusion that CPR Part 6 distinguishes the requirements for service of the claim form from 'other documents'. Section II of Part 6 sets out the rules for service of the claim form and Section III sets out the detail for service of 'other documents'. 'Other documents' are defined as all those documents that require service that are *not* the claim form. In this regard, Section II of Part 6 (which sets out the rules for service of the claim form) states that the 'claim form' includes other documents that can be used to commence an action, for example petitions.

Valid service of the claim form, in the manner specified by the court rules (and as it has been interpreted by case law), is a precondition to the exercise of the court's jurisdiction. In certain circumstances, the need to 'serve' the claim form may be dispensed with. It is also worth noting that what is sometimes described as the fiction of service is preserved—that is, the fact that a person has (or has not) *received* a document does not necessarily mean that the person has (or has not) been *served* with the document. The rules provide for a 'deemed service' rule. The 'deemed' date of service will be on the second business day after completion of the 'relevant step' required to effect service by the chosen method (CPR 6.14). The 'relevant step' for effective service for each method is set out in CPR 7.5. For limitation purposes the 'deemed' date of service of the claim form is less important than the date of 'dispatch' (which will be the 'relevant step' required for that method of service), as it is 'dispatch' that must be completed 'on time' (that is, within the limitation period). The deemed date of service is needed for the defendant to determine when the acknowledgement of service and/or defence is due.

Parties in an action must give an address for service when responding to a claim (CPR 6.23).

9.7.1.2 When does service take place?

9.7.1.2.1 *Time periods for serving the claim form*

The rules relating to the service of a claim form (which must be an original sealed claim form, not a photocopy of a sealed claim form—see *Hills Contractors & Construction Ltd v Struth* [2013] EWHC 1693 (QB); the only exception to this requirement is where the claim form is served by fax or email in accordance with PD 6A) are as follows:

- A claim form issued for service within the jurisdiction must be served within four months after the date of issue (CPR 7.5(2)).

- A claim form issued for service outside the jurisdiction must be served within six months after the date of issue (CPR 7.5(3)).

9.7.1.3 Can the parties extend the period of service of the claim form?

The parties can agree between themselves to extend the time for service of the claim form (CPR 2.11). This was extensively considered in *Thomas v Home Office* [2006] All ER (D) 243 (Oct).

In order to extend the time for service, the parties may:

- agree to the extension in writing (CPR 2.11)—and this must be more than an oral agreement to extend the time recorded by a written note on each legal representative's file. A specific exchange of letters is recommended, which includes a precise deadline; or

- create a single document—that is, an agreement, signed by both parties, which sets out the determination to extend to a precise deadline.

When such an extension is agreed, it will be the claimant who will bear the risk of the court subsequently concluding that the agreement to extend was not valid.

9.7.1.4 Extending the time of validity for service of the claim form and/or seeking an order for alternative service

The courts have traditionally not shown much sympathy for a claimant or legal representative who has issued his claim form and then waited until the end of the period of validity of that claim form to serve it, but then encountered difficulties. It is therefore vital to understand the rules of service and to adhere to them strictly, so that good service is achieved—especially when service has been left late and is very near to, or at, the end of the period of validity of the claim form.

9.7.1.5 Extending the period of validity of the claim form

CPR 7.6 states that an application to extend the period of validity of the claim form must be made 'within the period specified by rule 7.5' (that is, within the period of validity of the claim form). Only in exceptional cases can the life of the claim form be extended after the end of the period specified by CPR 7.5 (see CPR 7.6(3)). The case of *Cecil & Others v Bayat* [2011] EWCA Civ 135 is a recent case that emphasizes the fact that applications to extend the life of the claim form should not be used where the reasons for non-service are practical, and where an application is being made it should be made before the time of validity has expired.

9.7.1.6 Is it sensible to wait to serve a claim form?

Once the claim form has been issued, whether pre-emptively to avoid an issue arising from expiry of the limitation period or on occasions on which it has been issued, but the particulars of claim are not yet drafted, it is still usually better to serve promptly. The claim form could be served with an explanation, and where the parties can agree an extension of time for the claimant to serve his particulars of claim, this may be achieved, by consent, under CPR 2.11 (see paragraph 9.7.1.3). Clearly it would be safer to obtain this consent to extension of time for service of the Particulars of Claim *before* service of the claim form.

9.7.1.7 Seeking an order for 'alternative service'

In certain circumstances in which service may not have been effectively achieved within the period of validity of the claim form, it may be possible (including retrospectively) to seek an order that service has, in fact, been successfully effected by 'an alternative method'. CPR 6.15 enables the court, for good reason, to make an order permitting service by an alternative method or at an alternative place. The court has the power to order this *retrospectively*. By CPR 6.15(2), the court may order that steps *already* taken to bring the claim to the attention of the defendant by an alternative method or at an alternative place have the effect of being 'good service'. There is every reason to believe that the courts will entertain such applications sympathetically when it is quite clear that the defendant has had notice of the proceedings and that the failure of good service may have been by some *understandable or reasonable* misunderstanding. It is doubtful, however, that the courts will agree to rectify a position in which the claimant (or his legal representative) has failed to serve properly by a basic misunderstanding of the CPR.

 Example

In a personal injury claim in which the claimant's legal representative has been corresponding with the defendant's insurer, it may be that the legal representative has had many cases with this particular insurer and that, in previous cases, this insurer has nominated its in-house lawyer to accept service. However, in this particular instance, the insurer has not expressly done this, although the claimant had sent the documents to the inhouse lawyer in the 'normal' way, and the insurer had taken no issue on the point and continued to correspond on the claim with the claimant's legal representative. However, after the four-month period of validity has expired, the insurer takes the point, and declares that purported service is bad and that service has not been effected. It is thought that, in these circumstances, the courts *may* grant an order under CPR 6.15(2) allowing the 'service' on the insurers' in-house lawyer to be declared 'good [alternative] service'.

If and when the court makes an order under CPR 6.15(2) that service has been effected (by an alternative method), it must specify the date on which the claim form is deemed to have been served (by the 'alternative method'). This is contained in CPR 6.15(4)(b).

9.7.2 **THE METHODS OF SERVICE**

The methods of service that may be used are set out in CPR 6.3. Where the claim form is served within the jurisdiction, the claimant must complete the step required by Table 9.3 in relation to the particular method of service chosen, before 12.00 midnight on the calendar day four months after the date of issue of the claim form.

It is clear that it is the taking of the 'step required' that is the relevant time in which to determine whether service has been effected in time (that is, within the period of validity of the claim form), not the date on which the document is deemed served by the method chosen. If the claim form is posted or dispatched by midnight on any day within its validity period (four months within the jurisdiction), then it will be deemed served on the second business day after the 'step required' and it will not matter that the deemed date of service is outside the four-month validity period of the claim form. The relevant step required for different methods of service is shown in Table 9.3.

TABLE 9.3 THE METHODS OF SERVICE

Method of service	Step required
First-class post, document exchange, or other service that provides for delivery on the next business day	Posting, leaving with, delivering to, or collection by the relevant service provider
Delivery of the document to, or leaving it at, the relevant place	Delivering to, or leaving the document at, the relevant place
Personal service under CPR 6.5	Completing the relevant step required by CPR 6.5(3)
Fax	Completing the transmission of the fax
Other electronic method	Sending the email or other electronic transmission

9.7.2.1 The 'default' position of service—by the court

In the High Court (but not the specialist divisions) and the County Court, the court will serve the claim form and accompanying documents unless the party lodging the document *expressly* indicates that it wishes to effect service. When a party is legally represented, his legal representative will usually arrange service. If the court is to serve, it will decide the method of service and this will usually be by first-class post. After service, the court will issue to the claimant (or his legal representatives) a certificate of service, and if the documents are returned by post, notice will be given to the claimant (or his legal representatives). In the County Court Business Centre, for all money claims, if the claimant wishes to effect service himself, the court copy of the claim form must have the words 'SOLICITOR SERVICE' boldly printed on the front page.

 Practical Considerations

Before issuing proceedings, it will be necessary to obtain specific instructions from the client regarding the method of service that he wishes to employ, so that monies on account for service can be obtained—for example, for the costs of engaging a process server—and so that the express request can be made to the court for 'documents to be returned (to the legal representatives acting) for service'.

Where the claimant elects to serve the documents, he must file at court a certificate of service in Form N215 within 21 days of service.

9.7.2.2 A clarification of 'personal service' under CPR 6

CPR 6.5 clarifies 'personal service' under CPR 6.5(3). The claim form must be served personally if a court order, a Practice Direction, or another enactment provides that it must be personally served. In all other cases, a claim form may be served personally unless service is to be effected on a party's legal representative or upon the Crown.

Under CPR 6.5(3), personal service is effected on:

(a) *an individual by leaving it with that individual;*

(b) *a company or other corporation* (which will include an LLP) *by leaving it with a person holding a senior position* [defined in PD 6A.6.2] *within the company or corporation* [for example, a person in a 'senior position' of an incorporated company is defined as a treasurer, the secretary of the company (or corporation), the chief executive, a manager, or other officer—and the definition of a person in 'a senior position' of an unincorporated association is also defined in PD 6A.2(2)]; *or*

(c) *a partnership (where partners are being sued in the name of their firm) by leaving it with—*

(i) *a partner; or*

a person who, at the time of service, has the control or management of the partnership business at its principal place of business.

 Practical Considerations

Personal service will often be completed by a process server. The person serving the document(s) should hand the document(s) to the individual and inform the individual of the contents of the document(s) in general, not specific, terms. When instructing a process server or agent to effect service for the first time, ensure that he has the experience and knowledge to effect service according to the rules.

9.7.2.3 What happens if the document(s) being served are handed back to the process server by the person who is to be served?

This happens quite commonly in practice: quite often, the person against whom proceedings have been brought is not entirely happy about the event and he may simply, once he is told the general nature of the documents being served on him, hand them back (or throw them on the ground). There is no post-CPR authority on the point, but in *Nottingham Building Society v Peter Bennett and Co* (1977) The Times, 26 February, the Court of Appeal held that once the document was handed over and the person had been told of the general nature of the document, it had been duly served. There is no reason to suppose that the courts would make any different finding on the point under the provisions of the CPR.

9.7.2.4 Service by or on partnerships

Where the claim is by or against two or more persons who were partners and who had carried on business within the jurisdiction (at the time that the cause of action accrued), under the provisions of PD 7A.5A.2, the term 'partners' includes both those claiming to be entitled as partners and those alleged to be partners.

Further, under the provisions of PD 7A.5A.3, where a claim is commenced by a partnership, it should be in the name of the partnership that was in existence when the cause of action accrued.

When acting in a claim against a partnership, it may be necessary to obtain details of the names and last known addresses of each of the partners at the time that the cause of action arose. This is known as a 'partnership membership statement' and the partnership has 14 days in which to provide such a statement when requested to do so (PD 7A.5B). PD 7A.5A.3 provides that 'where the partnership has a name, unless it is inappropriate to do so, claims must be brought in or against the name of the partnership'. This is a rule of convenience; that is, the use of the name of the firm name is merely shorthand for listing the partners individually. It may be inappropriate to start proceedings using the partnership name where, for example, there have been multiple changes of the name of the partnership or multiple mergers so that it would be clearer to identify the partners by their individual names. Similarly, if it seems likely that your client may have to seek enforcement of any judgment debt against the personal assets of one or more partners it is safer to issue against the partners by name of the partners. A compromise solution to what may be a cumbersome claim form would be to sue in the firm name but to set out the individual names of the partners in an attached schedule (making reference to the schedule in the claim form).

This is required because CPR 6.9 provides that where partners are sued in the name of a partnership, service should be at the principal or last known place of business of the partnership or at the partners' 'last known residence'.

However, where service is being made on an individual as a partner of the firm being sued, a notice must also be given specifying whether the person being served, is being served as:

- a partner;
- a person with control or management of the partnership business; or
- both of the above.

This information is contained in Form N218. It is advisable to include this notice with the document(s) being served.

 Practical Considerations

Where service is being effected on a person who may not be a partner, but who is stated to have 'control or management', it would be prudent to include Form N218 with the documents for service on every occasion and also whenever a partner is being served at his home or 'last known residence'.

9.7.2.5 Companies and limited liability partnerships (LLPs)

Service on a company may be by any method permitted under CPR 6—(CPR 6.3(3) (claim form) and 6.20(3) (other documents)). Additionally, Section 1139(1) of the Companies Act 2006 (Commencement No. 8, Transitional Provisions and Savings) Order 2008 (SI 2008/2860) provides that 'a document may be served on a company registered under the act by leaving it at, or sending it by post to, the company's registered office'.

Service on a limited liability partnership (LLP) may be served by any method permitted under CPR 6 (CPR 6.3(3) (claim form) and 6.20(3) (other documents)) and, additionally, by any of the methods of service permitted under the Companies Act 2006 as applied by the Limited Liability Partnerships Act 2000.

Where service is to be to an overseas branch of a company registered in England and Wales or on an overseas registered company, s. 1139(2) will continue to permit a document to be served at the UK branch or a person who is authorized to accept service or at any place of business in England and Wales. In the recent case *SSL International plc v TTK LIG Ltd* [2011] EWCA Civ 1170, the court rejected an attempt by the claimant to rely on CPR 6.5(3)(b) to serve a claim form on an Indian company that did not carry on business within the jurisdiction and concluded that personal service on one of the directors who was present within the jurisdiction was not effective service on the company. It is a reminder that the rules of service will be strictly applied.

Section 1139 of the Companies Act 2006 also applies to a limited liability partnership (LLP). Therefore, an LLP can be served at its registered office. Service under the provisions of s. 1139 is an additional place of service on a company or LLP and is effective even if the company or LLP has legal representatives acting, who have signified that they have instructions to accept service of proceedings.

 Practical Considerations

Where service is to be effected under s. 1139 rather than the CPR, note that the 'deemed date of service' (see paragraph 9.7.6) does not apply. The wording in the statute is 'in the ordinary course of post' and service is assumed to have occurred 'unless the contrary is proved'. Because this is a rebuttable presumption, it is again different from the 'deemed date of service' rule in the CPR. Also, under the Companies Act 2006, service by second-class post is permitted, whereas it is not under the CPR.

CPR 6.5(3) provides that a document is served personally on a company or other corporation by leaving it with a 'person who holds a senior position'. A list of who is such a person is set out in PD 6A.6.2 (with regard to a registered company), and appears in paragraph 9.7.2.2.

For an unregistered company or corporation, such a person might include:

- the mayor;
- the chairman;
- the president;
- the town clerk; or
- a similar officer.

 Practical Considerations

When instructing a process server to effect service on such a body, it would be prudent to provide the process server with a list of the people who are eligible to accept service.

9.7.2.6 Service on the Crown
Personal service cannot be made on the Crown.

9.7.2.7 What steps must be taken to ensure that the address for service is the correct one?
Where a claimant has reason to believe that the address of the defendant—whether he is being served as an individual, or as a partner in an (unincorporated) partnership or in the name of a business—is an address at which the defendant no longer resides or carries on business, the claimant must take 'reasonable steps' (and make 'reasonable enquiries') to ascertain the defendant's current address (CPR 6.9(3)).

In *Smith v Hughes*, sub nom *Cranfield v Bridgegrove Ltd* [2003] EWCA Civ 656, [2003] 3 All ER 129, the Court of Appeal (CA) held that the words 'last known address' were plain and unqualified. It did not matter that the defendant was no longer there.

Since that case, however, it must be borne in mind that CPR 6.9 now states that where the claimant has reason to believe that the address is an address at which the defendant no longer resides, he must now make 'reasonable steps to ascertain the defendant's current address'. In *Davies (R on the application of) v Kingston Upon Thames County Court* [2014] EWHC 4589 the court determined that 'reasonable steps' would include knowing that the defendant was no longer at the address for service but had a 'postal re-direction' service in place.

 Practical Considerations

The practical effect of this is that, where the claimant does have reason to believe that the defendant no longer resides at the address that he has, it appears that it would be safer to make an application for an order for 'alternative service' under CPR 6.15 than to rely on the court's interpretation of the 'reasonable steps' that have been made under CPR 6.9(3). An application under CPR 6.15 could seek, for example, an order for service at an alternative place (such as place of work) or by an alternative method (for example, care of a relative).

9.7.2.8 Service by first-class post (or an alternative service that provides for delivery on the next working day)
By this provision, a courier service or any 'next day delivery service' can be used. But it would be prudent to obtain a 'proof of posting' receipt in order to establish the fact of deemed service by the method.

9.7.2.9 Leaving the document at a specified place
The provisions for this must be distinguished from personal service: personal service requires the document(s) to be handed to an individual, while leaving document(s) at a specified place requires that it be placed through the letterbox or left at reception. Confusing the two can result in ineffective service, as in *Cherney v Deripaska* [2007] EWHC 965 (Comm). In this case, the claim form was 'served' on a security guard at an address that was not 'the last known residence' of the defendant, nor was the security guard an agent for the defendant for personal service to be effective, nor was it effective service by being left at a specified place.

9.7.2.10 Service through the document exchange (DX) system
Service through the document exchange (DX) system may only take place when:

- the party's address for service includes a DX number;
- the DX number is on the party's writing paper; and
- neither party nor his representative has indicated that he will *not* accept service by this method.

9.7.2.11 Service by fax or other electronic means of communication

Under the provisions of PD 6A.4, service by fax or other electronic means may only take place when:

- a party or his legal representative has expressly (in writing) indicated that he is willing to accept service by this means; and

- a party has given the fax number or email address to which documents should be transmitted;

- a fax number on the legal representative's writing paper or on a statement of case is 'express notice', unless a contrary intention is given; and

- service on the party 'express notice' is satisfied by express prior written consent or by the number appearing on a statement of case or in a response to a claim that has been filed at court.

Thorne v Lass Salt Garvin [2009] EWHC 10 (QB) considered the requirement to obtain a party's express consent to serve by fax. The court held that service was invalid because the claimant had not first obtained the defendant's agreement, in writing, to accept service by fax. Although the defendant was a firm of solicitors, at the time of alleged service, it was not acting as its own legal representative; therefore, the existence of the firm's fax number on the notepaper did not (in these circumstances) indicate its agreement to accept service by fax. The judgment emphasizes the importance of strict compliance with the provisions relating to service.

There is no requirement to send a hard copy of a document served by fax, but if a hard copy does follow, it would be prudent to confirm which method of service is being employed, so that there can be no confusion as to the date of dispatch of the claim form for limitation purposes, or the 'deemed date of service' from which the defendant can calculate when his defence is due.

It is also worth remembering, in preparing to serve document(s) by fax or other electronic means of communication, that the fax number must be 'in the jurisdiction'.

 Practical Considerations

Previous correspondence by fax or email in a claim will not constitute 'express consent' (see *Kuenyehia v International Hospitals Group Ltd* [2006] EWCA Civ 21 and *Hart Investments Limited v Fidler* [2006] EWHC 2857, (TCC)). In the former case, the Court of Appeal confirmed that a failure to obtain express written consent could not 'happen' in this way, and in the latter case, service by fax on the second defendant's liquidator was held to be equally ineffective through lack of express consent. The detail of these cases goes to show quite how easily a mistake can be made, through a failure to abide by the strict letter of the procedural rules for service requirements.

9.7.2.12 Service by email

The appearance of an email address on notepaper is not deemed to be 'express consent', as it can be in some circumstances for service by fax. For this to be implied, the email address will need to appear on a statement of case filed at court.

For any situation in which service is proposed to be effected by email, it is good practice to check whether there are any limitations of format or size of document to be sent. It is also good practice to confirm whether incoming emails are checked on a daily basis and who checks them—it could be that the email does not reach its intended recipient as quickly as other methods of service.

Considering the potential for error in email transmission and the fact that the deemed time for service is the same day if a business day and sent before 4.30 p.m. or the next business day, many firms will not accept service by email. Despite the fact that express notice is strictly required where email addresses appear on a firm's notepaper, it will often be accompanied by a notice 'not to be used for service'.

As with faxes, there is no requirement to send a hard copy of a document served by email, but if a hard copy does follow, it would be prudent to confirm which method of service is being employed, so that there can be no confusion of the 'deemed date of service'.

9.7.2.13 Contractually agreed methods of service

CPR 6.11 provides that a claim form may be served by a contractually agreed method where:

- the contract provides that if a claim form is issued in relation to the contract, it may be served by a method specified in the contract; and

- the claim form contains only a claim in respect of the contract.

Practical Considerations

A contractual method of service is commonly used in contracts in which the transaction is based outside the jurisdiction, and in which it would save time and expense to serve in the agreed way (for example, on a nominated firm of solicitors). In using a contractually agreed method, it is prudent to check and take care that the claim arises out of the contract.

9.7.3 EXAMPLES OF THE EFFECT OF THESE SERVICE RULES

To help you understand these examples, remember that the date of dispatch is the key date for limitation and the deemed date of service is the key date from which the defendant calculates when his defence is due.

Example 1

A claim form expires on Friday 31 October. On that day, it is placed in a postbox at 11.30 p.m., addressed to the defendant at his usual address. The defendant is deemed served on Tuesday 4 November (the second business day after completion of the relevant step—see CPR 6.14 and 7.5). The claim form has been served 'in time'—that is, within its validity period—because the 'step required' was undertaken before the end of the period of validity of the claim form.

Example 2

A claim form expires on Saturday 1 November and is handed to the defendant personally on that day. The defendant is deemed served on Tuesday 4 November (see CPR 6.14 and 7.5). Again, the claim form has been served 'in time'—that is, within its validity period.

Example 3

A claim form expires on Friday 31 October. It is transmitted by fax that afternoon at 4.15 p.m. Provided that the transmission of the fax is completed, the claim form has been served 'in time'—that is, within its validity period—because the time given in which to complete the transmission of the fax is until midnight on Friday 31 October. The deemed date of service will be on the second business day after dispatch—that is, Tuesday 4 November.

Note: Under PD 6A.10, it is quite clear that the deemed date of service of 'other documents' by fax, email, and personal service must be completed before 4.30 p.m. This is not noted in any part of the CPR or the Practice Direction in relation to service of the claim form. The authors are therefore interpreting the rules in relation to the dispatch of a claim form to cover any method of service set out in Table 9.3 and that the step to effect service by the method chosen should be before midnight. There are no provisions in the new rules that indicate that the date when the 'step required' is made can ever count as the first business day, even when that step is effected before 4.30 p.m.

 Example 4

A claim form expires on Friday 31 October. At 3 p.m. that afternoon, the claim form is given to the accounts clerk at the defendant company's registered office in purported performance of effecting personal service. Here, there has not been valid service of the claim form, because the method chosen has not been done correctly—the accounts clerk not being within the definition of 'a senior person'.

Note: In this situation, CPR 6.15(2) may act to 'save' the situation.

 Example 5

In an action, the defendant has indicated that service may be on his nominated solicitor, but there has been no confirmation of this by the legal representatives. Service is duly effected on the firm within the time of validity of the claim form. Here, again, valid service has been effected, because for service on nominated solicitors where the nomination has been given by the defendant, there is no need to obtain the express consent of the legal representative for service on it to be good service (CPR 6.7). There has to be express consent for service on nominated solicitors, but that consent may be given by the defendant or the legal representatives.

 Example 6

Service has been effected personally on the defendant within the time of validity of the claim form, but, in this case, the legal representatives of the defendant had indicated that they have authority to accept service on their client's behalf. In this situation, there has not been good service, as consent to service on nominated legal representatives now excludes personal service on the defendant and service must be effected on the nominated solicitors (CPR 6.7).

9.7.4 WHEN MAY A PARTY SERVE DOCUMENTS ON A PARTY'S LEGAL REPRESENTATIVE?

It is important to know when service is required on a party or whether it may be effected on its legal representative. It is often more convenient to serve on an opponent's legal representative, because it will be with that representative that you will probably have had all of your correspondence. Usually, when service can be effected on the legal representative, no other form of service will be valid.

Where the legal representative works from within the EEA, service must still take place on the legal representative where service on the legal representative has been notified to the serving party as the means of service on their client.

9.7.4.1 Are there any occasions on which service cannot be effected on the legal representative of a party?

The general rule is that any document may be served personally (CPR 6.5(2)). However, when a solicitor has been properly authorized to accept service, this will override the general rule and service *must* be made on the firm of solicitors authorized to act unless:

- the document is one that must be served personally—this is when a court order requires it, or when the document or order contains a penal notice. In these situations, service on the person to be served is the only effective method of service;
- the contractual provision relating to the action provides for a method of service that excludes service on solicitors authorized to act; or
- under the provisions of s. 725(1) of the Companies Act 1985, the defendant is a company, and even where the defendant has provided an address for service (which may be those of the legal representative who is acting), the claimant has the additional option of serving at the company's registered office either by post or by leaving the documents there.

9.7.4.2 When does a legal representative have 'authority' to accept service?

CPR 6.7 operates to prevent any other method of service being effective where the legal representative, who is acting, is authorized to accept service except in the circumstances noted in CPR 6.5(1). The important point to note is that the legal representative must have the necessary express authority. Notice of this authority can be given:

- by the legal representative;
- by the party; or
- by the party's insurer when the action is subrogated to the insurer.

 Practical Considerations

Where notice has been given by the party to be served or his insurer, it is usual to seek confirmation from the legal representative in writing that he has that authority and will accept service, despite the implication from the CPR that notice may be given by the person to be served or his insurer.

An 'assumption' should never be made that a legal firm has the authority and instructions from its client to accept service on its client's behalf. Instructions authorizing a legal representative to accept service on his client's behalf must always be expressly given by the client (preferably in writing) and be expressly confirmed to the opponent wishing to serve documents. When a legal representative is acting in such a matter, and has been so acting during the course of all pre-action work and negotiations, it could be easy for an 'assumption' to be made that they will accept service on their client's behalf. But despite the fact that all correspondence on the matter has been directed to the legal representative, this does *not* mean that they have authority to, or will, accept service of proceedings—specific confirmation is required. It may be significant in the case of *Integral Petroleum Electrical Industries Ltd v Alstom UK* [2014] EWHC 430 (Comm) that the Commercial Court treated service of particulars of claim on the defendant's legal representatives by email as valid service, despite the fact that the legal representatives had not agreed to accept service by email and that the purported service was five days late. The court held that the case fell within CPR 3.10, which provides that an error of procedure does not invalidate any step in the proceedings unless the court so orders.

9.7.5 **WHEN SERVICE ON A PARTY'S LEGAL REPRESENTATIVE IS NOT AVAILABLE, WHO MUST BE SERVED AND WHERE CAN THEY BE SERVED?**

Save where service is to be on a person's (or firm's) legal representative who has been authorized to accept service on their behalf, service will be on the party, as set out in Table 9.3.

9.7.5.1 What steps must a party take to ensure that the address that they will use is a suitable place at which to serve?

The claimant must make 'reasonable enquiries' to ascertain the defendant's current address. 'Reasonable enquiries' is not specifically defined and will be given its natural meaning. The consequences of getting methods of service muddled or not taking enough care with ensuring proper service can be severe. In *Cherney v Deripaska* [2007] EWHC 965 (Comm), some problems arising with service were highlighted. In this case, among other things discussed, a defendant's 'occasional' residence did not fall within the definition 'usual or last known residence'. In *Cranfield v Bridgegrove Ltd* [2003] EWCA Civ 656, the Court of Appeal held that where the party had not provided an address for service, the meaning of 'last known address' could include a place at which the defendant used to live, even though it was known that he had left there (provided that 'reasonable enquiries' had been made to discover his current whereabouts).

In the case of *Relfo Ltd (in liquidation) v Varsani* [2009] EWHC 2297 (Ch), the court noted that it was possible for an individual to have more than one residence and that a party wishing to serve should look at the 'quality' of usage of the property, not simply how much time the defendant spent there.

If the defendant is in prison, he should be served in prison, not at his 'last known address'.

In effect, whenever the defendant's whereabouts is known and service on him could therefore be effected, it must be.

 Practical Considerations

If the defendant is thought not to be at his 'last known address', it may be more prudent to apply under CPR 6.15(2) for alternative service than to risk a conclusion that service has not been effective because the 'reasonable enquiries' were not sufficient. See examples in paragraph 9.7.3.

9.7.5.2 What happens if the documents are returned before the claimant has entered judgment?

If the document(s) served are returned undelivered before the claimant has obtained judgment, service will not be effective. In that situation, the claimant will have actual knowledge that the defendant has not received the document(s) and a valid certificate of service could not be completed.

Where this happens, the claimant will either have to try another method of service or apply to the court under the provisions of CPR 6.15 for an order for service by an alternative method.

However, if the document(s) are not returned before judgment is entered, service will be deemed to have taken place (provided that the provision as to 'reasonable enquiries' is met) even if, in fact, the defendant had never received them.

9.7.6 THE IMPORTANCE OF EFFECTIVE SERVICE

Provided that the 'step required' to effect service by the correct chosen method is achieved before the expiry of the period of validity of the claim form, it does not matter that the deemed date of service may be outside this period of validity. It is necessary to calculate the deemed date of service of the method chosen, because that is the date from which a party can calculate the appropriate period for taking a step in the action—for example, to seek a default judgment should the defendant fail to respond.

Remember, where service is by a method outside the CPR, the date of service may not have the benefit of the 'deemed service' rule.

The key to service is:

- do it on time; and

- do it properly.

9.7.7 CONTESTING EFFECTIVE SERVICE

Defendants need to be able to determine whether service upon them is valid service and if not, whether it is worth contesting jurisdiction on the ground that service is invalid. If the claimant has left it until near the end of the limitation period to issue, taking a point on invalid service could dispose of the claim for good. The decision has to be made quickly, and if arguing jurisdiction on this ground, the defendant must:

- acknowledge service on Form N9 with box 3 ticked ('I intend to contest jurisdiction') within 14 days. If the defendant files the acknowledgement of service without box 3 ticked, any defects of service are waived; and

- file an application within a further 14 days under CPR 11(4).

The following are examples where it may be possible to dispute jurisdiction on the grounds of ineffective service:

- where only a photocopy of the claim form has been served;

- where service has been by an inappropriate method (for example, service by fax or email without express permission or by the deeming provisions in PD 6A.4.1(2));

- where service has been out of time (that is, more than four months after issue for service within the jurisdiction or six months after issue for service outside the jurisdiction);

- where service has been out of time but the claimant has obtained an extension of time from the court under CPR 7.6(2), but where the defendant feels that there appears to be good reason for the failure to serve within the appropriate four- or six-month period;

- where service has been on the wrong person (for example, on the defendant, but the defendant's solicitors had indicated that service should be effected on them—CPR 6.7);

- where service has been at the wrong address and the claimant has made insufficient enquiry.

9.7.8 SERVICE OF DOCUMENTS OTHER THAN THE CLAIM FORM

CPR 6.20–6.29 provide separate rules for service of 'other' documents. These rules cover service of all other documents created in the action that require service *other than* documents used to initiate the proceedings (this, therefore, includes not only claim forms, but also petitions) other than the claim form. Essentially, many of the provisions for service of 'other' documents are repeated in these sections of CPR 6.

 online resource centre

KEY POINTS SUMMARY

- Understand the criteria that will be applied to cases to place them into one of the three tracks.

- Look out for Europe-wide procedures and Money Claim Online procedures.

- Make sure that all documents required to start an action are in place and correctly completed. Decide who the parties are and describe them correctly.

- Understand and apply the rules for joining parties or causes of action together in the one claim.

- In relation to service—decide on the appropriate method of service, and ensure it is carried out properly and on time.

Case Study *Bollingtons Ltd v Mrs Elizabeth Lynch t/a The Honest Lawyer*

Question

Assume that it is now 7 October 201?. There has been no response to the letter before claim. Locate a blank claim form and complete it. A debt action such as this is relatively straightforward and this is the kind of case in which it would be appropriate to include the particulars of claim on the reverse side of the claim form itself—that is, an indorsed claim form. You will need to consider, and deal with, the claim for interest. You do not need to complete any calculations for interest, but make any provision in your draft for what you would have done. You will need to consult Chapter 11 to inform your drafting.

Case Study *Andrew James Pike v Deep Builders Ltd*

The insurers of Deep Builders Ltd have indicated that they accept that Mr Deep was acting in the course of his employment at the time of the accident but deny any negligence, alleging that Andrew Pike was responsible for the accident. You have obtained a medical report from Mr Edgar Higgins. Please read this on the Online Resource Centre.

Question

Look at the draft particulars of claim available on the Online Resource Centre. Consider this partially completed document and complete the remaining sections so that it meets the requirements of the CPR. You will need to consult Chapter 11 to inform your drafting.

Any documents referred to in these case study questions can be found on the Online Resource Centre—simply click on 'Case study documentation' to access the documents that you need for Chapter 9 and to be reminded of the questions. Suggested answers to these case study questions can also be accessed on the Online Resource Centre when released to you by your lecturer.

10 DEFENDING A CLAIM

Relevant court forms relating to this chapter:

- N9 Response Pack
- N211 Part 20 Claim Form

Relevant parts of the CPR and its PDs: 10, 14, 15, 20, 24, and 18

10.1 INTRODUCTION

It would be wrong to believe that the defendant will take a reactive role in the action, seeking only to fend off the claimant's case, sitting back and waiting to see if the claimant can establish his case. In modern litigation, the defendant will take a more proactive role. Additionally, the expectation that the parties will have engaged in Protocol should ensure that only the cases where both parties believe that they have a reasonable 'claim' or 'defence' or 'defence and counterclaim' commence litigation and thus the defendant is very likely to have substantive responses to make to the claimant's claim. The Civil Procedure Rules (CPR) deny the defendant the right, in his defence, simply to deny the allegations against him.

LITIGATION TRAIN: ACTING FOR A DEFENDANT, RESPONDING TO THE CLAIM, THE CONSEQUENCES OF FAILING TO RESPOND

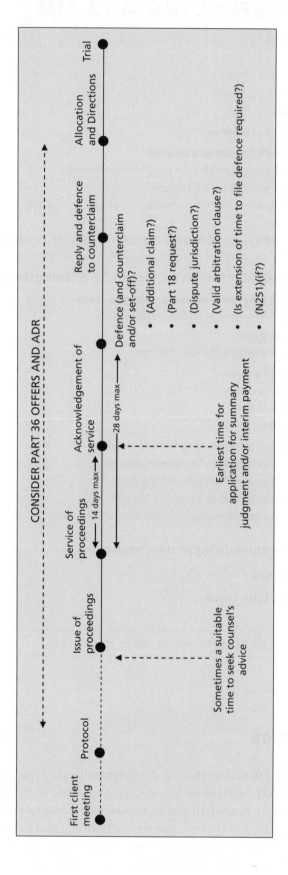

A defendant is charged with the duties of explaining any defence that he files and setting down why he submits that the claimant's allegations are false or cannot be substantiated.

Where the defendant makes an additional claim (which may be a counterclaim) in his defence (see paragraph 10.6.2), whether that be against the claimant or against another person not yet a party, he will be in the position of 'claimant' in that action, so will have the burden of proof for that claim.

Notwithstanding this more proactive role of the defendant, there are distinct differences and similarities in the way in which both the claimant and the defendant are 'involved' in the action.

The claimant, as a client, will, or may:

- take an active role in initiating the action, deciding on the cause(s) of action that he intends to pursue either alone or on the advice of his legal representative;

- decide who the defendant(s) will be in his action. It is never up to the defendant to join another party as a co-defendant in the action. That prerogative is the claimant's and only the claimant's;

- be motivated by a desire to seek justice and compensation, and to 'right a wrong' that he alleges has happened to him;

- exert some control over the action through the decisions that he takes;

- perhaps be less concerned with the costs of the action in that he hopes that the court will order the defendant to pay his costs if he is successful. This view may manifest itself despite all the costs information that the legal representative gives to his claimant clients and the advice on costs risks. The legal representative needs to be aware of managing this view at all times throughout an action; and

- potentially be 'economical with the truth' in order to maintain the strengths of his case.

The defendant, as a client, will, or may:

- have a defensive mindset, seeking to resist the claim, or at the very least to reduce significantly the financial consequences for him if the claimant should succeed in his claim;

- be seeking to limit the claimant's claim;

- have concerns for himself regarding the financial consequences of the action against him.

Note: The burdens for legal representatives in the advice they must give to their defendant clients on costs and the litigation risk is equally as important as the burden upon them to advise their claimant clients;

- have less control of the way in which the action is conducted. This 'difference' between the claimant and the defendant has been significantly reduced by the CPR and the requirement for cooperation between the parties in both the pre-action and the litigation stages. Also, under the terms of the overriding objective, the court will be looking to maintain an 'equality of arms' between the parties;

- simply be less 'engaged' with the action because he does not want to be involved in it at all. He may be angry at his involvement and find the whole procedure something with which he wants to have as little to do as possible. This can make the legal representative's job harder. Acting for defendants can often require more tact and perseverance in obtaining timely instructions; and

- potentially withhold information (that is damaging to him), and he may also be 'economical with the truth' in order to strengthen his case.

Whilst the procedural rules embodied in the CPR apply equally to claimants and defendants, it would be wrong to say that acting as legal representative for either is the same. In practice, legal representatives have had a tendency to specialize in 'claimant work' or 'defendant work', but this division is by no means universal. Firms that regularly handle both claimant and defendant work need to engage with the differing skills that apply to acting for one party and with the other.

It is unlikely in modern litigation that the service of a claim form upon the defendant will be the first that he knows of the claim being made against him. It is probable that he will have received earlier correspondence from the claimant and, if Protocol has been fully followed by the claimant and the defendant, the essence of each party's case will have been set out by each of them before proceedings have been started. This information will be formally contained in the letter of claim and in the response to the letter of claim, but also possibly in other pre-action correspondence. The parties may have engaged in some disclosure of evidence, had meetings, disclosed or exchanged experts' findings, and participated in some form of alternative dispute resolution (ADR) in the pre-action stage.

This chapter, in considering the options open to a defendant faced with a claim against him, will cover:

- the emotional responses of the defendant;

- the defendant's pre-action position;

- the way in which a defendant may fund the litigation;

- the essential steps needed to respond to a claim;

- the substantive responses to the action; and

- tactical responses to the claim.

10.2 THE DEFENDANT'S RESPONSE

There is a wide spectrum of responses that the defendant, as your client, may take to the action issued against him.

- He may **deny liability**—that is, he may entirely refute the liability allegations made against him. In order to do this, he will need to be able to proffer an alternate version of the story that the claimant has put forward. He will need to be able to give a version that satisfies the court that the claimant's case is not made. He may seek to achieve this by challenging the evidence of the claimant or by adducing evidence of his own that supports his version of how the 'event' (the allegations of the claimant) happened.

- He may **deny causation**—that is, he may accept some involvement in the events set out by the claimant, but deny that his actions either caused the breach or accident, or that the breach or event caused the damages and losses that the claimant alleges. To do this, he will need either to refute and challenge the claimant's case on causation, or to adduce evidence of his own that substantiates his denial.

- He may **deny quantum**, either by:
  - stating that he denies the nature and extent of the injuries or damage, and seek to suggest that the claimant contributed to his injuries; or
  - both admitting and denying—that is, by admitting parts of the claimant's case, but denying other parts of it.

- He may **seek a settlement**—in which case, he will be motivated to bring the action to an end as quickly as possible.

Clearly, in acting for a defendant, 'what' the defendant seeks to do will affect 'how' he will achieve it. A defendant can alter or affect the way in which the claim continues by the way in which he responds to it, and thus it is extremely important that the legal representative has clear instructions from the defendant and that the defendant fully understands the steps that will be taken on his behalf by the legal representative.

10.3 THE DEFENDANT'S PRE-ACTION BEHAVIOUR

10.3.1 WHAT IS A DEFENDANT'S LEVEL OF ENGAGEMENT IN PROTOCOL?

Chapter 8 deals with much of the pre-action work to be undertaken by the parties if they abide by Protocol. This section concentrates on, and will act as a reminder of, Protocol practice—but from the defendant's perspective.

Within Protocol, the defendant will need to ensure that he acknowledges the claimant's letter of claim (or letter before claim) within the time the letter has stipulated, because, under most Protocol practice, a failure to acknowledge the letter of claim will enable the claimant to proceed to issue proceedings. In those circumstances, it is highly likely that the defendant's failure to abide by Protocol practice will come back to haunt him in an unfavourable costs order within the litigation, especially if the court regards the failure to have significantly increased the costs or been the main reason why the action was started, when, had he cooperated, there may not have been a need for the action to have been started at all.

Having acknowledged the claimant's letter of claim, the defendant will then have a period of time in which to investigate the claimant's claim so that he can respond to the allegations. The period of time that the defendant should have to undertake these investigations will vary, but will be suggested in a Protocol applying to the action, or in the Practice Direction on Pre-Action Conduct and Protocols (PDPACP). The courts will expect the parties to act 'reasonably' and in accordance with the spirit of Protocol practice, and in accordance with the aims of the overriding objective. The parties may agree between themselves a reasonable time for the defendant to 'investigate' and be in a position at the end of that period to send a formal letter of response, or they may use the time suggested by the Protocol applying to the case. The steps taken by both parties in the pre-action stage should be 'reasonable' and 'proportionate'.

Once the defendant has investigated the claimant's allegation, he should reply fully to the letter of claim with a formal letter of response.

10.3.2 THE CONTENTS OF A LETTER OF RESPONSE

The letter of response should:

- say whether the claim is accepted in whole or in part, and make proposals for settlement; or
- state that the claim is not accepted.

In either of these two situations, the defendant needs to define which parts he accepts (if any) and which he refutes. Where he refutes the allegations, he needs to give detailed reasons for his conclusions.

- Where the claimant's allegations are being refuted, in addition to giving detailed reasons, the defendant should enclose documents for which the claimant has asked. If any documents requested by the claimant are not being sent, the defendant will need to give his reasons why they are not being supplied.
- The defendant may also request documents from the claimant (and the claimant should respond to this request within a reasonable time, and if the documents requested are not being sent, give reasons why not).
- The defendant should also state whether he is prepared to enter into a form of ADR, which might include:
  - discussion and negotiation;
  - early neutral evaluation (ENE) by an agreed third party; or
  - mediation.

- Although a party cannot be compelled to enter into a form of ADR, we have seen in Chapter 5 that the courts will take account of a party's response to the possibility of settling the dispute by a form of ADR when considering the appropriate costs order that may be made in the action (see also Chapter 15, which contains details of the powerful use that a defendant may make of CPR Part 36 offers to settle).

- The parties should also take steps to consider any expert evidence that may be required and seek to agree on the use of an independent expert. Any steps that the parties make towards agreeing the use of experts does not, however, preclude the court from making any order as to expert evidence that it feels is appropriate. Both claimants and defendants in litigation should be advised by their legal representatives that any expert engaged in Protocol may not be permitted in the litigation, and that the costs of engaging that expert may not be recoverable.

- The defendant may, if he wishes to do so, notify the claimant if he has entered into a relevant funding arrangement that falls within the meaning of CPR 43.2(1)(k).

10.3.3 IS THE DEFENDANT BOUND BY THE MATTERS THAT HE RAISES IN HIS LETTER OF RESPONSE IN ANY SUBSEQUENT LITIGATION?

In the Protocol phase, neither party is restricted to the matters and allegations that they raised in their letter of claim or letter of response. However, if the changes or additions to a party's case arise from an intent to mislead the other party during the Protocol phase, the court is likely to impose costs sanctions against the misleading party.

 Practical Considerations

Notwithstanding the professional conduct implications of inconsistencies between the defendant's letter of response and his subsequent defence, a significant departure from the defendant's original position contained in the letter of response can reduce his credibility. This may also encourage a claimant's application for summary judgment or strike-out (see Chapter 14, paragraph 14.3, and see paragraphs 10.7.1 and 10.7.2).

10.3.4 WHAT IS THE POSITION IF THE DEFENDANT MAKES AN ADMISSION DURING PROTOCOL?

Where the defendant makes an admission of liability during Protocol, he will be bound by any admission up to a value of £25,000. The CPR encourage admissions, because they narrow the issues between the parties, usually save costs, and they will perhaps aid settlement being achieved. However, legal representatives should be aware of the importance of admissions and the consequences of them.

10.3.4.1 What constitutes an admission?

An admission may be made of the truth of an allegation or of the facts stated, and it may be express or implied. It may be found in correspondence, or in oral discussions between the parties and their legal representatives, or between a party and a third party. An admission can also be inferred by conduct.

10.3.4.2 What are the consequences of a pre-action admission?

The consequence of a formal admission (for example, made in response to a notice to admit, in writing in open correspondence) will be that neither party will need to adduce evidence at trial of the issue or fact admitted. Informal admissions, such as an implicit acknowledgement of a state of affairs, are treated as pieces of evidence and further evidence may be adduced to disprove the informal admission or to explain away its apparent result. Equally, an admission made without knowledge of a material fact will have little evidential value.

10.3.4.3 Is a potential party always bound by a pre-action admission?

A party will not be bound by a previously made admission in the following circumstances:

- an admission made in previous proceedings that have not been placed before the current court as adopted and true;

- an informal admission that is not proved;

- an admission made by a person not authorized to make it unless there existed ostensible or apparent authority (of the agent), in which case the admission may bind (the principal), but he may have a right to claim an indemnity from the person who made the unauthorized admission; and

- an admission that is not clear and unambiguous.

10.3.4.4 Can admissions be withdrawn?

A formal admission may be withdrawn in certain circumstances, as follows:

- It may be withdrawn with the permission of the court. The court will consider the overriding objective when considering such an application and will consider such issues as prejudice to a party, the reasons why the admission was made, the stress that a party was under when the admission was made, the interests of the public in permitting the withdrawal of the formal admission, and the time at which the application to withdraw from the admission is made.

- Three important cases have considered the effect of formal admissions: *Sowerby v Charlton* [2005] EWCA Civ 1610; *The Governing Body of Charterhouse School v Hannaford Upright* [2007] EWHC 2718; and *Stoke on Trent City Council v John Walley* [2006] EWCA Civ 1137. These cases have held that:
  - permission may not be granted if it is made late (and close to the trial);
  - permission may be granted when the admission was made by mistake; and
  - permission will depend upon whether the admission was made pre action or not.

- Following the outcome of these cases and further consultation, CPR 14.1A states that a person may withdraw a pre-action admission:
  - with the consent of the person to whom the admission was made; and
  - after commencement of proceedings with the permission of the court.

- These conditions apply when:
  - the admission was made in proceedings listed under the rule—that is, personal injury, clinical disputes, and disease and illness claims; and
  - the admission was made after a letter of claim has been sent, or if before, the admission states that it has been made under the provisions of CPR 14.

- The rule also makes provision for these pre-action admissions to be dealt with in subsequent litigation as follows:
  - that any party may apply for judgment on a pre-action admission that is covered under the rule; and
  - the party who made the admission can apply to the court to withdraw it (and the court will apply the criteria noted here when considering the application).

The case of Moore v Worcestershire NHS Trust [2015] EWHC 1209 (Q3) is a recent reminder of this important concept. However, in this case the defendant was allowed to withdraw an admission because it 'arose by mistake'.

10.3.5 WHAT IS THE POSITION OF AN EXPERT ENGAGED BY A PARTY IN PROTOCOL?

It will be for the claimant to decide whether any expert report that he has obtained in Protocol will be disclosed to the defendant (see also Chapter 8, paragraph 8.11.2.9, and Chapter 18, paragraph 18.12.1). A favourable report may increase the chances of achieving a settlement, but it will also give the defendant plenty of time to 'pick holes' in the claimant's expert report. Although there is encouragement in Protocol to seek to agree the use of a jointly selected expert, this does not mean that the claimant is forced to do so and, in any event, he may have engaged an 'advisory expert' (see Chapter 18, paragraph 18.8.1) to help him to formulate his case. The defendant also may wish to engage the assistance of his own expert. The claimant should not unreasonably refuse to be examined by the defendant's nominated expert.

Where the claimant has proffered the names of experts in Protocol, and where the defendant has not rejected an expert from that list and the claimant so instructs that expert, the defendant will not be permitted to engage his own expert within proceedings unless the court permits.

10.4 HOW MAY A DEFENDANT FUND THE COSTS INCURRED IN DEFENDING THE CASE AGAINST HIM?

A defendant has the same methods of funding his action available to him as those that are available to the claimant and he may agree or negotiate any of these with his legal representative. Essentially, these include:

- a private retainer with his legal representative; or

- a conditional fee agreement (CFA)—the definition of what would be deemed a 'success' in such an arrangement (where a success fee is included in the agreement) will be specifically set down in the CFA contract with his legal representative. It may vary from succeeding in resisting the claim to attaining a reduction in the sum of the claim. Notice of such a funding arrangement may be given to the claimant. (The 'success' fee element of a CFA entered into after 1 April 2013 is not recoverable from the claimant and in such circumstances there is no requirement to give notice of the funding arrangement to the opponent.); or

- a damage-based agreement—probably only an option for a defendant as a method of funding for any substantial counterclaim he is pursuing—see Chapter 3, paragraph 3.3.8.5.

Further details of these funding arrangements are outlined in Chapter 3, paragraph 3.3.

Defendants are under the same obligations to abide by the principles of the overriding objective to ensure that the litigation is conducted with 'a view to controlling expenses' and in conducting the action 'proportionately'.

A defendant who is engaged in litigation, but feels that the claimant may be unable to satisfy any costs order made against him, may, in certain circumstances, apply to the court for an order for security for costs within the provisions of CPR 25.12 (see paragraph 10.7.3 and Chapter 14, paragraph 14.6).

10.5 THE STEPS AND TIME LIMITS FOR RESPONDING TO A CLAIM

The defendant need not take any action in response to the claim issued against him until the particulars of claim have been served on him. Remember that the claimant is not obliged to serve the particulars of claim at the same time as the claim form, but if he does serve the claim form without the particulars of claim, he must serve the particulars of claim within 14 days of serving the claim form (see Chapter 9, paragraph 9.3.5). When the claimant serves the particulars of claim, it will be accompanied with the response pack in Form N9A or Form N9C, which are supplied by the court. Form N9A will be used when the claimant's action is for a specified sum; Form N9C will be used when the claim is for an unspecified sum.

Time begins to run from the deemed date of service (see Chapter 9, paragraph 9.7.1.1) of the particulars of claim on the defendant (CPR 9.2). The defendant has 14 days from that date in which to:

- file or serve an admission; or
- file a defence (which may be combined with a counterclaim) (this may use Form N11 or be drafted separately); or
- file an acknowledgement of service.

Each of these options is now considered.

10.5.1 ADMITTING THE CLAIM AND REQUESTING TIME TO PAY

Forms N9A and N9C make provision for admissions to be made. Admissions may be made of the whole claim or a part of it. Where only part is being admitted, the defendant will need to file a defence to that part of the claim that is not admitted, otherwise the claimant will be able to apply for judgment in default of that part. In either case, the forms also make provision for the defendant to make provision to pay the sum admitted or to ask for time to pay.

Where the defendant seeks time to pay the sum admitted, he must also complete those parts of the form that require details of his assets, income, and outgoings. The completed form will be sent to the claimant, who may raise objections to the defendant's instalment payment offer that he will include in the form. Where the claimant raises objections to the offer, the court will either set the level of instalments or set the matter down for a disposal hearing. The specific detail and order of instalment offers and terms are set down in CPR 14.

Where the defendant admits the whole claim within 14 days of service of the particulars of claim, he will be liable for the fixed costs of the action. Details of the sum of these fixed costs will be contained in the bottom right-hand box on the front page of the Form N1 claim form. Where the defendant admits the whole claim, the admission in one of the Forms N9 will be sent directly to the claimant rather than filed at court and the claimant will be able to obtain judgment on the claim by filing a request for judgment in either Form N225 or Form N227.

Where the defendant has requested time to pay, the claimant will have to respond to the offer and either accept it or raise objections. If the admission is of the whole claim, or the claimant accepts the instalment offer, the court will proceed to issue the judgment order in Form N30. The judgment will include accrued interest and the fixed costs. The judgment is also registered in the Register of Judgments. Because registration of a judgment debt may affect a defendant's creditworthiness, it is worth noting that a defendant may avoid registration of the debt if he has admitted the whole claim and paid the sum due and fixed costs within 14 days of service of the particulars of claim.

If the defendant's admission is for part of the claim, but has an offer to satisfy the whole claim, the claimant has the option of accepting the sum offered. If he does accept the sum offered, the matter will proceed as stated and the court will proceed to make the judgment order. If the offer is rejected, the case will proceed as a disputed claim.

In unspecified sum claims in which the defendant has filed an admission of the claim, the matter will be stayed and set down for a disposal hearing for the court to determine the sum of the claim. Directions will be given as to the evidence to be filed and exchanged in advance of the disposal hearing.

Where the defendant is a child or protected party, the court must approve any admission, or part-admission, or offer to pay by an instalment option. (For further details of child or protected party applications, see Chapter 9, paragraph 9.5.)

10.5.2 FILING A DEFENCE

If the defendant intends to defend the action against him, he will need to file and serve his defence. The defence may be drafted on Form N11 or be a separately drafted document (see

Chapter 11, paragraph 11.5). CPR 15 contains the rules for the filing of the defence and service upon every other party in the action. These rules include provisions that:

- a defendant who wishes to file a defence should do so within 14 days after service upon him of the particulars of claim;

- a defendant who files an acknowledgement of service within 14 days (after service upon him of the particulars of claim) must serve his defence within 28 days after service upon him of the particulars of claim; and

- the time limits of 14 days and 28 days do not apply when the defendant resides outside the jurisdiction (the alternative time limits are set down in CPR 6.33), or when the defendant is disputing jurisdiction, he need not file a defence (CPR 11), or when the claimant makes an application for summary judgment, the defendant need not file a defence before the hearing of the claimant's application (CPR 24.4).

Forms N9A, N9C, and N9D provide space for a defence to the claim to be made. Where a party is legally represented, the defence will usually be separately drafted in the form and structure detailed in Chapter 11, paragraph 11.5.

 Practical Considerations

Acting for a defendant will require as many, if not more, matters to be discussed with the client than may be discussed with a claimant to establish whether he has a claim. Although the claimant will have formulated the substance of the claim, a defendant has a variety of options that may be available to him to respond and defend the claim (see further paragraph 10.6). A defendant should admit what should be admitted. Costs penalties and professional conduct Principles will apply if there has been any deliberate, or careless, intention to mislead the court or if a defendant is reluctant to admit those parts of the claim that clearly should be admitted. Ambiguous claims can be amended or put right, and it is important that you, as the legal representative, seek to balance the interests of the overriding objective and the need to be 'cooperative' in litigation with what may be in the 'best interests' of the client. Where a claim is being 'denied', the legal representative should consider whether there is evidence that is credible and admissible to support the defence. It is not simply a case of waiting to see if the claimant can establish his case.

Further, clients may not always understand the intricacies of their actions—for example, in claims for misrepresentation. Misrepresentation arises where something is said with the *intention* of inducing a contract and *does* induce a contract. Clients will not always understand the difference between pre-contractual enquiry and true misrepresentation. These misunderstandings have to be managed by the legal representative. These and many other matters may arise in acting for a defendant in even the simplest of actions.

10.5.2.1 Extending the time for service of the defence

The time limits for filing a defence may be extended by agreement between the parties. The parties can agree an extension up to a maximum of a further 28 days. When such an agreement is made, the defendant must inform the court of the period of the extension (CPR 15.5). If any greater extension of time is required, whether the claimant consents or not, an application must be made to the court. The application must be justified in terms of the overriding objective.

 Practical Considerations

In any dispute resolution department, any legal representative has to be more than simply able to undertake the procedural requirements of litigation—he must also be commercially aware. In commercial matters, one or both sides to the claim may be in business and an awareness of the implications of this are important if the legal representative is to 'serve' his client's best interests. The action may have a significant cash flow impact on the business; the parties to the action may need to, or wish to, continue their business relationship. These, and other, business-related issues need to be understood and 'managed' within the action.

Once the defence is filed, the court's case management role is started with the notification of intended allocation and direction of the issuing of the DQ (directions questionnaire) to all parties. Chapter 12 sets out the detail and consequences for the parties of this step.

10.5.2.2 If no defence is filed and served

If the defendant fails to file a defence within the period specified, in most actions, the claimant will be able to obtain default judgment. This precludes the defendant from defending the claim further (see Chapter 14, paragraph 14.2 for details of how the claimant can secure default judgment and what the defendant can do to have it set aside). Default judgment is not permitted if the claim is for delivery of goods that are subject to an agreement regulated by the Consumer Credit Act 1974, or in CPR Part 8 proceedings, or in any other case in which a Practice Direction provides.

If a defence is not filed and the claimant fails to seek default judgment, six months after the date on which the defence should have been filed, the claim will be stayed (CPR 15.11).

10.5.3 FILING AN ACKNOWLEDGEMENT OF SERVICE

The form of acknowledgement of service is used by a defendant for three reasons. The defendant will file and serve the acknowledgement of service when he is unable to file his defence within 14 days of the service upon him of the particulars of claim, but intends to defend some or all of the claim, or he may file it when he admits some or all of the claim, but wishes to have time to pay, or he may file it when he intends to signify (and take no other step in the action) that he disputes the jurisdiction of the court to hear the action.

The acknowledgement of service form is included with Form N9 (A, B, C, or D) and must be filed at the court out of which the claim is issued. It will ask for the following information:

- the defendant's full name—if the defendant's name has been incorrectly stated in the claim, the defendant will set out his correct name in the acknowledgement of service; and

- the defendant's full address for service, including postcode—this may be a personal or a business address, and if the defendant is legally represented, his legal representative will state the firm's address for service. Service of the claim on a partnership may be acknowledged by any of the partners served or someone authorized to acknowledge on behalf of the partnership, and if served on a company, the form of acknowledgement may be signed by a director or a person holding a senior position in the company (the person signing also indicating his position in the company).

See the Online Resource Centre for a copy of the acknowledgement of service.

10.5.3.1 Disputing all or part of the claim

The defendant must tick one of two boxes on the form confirming whether he intends to defend all or part of the claim. He must then file his defence within the time limit now available to him by having filed the acknowledgement of service (see paragraph 10.5.2). The filing of the acknowledgement of service is also the trigger point for some interim applications—for example, either party may make an application for summary judgment, or the claimant may make an application for an interim payment. If the defendant admits the claim but wishes to have time to pay or pay by instalments he will complete a means form with the form of acknowledgement.

10.5.3.2 Contesting jurisdiction

If the defendant intends to contest the jurisdiction of the claim against him, he must tick the box confirming this. If a defendant intends to do this, he must take care not to take steps in the action beyond acknowledging service of the claim form (CPR 11). He must then, within 14 days, make an application, supported with written evidence, disputing the jurisdiction of the court (CPR 11(4)). The defendant need not—in fact, should not—file his defence until after the court has heard his application. A defence will be required from him if his application disputing jurisdiction has failed, usually within 14 days of the court's decision declaring that the action is correctly being dealt with within the jurisdiction. Sometimes, the application is clear: for example, there may be a valid agreement for the matter to be submitted to arbitration. Sometimes, the application disputing the jurisdiction of the court may be made because there is a choice, in which case, the court will exercise its discretion in accordance with the principles of the overriding objective.

If the defendant does not make an application to the court under the provisions of CPR 11(4), he will be treated as if he has accepted that the court does have jurisdiction to hear the claim.

See also Chapter 9, paragraph 9.7.7 for examples where the defendant may seek to challenge jurisdiction on the grounds of ineffective or invalid service of the claim form.

10.6 THE DEFENCE OF A CLAIM

10.6.1 COMMON DEFENCES

A defence is required when a defendant wishes to defend all or part of a claim. Once filed, a copy of the defence must be served on every other party. The time limits for the filing of a defence are set out at CPR 15.4 and in paragraph 10.5.

'Defences' can be broadly subdivided into the following categories, which can be used exclusively or concurrently if appropriate:

- **Procedural defences.** These could include, for example:
  - a submission that the court does not have jurisdiction; or
  - a submission that the claim is outside the limitation period.
- **Defences to the cause of action.** These could include submissions that state:
  - that the claim does not disclose a cause of action; or
  - that, on the evidence, the cause of action is not established on the balance of probabilities; or
  - that, on the grounds of the defence, the defendant is absolved from liability.
- **Defences to the claim for damages.** These could include submissions that:
  - the claim does not set out all of the required elements for a claim for damages; or
  - on the evidence, the elements of the remedy sought are not, on the balance of probabilities, substantiated; or
  - on the facts, the loss was not caused by the breach (causation); or
  - on the facts, the loss was not foreseeable; or
  - on the facts, the claimant has failed to mitigate his loss; or further
  - in a negligence or breach of contract action, the claimant was also negligent or in breach, and contributed to his loss and damage.

It can be seen that some of these defences will act as defences to the claim itself, while others will seek to reduce (or eliminate) the liability that the claimant alleges has arisen, but 'liability' itself is accepted. We refer to the latter case as an admission of 'primary liability' coupled with an allegation of contributory negligence against the claimant. (See Chapter 11, paragraph 11.5, for details on how to draft some of these defences.)

One of the options that may be part of the defendant's case may be to seek to pass the blame or liability of the claimant's action to another. This is dealt with next.

10.6.2 **PART 20 CLAIMS**

A defendant faced with an action against him may have:

- no issue with the fact that the claimant has suffered a loss, but he may feel that responsibility for some or all of those losses does not lie with him, but with somebody else;

- a claim of his own that he would like to bring that arises out of the same set of circumstances.

In these circumstances, a defendant can use the provisions set out in CPR 20. CPR 20 has, however, been drafted poorly and many new to practice find its categorization of claims unhelpful. CPR 20 essentially enables the defendant to make four types of additional claim, the nature of each of which is examined here. The correct terminology for this type of claim is an 'additional claim', but you will often see it referred to as a 'Part 20 claim'.

By way of definition, an 'additional claim' is any claim other than that initiated by the claimant against the defendant. This could also be called the 'main action'. Although CPR Part 20 claims are procedurally connected with the main action, they can be entirely separate claims. A settlement or action terminating the main action will not usually terminate an additional claim unless it is included in the agreement or order terminating the main action. It will depend on the nature of the additional claim and whether it is worth pursuing it after the settlement or termination of the main action. For example, if the defendant has sought a contribution or indemnity, the dismissal or striking out of the main action will render it pointless continuing with the claim for a contribution or indemnity, because there will be no sum to which to contribute or to indemnify.

10.6.2.1 A counterclaim brought by the defendant against the claimant (CPR 20.4)

A counterclaim is a claim in its own right that lies against the claimant in the action. It could form the basis of a separate claim by the defendant against the claimant in separate proceedings, but in these circumstances the defendant does not have the choice of issuing his own proceedings against the claimant, because when there is already litigation existing between the parties (because of the main action started by the claimant), the defendant must—apart from for reasons of convenience, efficiency, and cost-effectiveness—bring his counterclaim in the same set of proceedings where the counterclaim arises from the same—or substantially the same—set of facts as the claimant's claim.

The subject matter of the counterclaim need not be precisely the same as the proceedings started by the claimant against the defendant, but the claimant and the defendant must sue and be sued in the same capacity.

Determining whether the defence has a true counterclaim requires careful legal and factual analysis, as follows:

- A defendant's case that amounts to a simple dispute of the facts set down by the claimant in the action is not a counterclaim. An example of this could be where the defendant disputes the terms of the contract that form the basis of the claimant's case.

- If the defendant's case against the claimant amounts to a simple defence to the allegations against him, these are matters that would be raised in the defence, not in any counterclaim. An example of this situation would be where the defendant alleges contributory negligence on the part of the claimant. This also is not an 'additional claim' under CPR Part 20. In this situation, the defendant should set out his allegations in the defence, stating what duty or act the claimant failed to discharge or undertake that contributed to the losses that he sustained.

- Any situation in which the defendant has a separate claim that has all of the requirements of a true action against the claimant (where related to the facts of the main action), would be a counterclaim within the provisions of CPR Part 20.

- Where the defendant blames someone else and claims to have no personal responsibility for the claimant's loss or damage, such a claim would be included in the defendant's defence and would not be a counterclaim. An example of such a situation would be if, in a road traffic accident (RTA), the defendant were to claim that the RTA was wholly caused by the claimant or someone else, or in a breach of contract action, if the defendant were to claim that he acted as agent rather than principal, or where the defendant claims to be absolved from the claim by an exclusion clause. These are defences, not counterclaims.

 Example

A claimant issues proceedings against a defendant for non-payment on an information technology (IT) service and maintenance contract. The defendant denies the allegations, stating that the IT works had not been effected correctly and that, as a result, his company has suffered loss of production.

The defence here is the allegation that the claimant had not performed his part of the contract properly and the counterclaim is the monetary losses to the defendant, which he incurred as a result of those breaches by the claimant. The flowchart in Figure 10.1 at the end of this chapter illustrates this.

Therefore, the key features of a counterclaim are as follows:

- It is brought by an existing defendant in an action against the claimant.
- It arises out of the same, or substantially the same, facts as the claimant's claim against the defendant.
- It is a monetary claim in its own right.
- It is not a defence.
- The court heading identifying the parties will not change. It will be identical to the court heading on the particulars of claim.

A 'simple' counterclaim by the defendant against the claimant (such as that described in the previous example) is a situation in which it can be seen quite clearly that the party's claims against each other should be heard in the same action, avoiding the potential situation of two courts reaching different conclusions based on the same facts. However, if the claims are so different from one another that there is no overlap of evidence or facts, and the combining of the actions is unlikely to result in a saving of costs or time, it may indicate that the claims should be independently processed.

See Chapter 11, paragraph 11.6.1, for an example of a drafted counterclaim.

10.6.2.2 A counterclaim brought by the defendant against a person other than the claimant (CPR 20.5)

This type of additional claim is against a person who is not already a party to the action, but against whom the defendant has a monetary claim that arises out of the same set of facts. Therefore, much of paragraph 10.6.2.1 will apply in terms of identifying a true counterclaim as opposed to a defence, but, of course, the additional party will not be the claimant, because it must be a person who is not already involved in the proceedings.

The easiest way to explain this is by way of an example.

 Example

The claimant, Pearl Fisher, is injured in an RTA whilst driving in the course of her employment with Purcell Logistics Ltd and issues proceedings against the defendant, Scott Butler. The defendant denies negligence and alleges contributory negligence against the claimant. The defendant wants to make a counterclaim, because his truck was badly damaged, as were the materials in the truck. The counterclaim technically lies against the claimant's employer, due to the principle of vicarious liability, but the employer is not a party to the action. If the defendant wants to pursue a counterclaim formally, then he will need to issue a Part 20 claim against the claimant's employer under CPR 20.5. The flowchart in Figure 10.2 at the end of this chapter illustrates this.

Practical Considerations

In practice, as would have been identified during Protocol correspondence between the claimant and defendant, what, in fact, would happen in this example is that the claimant's legal representative would have passed details of the counterclaim on to her employer's insurer, which would subrogate the counterclaim. It would confirm that the claimant was driving in the course of her employment and, in order to deal with the defence of the counterclaim proportionately and reasonably in this case, it would agree with the claimant's and defendant's legal representatives that it would allow the claimant's legal representative to conduct the defence to the counterclaim, indemnify them in respect of any costs, and abide by any judgment and costs orders made in respect of the counterclaim.

In such actions, the title of the action will change. The heading of a claim with a CPR Part 20 claim could look like that detailed here. (Note that the defendant refers to the Part 20 defendant as a 'third party'.)

MRS PEARL FISHER   Claimant

     and

MR SCOTT BUTLER   Defendant

     and

PURCELL LOGISTICS LTD   Third Party

These additional claims do not operate as a defence to the action either.

10.6.2.3 An additional claim brought by the defendant seeking a contribution or an indemnity (CPR 20.6)

A defendant may make such a claim for a contribution, or an indemnity or other remedy, from an existing party, usually another defendant, in which case the claim will be called a 'Contribution Notice'. Such a claim may arise between joint tortfeasors, joint contractors, joint sureties, joint debtors, or joint trustees. The sum of the 'contribution' will be based either on the facts of the joint responsibility, or on the basis of the degree of blame for the claimant's loss and damage. A claim for a contribution will usually seek to share the liability. A claim for an indemnity, however, seeks to pass on the entire liability to the indemnifier; an indemnity may arise under a contract, under statute, or by virtue of the relationship between the defendant and additional party. A party can also seek to claim both a contribution and an indemnity from its co-defendant.

 Example

Claims for contribution are frequently found in road traffic actions, as follows:

The claimant had emerged from a set of traffic lights at a crossroads and was waiting to turn right in the junction. He was stationary. Two vehicles travelling in the opposite direction collided with him. The claimant issued proceedings against both defendants. The first defendant served a contribution notice, requesting that the second defendant agree to a 60:40 liability split in favour of the first defendant, in accordance with CPR 20.6.

Claims for indemnity are frequently found in commercial claims, as follows:

The claimant contracted with an architect to design a home for him. He also engaged a building company to construct the property. The property was defective, and the claimant issued proceedings against both the architect and the building company. In the architect's defence, he denied the claimant's claim and blamed his co-defendant for all of the claimant's losses. The architect in this situation served an additional claim for an indemnity against the building company. The flowchart in Figure 10.3 at the end of this chapter illustrates this.

In such actions, the court headings identifying the parties will not change. These additional claims do, however, operate as a type of defence to the claimant's claim.

10.6.2.4 An additional claim brought against other persons (CPR 20.7)

Such a claim is made in the first instance by a defendant to the action who wishes to blame someone other than the claimant for the claimant's losses. The new additional party will be called a 'third party'. If that third party then wishes to blame someone else, whether that 'someone else' is a party to the action or not, then that 'someone else' is called a 'fourth party'—and so on. These allegations and counter-allegations can become complex in, for example, large building and construction contracts—although the number of additional parties continues with the allegations and counter-allegations, it remains 'convenient' to hear all of the claims together (or as managed by the court), because all relate to the same facts (that is, the subject of the construction contract).

 Example

A garden centre contracted with a greenhouse supplier to supply and install two large warehouse greenhouses for indoor plants. The heating system did not work, to the extent that it overheated and killed the plants. The garden centre issued proceedings against the greenhouse supplier for loss of revenue. The greenhouse supplier defended the claim, blaming the electrical contractor that it had engaged to install the heating system. The electrical contractor denied liability and blamed its subcontractor—an individual who had actually undertaken the works. The flowchart in Figure 10.4 at the end of this chapter illustrates this.

When this occurs, the heading of the action will continue to 'evolve' as new parties are added and additional claims are made, and it might look like this:

DALE GARDEN CENTRE LTD   Claimant

      and

WIRRAL GREENHOUSES LTD   Defendant

      and

S & S ELECTRICAL SOLUTIONS (A FIRM)   Third Party

      and

MR BERNARD TALBOT T/A TALBOT ELECTRICIANS   Fourth Party

See Chapter 11, paragraph 11.6.2.1, for a drafted third-party claim.

These additional claims do operate as a defence to the claimant's claim.

10.6.2.5 How to issue an additional claim

10.6.2.5.1 *A counterclaim against the claimant*

Where the counterclaim is a 'simple' one, being a counterclaim made by the defendant in the main action against the claimant, the defendant may raise the counterclaim:

• without the permission of the court, provided that he files it with, or at the same time as, his defence (CPR 20.4.2(a)). Practically, the counterclaim is drafted so that it follows directly on from the defence. This can sometimes be confusing for those new to practice, as the counterclaim has the appearance of being part of the defence. It is, however, a separate legal document with its own cause of action and loss claimed. Again, see paragraph 11.6.1.1 in Chapter 11 for a draft counterclaim attached to a defence; or

• at any other time with the court's permission (CPR 20.4.2(b)). Here the counterclaim will more obviously stand alone as a separate legal statement of case. The only difference to the example given in paragraph 11.6.1.1 is that the full title of the action and the heading will need to be inserted at the top of the document.

In either of these cases a fee is payable for the counterclaim that is equivalent to the fee for issuing a fresh claim, although there is no claim form to complete.

10.6.2.5.2 *A counterclaim against a person other than the claimant*

Where the defendant wishes to seek an additional claim by way of a counterclaim against a person who is not a party to the proceedings, he must apply to the court for permission to do so (CPR 20.5). When he makes an application, it must be accompanied by a statement of case (of the additional claim), and will set out details of the stage that the main proceedings have reached, the nature of that claim, and details of the nature of the claim against the new party. The statement of case will be headed 'Defendant's Counterclaim against a Third Party'.

If the court makes an order permitting the addition of the new party, it will also give directions for managing the case. These directions are likely to include provision for service of all statements of case on the new party, together with a response pack and an order stating the time allowed for responding to the additional claim, together with directions of the role that the new party will take in the action (if any). Further case management directions will also be given for disclosure, exchange of witness statements, etc.

A fee is also payable here and, again, there is no claim form.

10.6.2.5.3 *An additional claim for a contribution or indemnity*

Where the defendant seeks a contribution or indemnity from someone who is already a party to the action, he may file a Contribution Notice setting out the grounds of the additional claim, and serve that on the claimant and the additional party without the permission of the court, provided that he files the notice and claim at the same time as filing his defence (CPR 20.6). He may also serve notice of an additional claim for a contribution or an indemnity against a person who later becomes a party to the proceedings, provided that he serves the notice within 28 days of the new party being added to the claim. In any other circumstances, the defendant must seek the court's permission, by way of an application, to seek a contribution or indemnity.

No fee is payable and no claim form is issued.

10.6.2.5.4 *An additional claim against persons not party to the proceedings*

Where an additional claim is made against someone who is not yet a party to proceedings, the defendant can make this additional claim without the court's permission if the additional claim is issued before or at the same time as he files his defence, or at any other time with the court's permission on a without-notice application (CPR 20.7). The statement of case could be headed 'Defendant's Additional Claim against a Third Party'. Again an example of how to draft this document can be found at paragraph 11.6.2.1 in Chapter 11.

A fixed fee is payable, though the sum differs in the High Court and the County Court. There is also an additional (Part 20) claim form to complete.

Please see the Online Resource Centre for a copy of a Part 20 claim form.

 online resource centre

10.6.2.6 The service of additional claims

When permission of the court is not required, a counterclaim made in these situations in which the permission of the court is not required must be filed at court with the defence and served on each party. Any additional claim issued by the court at a later date must be served on the person against whom it is made within 14 days of issue by the court.

When permission of the court is required, the court will make directions for the service of the additional claim when it gives permission for the additional claim to be made within the main action.

In either case, service of the additional claim will be accompanied by:

- a form for defending the claim;
- a form for admitting the claim;
- a form for acknowledging service; and
- a copy of every statement of case already served in the main action and any other documents that the court has directed should also be served (CPR 20.12).

10.6.2.7 What response does a claimant or other person give to the counterclaim (CPR 20.4 and 20.5)?

Save where CPR Part 20 states to the contrary, the provisions of the CPR apply to counterclaims as if they were claims. In this way, a 'defence to the counterclaim' must be served within 14 days of the date of service of the counterclaim. Failure to do this will enable the defendant to seek judgment in default on the counterclaim.

Whilst defending the counterclaim, a reply to the defendant's defence can be raised. The statement of case is known as a 'reply and defence to counterclaim' and forms one document. The reply is optional and is only usually prepared where something has been raised in the defence (and counterclaim) that requires a response, so that the issues between the parties are defined. PD 15 at paragraph 3.2A, however, states that the deadline for filing a defence to counterclaim (where a reply is also to be filed) may be extended by the court to correspond with the date for filing the DQ where that date is more than 14 days after the notice of proposed allocation is deemed served for small claim track cases, and 28 days for fast-track and multi-track cases, in accordance with CPR 26.3(6)(b). When there is no counterclaim, the usual time for service of the reply is on the filing of the DQ with the court. Once a reply and defence to counterclaim has been served, the court is very likely to case manage the claim and the counterclaim together.

See Chapter 11, paragraph 11.7, for a drafted reply.

10.6.2.8 What action must an additional party take in an additional claim (CPR 20.6 and 20.7)?

For additional claims brought by the defendant, the additional party must serve a defence (if already a party to the action), or an acknowledgement and defence if not already a party to the action.

If the additional party fails to acknowledge or defend the additional claim, he will be deemed to admit the main action and be bound by the outcome of it so far as it relates to him by the additional claim made against him by the defendant.

See Chapter 11, paragraph 11.6.2, for a drafted additional claim.

10.6.2.9 CPR Part 20 claims and costs

The general rule is that the loser should pay the winner's costs. As we have seen in Chapter 4, there are many factors that influence the order for costs that the court will make. Where an action has included additional claims, then the issue of costs demands special attention. In some situations, with additional claims, the defendant may be in the unenviable position of incurring costs in defending the main action, but also incurring costs in pursuing his additional claim. The issue of who has 'won' an action in which there are multiple claims may make it difficult to deal with the issue of costs orders between the parties, as well as the sum of those costs orders. These types of costs order are outside the scope of this book, but are 'flagged up' here as an area in which careful study and attention must be paid in any dealings with an action that includes an additional claim.

10.6.3 **THE DEFENCE OF 'SET-OFF'**

The law relating to set-off is complex, because it is based on legal doctrines (legal set-off and equitable set-off) and case law. Here, we set out only the basic principles in relation to the simplest and most common type of set-off: the legal set-off.

A legal 'set-off' is a money claim that a defendant has against the claimant. It is for an ascertainable amount and is usually used as a defence with a view to reducing significantly, or even extinguishing, the claimant's claim against the defendant. Another feature of a set-off is that it is 'separate' to the cause of action that the claimant has brought against the defendant in his particulars of claim.

Example

Sole Trader A supplies goods totalling £20,000 to Limited Company B in July. In August, Limited Company B supplies goods to the value of £30,000 to Sole Trader A. Neither company pays for the goods. Both transactions had a separate written contract. If A were to sue B, it is likely that B would raise a defence of set-off that, in this case, would completely extinguish A's claim if successful. B would then counterclaim, seeking the remaining £10,000. Therefore, in this example, B has both a defence of set-off and a counterclaim.

Here, the court could award the claimant judgment on his claim, but order a stay of execution pending the determination of the counterclaim.

 Practical Considerations

In practice, you may come across contracts that stipulate that the debtor has no right of set-off against the creditor. You will need to consider the clause carefully, taking into account whether it may be held to be unreasonable and rendered ineffective under the Unfair Contract Terms Act 1977. The purpose of these clauses is to cover the situations in which contracting parties undertake reciprocal business.

A defendant who has an unquantified set-off against the claimant that is not connected with the claimant's claim is not usually entitled to a set-off, although the doctrine of equitable set-off would need to be examined. This is outside the scope of this manual.

Legal set-offs are therefore most successfully used by defendants in mutual debt-type claims as in the previous example—but compare the following example.

 Example

A building contractor undertakes building works for a homeowner. The homeowner alleges that the works are of unsatisfactory quality and refuses to pay. The contractor issues proceedings for the amount owed, and the homeowner defends on the basis of poor workmanship and seeks to set-off, by way of a counterclaim, the value of the remedial works to rectify the job against what he owes the contractor.

This second example can be distinguished for two reasons: firstly, the second example concerns a set-off for an unquantified amount, because the value of the remedial works would need to be ascertained; and secondly, the counterclaim operates as a set-off within the claimant's action. Although the situation of the homeowner in this second example is not strictly a set-off, these types of scenario can also be treated as set-offs in practice.

10.7 COMMON TACTICS AVAILABLE IN DEFENDING A CLAIM

In addition to defending a claim, a defendant has a selection of tactics to employ where appropriate and proportionate to do so. The tactics listed here are not exhaustive, however, and all are also available to a claimant, save for the security for costs application (unless the claimant is defending a counterclaim), which rests exclusively with the defendant.

10.7.1 MAKING AN APPLICATION FOR SUMMARY JUDGMENT

An application for summary judgment may be made by the defendant under the provisions of CPR 24 when he believes that he can show that the claimant's case is so weak on the facts that it has no real prospect of succeeding. (See Chapter 14, paragraph 14.3, which deals with applications for summary judgment.)

An application for summary judgment can also be made for part of a claim, and in this way, the issues between the parties can be narrowed and be used by a defendant who wishes to restrict the claim being made against him. The requirements for summary judgment for part of a claim are the same as an application for summary judgment on the whole.

A defendant's application for summary judgment can be made at any time after he has filed his acknowledgement of service indicating an intention to defend the action (in whole or in part).

10.7.2 MAKING AN APPLICATION TO DISMISS THE CLAIM

A defendant may make an application to dismiss the claim under the provisions of CPR 3 (to strike out the claim or to dismiss the claim as a sanction). This could arise if the claim raises no proper cause of action, or is an abuse of process, or on the basis that there has been a failure to abide by an order of the court.

Examples of each of these could include:

- that the claim sets out no known 'cause of action' in law;
- that withdrawing, in bad faith, an admission previously made could be construed as an 'abuse of process';
- that attempting to relitigate a cause of action previously tried could also be an example of an 'abuse of process'; and
- a failure to abide by a court order or inordinate delay on the part of a party.

The court has the power to make orders under the provisions of CPR 3 on its own initiative, but the provisions can be used upon the application of a party. On occasion, an application under CPR 3 will be made in conjunction with an application for summary judgment under CPR 24— but note the distinction between the two applications set out in Chapter 14, paragraph 14.3.2.

 Practical Considerations

The provisions in CPR 3 will be exercised sparingly. In situations in which CPR 3 may apply, the court may determine that it would be more 'just' or appropriate to use the provisions of CPR 18 (see paragraph 10.7.4) to clarify the inadequate case. Alternatively, in the interests of 'justice', a court may also allow a party to amend its case rather than impose an order to strike out the claim.

10.7.3 MAKING AN APPLICATION FOR SECURITY FOR COSTS

A defendant has often not chosen to be embroiled in the litigation (although his behaviour may have been deliberately such that the claimant had no other option but to commence proceedings). Defending his position against the claim will cost him money. These costs can be considerable. Equally, a defendant will be at risk of an order for damages being made against him.

A defendant's armoury to protect against a judgment for damages against him will be in the steps that he can take to:

- prove his version of the 'story' that gives rise to the claim and absolve himself from any liability;
- show that a head of damage or a part of the loss is not recoverable so as to limit the claim against him; and
- show that the sum claimed should be as low as possible—that is, by showing a failure to mitigate by the claimant.

A defendant's armoury to protect him from the legal costs that he may incur in defending his claim includes:

- making a carefully pitched CPR Part 36 offer to transfer some of the risks of the costs of the action to the claimant (offers to settle and the consequences of such offers are detailed in Chapter 16);

11 DRAFTING STATEMENTS OF CASE

Relevant parts of the CPR and its PDs: 1, 14–20, 22, 31, and 32

11.1 INTRODUCTION

Drafting statements of case requires a logical and clear mind. Legal representatives will draft many statements of case, with the aim of producing accurate, relevant, and compelling formal court documents. This chapter provides key formulae to help those new to practice produce competent statements of case.

Whilst a claim form is a statement of case, how to complete this standard form has been dealt with in Chapter 9, paragraph 9.3.2. The Online Resource Centre features the claim form N1, accompanied by drafting tips on the form itself.

Here, we examine some statements of case. This list is not exhaustive, but represents those statements of case that you will come across most frequently in practice:

- particulars of claim;
- defences;
- additional claims;
- replies; and
- Part 18 requests.

11.2 THE PURPOSE OF A STATEMENT OF CASE

Whenever preparing a statement of case, there are a number of cardinal rules to remember in relation to the purpose of the statement of case, as follows.

11.2.1 PROVIDE AN OUTLINE

The court requires only an outline of a party's case on liability, causation, and quantum. In essence, this means the statement of case needs to set out the cause of action, the exact nature of the allegation(s) being made, and the financial consequences. The temptation is to provide each and every detail that you have in relation to each of these points, but these are to be left to form the basis of the main witness statements in the action.

11.2.2 PROVIDE CLARIFICATION

The purpose of the statement of case is to clarify matters in dispute so that the issues can be clearly identified by the court and the parties to the action.

11.2.3 SET OUT FACTUAL DETAILS

All matters being alleged are stated so that all parties in an action know in advance what is being alleged by each party against them. Generally, it is only the facts of a case that are 'stated'—that is, facts relating to the nature or background to a case, the issues, the allegations, and losses.

However, because the CPR encourage considerable pre-action work being undertaken, the parties will normally be in a position to refer to some evidence in the statement of case and, on occasions, to exhibit it. There are some CPR requirements, for example PD 16.7.3(1), which stipulates that a written contract should be attached to the particulars of claim.This makes the art of drafting considerably simpler. It will also have the benefit of adding weight to a case for the party who can refer to or exhibit strong evidence in favour of his case. It may, however, be a question of reasonableness, judgment, or a mandatory requirement as to the relevancy or the inclusion of the evidence to be included or annexed.

11.2.4 IDENTIFY LEGAL REQUIREMENTS

Every piece of litigation must have a legal basis upon which a claim can be founded: for example, a claim in tort must be considered to exist before a negligence claim can proceed. However, generally, the law is not to be stated in the statement of case, because the judge is presumed to know it. Nevertheless, there is no prohibition against doing so and the law, in terms of a statute or regulation, may be stated where it is thought necessary. For example, if there is a particularly unusual point of law to be taken, or a little-known piece of legislation or a statutory defence, then the relevant law can be stated. This is particularly prevalent in accident at work claims (see the example in paragraph 11.4.1.3).

11.3 THE STANDARD REQUIREMENTS OF A STATEMENT OF CASE

In paragraph 11.4, we have set out a series of 'formulae for drafting' specific to different types of civil action. Here, it is the intention to highlight some general practical, but important, drafting hints that are particular to all statements of case, as follows:

- The statement of case should import the court heading of the action and state what type of statement of case it is directly below the court heading.
- The statement of case should always be in the third person: 'the claimant', 'the defendant', etc.
- Numbered paragraphs should always be used, frequently with subparagraphs or even subheadings if a paragraph is long. The judge, opposing lawyers, and any expert witnesses in the case do not want to lose the 'thread' and have to reread the statement of case. This may only irritate those who read it. Paragraph numbers also make reference to specific parts of a statement of case much simpler.
- The statement of case is the draftsman's opportunity to be articulate and clear on paper. When reading older statements of case, take care not to pick up on and replicate antiquated language such as 'hereinbefore' and 'bequeath'.
- There is a requirement to include a statement of truth on every statement of case. The statement of truth is said to add weight to a statement of case and should act to restrict the action to legitimate issues rather than statements of 'hopeful' allegations, which may have little chance of succeeding at trial. Increasingly, the judges are making costs orders (CPR Part 44) that reflect the numbers of issues with which a party may have proceeded to trial, and considering whether this was a sensible, proportionate, fair, and just thing to do (CPR Part 1).

11.3.1 THE STATEMENT OF TRUTH

All statements of case must contain a statement of truth in accordance with CPR 22, which also provides additional occasions when a statement of truth must be provided in other documents.

A failure to provide a statement of truth on a document where one is required will mean that although the document will remain effective unless it is subsequently struck out, the party may not rely on the statement as evidence of any matter set out in it (CPR 22.2).

The form of the statement of truth for a statement of case is set out in Practice Direction (PD) 22.2.1 and 22.2.2 as follows:

> [I believe] [the (claimant or as may be) believes] that the facts stated in this [name the document being verified] are true.

11.3.2 WHO SHOULD SIGN THE STATEMENT OF TRUTH?

Practice Direction 22.3 sets out who should sign the statement of truth. In general, it should be the party or his legal representative, but best practice indicates that, for all statements of case, the party itself should sign the statement of truth. PD 22.3 will need to be looked at where the party is a company, a partnership, or an insurer.

11.3.3 WHAT ARE THE CONSEQUENCES OF MAKING A STATEMENT OF TRUTH WHEN THE CONTENTS OF THE DOCUMENT, OR ANY PART OF IT, ARE KNOWN TO BE FALSE?

Proceedings for contempt may be brought against a person if he makes, or causes to be made, a false statement of truth. Proceedings for contempt may only be brought by the Attorney General or with the permission of the court (CPR 32.14 and PD 32.28).

11.4 THE PARTICULARS OF CLAIM

The principal rules surrounding the drafting of a particulars of claim can be found in CPR 16 and its Practice Direction. On the reverse side of Form N1 can be found a space in which to draft the particulars. It is not mandatory and usually not sensible or appropriate to draft the particulars of claim in that section of the claim form in every case; rather, it will be a question of common sense in terms of how much you have to say and whether there is enough room to set out your case clearly. It will usually only be a fairly straightforward claim, such as a debt claim, that can be fitted on the reverse side of the claim form.

Drafting can get quite technical, but it is important to remember a guiding principle— that is, 'tell the story'. The story is told to the defendant from the claimant's point of view, and is essentially very simple, as follows:

1. 'This is who we are ...'
2. 'This is who you are ...'
3. 'This is what happened ...'
4. 'It is your fault/breach ...'
5. 'This was the result of what happened ...'
6. 'And so this is what I want from you ...'

Remember, the claim must set out those facts and allegations that, if proved, would give the claimant the right to the remedy sought as a matter of law.

Against this simplistic theory of drafting a particulars of claim, the drafting formulae can now be brought into play. These will assist in the drafting of each of the most common statements of case and, if followed, can provide a good basic structure for even the most complex of cases, whether of high or low value.

11.4.1 THE FORMULAE

11.4.1.1 A claim for a breach of contract

A claim for a breach of contract should deal with the following matters in the following order:

1. The parties (and, if appropriate, the name of the parties' representatives) to, and the date (if written) or approximate date (if oral) of, the agreement.

2. The nature and purpose of the agreement and the consideration.

3. Any relevant express or implied terms of the contract that the claimant alleges have been breached by the defendant, generally stating any express terms first and then any implied terms.

4. The facts concerning each breach alleged (with sufficient details to identify what is the alleged breach).

5. Losses that flow from the alleged breach (with particulars of the losses).

6. Interest (see the worked example in paragraph 11.10 for a fuller consideration).

7. The 'prayer'—that is, a brief summary of what is being claimed. It does not add anything new to the document. For example:

AND THE CLAIMANT CLAIMS—

  1. The sum of £ … …;

  2. Interest.

8. A statement of truth and relevant authorization paragraph, if appropriate.

9. The date of the document and the 'author' (which may be the firm acting).

A detailed discussion of a worked example of a breach of contract claim is examined in paragraph 11.10. An example of a particulars of claim in a breach of contract claim is also included in Appendix 4.

11.4.1.1.1 *Example of breach of contract claim*

IN THE COUNTY COURT MONEY CLAIMS CENTRE   Claim No. CM67Y34566

BETWEEN

DALE AND CO LTD   **CLAIMANT**

AND

MPR LTD   **DEFENDANT**

PARTICULARS OF CLAIM

1. The Claimant is a private limited company carrying on business as a manufacturer of wood products.

2. The Defendant is a private limited company supplying woodworking machinery.

3. By a written Purchase Order dated 10 . . . . , the Defendant agreed to supply and the Claimant agreed to purchase an MPR X20 woodcutting machine ('the X20') for the total cash price of £45,000 plus VAT payable by an initial deposit of 20% on the placement of the order and the balance due on delivery of the X20. The Claimant made the deposit payment on 25th . . . . in the sum of £9,000 plus VAT and paid the balance plus VAT on 1st . . . . Payment was therefore made in full by the Claimant. A copy of the Purchase Order is attached to this Particulars of Claim.

4. There were implied terms of the agreement that the X20 would be of satisfactory quality and fit for the purpose for which it was provided—namely, as a specialist woodcutting machine capable of achieving a high degree of accuracy and speed.

5. The X20 was delivered on the due date, and installation and commissioning of the X20 was completed on or about 17 . . . .

6. In breach of the implied terms, the X20 was neither of satisfactory quality nor fit for the purpose for which it was supplied.

PARTICULARS OF BREACH

6.1. The X20 seized up within five hours of installation.

6.2. The speed of the X20 was much slower than the more inferior model (the X18) in the range.

6.3. The operating cycle had been jarring, which caused the head synchronization and changing process to become significantly slower than the X18.

6.4. The X20 was supplied as a precision piece of machinery with four adjustable heads, but two of those adjustable heads regularly fell out of alignment by 0.3mm during the production process, with the result that the X20 was rendered unsuitable for the production of products that required precision woodcutting.

The Claimant will seek to rely on the engineer's service reports for the period January . . . . , October . . . . , and the evidence of a jointly instructed expert at the trial of the matter.

7. By reason of the breach of the implied terms, the Claimant has suffered loss and damage.

PARTICULARS OF LOSS AND DAMAGE

The purchase price plus VAT	£52,875
Loss of production costs resulting from 125 hours of down time due to the failure of the X20	£10,000
Loss of business and goodwill	To be quantified

8. Further, the Claimant claims interest pursuant to s. 69 of the County Courts Act 1984 on the amount to be found due to the Claimant at such a rate and for such a period as the court thinks fit.

AND THE CLAIMANT CLAIMS—

(1) Damages pursuant to paragraph 7 above;

(2) Interest pursuant to s. 69 of the County Courts Act 1984.

STATEMENT OF TRUTH

I believe the facts stated in these Particulars of Claim are true. I am duly authorized by the Claimant to sign this statement on its behalf.

Signed . . . .

Managing Director

Dated this . . . .

11.4.1.2 An action in negligence—a road traffic accident (RTA)

An action in negligence relating to a road traffic accident (RTA) should deal with the following and usually in this order:

1. Sufficient details to identify the incident should be set out, including a simple description that a collision occurred, on a particular date, at a particular time and place, and between the parties. Where an existing duty of care applies by implication, there is no need to state this: for example, where the RTA occurred on the public highway, then there arises a clear duty of care by all road users to other road users and pedestrians.

Where the existence of the duty of care is less obvious, it may be necessary to state it in the document.

2. A statement, with details of the negligence of the defendant, including specific examples of his negligence.

3. Any relevant previous convictions. When a conviction of an offence is relevant to the issues of the case, it may be pleaded. When this occurs, details of the conviction, its date, the court in which it was made, and the relevance to the cause of action in which that conviction is stated should be stated.

4. The fact that the claimant suffered injury as a result of the negligence, along with brief details of those injuries, referring to the appended medical report(s).

5. That losses have been sustained as referred to in a schedule of losses containing full details of those losses.

6. Interest pursuant to the relevant statute.

7. The 'prayer' for the relief sought, as earlier: damages and interest.

8. A statement of truth and authorization (if appropriate), as earlier.

9. The date of the document and the 'author' (which may be the firm acting).

11.4.1.2.1 *Example of a particulars of claim*

IN THE COUNTY COURT MONEY CLAIMS CENTRE   Claim No. CR345267

BETWEEN

Miss Chloe Whitfield   Claimant

and

Mr Stephen Broad   Defendant

PARTICULARS OF CLAIM

1 The Claimant was the driver of an Audi A4 motor car, registration number GH51 OLM. The Defendant was the owner and driver of a Ford Focus, registration number VG52 BLU.

2. On 16 July 201?, in the vicinity of the Cloversmead Shopping Centre, the Claimant was driving down Hayhurst Avenue and turned left into Warrington Way, when a collision occurred with the Defendant's car. The position of impact is indicated on the attached map.

3. The collision was caused by the negligence of the Defendant.

PARTICULARS OF NEGLIGENCE

(1) The Defendant failed to keep any or any proper lookout.

(2) The Defendant failed to stop, or slow down, or swerve, or in any other way to control his motor car so as to avoid the accident.

(3) The Defendant was driving at a speed that was excessive in the circumstances.

(4) The Defendant drove through a red light on Warrington Way.

(5) The Defendant was speaking on his mobile phone.

4. As a result, the Claimant has sustained injuries and suffered loss and damage.

<hr>

PARTICULARS OF INJURY

The Claimant's date of birth is 20 November 1983. The Claimant suffered a whiplash injury and fractured her sternum. She suffers from headaches, pain in the neck and chest, and numbness in the outer upper arms. The Claimant held twice-weekly yoga classes at the local community centre, but has been unable to resume these classes since the accident. The injuries and symptoms are fully described in the attached medical report, prepared by Mr Christopher Kartby, consultant orthopaedic surgeon, dated . . . . . .

PARTICULARS OF LOSS AND DAMAGE

The Claimant refers to the attached Schedule of Losses for details of her special damages.

5. The Claimant claims interest pursuant to s. 69 of the County Courts Act 1984 at such a rate and for such a period as the court thinks fit.

AND THE CLAIMANT CLAIMS—

(1) Damages;

(2) Interest pursuant to s. 69 of the County Courts Act 1984.

STATEMENT OF TRUTH

I believe that the facts stated in these Particulars of Claim are true.

Dated this . . . .

<hr>

11.4.1.3 An action in negligence—a factory accident

An action in negligence relating to a factory accident should deal with the following matters, and usually in this order:

1. The relationship of the employer and employee should be established (or that of the factory owner and the visitor), and the application of any relevant statutory provisions (for example, the Factories Act 1961, but only for accidents which occurred before 1 October 2013. For employer liability claims after this date, the Enterprise and Regulatory Reform Act 2013 has removed the possibility of a claim for breach of statutory duty unless that breach amounts to an act of negligence) should be set out.

2. Details of the accident at the premises, with brief particulars as to how it happened.

3. An allegation that the accident was caused by the negligence or breach of statutory duty of the owner, or employer, or employee, with particulars and any specific statutory provisions. Again, here it is now only permissible to plead breach of statutory duty at all if the breach of duty giving rise to the claim occurred before 1 October 2013, or the breach 'amounts to an act of negligence'.

4. That, as a result of the alleged negligence/breach of statutory duty the claimant suffered injury and loss, with particulars of both and annexed medical report(s) and schedule of losses.

5. Interest.

6. The 'prayer' for relief—damages and interest (as earlier).

7. A statement of truth and authority (if appropriate).

8. The date of the document and the 'author' (which may be the firm acting).

Professional Conduct

Often, accidents at work are caused by the incompetence of a fellow employee. Consider the situation in which, acting for a claimant employee, you enter into Protocol with a potential employer defendant claiming damages for personal injuries. The employer fails to confirm that the fellow employee was acting in the course of his employment. If it is necessary for you to commence proceedings, you will need to issue against both the fellow employee and the employer until such time as the employer confirms vicarious liability either in correspondence or on the filing of his defence, at which point you can amend your particulars of claim to remove the fellow employee. This course of action is necessary to ensure that you have a cause of action against an appropriate party.

11.4.1.3.1 *Example of a particulars of claim*

IN THE HIGH COURT OF JUSTICE   201?-D-8976

QUEEN'S BENCH DIVISION

STOKE ON TRENT DISTRICT REGISTRY

BETWEEN

MR SIMON HERBERT	Claimant
and	
ARISTA LOGISTICS LIMITED	Defendant

PARTICULARS OF CLAIM

1. The Claimant was employed by the Defendant as a forklift truck driver at Gladstone Lock warehouse, Regent Road, Stoke on Trent. The nature of the Claimant's work is regulated by the Provision and Use of Work Equipment Regulations 1992, SI 1992/2932, and the Manual Handling Operations Regulations 1992, SI 1992/2793.

2. On 29 September 2013, in the course of his employment, the Claimant was loading a steel rod of approximately 3.5 metres in length and weighing just over 100 kilos onto his forklift truck. By reason of the weight of the rod, it had to be loaded mechanically, and by reason of its length, it had to be placed on the forklift truck lengthways. Accordingly, it could not be placed across the forklift truck, but had to be positioned on the forks pointing away from the mast of the forklift. By reason of its length and despite using long forks, it would not stay on the forks unless strapped on. The Claimant and his colleague were attempting to strap the steel rod onto the forks of the forklift truck in order to secure it for transportation to the back of a lorry when it rolled off the forks and dropped directly onto the arch of the Claimant's left foot.

3. The accident was caused by the negligence and/or breach of statutory duty of the Defendant or its employees.

PARTICULARS OF NEGLIGENCE/BREACH OF STATUTORY DUTY

The Defendant was negligent in that it—

(i) Failed to devise and implement for the Claimant a safe system of work;

(ii) Failed to ensure that the Claimant had received adequate training and/or health and safety information, negligently and/or in breach of its statutory duty under regs 8 and/or 9 of the Provision and Use of Work Equipment Regulations 1998;

(iii) Failed to provide competent staff (the Claimant's case is that an overhead crane ought to have been used in order to load the metal rods onto the lorry);

(iv) Failed to exercise any or any adequate care for the safety of the Claimant;

(v) Failed, so far as was reasonably practicable, to avoid the need for the Claimant to undertake the said manual loading operation, in particular by not providing any, or any suitable, mechanical lifting equipment, negligently and/or in breach of its statutory duty under reg. 4(1)(a) of the Manual Handling Operations Regulations 1992;

(vi) Failed, so far as was reasonably practicable, to make a suitable and sufficient assessment of such manual handling operation, negligently and/or in breach of its statutory duty under reg. 4(1)(b) of the Manual Handling Operations Regulations 1992;

(vii) Failed to ensure that lifting equipment—namely, the forklift truck—was suitable for the purpose for which it was used, negligently and/or in breach of its statutory duty under reg. 5 of the Provision and Use of Work Equipment Regulations 1992;

(viii) Failed to ensure that the said forklift truck was used only for operations, and under conditions, for which it was suitable, negligently and/or in breach of its statutory duty under reg. 5 of the Provision and Use of Work Equipment Regulations 1992.

4. By reason of the above, the Claimant has suffered personal injury, loss, and damage.

PARTICULARS INJURY

The Claimant, who was born on 26 January 1950, sustained two broken bones in his left foot. Full details of the Claimant's orthopaedic injuries are contained in the medical report of Mr Mark O'Brien, dated 15 September 201?, annexed. The Claimant also now suffers from post-traumatic stress disorder as a result of the crush injury to his left foot. A psychiatric report of Dr Nichola Davies, dated 29 October 201?, is also attached.

PARTICULARS OF LOSS AND DAMAGE

The Claimant sustained a variety of financial losses and these are detailed in the attached Schedule of Losses.

ANDTHE CLAIMANT CLAIMS—

(1) Damages;

(2) Interest at such rates and for such periods as the court deems fit.

Dated this . . . .

STATEMENT OF TRUTH

I believe that the facts in these Particulars of Claim are true.

Note: These particulars of claim include a claim for breach of statutory duty because the accident occurred before 1 October 2013. For accidents that arose after this date, it is thought that breaches of statutory duties will not be formerly pleaded in a particulars of claim. See paragraph 11.4.1.3.

11.4.1.4 A debt action for goods sold and delivered, but not paid for

A claim for goods sold and delivered, but not paid for, should deal with the following matters and usually in this order:

1. The nature of the goods sold and delivered, the date of the delivery, any invoice details (with attached copy), and the price.

2. The fact that the goods have not been paid for, and that payment is still due and owing.

3. Interest pursuant to statute or under the terms of the contract.

4. The 'prayer' for relief—the price of the goods and interest.

5. A statement of truth with relevant authorization (if appropriate).

6. The date of the document and the 'author' (which may be the firm acting).

The particulars for debt claims are usually very short and appear on the reverse of the claim form.

The following example shows the particulars as seen on the reverse of a claim form in a straightforward debt action. A claim form that contains the particulars of claim in this way is known as an 'indorsed claim form'.

11.4.1.4.1 *Example of an indorsed claim form*

---

1. The Claimant claims the sum of £15,000 plus VAT in respect of electrical components supplied and delivered to the Defendant in accordance with the terms of a written contract made between the parties dated 25 April 201?, a copy of which is attached to these particulars of claim.

2. The Claimant delivered the goods on the agreed delivery date of 1 February, but the Defendant has failed to pay the invoice, a copy of which is attached.

3. The total sum of £15,000 plus VAT of £3,000 remains due and owing.

4. The Claimant claims interest at the contractual rate of 8% per annum from the due date of payment to judgment or sooner payment in the sum of £xxx and continuing at a daily rate of £x.

AND THE CLAIMANT CLAIMS—

 (1) The sum of £18,000;

 (2) Interest in the sum of £xxx and continuing at a daily rate of £x, pursuant to the contractual interest rate.

I believe the facts stated in these Particulars of Claim are true. I am duly authorized by the Claimant to sign this statement on its behalf.

. . . .

Dated . . . .

11.5 THE DEFENCE

The principal rules concerning the drafting of the defence can be found in CPR Parts 15 and 16, and their associated Practice Directions. The use of Forms N9B (a claim for a specified sum, N9D (a claim for an unspecified claim or a non-money claim), or N11 (a general defence), included in the response pack and served with the particulars of claim, may be used to file a defence. These forms can be found on the Online Resource Centre.

online resource centre

The use of these forms is not mandatory and often there is insufficient space in any but the simplest claim to prepare a fully pleaded defence on the forms. These forms are usually only ever completed by litigants in person—that is, those without legal representation. In practice, the defence will be prepared as a separate document.

A defence is required when a defendant wishes to defend all or part of a claim. Once filed, a copy of the defence must be served on every other party. The time limits for the filing of a defence are set out at CPR 15.4 (see also Chapter 10, paragraph 10.5).

Under CPR 15.5, the defendant and the claimant may agree that the time for filing a defence be extended for a period up to a maximum of an extra 28 days. Where the claimant consents to the requested extension, the defendant must notify the court in writing of the agreement to extend time. Any need for further time must be made by application to the court under CPR 3.1, because the CPR do not afford any authority to the claimant to agree to any further extensions of time (see also Chapter 10, paragraph 10.5.2.1).

11.5.1 THE FORMULA

The defence should deal with every material allegation contained in the particulars of claim. The simplest way in which to do this is to respond to each paragraph of the statement of case in the order in which it appears, and to deal with each allegation in each paragraph.

For each response, the defendant has four options:

- he may **admit** the allegation;
- he may **deny** the allegation with reasons;
- he may **refuse to admit or make no admissions** to the allegation and request the claimant to prove such allegations or facts; or
- he may seek to **shift the blame to another party or third party**.

11.5.1.1 Admissions

Allegations that can be admitted *should* be admitted: for example, if there was a collision or a contract, in accordance with your client's instructions, you should be able to admit that fact. However, care should be taken not to admit that which should not be admitted (see the 'Professional Conduct' box). Conversely, a failure to admit statements that should have been admitted may have costs consequences for the defendant (see Chapter 10, paragraph 10.3.4.2).

 Professional Conduct

If, in drafting a defence, you admit an allegation that should not have been admitted, then, depending on the nature and extent of that which has been admitted, this may have a profound effect on the ability to continue to defend either part or all of the case on liability, causation, and quantum. It may be possible to amend the defence under CPR 17, but this, again, will depend on the nature of the erroneous admission made. Needless to say, you may need to cease acting for your client, because a conflict is likely to arise under the Code, Chapters 1 and 3, on the basis of not being able to provide a good standard of service to your client.

11.5.1.1.1 *Example of an admission in an RTA claim*
'Paragraph 1 of the Particulars of Claim is admitted.'

11.5.1.2 Denials

Where an allegation is denied, in accordance with your client's instructions, the defendant needs to put his side of the story forward. A bare denial is not acceptable under the CPR. It is therefore important to remember, when drafting the defendant's version of events, that he needs to give an explanation of *how* and, in some cases, *why* the event happened, not simply to justify his own position. This will often involve allegations that the accident or breach and the resultant losses were caused by the negligence or breach of either the claimant or somebody else.

For example, in an action for damages arising from an RTA, it is likely that the *fact* of the collision can be admitted. The defendant, in his defence, may be saying that the collision was not his fault (that is, he may be denying the allegation), but if he has admitted that a collision occurred, his defence needs to explain how the accident happened. Simply denying the allegations of the claimant does not do this; rather, the defendant needs to explain by blaming someone else or by some other event *how* the accident did happen. This explanation in this example will need to set out clearly allegations of contributory negligence.

can do is to state that he seeks to recover the amount which the claimant may recover against him in the main action. This is done by way of an indemnity or contribution in the prayer, or by a request for damages generally.

11.6.2.1 Example of a defendant's additional claim against a third party

---

IN THE HIGH COURT OF JUSTICE   201?-R-2456

QUEEN'S BENCH DIVISION

MANCHESTER DISTRICT REGISTRY

BETWEEN

MILLARD AND CO LTD   CLAIMANT

AND

SMT LTD   DEFENDANT

AND

COLVILLE CONTRACTORS (A FIRM) THIRD PARTY

DEFENDANT'S ADDITIONAL CLAIM AGAINST THIRD PARTY

1. This action has been brought by the Claimant against the Defendant. The Claimant claims from the Defendant damages and interest for an alleged breach of contract for the manufacture and supply of stainless steel cladding ('the Cladding'), as appears from the Particulars of Claim, a copy of which is served with this Additional Claim, along with the written contract, dated 17 September 201?.

2. The Defendant denies that it is liable to the Claimant on the grounds set out in its Defence, a copy of which is also served with this Additional Claim. These Particulars of Additional Claim set out the Defendant's Additional Claim against the Third Party on which the Defendant will rely if it is found liable to the Claimant.

3. By a written purchase order no. 55648 dated 1 October 201?, a copy of which is annexed to this Additional Claim made between the Defendant and the Third Party, the Third Party agreed to manufacture and deliver the Cladding for a price agreed at £132,500.

4. It was an implied term of the agreement that the Cladding would be of satisfactory quality and fit for its purpose.

5. On 5 January 201?, the Third Party, pursuant to the purchase order, manufactured and delivered the Cladding to the premises of the Claimant at Runcorn Works.

6. In breach of the above implied term, the Cladding was neither of satisfactory quality nor fit for purpose.

PARTICULARS OF BREACH

6.1. The Cladding buckled when fixed to the rear elevation of the Claimant's commercial unit at Runcorn Works.

6.2. The Cladding rusted and detached from the entrance area to the said commercial unit.

> 6.3. Over the entire unit, the Cladding has discoloured and deteriorated to the extent that water ingress has occurred.
>
> 7. As a result of the matters set out above, the Defendant has suffered loss and damage to the extent of its liability (if any) to the Claimant, any costs that it may be ordered to pay to the Claimant, and its costs incurred in defending the Claimant's claim.
>
> **AND THE DEFENDANT ADDITIONALLY CLAIMS—**
>
> (i) An indemnity or contribution in respect of the Claimant's claim;
>
> (ii) Alternatively, damages.
>
> STATEMENT OF TRUTH
>
> I believe that the facts stated in these Particulars are true. I am duly authorized by the Defendant to sign this statement.
>
> Signed . . . .
>
> Dated. . . . .

11.7 THE REPLY

11.7.1 WHAT IS A REPLY?

A 'reply' is a statement of case that responds to a defence, as discussed in CPR 15 and 16 and in Chapter 10, paragraph 10.6.2.7. It deals in essence with any matters raised in the defence to which the claimant feels that he should respond and which were not covered in the particulars of claim. There is no obligation on the claimant to serve a reply and, as such, no admissions are to be implied from the absence of one.

As with the drafting of a defence, the reply can respond to each, but not necessarily all, of the paragraphs of the defence in a structured and clear manner, explaining and clarifying (both by way of additional factual information) and taking issue with its contents.

 Example

In a simple debt action for the supply of flour to a commercial bakery, in which the formula described in paragraph 11.4.1.4 has been followed correctly, no details of any contract terms other than type of goods, delivery date, and price are relevant to the pleaded claim at this stage. The defendant defends the claim and refuses to pay the amount due, on the basis that the flour supplied and delivered was not of satisfactory quality, and he particularizes the problems—in this case, mite infestation.

Whilst there is no counterclaim raised in this scenario, the claimant may wish to respond by way of a reply and set out any relevant facts that could be brought to the attention of the court that might have a bearing on the success of his action, such as a contract term that the quality of the flour be maintained by storage in airtight containers and, in his reply, asserting the fact that the defendant kept the flour in open sacks.

A reply is not, however, an opportunity for the claimant to rectify any mistakes made in the particulars of claim; that is something that is left to the formal process of amendment (see paragraph 11.9).

11.7.1.1 Example of a reply based on the 'Example' box

1. Save as is expressly admitted or not admitted below, the Claimant joins issue with the Defendant on its Defence.

2. As to paragraph . . . of the Defence, the Claimant avers that a term of the said agreement, at clause . . . , between the parties was that the quality of the flour was to be maintained by storage in airtight containers.

3. As to paragraph . . . of the Defence, the Defendant refers to a report from a Mr . . . , an independent quality assurance inspector, who examined the flour for contamination. At paragraph 7 of the report dated . . . ., Mr . . . states that 'the flour was contained in open sacks . . . .'.

I believe that the facts stated in this Reply are true. I am duly authorized to make this statement on behalf of the Claimant.

. . . .

Dated . . . .

11.8 THE PART 18 REQUEST FOR FURTHER INFORMATION

For a reminder of what a Part 18 request is, see Chapter 10, paragraph 10.7.4.

The doctrine of proportionality and the greater burden under the CPR for parties to state their cases in detail should mean that requests for further information are needed less frequently. They should be used with some caution.

 Example

A particulars of claim alleges that an agreement was made whereby the defendant agreed to supply the claimant with a quantity of mixed Mediterranean vegetables at a price of £10 per box and that, despite numerous requests by the claimant, the defendant has refused to supply any of the vegetables. The defendant therefore had to buy them elsewhere at a greater cost. The particulars are vague and incomplete in relation to the date of the agreement, whether it was written or oral, who made it, the amount of the order in terms of number of boxes and overall price, and the delivery date.

11.8.1 WHAT IS THE FORM AND CONTENT OF THE PART 18 REQUEST?

There is no requirement that the Part 18 request should be in a particular form, although guidance is given in PD 18.1.2–18.1.7. It should be expressed to be a request under the provisions of CPR 18.

It may be in a letter form, as suggested previously, or drafted as a stand-alone formal document with the court heading. It is often thought helpful to make the request in formal form, so that if there is no response to the request, it can form the basis of the application to the court for an order for the information sought.

In formal form, the document can also allow space for the recipient's reply (this is a different document from the reply discussed in paragraph 11.7) and therefore be prepared in tabular form. The reply to a CPR 18 request must contain a statement of truth, because it is a statement of case in its own right.

Whether made by letter or in formal form, the request must:

(a) be headed with the action title and number;

(b) state that it is a request made under CPR Part 18;

(c) identify the party making the request and the party to whom the request is made;

(d) set out, in numbered paragraphs, each request and identify which part (by repeating the words) of the other party's statement of case is either unclear or upon which clarification is sought; and

(e) state the date by which a response is expected and state that an application will be made to court if there is a failure to respond.

11.8.1.1 Example of a Part 18 request in respect of the 'Example' box

IN THE COUNTY COURT AT CARDIFF   CLAIM NO. 1NT 443576

BETWEEN

MR CAMERON STUART

AND

MR WILLIAM STODDARD

DEFENDANT'S PART 18 REQUEST FOR FURTHER INFORMATION OF THE PARTICULARS OF CLAIM

Under paragraph 1—'By an agreement made in or about March 201?, the Defendant agreed to supply the Claimant with a quantity of mixed Mediterranean vegetables at a price of £10 per box.'

Please state:

1. The alleged date of the agreement;

2. Whether it is alleged that the agreement was oral or written;

3 (a) If the agreement was oral, who made the agreement and what was said;

3 (b) If the agreement was written, the terms of the agreement, along with a copy of the contract or documentation relied on in support thereof;

4. The date on which it is alleged that the Defendant agreed to supply the boxes of mixed Mediterranean vegetables;

5. The quantity of the said vegetables to be supplied.

Under paragraph 3—'notwithstanding several requests to do so . . . . . .'

Please give full particulars of:

6. The date/s of every such request;

7. Whether such requests were made orally or in writing;

8 (a) If orally, by and to whom the requests were made, the content of the request/s and the answer/s;

8 (b) If in writing, the details of the request/s and any documentation in support thereof.

Under paragraph 6—'. . . . the Claimant had to purchase the same elsewhere at a greater cost.'

Please state:

9. From where is it alleged that the Claimant purchased the mixed Mediterranean vegetables;

10. The quantity and price of the mixed Mediterranean vegetables.

Dated . . . .

11.9 AMENDMENTS TO STATEMENTS OF CASE

CPR 17 generally sets out the position on amendments to statements of case. A party may amend a statement of case at any time before it has been served on any other party. Once served, a statement of case may only be amended with the consent of all parties or the permission of the court, unless the amendment relates to the removal, addition, or substitution of a party, in which case, the procedure set out in CPR 19.4 must be followed.

An amended statement of case must be marked as amended and set out as under PD 17.2.1. The original text need only be shown if the court considers it appropriate and desirable. If the substance of the statement of case is changed by the amendment, it should be reverified by a statement of truth.

The judge is not permitted to give judgment on the basis of a claim not set out in the statement of case. If this is done, a retrial will be ordered.

For the purposes of the Limitation Act 1980, an amendment to add or substitute a new party or to add a new cause of action is deemed to be a separate claim and to have been commenced on the same date as the original claim.

 Costs

The party applying to amend its statement of case will usually be responsible for its own costs, as well as any costs of the opponent, especially if the opponent then needs to amend his statement of case as a result of the amendment. Again, it is good practice to ask your opponent to agree to the proposed amendment before making an application to the court for permission. If your opponent unreasonably refuses, then it will be incumbent on you to raise this at the hearing on the question of costs, because the time and cost incurred by you and your client may have been unnecessarily incurred.

11.10 A DETAILED WORKED EXAMPLE

To demonstrate the thought processes behind drafting a statement of case, a detailed worked example of what should be considered when drafting an effective breach of contract claim is set out here. There are eight important stages.

11.10.1 THE ESSENTIAL INGREDIENTS

The essential ingredients of a successful claim for damages for breach of contract, leading to full recovery, are as follows:

1. That there was a contract, which involved:
   • an agreement;
   • between C and D;

- a promise;
- consideration; and
- an intention (to create legal relations).

2. That there was, in the contract, a material term—that is, one that D is alleged to have breached, or one that entitles C to the relief sought.

3. That C has performed any obligation that was a precondition to the performance of D's obligation, or to his entitlement to relief.

4. That D was in breach of his obligation.

5. That C has suffered loss and damage.

6. That such loss and damage was caused by D's breach.

7. That the loss is not too remote—that is, that it was reasonably within the contemplation of the parties at the time that they entered into the contract as a likely consequence of the breach, in the light of their knowledge at that time.

8. That the claim is not statute-barred.

11.10.2 THE PARTIES

This stage is partly a matter of setting out essential ingredients to do with the parties and partly a matter of story-telling. If either party has a business or is a company, then you will almost always state what that party's business is. This may be an essential ingredient if you have to establish any of the following—for example:

- that a party entered into the contract in the course of his business;
- that a party was dealing as a consumer;
- that a term should be implied into the contract; or
- that a party held himself out as having a particular skill or expertise.

If the terms of a contract are to be inferred from the previous course of dealing between the parties, then this will need to be established. If there have been significant pre-contract negotiations, then these will have to be set out. If the claimant is making a claim for the loss of or damage to his property, then he needs to state his ownership of the property.

11.10.3 THE CONTRACT

To set out the contract properly, you must:

- state that there was a contract (or agreement);
- state the date (or the approximate date) of the contract;
- identify the parties to the contract;
- state whether either party acted through employees and, if so, identify them;
- confirm the form of the contract, whether written or oral, or partly both, or implied from a number of circumstances;
- attach any documents evidencing the contract;
- if the contract is oral, state how it was made (for example, by phone), between whom, and when and where;
- confirm the subject matter of the contract—that is, what it sought to do or what was promised; and
- identify the consideration.

11.10.4 THE DEFENDANT'S KNOWLEDGE

Where you are relying on the defendant's knowledge of certain facts to show that the loss and damage that you seek was within the contemplation of the defendant and so is not too remote, you need to state those facts and allege that he had that knowledge. The material time is the time at which the contract was made, so it is usual to confirm the date of the contract.

11.10.5 THE TERMS

At this stage, you should set out any material terms that have not already been covered when setting out the contract (see paragraph 11.10.3). It is a matter of judgment whether a term is really part of the basic subject matter of the contract (in which case, it belongs in the setting out of the contract) or whether it is a separate term. You should state whether the term is an express or implied term, and then set out its effect. The best practice is to paraphrase concisely, rather than to copy out the exact words of the term—but this is pointless if it will not make the term any more clear or concise. Do not set out terms that are not relevant.

If relying on an implied term, you should state the basis on which it is implied, unless it is obvious, or is implied by statute.

Where relying on express terms and implied terms, it is usual to set out the express terms first.

11.10.6 PERFORMANCE OF THE CONTRACT

It may be that the defendant was only obliged to carry out his obligations under the contract if the claimant had first performed his part of the bargain. If this is the case, then these obligations need to be set out.

11.10.7 THE BREACH

Breach of contract must be expressly alleged and particularized. You should start by alleging that the defendant was in breach of contract and then set out in full what it is that constitutes the breach. It may be an act or an omission, or a state of affairs, or the fact that some representation was untrue. If the defendant's breach brought the contract to an end, then this must be expressly stated by using the word 'repudiated'. If the defendant has repudiated the contract, thereby giving the claimant the right to treat the contract as at an end and the claimant has done so, it will be necessary to state that the claimant accepted the repudiation.

Where the breach consists of an act, omission, or event, you should state the date on which it occurred.

It may also, at this stage, be necessary to state any additional facts that entitle the claimant to the relief sought.

11.10.8 THE LOSS AND DAMAGE

It is essential to allege causation, as well as damage. This may take a considerable amount of explanation. It is sometimes not obvious why the breach alleged should have led to the loss claimed.

Particulars of the loss and damage must be given. You should state the nature of the loss and the basis on which the claimant wants damages to be assessed, set out the financial losses in an itemized schedule (if there are many), and quantify each item as far as possible.

11.10.9 INTEREST

Interest must always be stated in the particulars of claim. If it is not, the court is unlikely to award interest.

The sum of interest accrued in a specified sum claim only must be stated on Form N1, as well as in the particulars of claim.

Interest may be pleaded as follows:

- under the terms of the contract, if there was a contractual provision;

- under s. 35A of the Senior Courts Act 1981 (if the action is a High Court action)—that is, at 8 per cent;

- under s. 69 of the County Courts Act 1984 (if the action is in the County Court)—that is, at 8 per cent; or

- under the Late Payment of Commercial Debts (Interest) Act 1998 (as amended by the Late Payment Directive 2011/7/EU)—that is, at 8 per cent above base rate. Compensation can also be claimed under the provision of this statute in addition to interest depending on the value of the claim.

If there is a contractual provision for interest, then there is a choice as to whether interest is stated under the contract or the Court Acts. It is not, however, permitted to state the Late Payment of Commercial Debts (Interest) Act 1998 (as amended) as an alternative to a contractual term for interest. If there is no contractual provision, then any one of the applicable statutes mentioned here can be applied.

If interest is stated on the terms of a contract, then express reference to the term in the contract needs to be made. Also, the rates of interest set out in the contract must be stated and the calculations given (both the total interest that has arisen and the continuing daily rate).

If interest is claimed under one of these statutes, then the claim must be for a specified sum. The statement for interest must state the authority (the relevant statute) and must also calculate the amount of interest that has accrued since the accrual of the cause of action (that is, the date of the breach) to the date on which the proceedings are issued, and thereafter a daily rate is calculated so that the court can readily calculate the sum due when judgment is given (if that is the outcome).

If the claim is for an unspecified sum (for the court to award), then interest is simply pleaded generally, requesting the court to award an appropriate amount.

KEY POINTS SUMMARY

- Remember that all statements of case are designed to provide an outline. Do not be tempted to include all of the details of your case.

- Even in the more complex cases, if you stick to the 'formulae', they will serve as a good basic structure for your case.

- Be ready to acknowledge that some drafting may be very complicated and best left to counsel. This is not 'passing the buck', but rather acting in your client's best interests by avoiding unnecessary amendments and adverse costs orders.

- Well-drafted statements of case will reflect well on you in the eyes of the judge if the matter ever gets to trial and should help to clarify the main issues in the case.

- In practice, it is common for practitioners to rely on precedent statements of case. Be aware of antiquated language and ensure that every paragraph used has a purpose for your own statement of case—such reliance must be undertaken intelligently.

online resource centre

- Do not forget the strategic use of a Part 18 request when acting for either the claimant or the defendant on service of their particulars of claim or defence. (See the Online Resource Centre.)

Case Study *Andrew James Pike v Deep Builders Ltd*

Question

The insurer of Deep Builders Ltd has indicated that it accepts that Mr Deep was acting in the course of his employment, but denies negligence, alleging that Andrew Pike was responsible for the accident. Andrew Pike's solicitors have obtained a medical report prepared by a consultant orthopaedic surgeon. You undertake research and the information provided by the client leads you to believe that total damages on a full liability basis would be in the region of £45,000–55,000. Settlement was not achieved in the Protocol.

The claim form has already been drafted. You will also have drafted the particulars of claim (see the Andrew Pike case study question in Chapter 9).

Now, acting for the defendant, consider the points that you believe the defendant needs to raise to defend this case and how it can deal with its own losses. Then draft the defence and any other statement of case that you feel is appropriate.

online
resource
centre

Any documents referred to in these case study questions can be found on the Online Resource Centre—simply click on 'Case study documentation' to access the documents that you need for Chapters 9 and 11 and to be reminded of the questions. Suggested answers to these case study questions can also be accessed on the Online Resource Centre when released to you by your lecturer.

Relevant court forms relating to this chapter:

- Forms N180 and N181 Directions Questionnaire

- Form N263 and N264 Directions Report and the Electronic Disclosure Questionnaire

- Form N170 Pre-Trial Checklist

> Relevant parts of the CPR and its PDs: 3, 26, 27, 28, and 29

12.1 INTRODUCTION

This chapter considers the way in which the court 'actively manages' cases. All disputed cases will be subject to a level of court management and enforcement of its directions orders.

The chapter aims to give you an understanding of the time at which active case management commonly occurs and will address:

- the ethos of case management;

- allocation (to track);

LITIGATION TRAIN: CASE MANAGEMENT OVERVIEW

CONSIDER PART 36 OFFERS AND ADR

Issue of proceedings	Service of proceedings	Acknowledgement of service	Defence (and counterclaim and/or set-off) (• additional claim) (• Part 18 request)	Reply and defence to counterclaim	Notice of Proposed Allocation		Possible Directions	Trial

Service of proceedings

Case 'in litigation' but court will not proactively case manage unless an early interim application is made

Notice of Proposed Allocation

Court will proactively manage from now by sending to parties the Notice of Proposed Allocation and request to complete DQs

- DQ
  - N181
  - Fee
  - Cost estimate or costs budget (H)
  - Cooperation between parties to complete N181

Confirmed Allocation and Directions Order with potential costs budget filing order, or CMC (MT and non PI) with Disclosure Report (N263) (and Electronic Documents Questionnaire where relevant), costs budget (Precedent H) to be filed 7 days prior to CMC, and case summary

Possible Directions

- stay for ADR
- disclosure and inspection
- witness statements
- expert evidence
- PTC with residual direction to trial or
- further CMC with directions set for filing a PTC to trial

Parties should review costs budgets and apply for approval if they have changed

- case management directions through the tracks; and
- the ways in which the court will seek to ensure that its orders for the management of a case are complied with.

12.2 WHAT IS CASE MANAGEMENT AND WHEN DOES IT OCCUR?

'Case management' includes all of the ways in which the court will control the progress and disposal of actions. The bulk of the rules relating to these processes are contained in Civil Procedure Rules (CPR) Parts 3 and 26–29, and the Practice Directions that accompany them. Case management can be exercised at any time in an action's process through to trial, but there are times in the litigation process when it most commonly occurs:

- at allocation (when the court will confirm or allocate the case to a track and when the court will commonly make a directions order);
- at further case management conferences (CMCs);
- whenever a party makes an interim application and the court makes further or amended directions at the conclusion of the interim application hearing; or
- on—the few—occasions when the court will impose orders or sanctions of its own volition.

Once a case is issued the court will 'manage' (in other words 'control') the action throughout, from beginning to its end—this may include management decisions made after trial where continued directions are needed to resolve remaining issues concerning costs or enforcement. It is important to understand that case management is management by the court. This management will be exercised by the district judges, masters, and circuit judges. LJ's interim report (published on 12 January 2016) recommended that some of the more routine management decisions could be taken by case officers. This recommendation is already in place in some courts. Any orders made in this way will read 'Before legal advisor –*surname of case advisor*– *sitting at* – *named County County* on the .... Day of .... 201x it is hereby ordered ....'.

The case advisors will be supervised by the judge. The type of orders that case advisors can make may include consent orders or other such orders that are unlikely to be appealed.

12.2.1 HELPING, OR INFLUENCING THE COURT, TO MAKE THE APPROPRIATE DIRECTIONS ORDER FOR A CASE

Parties (and their legal representatives) usually have a voice in the case management decisions and the directions order on that is made for a case. The parties will usually seek to influence the court's decision in the information (or requests) they include in their completed DQ. It is ultimately the court that will control how a case will progress. But the court will have regard for, and consider, all justified requests by a party. Any request for a specific order or particular timescale for a case should be fully justified according to the principles of the overriding objective (CPR 1.3). In order to assist the court to make the right directions order for a case, legal representatives should have or include (probably in their DQ):

- a good understanding of the issues in the dispute;
- provide relevant information to the court promptly when such information is required;
- respond promptly to any contact from the court to monitor compliance with directions;
- ensure that any necessary applications are made promptly;
- keep the court informed of any significant delays in the implementation of any directions orders made; and
- continue to try to resolve the dispute.

The range of ways in which the courts will monitor and control cases can include:

- identifying disputed issues at an early stage, and how those issues are to be presented and proved;

- giving directions to ensure that the progress of the case is efficient;

- fixing dates and a timescale for each step to be undertaken to make the case ready for trial (essentially these comprise the directions order that sets out the steps that each party must take as the case progresses to trial);

- combining several aspects of management in one stage;

- controlling costs (which may include the filing of costs budgets in the form of Precedent H);

- disposing of cases summarily where they disclose no case or defence;

- expecting the parties to cooperate with each other on a number of fronts (see Chapters 3–6 and 16);

- dealing with matters without the parties having to attend court; and

- ordering a stay to encourage the parties to settle.

The aim of 'case management' is included within the ethos and the aims of the overriding objective—(CPR 1.1)—that is, ensuring that cases are dealt with justly (which includes 'enforcing compliance with rules, practice directions, and orders'), fairly, expeditiously, and proportionately (to the value and as to costs). To accommodate these objectives, in multi-track non-PI cases a menu approach will be taken to the directions orders a case may need, and for cases in the fast track and PI multi-track, fixed or standardized management directions and timetables are used as much as possible. In both the fast track and the multi-track, it will be for the parties to seek directions and management decisions that better suit their cases if these can be justified (within the provisions of the overriding objectives). Requests for 'tailor-made' directions will usually be set out in, or accompany, the directions questionnaire, Forms N180 or N181 (see paragraph 12.3). The courts can entertain requests for specific directions at any time, but if an application is made late, the justification for it will have to be strong and very persuasive.

The court has power to encourage and to compel parties to comply with court decisions. A failure to meet the directions and orders set can result in a variety of costs penalties. These may include an order to pay the other party's costs of a hearing or application a 'wasted costs' order against the legal representatives (see Chapter 4, paragraph 4.8), an 'unless' order (in which the penalty for failing to comply is set down in the order), or an order to strike out that party's case or defence. CPR 3.9 requires the court to consider 'all the circumstances' of the case, so as to enable it to deal justly with any application for relief from a sanction the court has imposed on a party, including the need (a) for the litigation to be conducted efficiently and at a proportionate cost and (b) to enforce compliance with rules, practice directions, and orders. (See also paragraph 12.9.)

 Professional Conduct

The Code, Principles 1, 2, 6, and 7 need to be upheld. Chapter 5 of the Code requires that a legal representative (or a registered European or foreign lawyer) must adhere to all the Outcomes set down in that Chapter in his dealings with the court on behalf of a client. CPR 1.3 requires parties to help the court to further the overriding objective (and this includes compliance with court orders). If the client's instructions would involve the legal representative in knowingly deceiving the court, then the legal representative must stop acting. Section 27 of the Courts and Legal Services Act 1990 provides that any person exercising a right of audience before a court has 'a duty to the court to act with independence in the interests of *justice*' [emphasis added] and that this duty shall 'override' any other obligation.

12.3 THE 'FIRST STEP' OF CASE MANAGEMENT—THE DIRECTIONS QUESTIONNAIRE (DQ) (FORMS N180 OR N181)

The first step in case management by the court will usually be taken once a defence is filed. Refer to the 'litigation train' at the beginning of this chapter. On the filing of the defence the court will send a Notice of Proposed Allocation to all parties indicating the track to which the case is likely to be allocated. This will be accompanied with a Notice to download and complete the appropriate DQ (N180 for the small claims track and N181 for fast-track and multi-track cases). These must be completed and filed at the court and on each party within 28 days of the deemed date of service of the Notice. Litigants in person will receive a paper copy of the DQ from the court rather than a notice.

online
resource
centre

12.3.1 CAN THE COURT EVER CASE MANAGE BEFORE ALLOCATION?

In some circumstances, steps will be taken on a case *before* the Notice of Proposed Allocation and the notice to file DQs are sent out to the parties. These provisions are listed in CPR 26 and predominantly include the occasions on which a case may be *automatically* transferred to the defendant's 'home court' (CPR 26.2).

CPR 26.2 (for cases in the High Court) and CPR 26.2A (for cases in the County Court) deal with the provisions for the automatic transfer of a case to the defendant's home court once a defence is filed:

- those that are defended;
- those that are for a specified sum; and
- those that are against individuals.

If there is more than one defendant, then the transfer will be to the home court of whichever of the defendants is an individual, or if there is more than one defendant who is an individual, the transfer will be to the home court of the first defendant to file his defence.

The definition of the defendant's 'home court' includes:

- for the High Court, the district registry for the district in which the defendant resides or carries on business, or where there is no such district registry, the Royal Courts of Justice; and
- for the County Court, the County Court in the jurisdiction in which the defendant resides or carries on business.

Other than the provisions mentioned that deal with an automatic transfer to another court, the procedure for and transfer between courts of other claims is dealt with in CPR 30. These provisions provide that a case may be transferred to another court when it has been commenced in the wrong court, or it may be struck out. Having regard to the provisions of the overriding objective, the court will not lightly strike a case out if it has been commenced in the wrong court, but it will probably impose costs sanctions (of the costs of transfer and any other costs incurred incidentally) against the claimant for the error.

Where the court orders a transfer, the court from which the claim is to be transferred must give notice of the transfer to all parties.

12.3.2 WHEN WILL THE COURT CONVENE A CMC BEFORE CONFIRMING THE ALLOCATION OF THE CASE TO A TRACK?

In most fast-track cases, there will be no need for a CMC. The case will be confirmed to the fast track and the directions order made after the filing of completed DQs by the parties (this will be within 28 days of the deemed date of service of the Notice of Proposed Allocation). Equally in many (less complex) multi-track PI cases there may be no requirement for a

CMC to be listed. However, for more complex high-value PI cases and for most non-PI multi-track cases the courts will list the case for a CMC after the Disclosure Report (and potentially the Electronic Disclosure Questionnaire) and costs budget have been filed. Where a CMC has been listed, the Disclosure Report must be filed at least 14 days before the CMC and the costs budget at least 7 days before the CMC. When a CMC has been listed, the court will then deal with case management and make the directions orders. The court may also treat any hearing that has occurred *before* it has received completed DQs as a CMC, and thus may dispense with the filing of completed DQs. In this way, the court will use some of the time of the hearing that is being heard to allocate the case to a track and make a directions order. This might happen if, for example, a party has made an application to the court for an interim injunction or for summary judgment (see Chapter 14): such applications can be made before a defence has been filed and so could be heard before the Notice of Proposed Allocation and the completed DQs have been sent.

A CMC may also be ordered in a case if the requests by the parties in their DQs (or by one party) for specific, tailor-made directions are either not agreed, or the request does not seem sufficiently justified.

12.3.3 THE COURT'S GENERAL PRACTICE ON ALLOCATION TO TRACK

After a defence is filed (or in a case in which there are multiple defendants, when the time limit for the filing of defences by all defendants has expired), the court will send each of the parties a Notice of Proposed Allocation to track and request that they download, complete, and file a DQ in Form N180 (for cases in the small claims track) or in Form N181 (for all fast-track and multi-track cases) (as stated above, litigants in person will receive a paper copy of the DQ from the court rather than a notice to download the form and complete it).

Fees are not required on the filing of DQs (they are included in the issue fee). Details of fees to be paid in litigation are contained in the Civil Proceedings and Family Proceedings Fees (Amendment) Order 2015 which sets out details of the fees payable in both the High Court and the County Court.

The notice to download, complete, and file a DQ will usually give the parties 28 days in which to complete and return the DQ. Parties may not, of their own accord or by agreement between themselves, vary the time permitted for the completion and filing of the form. Parties are expected to complete DQs, because the information sought from the parties on this form will enable and assist the court to make the best use of the available resources, including the amount of 'judicial time' that should be spent on the case, and order the appropriate directions for the case. In this way, the procedural judges will be able to make decisions and directions for the future conduct of the case that are 'proportionate (to the value of the claim and to the costs of pursuing it)', 'fair', and 'expeditious'. Normally, if the parties have completed the sections in the DQ properly and fully, it will provide the court with additional information about the progress (if any) that the parties have made towards resolving the dispute through alternative methods, and the progress that has been made in preparing evidence and settling the identity of any expert that may be needed and details of the appropriate directions order that the parties themselves feel are appropriate for the case.

12.3.4 WHAT HAPPENS IF ONE OR BOTH PARTIES FAIL TO FILE A COMPLETED DQ?

In practical terms, it is unlikely that the claimant will fail to complete his DQ. There are many rules and safeguards within the CPR that are intended to prevent parties from filing cases in court as 'threats' to their opponent, but with which they have, in reality, no real intention of proceeding. These include the need to sign statements of truth, and the costs penalties of unreasonably starting a case or raising issues that are not, or should not, be proceeded with. These sanctions and safeguards should mean that the number of cases in which the claimant intentionally fails to complete and file the DQ is few. It could happen that the claimant has simply failed to diarize the date on which the completed DQ should be filed at court, but even in these circumstances, the provisions requiring parties to consult with one another and to cooperate in completing their DQs (PD 26.2.3) should mean that where one party may have forgotten the deadline date, they are likely to be reminded of the need to complete and file it by the other party. It is important to note that even though the CPR seek to ensure that the parties consult and cooperate in the filing of the DQs, this consultation process cannot be used to delay the filing of the completed forms. In genuine cases in which there is a good reason for the delay in completing and filing the forms, and more time is needed (and can be fully justified), then the party (or parties) may apply to the court for further time. With the court's increased emphasis on compliance with court rules, legal representatives should never consider that extra time will be readily granted.

12.3.4.1 If completed DQs are not returned by any of the parties

If completed DQs are not returned by any of the parties, the court will order that unless a DQ is filed by a certain date (usually within seven days from the date of service of the order), the claim, defence, and any counterclaim will be struck out (PD 26.2.15(1)).

12.3.4.2 If completed DQs are filed by one (or some) of the parties, but not the other(s)

If the completed DQs are filed by only one (or some) of the parties, but not all involved, the case will be referred to the procedural judge and he may:

* confirm the proposed allocation to track should he feel that there is enough information supplied within any DQs that have been returned; or

* order that the parties attend a CMC. These are now automatically conducted by telephone (PD 23.6(2))—see paragraph 12.6. The court may also order that the costs of the parties attending be paid by the party that failed to file its DQ.

In reality, if it is the claimant who has failed to file his DQ, the more likely order will be along the lines of that in paragraph 12.3.4.1, because the court is unlikely to see any benefit in progressing a case which the claimant does not seem to wish to pursue. Where the defendant has included a counterclaim in his defence and he has filed his completed DQ, then the court may, if it is appropriate to do so, either order an allocation hearing that all parties must attend, or make an order that will enable the defendant's counterclaim to proceed.

12.4 FORMS N180 AND N181—THE DQs

Form N180 is used in all cases in the small claims track and Form N181 for all cases in the fast track and multi-track. DQs are not required in the specialist courts—claims in the Commercial Court, Technology and Construction Court, and Mercantile Courts use different forms and procedures. Legal representatives in any claim issued in the specialist courts should consult the specialist court guides for details of the procedure in these courts.

Please see the blank DQ in Form N181 on the Online Resource Centre. See also the 'Case study documentation' section of the Online Resource Centre and the 'Annotated forms' section, in which there are some practical notes to aid completion of the form.

12.5 COSTS INFORMATION ON THE DQ OR THE REQUIREMENT TO FILE A COSTS BUDGET IN PRECEDENT H

Chapter 20 on 'Assessment of Costs Proceedings', at paragraph 20.3.5.8, notes that a legal representative's costs estimate made in the DQ may be binding in fast-track and multi-track cases where there has been no Costs Management Order (CMO) (this is where the court has formally recorded the extent to which the costs budgets are agreed or approved by the court). CPR 6.5A states that if there is a difference of 20 per cent or more between the estimate given and the final costs being claimed, that party may be asked to provide a statement of the reasons for the difference. It will also be very pertinent to any costs recovery that the client had been made aware of the difference and had authorized it. CPR PD 44.3 also provides that the court 'may' take the estimate into account.

In cases where there are no CMOs, a costs estimate made in the DQ should be as accurate as possible and must be served on the client. If steps are taken on the case that would increase this estimate, a full file note should be made, the client informed, and his instructions to incur the additional costs obtained.

As suggested previously, for all multi-track cases the parties will have been ordered to file a cost budget in Precedent H, but there may not always be a residual CMO. (See Chapter 4, paragraph 4.6.3.)

12.6 **ALLOCATION TO TRACK**

Once a defence has been filed, the court will give Notice of the Proposed Allocation to track (see Chapter 9, paragraph 9.2, and paragraph 12.6.2 in this chapter) and direct that the parties download and complete the appropriate DQ. The court may dispense with the need for DQs to be completed; this may happen when another application (for example an application for summary judgment or for strike-out) has been treated as an allocation hearing (see paragraph 12.3.2). The specified date for filing any documents required by the Notice of Proposed Allocation (and this will usually be a requirement to complete and file the DQ) will be at least:

- 14 days after the Notice of Proposed Allocation is deemed served (for small claims track cases); or

- 28 days after the Notice of Proposed Allocation is deemed served (for fast-track and multi-track cases).

On receipt of the completed DQ, the procedural judge will either confirm the track and make a directions order or will order a CMC to be listed. Where a CMC is listed, the parties will also be ordered to file a Disclosure Report (and possibly an Electronic Disclosure Questionnaire) and costs budget (see paragraph 12.3.2). A case can be 'down-tracked' in a case where both parties and the court agree that this is appropriate (see paragraph 12.6.3). A 'procedural judge' may include a master (for cases proceeding in the Royal Courts of Justice), or a district judge and circuit judge in the district registries and county courts. The parties have the opportunity in their replies to the questions in the DQ to influence the directions order that the judge will make to manage the case. Any request for a tailor-made directions order for the particular case will need to be justified by the party requesting it. The ultimate power to make case management decisions rests with the procedural judge.

The court will now automatically hear CMCs over the phone wherever possible. (See the Additional Chapter 'A Practical Guide to Court Hearings' on the Online Resource Centre).

 online resource centre

On occasions, the hearing of another application could be *treated* as the first CMC where the court will confirm allocation to track and make the directions order. Legal representatives should always attend any such hearings fully prepared to discuss with the judge issues of allocation and the appropriate directions order to be made for the future management of the case. Where such a first CMC is listed or a hearing has been heard before the court has formally confirmed the allocation to a track, a legal representative who attends the hearing should, wherever possible, be the person who is responsible for the case (or at least part of the legal team responsible for the case). In any event, he must be familiar with the case, and have sufficient authority to deal with issues that may arise so as to be able to provide the court with any information that it might seek in order to make its decision on matters of allocation to track and the directions order appropriate for the case.

The majority of cases proceed between the filing of the defence and trial with a directions order that is more or less in standard form, but, when necessary, tailored to the needs of the particular case.

12.6.1 WHEN WILL ALLOCATION TAKE PLACE?

Generally, confirmation of the allocation to track—which includes both the allocation to track and any directions—will be made once the procedural judge has considered the DQs returned or, in cases where a first CMC has been listed at this hearing after the Disclosure Report, Electronic Disclosure Questionnaire, and costs budget have been filed, or possibly when the time limit for the filing of DQs has expired (see paragraphs 12.3.4.1 and 12.3.4.2).

If one or more of the parties have requested it, or if the court decides that it is appropriate to do so, the action can be 'stayed' for a period of time (in the fast track often for a period of one month) to enable ADR to be tried. In these circumstances, confirmation of allocation will not be made until after the period of stay ordered.

In cases in which the case is to be transferred to another court or hearing centre or to a specialist court, allocation decisions will be taken after the transfer by the procedural judge in the court or hearing centre to which the case is transferred—although note CPR 26.3(3), under which the court in which the claim was started will issue the Notice of Proposed Allocation request to the parties to file DQs before transferring the case. Unless the transfer is to one of the specialist courts, the notice will instruct that the completed DQs be returned to the court or hearing centre to which the case is transferred. A case transferred to a specialist court will be processed in accordance with the rules and procedures of the specialist court to which the case has been transferred.

12.6.2 WHAT DOES THE COURT CONSIDER WHEN ALLOCATING TO TRACK?

There are nine basic principles that the court will consider when allocating a case to the appropriate track. These are set out in CPR 26.8(1) and they include:

- the financial value of the claim—that is, the sum that represents the 'financial value' of the case for tracking purposes, disregarding any amount not in dispute, any claim for interest or costs, and any claim of contributory negligence. This principle is important to bear in mind in practice at all times. Both the Protocol phase of litigation, the rules of litigation and drafting statements of case, are designed to encourage parties to narrow the issues between them and, in doing so, the value of the claim may well be reduced. Narrowing the issues, admitting or agreeing what can be agreed, or being realistic in terms of the sum claimed in the Protocol phase can have significant impact on the 'value' of the claim for tracking purposes. Where the court believes that the amount being claimed by the claimant (or the defendant in any counterclaim) exceeds what that party may reasonably be expected to recover, it can make an order directing that the party justify the amount being claimed (CPR 26.5(3));

- the remedy sought;

- the complexity of the claim—which may include complexities of law, fact, and/or evidence; and

- where there is no financial value, the court will allocate the case to the most appropriate track, having regard to matters such as complexity, numbers of witnesses, the importance of the claim to persons who are not parties (in effect, those matters listed in CPR 26.8(1)).

12.6.3 CAN A CASE BE PLACED IN A TRACK THAT IS ABOVE, OR BELOW, ITS INDICATIVE TRACK?

A case can be placed in a different track. The criteria for cases to be heard in the small claims track should not be seen only as a question of value, although 'value' is the guiding

principle that sets a case in that track. The small claims track is intended to provide a proportionate procedure for the most straightforward claims. Although a claim may exceed the
small claims track financial limit, parties should consider whether it would, in fact, be more
proportionate, more just, and more efficient for the case to be heard in the small claims
track rather than the track that its value would indicate. If this occurs, the parties could still
also agree that the costs provisions that apply in the fast track should apply to the claim
so 'down-tracked' to the small claims track (CPR 27.14(5)), so a party is not prejudiced by
the more restricted costs rules applicable in the small claims track. This applies equally to
claims with a financial limit above £25,000 that, for similar reasons, might be better placed
in the fast track rather than the multi-track.

The court may also place a case in a track higher than its financial value would indicate if
it is appropriate to do so (having regard to the matters listed in CPR 26.8(1)).

In practice, there may be cogent reasons why a party may wish to have his claim allocated
to the 'highest' track, because it may mean that:

• the matter will be determined by a more senior judge;

• there may be more flexibility to recover more costs; and

• there may be more flexibility in the directions orders that can be made, and more flexibility in the amount of oral evidence to be given and the amount of expert evidence that
may be permitted.

12.6.4 REALLOCATION

The court has discretion to reallocate a claim to a different track (CPR 26.10). This may happen if there has been a change in the circumstances, or nature, or value of the claim.

If a party is unhappy with the allocation order that has been made, he may appeal the
order if he (or his legal representative) had been present at a CMC hearing (if such took
place), or apply to the court to reallocate. In either case, the party should have clear reasons
for asking the court to reallocate. An appeal would be with permission to a circuit judge, or,
if by application, either by letter or Form N244, usually to the district judge who made the
original order.

If a reallocation order is made, it is also likely to result in a change of the directions order
made for the future management of the case. Any appeal or application by a party for reallocation should therefore also take account of, and suggest where appropriate, the changes
that may be needed in the case management directions.

12.7 CASE MANAGEMENT: THE DIRECTIONS ORDER

Once the judge has confirmed or allocated a case to track he will then also make the case
management directions order. This will set down all of the steps which the parties need to
comply with, and when they must comply, in order to make the case ready for hearing. The
directions order may indicate the steps which the parties need to comply with all the way to
trial, or (more commonly) will set directions orders up to the point of the issuing of pre-trial
checklists (Form N170—see paragraph 12.7.3.3), at which time the court will undertake a
similar review of the action and set a further directions order of the steps that are required
to manage the case on to trial.

12.7.1 WHAT TYPE OF DIRECTIONS ORDER WILL GENERALLY BE MADE?

Details of the most likely directions that may be made in an action will be contained in the
CPR applicable to the track in which the case is placed (CPR Parts 27–29).

When making directions, the court will be seeking to apply the principles of the overriding objective. The aim of the directions made will be to ensure that the case proceeds on its

path to trial properly, efficiently, and proportionately. Accordingly, every attempt will be made to clarify the issues in dispute (and encouragement is evident for the parties to seek to narrow the issues in dispute) and to control the evidence.

In the DQ, parties must either set out agreed directions or proposed directions. Parties can have reference to the 'standard directions' (contained in PD 28) or in the schedule of typical directions orders contained in the menu options found in the CPR for multi-track non-PI cases (PD 29). Where inadequate information has been given in the DQs, the court is likely to set down standard directions and timescales.

12.7.2 WHAT INFORMATION SHOULD BE GIVEN BY THE PARTIES IN THEIR DQs?

If the parties have cooperated with each other, as they are required to do, in the preparation of their DQs, and, further, they have agreed the directions that they feel are needed for the management of the case either to trial or to the next CMC (which will probably be a pre-trial review), the procedural judge may simply endorse their proposals and make the directions order proposed.

In order to obtain the court's approval in this way, any proposals should:

- if appropriate, deal with the filing of a reply to a defence;
- if appropriate, deal with any amendments to a statement of case;
- make provisions for disclosure and inspection—its extent, as well as the time allowed;
- propose directions concerning the exchange of evidence of fact and expert evidence (if any). If there is expert evidence, the proposals should include a direction concerning the type of expert permitted, the timing of exchange of reports (if more than one), questions to the expert, and any meeting between experts (again if more than one expert has been permitted). In the fast track, the normal order for any expert evidence will be for a single joint expert;
- include dates on which any requests for further information may be made and complied with;
- state when the trial period should be set and the date for the sending out of pre-trial checklists (PTCs, Form N170) and the pre-trial review or hearing;
- if appropriate, set a date for a further CMC; and
- consider a stay for ADR.

The court may accept or reject the proposals, but, in making its directions order, will have regard to the proposals put forward by the parties. The ultimate responsibility for case management directions remains with the court.

In the fast track and PI cases in the multi-track, the order will normally be for 'standard directions'.

12.7.3 WHAT ARE 'STANDARD DIRECTIONS'?

'Standard directions' are established under the CPR. They represent the case management directions that apply generally to the average, relatively un-complex, claim. These can be found in the PD for each track. They seek to ensure that the claim will progress efficiently, proportionately (as to the value and costs), and justly.

12.7.3.1 In the small claims track

Standard directions in the small claims track are set out in CPR 27.4(3) and PD 27, Appendix B. These include:

- the requirement to exchange copies of all documents on which a party will rely usually at least 14 days before the hearing;

- a requirement that the parties should file at court (for cases which will be determined as 'paper' hearings without the parties attending) or to bring originals of the documents to a hearing (where the court has determined that a hearing be listed);

- if appropriate a notice of the date and time of, and time allowed for, any final hearing;

- a note encouraging parties to communicate with each other, with a view to settling the dispute, coupled with a requirement that they should notify the court in writing if they do settle; and

- a note that no expert report will be permitted unless express permission has been granted.

PD 27, Appendix C, sets out the special directions that may be made or requested in this track. The purpose of special directions is to enable the case management of these low-value claims to be more effective, just, and proportionate (to their value and to the amount of costs being incurred). They may include directions regarding the issues on which the court requires evidence, the nature of the evidence required, and the way in which the evidence will be presented. (This is not a definitive list of special directions that could be made, but it gives useful guidance to any practitioner who is assisting a party who is conducting or defending a claim in this track, or a party who is acting in person.)

Because some of the CPR on matters relating to expert evidence, witnesses of fact, disclosure, and inspection do not apply to the small claims track, it may be necessary for the court to specify, or for the parties to seek, special directions because of the particular needs of the case, although it must be borne in mind that the overriding objective applies to the small claims track and that any request for special directions must meet with this objective. If the number of special directions needed, or some other reason, means that it is appropriate to do so, the court may, of its own initiative or upon the application of a party, reallocate a case from the small claims track to the fast track. It may also add, vary, or revoke any special directions made.

One of the most common special directions that may be sought may be a special direction that the parties exchange witness statements before the final hearing (this being a standard direction in both the fast track and the multi-track). Before making any such order, the court will have regard to the matters set out in the PD 27.2.5. These considerations include:

- whether there is to be a hearing and whether either or both parties are represented;

- the amount in dispute;

- the nature of the matters in dispute;

- whether it would be better for a party to be asked to clarify his case better before the hearing;

- the need to provide for 'justice' without undue formality, cost, or delay.

12.7.3.2 In the fast track

The case management directions order in cases allocated to the fast track will generally (but not always) be given in two stages:

(a) when allocation to track has been confirmed and the first directions order is made; and

(b) on the filing of pre-trial checklists (PTCs) in Form N170—(see paragraph 12.7.3.3).

On both occasions, the court will expect a degree of cooperation between the parties and will make the directions order wherever possible without a CMC. Where a CMC does have to take place, this will be by telephone (PD 23.6.2). The court will also readily impose costs sanctions if the requirement for a CMC has been necessitated by either a lack of cooperation of a party or the default of a party in the completion of the DQs. Also, if a CMC has to take place, the parties have a duty to attend that hearing, having considered what directions order they wish the court to make.

The court will take account of the steps that the parties have already taken in the Protocol period to make the case ready for trial.

The Appendix in PD 28 contains the form of fast-track standard directions and, wherever possible, the court will base its directions order on those set out in the Appendix.

One of the principles that guide the decisions that the court will make for a fast-track case directions order will be the court's duty under CPR 28.2(2) to set a case management timetable and to fix a trial date (or trial period). This trial date or trial period shall not be longer than 30 weeks from the date of the directions order. Where parties recommend an agreed directions order to the court, they must equally ensure that the agreed directions order provides specific dates for steps to be completed, include a trial period (that must not be longer than 30 weeks from the date of the directions order), and include provisions about disclosure of documents and the management of both fact and expert evidence.

A typical timetable for the preparation of a fast-track case to trial would be a directions order that provided for:

- disclosure within four weeks (from the date of the directions order);
- an exchange of witness statements within ten weeks (from the date of the directions order);
- an exchange of expert reports within 14 weeks (from the date of the directions order), together with any additional directions that may be needed—for example, concerning questions to the expert, or who is to pay the expert's fees;
- the date on which PTCs will be sent out by the court—typically, 20 weeks (from the date of the directions order);
- the date on which the PTCs must be returned—typically, 22 weeks (from the date of the directions order); and
- the date of the trial or trial period—typically, 30 weeks (from the date of the directions order).

If a party is dissatisfied with the directions order, or the parties have agreed that there should be changes made to the order, or if, for other reasons, changes are appropriate, an application for the change should be made at the earliest opportunity. This would be by notice of application to the court on Form N244, with reasons. Such an application will usually be heard by the master or district judge who made the original order. If an application is made later than 14 days from the date of the order, the court will assume that the directions order made was appropriate at the time and therefore any changes will need to be justified. If the original directions order was made at a CMC at which the party was present or represented (or at which the party had had due notice of the hearing), he must appeal the order if he seeks changes. In any other circumstance, the party may apply to the court to reconsider the directions order made. In these circumstances, the application will usually be heard by the judge (or at least a judge of the same level) who made the original directions order.

 Practical Considerations

If a case requires special directions, it will be essential in practice to be prepared to state, and justify (within the provisions of the overriding objective), what special directions you think your case needs and make a request to the court for the special directions at the earliest opportunity. This will probably be in or accompanying the DQ.

12.7.3.3 The pre-trial checklists (PTCs) Form N170

Where the case management directions order for a case allocated to the fast track has been given in two stages, the initial directions order will usually give directions up to the point at which the court sends out PTCs to the parties. This form has a similar function to the

DQ—that is, it seeks information from the parties that enables the court to determine the appropriate directions order that should be made guiding the case from that stage and on to trial. It also enables the parties to seek specific tailor-made directions if justified. Again, the parties should cooperate with one another in the completion of the PTC.

There is a fee for the filing of the PTC, this is the first part of the trial fee, (the 2nd part is payable prior to trial as directed by the court). If the case settles or is discontinued a part (or in some situations, the whole) of the fee can be reclaimed. This is set out in paragraph 2.1 of the Civil Proceedings and Family Proceedings Fees (Amendment) Order 2015. Even when the court has not made a two-stage directions order to trial both, the pre-trial fees will be payable by the claimant within 14 days of the specified dates. If the case is proceeding on a defendant's counterclaim alone, he will need to pay this hearing fee. If the hearing fee is not paid, the court will issue a reminder to the party, but CPR 3.7 enables the court to strike out the claim for non-payment after the reminder.

The purpose of the PTC is to:

- check the directions order to date has been complied with; and
- provide more detailed information about the trial requirements so that it can make a directions order dealing with the steps necessary to make the case ready for the trial and to include any directions for the trial itself.

The completed PTCs will be placed before the procedural judge, who will decide whether to make a trial directions order from the completed lists or to call a pre-trial review (or pre-trial directions) hearing or CMC. The court will also again consider whether there should be a stay for any further attempt at settlement by a method of ADR.

A typical directions order that may be made on receipt of the completed PTCs includes:

- confirming or fixing the trial date;
- directions concerning evidence, the number of witnesses, expert evidence (if permission has been granted at allocation directions or subsequently), or for expert evidence to be adduced;
- indicating whether a trial timetable and trial estimate are required;
- provisions concerning the preparation of the trial bundle; and
- any other relevant directions (for example, the provision of an interpreter, specific IT facility, etc.).

The trial judge can be pragmatic in his requirements for individual trials and such 'hands-on' directions were given in the *Wembley* litigation in 2008, in which the TCC trial judge ordered that each party were to share the time allocated for the trial equally, that parts of the evidence were to be left to the trial judge's private reading, and that post-trial hearings were to take place to provide the parties with parts of his judgment and to discuss issues in the case. This style of case management is becoming more prevalent in the specialist courts.

12.7.3.4 In the multi-track

A multi-track directions order is, in practice, appropriate for cases in this track:

- that are worth more than £25,000;
- in which the trial is estimated to last for more than a day; and
- in which each party will need to adduce expert oral evidence either in more than one field of expertise, or from more than one expert in a particular field.

Multi-track claims can be heard in either one of the County Court hearing centres or the High Court, or one of its district registries, but unless there are particular factors of the case (complexity, legal principle), any case that is worth less than £100,000 will invariably be listed *for trial* in a County Court hearing centre. Cases on the multi-track will generally be dealt with either in the Royal Courts of Justice or other trial centres in the district registries.

12.7.3.4.1 *Case management directions in the multi-track*

Cases on this track are typically more complex and are of higher value than the cases in the small claims track or the fast track; accordingly, the case management directions order for these cases is likely to be more flexible and more likely to be tailored to meet the specific requirements of the case. The degree of flexibility available for actions within this track will reflect the wide variety of actions—from complex but quite low-value claims to claims involving great sums of money, or claims that raise matters of public importance. The emphasis is again on 'efficiency', 'fairness', and 'proportionality (to the value and to costs incurred)', and in claims that are less complex, the court will seek to make standard directions without the need for a CMC. Such claims will be given a directions order with tight timetables that are similar to the standard directions in the fast track. As in the fast track, parties are under a duty to be well prepared for hearings and to give consideration to the directions orders that they may require. Again, parties are expected to cooperate with one another in agreeing the directions that they seek.

At the time that the DQ (in Form N181) is filed for cases in this track, the procedural judge will decide whether to make the directions order or to fix a CMC and direct that the parties file a Disclosure Report, Electronic Disclosure Questionnaire, and costs budget before that CMC (see paragraph 12.3.2). The procedural judge will also consider whether to order a stay (whether sought by one or more parties in the action or not) while ADR procedures are attempted to settle the case or to narrow the issues.

If a party feels that the directions order is wrong or wishes to seek amendment to it, the rule that applies in the fast track concerning the directions order (that the court will assume that the directions order was correct for the circumstances of the case when made) applies equally in the multi-track and unless a prompt application to vary is made (within 14 days, under PD 29.6.2(2)), and is fully justified, changes are unlikely to be made.

12.7.3.4.2 *What is a 'usual directions order' in a multi-track case?*

The directions order in cases allocated to the multi-track will generally (but not always) be given in two stages:

(a) when the court has confirmed the allocation and makes its first directions order with all the steps the parties must comply with up until the date of filing of the PTC; and

(b) on the filing of PTCs (Form N170—see paragraph 12.7.3.3) where the court will then make the directions order with the steps the parties must comply with from then on to make the case ready for trial (including orders for the trial itself).

As in the small claims track and the fast track, the court aims to set an efficient and proportionate and fair path for the action to trial. The court will usually consider:

• whether there is a need for an order to clarify the points in issue. This may be undertaken either by making orders for further information to be filed (CPR 18), or for amended statements of case to be prepared and filed and served;

• whether there should be an order for a stay to enable the parties to engage in a form of ADR;

• Whether a Costs Management Order (CMO) should be made;

• what should be the scope of any disclosure and inspection;

• the number of witnesses of fact that are required and provision for the exchange of witness statements. Orders can be made to restrict the issues on which evidence will be given;

• whether there is a requirement for expert evidence. The court will further consider whether this should be by single joint experts or by each party having their own expert, and consider in which fields of expertise expert evidence is required. The court will consider what provisions need be made concerning expert evidence (for example, 'questions to an expert' or 'meetings between experts') and whether there needs to be a provision for oral evidence by the expert(s) at trial. As with witnesses of fact, orders can be made to restrict the issues on which expert evidence will be given;

- whether it is appropriate, on grounds of costs, efficiency, fairness, or proportionality, for there to be an order for a 'split trial' (between matters of liability and quantum), or whether there should be a trial of one or more preliminary issues (see Chapter 16, paragraph 16.2.2);

- whether there should be another CMC or pre-trial review hearing and when;

- whether it is possible to fix a trial period; and

- at which court, or before which calibre of judge, the matter should be listed for trial.

Parties will refer to the suggested draft directions contained at http://www.justice.gov.uk/courts/procedure-rules/civil/standard.directions/list-of-cases-of-common-occurrence when drafting their proposed directions order submitted with their completed DQs.

12.8 CASE MANAGEMENT CONFERENCES (CMCs)

A first CMC may be held after the filing of DQs, the disclosure report, and the costs budget where the court will confirm allocation to a track and consider a directions order (usually in two stages; see paragraph 12.7.3.4.2). It may also have arisen immediately after the hearing of an early interim application (see paragraph 12.3.2). Often, the parties will also be prompted to try (or to try again) some form of ADR procedure to settle the case. In any event, the procedural judge will seek to use the hearing to progress matters efficiently, justly, and proportionately, and not only to make a directions order but also, for example, by encouraging parties to narrow the issues in dispute, or to order that certain issues shall not be proceeded with. CPR 32.2(3) gives the court power to limit evidence and the issues that the case proceeds with.

 Practical Considerations

It is important to remember that no mention must be made by the parties at the CMC of any CPR Part 36 offers that have been made in the action, or the details of any attempts at ADR.

Attendance at CMCs should be by a legal representative who is familiar with the issues of the case and who has the appropriate authority to deal with matters arising at it.

 Practical Considerations

If the person attending the CMC does not have sufficient knowledge, or experience, or authority to deal with matters arising at the hearing, and the hearing has to be adjourned because of that lack of knowledge or authority, then a wasted costs order will usually be made.

If parties have been ordered to attend and the party is a company, it should be someone from the company who has knowledge of the history of the case.

At the CMC, the court will:

- make a review of the steps taken by the parties to progress the action;

- review how far the parties have complied with any previous directions or orders;

- decide on further directions or orders (that are within the spirit of the overriding objective);

- seek to encourage consensus, wherever possible, on issues, directions, orders, or future conduct; and

- record any agreements.

If the court feels that it will assist the efficiency of the CMC or the progress of the action, an order may be made in advance of the CMC, or before the hearing of any next CMC, for a case summary to be prepared by the parties and lodged at court. The court may equally order that certain documents (in a 'case management bundle') be prepared and lodged for the hearing. The Court Guides for High Court matters may also specify certain requirements for CMCs.

12.9 WHAT HAPPENS IF A PARTY FAILS TO COMPLY WITH A CASE MANAGEMENT DIRECTION?

The court retains control of actions, and has powers of coercion and sanctions to ensure that, so far as possible, parties comply with the orders made. These include the following provisions and powers to:

- strike out a party's case—that is, the most draconian measure that is used in only the most serious cases of default or breach;

- make an 'unless order'—that is, the court will make an order against the defaulting party to compel compliance, but if they fail to do so, the 'unless' provision will apply. This 'unless' provision could be an order to strike out all or part of that party's case. In either track, where the directions order for trial has been set and the times allowed are 'tight', the court will be prepared to impose an 'unless' order on a party even after only one breach (see Chapter 13, paragraph 13.9);

- make adverse costs orders—the court may also provide that those costs orders be payable immediately;

- make an order for indemnity costs or increased interest on damages or costs;

- make an order that a defaulting party pay money into court;

- debar a party from proceeding with an issue, or from amending its statement of case, or from filing additional evidence;

- restrict the numbers of witnesses that may be called (including an expert witness); and

- refuse to grant any application for further time.

In respect of any of these orders and sanctions, the court will consider wasted costs orders against the legal representative if the reason for the party's default rests with the legal representative.

If both parties, or more than one party, in an action are in default, the court will consider a sanction order against either or both parties in default.

CPR 3.9 is intended to ensure that the parties focus on compliance with rules and court orders ('compliance' is part of CPR 3.9). The case of *Mitchell v News Group Newspapers Ltd* [2013] EWHC 2355 (QB) gave the following guidance on the approach the courts should follow where a party applies for relief from a sanction imposed following a breach of a court rule or an order:

- Where non-compliance is trivial and an application for relief from sanctions is made promptly, the court will often grant relief.

- The defaulting party must persuade the court that there was good reason for the default.

- If the party believes that the order was wrong when made, then the appropriate application is an appeal or an application to revoke or vary the order.

Generally any application for 'relief from sanctions' should only be made where there has been 'a material change of circumstance'. The more recent case *Thevarajah v Riordan* [2015] EWCA Civ 14 has added detail to this general overview of the courts' approach to an application for 'relief from sanctions'—and stated that a party who has—finally complied with an order cannot use this as a reason for being relieved of sanctions the court had imposed on it for failing to abide by an order on time or as directed.

CPR 3.8 should be noted and does provide some leeway as it enables parties to agree extensions of time (to comply with an order), in writing, for up to 28 days, without court approval, *provided* such extensions do not put a hearing at risk.

Practical Considerations

Legal representatives have a duty to help to further the overriding objective (CPR 1.3). It is therefore inappropriate to 'sit back' and let an action stagnate: delay by one party does not justify any delay by any other party.

12.10 **THE CASE MANAGEMENT FLOWCHART**

Figure 12.1 will guide you through the most significant aspects of case management.

FIGURE 12.1 CASE MANAGEMENT

KEY POINTS SUMMARY

- Often the court's first step in 'active case management' will occur when a case is allocated to track and the court makes the first directions order to provide a timetable of the steps the parties must comply with, either in one stage (to trial) or in two stages: firstly, those steps to be undertaken up to the filing of form N170, and then secondly, from then on to (and including) the trial.

- Parties are expected to cooperate in completing their DQs and to assist the court in the preparation of the directions order.

- The court will look to impose 'standard directions' wherever possible.

- Details of the standard directions applicable to each track can be found in the CPR and accompanying Practice Directions pertaining to the track (CPR 27–29).

- Any directions outside standard directions will need to be justified within the provisions of the overriding objective.

- Parties must be prompt in applying to the court for tailored directions orders and fully justify their request.

- The court will impose sanctions if a party fails to comply with the directions order set down unless extensions of time have been agreed in accordance with the amended CPR 3.8.

Case Studies *Andrew James Pike v Deep Builders Ltd/Bollingtons Ltd v Mrs Elizabeth Lynch t/a The Honest Lawyer*

Question 1

Complete the DQ for the claimant in each of the two case studies. When completing the form consider whether the defendant (in each of the case studies) would be likely to agree the order sought or may seek to ask for a different order. (You do not need to complete the DQ for the defendant).

Question 2

Prepare a suitable directions order that you feel the claimant could seek from the court for each of the two case studies.

---

online resource centre

Any documents referred to in these case study questions can be found on the Online Resource Centre—simply click on 'Case study documentation' to access the documents that you need for Chapter 12 and to be reminded of the questions. Suggested answers to these case study questions can also be accessed on the Online Resource Centre when released to you by your lecturer.

- If there is a time limit for making an interim application, the application is treated as being made on the day on which the application notice and fee are received by the court (CPR 23.5).

- All of the evidence being relied on for the interim application should be filed at court, ideally at the same time as filing the application notice (PD 23.9.4). If the evidence is already with the court, then further copies need not be filed.

- The application notice, evidence, and order should be served at least three clear days before the hearing (CPR 23.7(1)(b)). If the matter is to be heard by way of a telephone conference hearing, then these documents should be served within five days of the hearing date.

- A draft order (of the application sought) should be filed at court, and if it is long or complex, it should also be supplied on disk (PD 23.12.1). If the matter is a multi-track case, then a case summary must also be served. Both the draft order and a case summary must be filed and served no later than 4 p.m. at least two clear days before the hearing.

- Supporting evidence is not always required when it is a case management directions order that is being sought, although reasons and costings should normally be given that seek to justify the application.

- The court may allow urgent applications to be dealt with on short notice (PD 23.3 and 23.4).

- Most interim applications are dealt with by the master or district judges, although some applications may be referred to a judge for hearing (CPR 23.1). If a particular master, or district judge, or judge has heard an earlier interim application, the matter can be referred to that master, district judge, or judge if it would be helpful to do so. The master or district judge may also refer the matter to a judge (PD 2 and PD 23.1).

- A fee is payable unless the applicant can obtain exemption on the ground of financial hardship.

- If the court is to serve the respondent, the applicant must file sufficient copies of the application notice, supporting evidence, and draft order for it to do so. The court will then serve these documents, together with notice of the hearing date and time.

- If the respondent wishes to rely on evidence to respond to the interim application, such evidence should be filed at court at least two days before the hearing. This would include a case summary if the case is a multi-track case, as stated earlier.

- If an application for costs is being made in the application, the party's cost schedule (Form N260) must be lodged at court and served on the other party at least 24 hours before the hearing.

Note: Reference should be made to Chapter 4 for detail of the most common costs orders and cost procedure in interim applications.

13.6 TIME ESTIMATES

The court will expect the applicant to give an assessment of the likely time that the hearing of the interim application will take. Where the application is to be on notice, the court also expects the parties, wherever possible, to cooperate in agreeing a time estimate for the hearing. The estimated time is included in the application notice (Form N244).

 Practical Considerations

The time estimate should not only include the time for both parties to make their representations, but should also include time for the judge to make a decision and time for any applications for costs to be considered. In more complex matters, the estimate should also include time for the judge to read the papers.

13.7 **NOTICE AND HEARING PROVISIONS FOR INTERIM APPLICATIONS**

13.7.1 **APPLICATIONS WITH NOTICE**

Applications on notice may occur with a hearing. They may also occur without a hearing when, for example, the parties have agreed that the order sought should be made or the court considers that a hearing is not appropriate (CPR 23.8). Most of the applications for which a hearing is listed will be heard by telephone, or by video conferencing (see the Additional Chapter 'A Practical Guide to Court Hearings' on the Online Resource Centre).

These general rules apply, but remember that the procedure set out in a CPR specific to the interim application being made will take precedence over the general rules in CPR 23.

✓ Practical Considerations

The CPR state that the notice of the interim application, the supporting evidence, notice of the hearing date, and the draft order should be served on the respondent 'at least three days before the hearing' (note: five days if the matter is being heard by way of a telephone conference hearing). However, it is important also to note the words 'as soon as practicable' that are contained in PD 23.4.1. If, as the legal representative for the applicant in an interim application, you have filed your application at court in good time, and have received back from the court the date and time of the hearing that is some time ahead (for example more than five days), you could be severely criticized by the court for holding back serving the application and notice of hearing on your opponent until much nearer the time of the hearing or telephone appointment (the aim being to gain the tactical advantage of time and giving the respondent limited time in which to respond). It would be wrong to choose to comply with that part of the rule for service that requires service 'at least three clear days before the hearing' and not that part which expects service 'as soon as practicable' in order to gain a perceived advantage of surprise. The criticism by the court could mean that the application is dismissed or adjourned, or, if the master or district judge does hear the application in these circumstances, he may make adverse costs orders against the applicant for the failure to serve 'as soon as practicable'.

13.7.2 **APPLICATIONS WITHOUT NOTICE**

Applications without notice can be made. These may be with or without a hearing.

The basic principle of litigation is that an order should not be made against a party without him having an opportunity to be heard. However, there will be occasions on which it is necessary to do so, such as:

- when giving notice may defeat the purpose of the application, or could create an injustice through delay or action that the respondent may take to defeat the application—examples include search orders and freezing injunctions (for further details of these, and other, injunctions, see the Additional Chapter 'Injunctions and Other Equitable Remedies' on the Online Resource Centre. See also Chapter 14, paragraph 14.7);

- when the opponent is not yet on the court record—examples of this could be when the claimant seeks more time in which to serve the claim form, or when a defendant seeks permission of the court to issue an additional claim (CPR 20) (on the occasions on which permission is needed); or

- when the defendant can only be identified by description and not by name—an example may occur in intellectual property claims.

PD 23.3 sets out a list of occasions on which an interim application may be made without notice. These include when:

- there is exceptional urgency;

- the overriding objective is best furthered by the application being made without notice;

- the parties consent;
- the court grants permission;
- a date for a hearing has been fixed and a party wishes to make an application at that hearing, but does not have sufficient time to serve an application notice; and
- where a rule, PD, or court order permits.

The evidence in support of an application without notice must include the reasons why notice was not given (CPR 25.3(3)). For further detail of without notice applications see Chapter 14, paragraph 14.7. Please also refer to the Additional Chapter 'Injunctions and Other Equitable Remedies' on the Online Resource Centre.

13.7.2.1 What may happen if an application is made without notice when it is not appropriate to do so?

If an application is made without notice in circumstances when the court concludes that it was not appropriate to have done so, the application will probably be dismissed or adjourned until proper notice is given. A wasted costs order is likely to be imposed if the legal representative is at fault.

13.7.2.2 When does the respondent hear of the order made?

CPR 23.9 states that when an order has been made on a without-notice application, unless the court orders otherwise, it must be served on the respondent. This service will include the application notice, the evidence that supported the application, and the order that has been made. Usually, the court will effect service—but see CPR 6.3 and 40.4 for details of these service provisions, and the option that the applicant has of effecting service himself.

The notice to the respondent will include a statement setting out the respondent's right to make an application to set aside or vary the order that has been made (CPR 23.10), but such application by the respondent must be made within seven days after the date of service.

13.7.3 APPLICATIONS WITHOUT A HEARING

Applications without a hearing are otherwise known as 'paper applications' and are discussed in some detail in the Additional Chapter 'A Practical Guide to Court Hearings' on the Online Resource Centre.

13.8 'CARELESS' NEGOTIATIONS—THE STATUS OF THINGS SAID IN THE PRE-HEARING DISCUSSIONS

It is important to make a careful file note of any discussions between the legal representatives that take place either on the telephone before the hearing, or, if an attendance at court is required, whilst waiting. It is important to note that no form of privilege will cover the pre-hearing discussions unless they are stated to be 'without prejudice'. Care needs to be taken, in any pre-hearing discussions, not to make careless concessions or unsubstantiated assertions of fact, because these could come back to haunt you as informal admissions and may bind the client, or be used to challenge your client's or another witness's testimony at the trial. Please see the Bollington Beer case study on the Online Resource Centre, as this demonstrates how pre-hearing discussions can be misconstrued.

 Practical Considerations

It is important to remember that the 'without prejudice' rule only covers discussions that take place 'with a view to settlement' and that this will not, therefore, cover general case management discussions. This is important to remember so as to avoid making an 'informal admission', or an acknowledgement of a state of affairs in an 'open', not 'without prejudice', forum—a reminder that was reinforced in *Stax Claimants v Bank of Nova Scotia Channel Islands Ltd* [2007] EWHC 1153.

13.9 **AN UNLESS ORDER**

13.9.1 **WHAT IS AN 'UNLESS ORDER'?**

If the court concludes that the opponent in an interim application has failed adequately to comply with the obligations of a previous order or within the general ethos of litigation practice (he may have failed to respond to an early request to comply), or if the court doubts the bona fides of the opponent, it will often make an order and, at the same time, specify a sanction to be imposed if the order is not complied with—this is an 'unless' order. An order that imposes a sanction for non-compliance will specify the date and time by which the steps of the order must be complied with (CPR 2.9). The sanction part of the order may take the form of an 'unless' provision. PD 40B.8.2 lays down formulae for drafting unless orders. Compliance with the time limits set in court orders is regarded as fundamental to litigation practice under the CPR, and the courts will not shirk from making unless orders within the terms of a first order so as to ensure that the strict timetable for the action can be met.

 Example

Your opponent has failed to serve his list of documents in accordance with the direction of the court for standard disclosure made at a recent CMC. You have requested the list and warned that an application will be made to the court if it is not forthcoming. The list still does not materialize and you are forced to apply to the court, requesting an order that your opponent be compelled to serve his list of documents within 14 days, failing which he should be deprived of the opportunity to defend the action.

If your application is successful, the order might be drafted as follows:

- 'The defendant is to serve its list of documents by 4 p.m. on 25 May 201?, failing which he shall be debarred from defending the claim further ...'; or

- 'Unless the defendant serves its list of documents by 4 p.m. on 25 May 201?, its defence will be struck out ...'.

 Costs

If, in your warning letter, you had also said that if you had to make an application to the court for an order compelling your opponent to comply you would seek an order for costs on the 'indemnity' basis, the court may also consider making a costs recovery order on the application on this enhanced basis.

13.9.2 **RELIEF FROM SANCTIONS—CPR 3.9 AND CPR 3.8**

If an unless order is made against a party and the order is not complied with, the sanction will automatically be imposed, even if, at a later date, the party complies with the order. Consider the previous example: if the defendant did not serve his list by 25 May, but served it on 29 May, his defence would still be struck out by virtue of the breach of the 'unless' order.

To try to remedy the situation, the defendant and his legal representative should consider making an application under CPR 3.9 for relief from sanctions—that is, ask the court to consider CPR 3.9(1) and not to strike out the case, nor to make the adverse costs order. The application must be made as soon as practicable and be supported by evidence. The court is very likely to take a robust and 'minimal tolerance' approach to any failure to comply with a court order. See Chapter 12, paragraph 12.9 for further details of the application of CPR 3.9.

In *Denton v TH White Limited, Decadent Vapours Limited v Bevan, Utilise TDS Limited v Davies* [2014] EWCA Civ 906 (*Denton*) the Court of Appeal has set out guidance on how the courts will consider applications for relief from sanctions under CPR 3.8.

14.2.2 **WHEN MAY AN APPLICATION BE MADE TO SET ASIDE A DEFAULT JUDGMENT?**

Whilst the request for default judgment may not be an 'interim application', an application by the defendant to set aside the default judgment obtained *is* an interim application and requires a 'judicial decision' before it can be granted. CPR 13 sets out the rules and procedure for applications to set aside a default judgment. It makes a distinction between the two sorts of default judgment that may be sought under CPR 12—that is, those that the court *must* set aside (CPR 13.2) and those that the court *may* set aside (CPR 13.3).

The court *must* set aside a default judgment when a ground listed in CPR 13.2 has been established—that is, when the defendant can show that the default judgment was wrongly entered by the claimant in that:

- it may have been entered too early;
- it was made after the defendant had made an application to strike out the claim or had applied to dismiss the claim summarily, but where the application by the defendant has not yet been concluded;
- it may have been entered even though the whole claim (including interest and costs) had already been paid or settled; or
- it was entered after the defendant had filed an admission, but had made a request for time to pay, and that request has not yet been dealt with.

In each of these situations, the defendant's request to set aside the default judgment need only establish one of the grounds listed and the default judgment will be set aside.

The court *may* set aside a default judgment that has been entered by the claimant in all other situations. CPR 13.3 provides that the court has discretion to set aside the default judgment entered. A defendant who wishes to seek an order to set aside a default judgment will need to act promptly and satisfy the two grounds set out in CPR 13.3.1—that is, in addition to 'acting promptly', he must:

- show that he has a real prospect of successfully defending the claim; or
- establish some other good reason why the judgment should be set aside and the defendant be permitted to defend the claim.

Additionally, under CPR 13.3.2:

- in considering whether to set aside or vary a judgment entered under CPR 12, the matters to which the court *must* have regard include whether the person seeking to set aside the judgment made an application to do so promptly. (Emphasis added)

The case of *Standard Bank plc v Agrinvest International Inc*, 14 January 2011, CA, is a case which clearly demonstrates that 'acting promptly' is every bit as important as the other criteria set down in CPR 13.3. In this case Lord Justice Moore-Bick set out some important observations on the necessity of timeliness in making applications to set aside default judgment. He confirmed that where there had been a lack of timeliness, even when a potentially successful defence had been put forward, the application may still be rejected.

14.2.3 **WHAT EVIDENCE IS REQUIRED TO SET ASIDE A DEFAULT JUDGMENT?**

14.2.3.1 **Where the court must set aside the default judgment**

An application need only submit the chronology or the facts that bring the application under the provisions of CPR 13.2. These facts may include copies of supporting evidence and, usually, there is sufficient space within Part C of the application notice (Form N244) in which to set out this detail. The court may be prepared to consider the application as a 'paper hearing' without notice (see the Additional Chapter 'A Practical Guide to Court Hearings' on the Online Resource Centre). In any application to set aside default judgment under the provisions of CPR 13.2, the consent of the other party should be sought, and if

online
resource
centre

it is obtained, the application can be submitted as an agreed application. The court will then almost certainly consider the application as a paper application and no hearing will be listed. In all cases in which it is clear that the defendant can establish a ground under CPR 13.2, the claimant would be well advised to consent to the application, because he may otherwise incur penalty costs for his failure to cooperate in such an application.

14.2.3.2 Where the court has discretion to set aside a default judgment

For applications to set aside under CPR 13.3, evidence must be submitted. The evidence that the defendant needs to produce to succeed in the application will need to address the court's discretion, which will be used to consider whether to make the order. The supporting evidence will therefore need to address the following:

- The prospects of success of the defence—this could be achieved by presenting a witness statement that sets out the basis of the intended defence. One of the most persuasive ways of doing this would be to exhibit a draft of the intended defence to the witness statement (provided that the legal representative has the client's approval to incur the additional costs of drafting the defence).

- If the ground set out in CPR 13.3.1(b) is being relied on, the witness statement needs to address the 'other good reasons' why the defendant should be permitted to proceed and defend.

- The defendant will also need to set out in what way he has acted 'promptly' in making the application, or provide any valid and excusable reasons that he may have for any delay.

In the case *Hockley v North Lincolnshire & Goole NHS Trust* (unreported, 19 September 2014) the defendant had failed to file an acknowledgement of service within the 14 days permitted by CPR 10.3(1). The claimant made a request, and obtained, default judgment on his claim. The defendant made a successful application to set aside the default judgment under CPR 13.3(1). The claimant appealed, seeking to restore the default judgment. In considering this appeal the court considered CPR 3.9 (see Chapter 13, paragraph 13.9.2 on relief from sanctions) and held that the defendant's breach (failure to adhere to the time limits of CPR 10.3(1) and file his acknowledgment of service on time) was 'serious'. The judge also noted that in making the application to set aside the default judgment the defendant had not filed a draft defence (or other document) with the application so as to allow the court to conclude that there was 'a real prospect' of defending the claim. It was held that the three-stage 'test' in *Denton* (see Chapter 13, paragraph 13.9.2) had considerable relevance. The case serves as a reminder that evidence in support of an application to set aside under this ground is crucial.

14.2.4 **THE PROCEDURE FOR MAKING AN APPLICATION TO SET ASIDE A DEFAULT JUDGMENT**

The claimant may still be invited to consent to the application before it is made. An application to set aside a judgment in default is made in the normal way in Form N244. Under CPR 13.4, the application will be transferred automatically to the defendant's home court if not already issued from that court when:

- the claim is for a specified sum; and

- the defendant is an individual.

If the defendant does not fall within the criteria of CPR 13.4, he could apply for a transfer to his home court as part of his application to set aside, but the application will be heard in the court in which the claim was issued; if the defendant makes this application it will be transferred to the preferred hearing centre for the hearing of the defendant's application.

Supporting evidence may be contained in Part C of Form N244 or in a separate witness statement. It is unlikely that the evidence will be contained in a statement of case available in the case, because at this stage, the only statement of case is likely to be the claimant's particulars of claim. The application must be submitted promptly and will, in nearly every case, be 'on notice' with the requisite current fee. Please see the witness statement in the Bollington Beer case study in the Online Resource.

14.2.5 ORDERS THAT MAY BE MADE IN AN APPLICATION TO SET ASIDE A DEFAULT JUDGMENT

Where the application is made in a case in which the court must set aside, any order made for payment to the claimant will also be set aside.

In applications in which the court has a discretion to set aside, the court will consider the evidence supporting the application, and may make such orders and directions as it thinks are appropriate. This can include dismissing the application or granting the application, either conditionally or unconditionally. If the application is granted, the action will proceed as directed.

14.3 SUMMARY JUDGMENT

14.3.1 SUMMARY JUDGMENT AND THE EUROPEAN CONVENTION ON HUMAN RIGHTS (ECHR)

Summary judgment is available both to claimants and to defendants. It seeks to avoid the occasions on which an opponent's case shows no reasonable prospects of success. It provides a quick and efficient solution to the case. It is therefore clearly distinguished from a default judgment, which relies on a 'default' on the part of the defendant.

An order for summary judgment will prevent the opponent from having 'his day in court' and would therefore potentially be a breach of Art. 6 of the ECHR; the court's powers are therefore strictly controlled and it will only make the order when the criteria for it are precisely met. Unless the strict criteria have been met, the court *cannot* make an order for summary judgment. In these situations, the court does, however, have the power to make lesser orders (see paragraph 14.3.5.2).

Any judgment or order made that denies a party a trial of the issues contravenes the basic core principle of domestic law and human rights. But this right is not an absolute one: the courts will frequently require the party who wishes to avoid an order for summary judgment against them to show that they have a claim or a defence with 'real prospects'—and that there is 'no other compelling reason' why the matter should be heard at a trial. Article 6 of the ECHR does not say that every piece of evidence must be tested at trial. The fact remains, however, that in any situation in which an injustice may occur, the court must be careful to ensure that due regard is given to these points before refusing a party a right to a 'fair hearing'. The CPR seek to embrace these issues. But the courts have limited scope to make an order that could breach the human right to a fair trial. This arises most clearly in applications for summary judgment. There will be occasions in applications for summary judgment on which the court can only make an order that is, in reality, a compromise—a balancing act, ensuring that cases are dealt with efficiently, but also fairly.

There is an advantage in a successful application for summary judgment in that it secures a quick determination of the action. But the disadvantages of a failed application must also be borne in mind. An application for summary judgment that has failed may, in addition to the likelihood of bearing an adverse costs order (these can be substantial and will be payable promptly), also result in delays, because until the application has been heard, further progress of the action is suspended.

14.3.2 WHEN IS SUMMARY JUDGMENT USED?

CPR 24 sets out the procedure when the court may make a decision on a claim or a particular issue without the delay and expense of trial. This has the benefit of precluding a claim that has no real merit proceeding to trial. It may apply at the same time as an application to strike out under CPR 3.4. Sometimes a combined application can be made under both CPR 3.4 and CPR 24. It is worth making a note of the differences between CPR 3.4 (applications to strike out a claim) and CPR 24.2 (applications for summary judgment).

CPR 3.4 provides that a claim, or part of a claim, may be struck out when:

- the statement of case discloses no reasonable grounds for bringing or defending the claim; or
- the statement of case is an abuse of the court's processes; or
- where there has been a failure to comply with a rule, Practice Direction (PD), or order.

CPR 24.2 provides that the court may grant summary judgment against a claimant or a defendant (for all or part of a claim) when:

- the claimant has no real prospect of succeeding on the claim or issue; or
- the defendant has no real prospect of successfully defending the claim or issue; and
- in respect of either of the grounds above, there is no other compelling reason why the case should be disposed of at trial.

In an application for summary judgment, the court may strike out the claim or defence if it is so weak on the facts that it will not succeed.

There is clearly an overlap between the two provisions, but the substance for each is not identical. Although there will be situations in which a combined application can be made, this will not always be the case and the practitioner must not assume that an application for summary judgment should always be conjoined with an application to strike out, or vice versa.

 Practical Considerations

If a combined application is being made, then the general requirements for any interim application set out in Chapter 13, paragraph 13.4 will apply, and the exact wording of each provision will have to be stated and the evidence submitted to establish both applications. The witness statement supporting a combined application will need to show, for example, both that a statement of case discloses no reasonable grounds for bringing or defending the claim (CPR 3), and also that there is no real prospect of successfully defending the claim or issue and that there is no other compelling reason why the case should be disposed of at trial (CPR 24). A failure to address the exact requirements of both CPR 3 and 24 will result in a failure of that part of the application not complied with.

14.3.3 THE PROCEDURE FOR SUMMARY JUDGMENT

An application for summary judgment is one of the interim applications the procedure of which is neatly contained in a part of the CPR designed specifically for that interim application. In this case, procedure is set out in CPR 24.4, which includes provisions that:

- either party can make the application, although it may not be made by the defendant until the claimant has served his particulars of claim, and the defendant has served either his acknowledgement of service or his defence;
- if the claimant has failed to comply with any Pre-Action Protocol, an application for summary judgment by the claimant will not usually be entertained by the court until after the defence has been filed or the time for doing so has expired (in the latter situation, the application will often be an application for default judgment rather than summary judgment);
- if the application is made by the claimant on the defendant lodging his acknowledgement of service and before the defence is filed, then the defendant need not file his defence until after the hearing of the summary judgment application;

The written evidence supporting the application must comply with PD 25B.2.1 and include details of:

- the sum of money sought;

- the items or matters in respect of which the payment is sought;

- an estimate of the likely sum of any final judgment (and reports that support that estimate, such as medical reports, should be exhibited);

- the reasons why the application meets the requirements of CPR 25.7;

- any other relevant matters;

- in claims for personal injury, details of the special damages, and past and future loss, and in a claim under the Fatal Accidents Act 1976, details of the person(s) on whose behalf the claim is made and the nature of the claim; and

- a costs schedule in Form N260 must be filed 24 hours before the hearing.

 Practical Considerations

Applications for an interim payment may, when it is appropriate to do so, be combined with an application for summary judgment. For example, where a claimant has sought, and obtained, summary judgment in a claim for personal injuries and for damages to be assessed at a later hearing, it would be an advantage to the claimant to seek an interim payment pending the assessment hearing. The application for an interim payment would then proceed immediately after a successful (or partially successful) application for summary judgment. Where this is done, care should be taken when indicating the time estimate for the hearing to allow sufficient time for the application to deal with both interim applications.

As this section has stated, the evidence supporting an application for an interim payment will usually be in the form of a witness statement. Please see the Online Resource for the witness statement for Andrew Pike. For applications that are made under the grounds set out at CPR 25.7.1(a) and (b), the main emphasis of the witness statement will be to set out how the particular ground being relied on applies (that is, to state the admission or judgment) and then continue with the most up-to-date evidence to support the damages claim, so that the district judge can consider the sum of the award that he wishes to make and ensure that he does not award too much.

For applications made under the grounds set out at CPR 25.7.1(c) and (e), there is a risk that the claimant may fail in his case, so in these circumstances, the witness statement will need to state arguments that directly address the district judge's concern not to make an award when failure by the claimant is a real possibility, as well as contain detail and evidence of the damages claim.

Chapter 17, paragraph 17.4 sets out further guidance on the form of witness statements.

14.4.4 ORDERS THAT MAY BE MADE IN AN APPLICATION FOR AN INTERIM PAYMENT

14.4.4.1 How much can be awarded?

The court must not make an award of an interim payment that is more than a reasonable proportion of the likely amount of the final judgment (CPR 25.7.4). In assessing the sum to award, the court must take account of contributory negligence, as well as any set-off or counterclaim (CPR 25.7.5).

In *Fiona Jordan and Philippe Jordan v Dean Geason (No 2)* [2007] EWHC 2270, the Technology and Construction Court (TCC) set out some relevant guidelines to consider the amount of an interim payment award. These include:

- a consideration of a sum that was just and would not exceed a reasonable proportion of the estimated final judgment award (in this case, the TCC awarded an interim payment approximately 15 per cent below the sum sought by the claimant);

- the claimant's ability to repay the sum, as well as the financial position of the defendant to make a payment (a provision that is only likely to have any real significance in interim payments made under CPR 25.7.1(c)); and

- the court should not be overly (or at all) concerned with the claimant's 'need' for the money, nor should it be concerned with what the claimant intends to do with the money.

 Practical Considerations

It would be a very brave applicant, making his application under CPR 25.7.1(c), who did not seek to add weight to his application by setting out what the money was needed for and how it might ultimately benefit the claimant. Equally, if it can be shown that an interim payment now might have the outcome of assisting the claimant's recovery and might help to reduce the sum of the final award, it would be prudent to include such evidence.

14.4.4.2 Can payments by instalment be ordered?

The court has the power to make an interim payment award payable by instalment under CPR 25.6.7, and where such an order is made, the order should contain:

- details of the total sum awarded;

- the amount of each instalment;

- the number of instalments; and

- to whom the payments should be made.

14.4.4.3 Social Security benefit payments

In the making of an interim payment award in a personal injury claim, the defendant should notify the court of any sum that is to be deducted under the Social Security (Recovery of Benefits) Act 1997. These are amounts that the claimant has received in respect of certain benefits, such as statutory sick pay. Any amount of an interim payment will be net of those (relevant) benefits that the claimant has received and with the relevant sum so deducted being repaid. The defendant will do this by obtaining a 'certificate of recoverable benefits' and filing this at court before or at the hearing of the application. (For further detail of the operation of the CRU see Chapter 7, paragraph 7.6.3.3.1.)

14.5 AN APPLICATION FOR SPECIFIC DISCLOSURE

Note: This section should be read in conjunction with Chapter 16 and Chapter 8, paragraph 8.7.

14.5.1 WHAT IS 'SPECIFIC DISCLOSURE'?

The purpose of disclosure generally is to make available documents that either support or undermine the respective parties' cases. It is designed to maintain the 'all the cards on the table' approach to litigation. As part of its management role, the court will usually make an order for standard disclosure (see Chapter 16, paragraph 16.4.1). The court can also order that certain specific documents, or classes of document, are disclosed, or it may order that further specific searches are conducted where there is evidence that a party is in breach of its disclosure obligations. The underlying purpose of specific disclosure is to ensure that justice is done between the parties and to avoid a situation in which a party may have, or obtain, an unfair advantage, or suffer an unfair disadvantage as a result of a document not being produced for inspection under standard disclosure.

Under PD 31.5.5(1)(b), the court can make a specific disclosure order requiring a party to disclose, or to search for and disclose, documents that:

- 'it is reasonable to suppose may contain information' that will assist the applicant's case or damage the respondent's case; or
- 'which may lead to a train of enquiry which has either of those consequences'.

Where a party believes that another party's disclosure is inadequate, he can apply to the court for an order for specific disclosure under CPR 31.12(1).

14.5.2 WHEN CAN AN APPLICATION FOR SPECIFIC DISCLOSURE BE MADE?

An application for specific disclosure is usually made after standard disclosure under CPR 31.5 has taken place. However, it may be made before service of the list of documents (CPR 31.12—see *Dayman v Canyon Holdings* (unreported, 11 January 2006, Ch D)). This will be subject to the specific procedural requirements in each track and any specific requirements in each of the divisions of the High Court.

14.5.3 APPLICATIONS AT A LATE STAGE OF PROCEEDINGS

There is no reason why the court will not order specific disclosure even a couple of weeks before trial, or even at trial, provided that it can be shown that the likely significance of the specific disclosure sought is substantial, the cost of complying is not disproportionate, and compliance with the order is within the capabilities of the respondent to the application even at a late stage in the proceedings (*Legal & General Assurance Society Ltd v Taulke-Johnson* [2002] EWHC 120).

14.5.4 IN WHAT CIRCUMSTANCES IS THE COURT LIKELY TO MAKE AN ORDER?

Under CPR 31.12, the court may make an order for specific disclosure if the court believes that the disclosure given has been inadequate (PD 31.5.1). 'Inadequate' has not been precisely defined, but it may arise when:

- it is clear on the face of the opponent's list of documents that it is inadequate—for example, if there are gaps in dates in a list of chronological documents;
- important documents that are known to exist, or to have existed, have not been disclosed;
- it is apparent that the search undertaken by the opponent was inadequate—for example, if there are documents that fall into a specific category, or which were created before or after a certain date that were not searched for, but which you believe support your case or adversely affect your opponent;
- documents are referred to in a statement of case, but not provided following a request under CPR 31.14;
- documents are referred to in correspondence, but are not included;
- documents to which your client or your potential witnesses have referred as existing, but which do not appear in the list;
- the disclosure statement is limited in a way that would mean that relevant documents would not be disclosed—for example, where your opponent objects to you inspecting on the grounds of proportionality and you believe that inspection would be proportionate; or
- there appear to be documents set out in your opponent's list in the section withheld from inspection on the grounds of privilege, but which you believe may not be privileged (see Chapter 16, paragraph 16.9).

It should be remembered that standard disclosure is not now the norm in multi-track non-PI claims. These claims will apply the 'menu option' approach to disclosure. It is yet to be seen whether this will result in fewer applications for specific disclosure made in these actions.

Practical Considerations

Was the opponent's search unreasonably limited? Look carefully at the disclosure statement. Was it unreasonable to exclude documents pre or post a certain date, or in a certain category?

Remember also that the disclosure obligation is a continuing one. Documents that may have come to light after your opponent has served his list of documents still need to be disclosed. In practice, the list of documents is amended mutually. If the documents are not forthcoming, then an application for specific disclosure may follow.

14.5.5 WHAT WILL THE COURT ORDER?

Under CPR 31.12(2), if an order for specific disclosure is granted, the court may order a party to do one or more of the following:

- disclose documents or classes of documents specified in the order;
- carry out a search to the extent specified in the order;
- disclose any documents located as a result of that search.

However, in deciding whether to grant an order, the court will (under PD 31.5.4):

Take into account all the circumstances of the case and, in particular, the overriding objectives. But if the court concludes that the party from whom specific disclosure is sought has failed adequately to comply with the obligations imposed by an order for disclosure (whether by failing to make a sufficient search for documents or otherwise) the court will usually make such order as is necessary to ensure that those obligations are properly complied with.

14.5.6 THE FORM OF AN ORDER FOR SPECIFIC DISCLOSURE

Under CPR 31.12, the court may order specific disclosure by ordering a party to:

- prepare a supplemental list of documents, specifying the documents available for inspection;
- give disclosure of specific documents, or a specific class of documents;
- carry out a new specified search and disclose documents revealed by that search.

14.5.7 'FISHING EXPEDITIONS'

When you have a belief that documents exist, but have no substantive evidence, your application for specific disclosure may be more akin to a 'fishing expedition' (that is, a search undertaken only in the hope that the documents will show up). This is known as the '*Peruvian Guano* test' (after *Compagnie Financière du Pacifique v Peruvian Guano Co* (1882) 11 QBD 55).

PD 31.5.5(1) provides that, in appropriate cases, the court may direct a party to carry out a search for documents that may:

(a) enable the party applying for disclosure either to advance his own case or to damage that of the party giving disclosure; or

(b) lead to a train of enquiry which has either of those consequences.

Under the CPR and the definition applied to 'standard disclosure', the ability to insist on a search that could lead to relevant, but as yet unknown, documents being discovered was effectively removed. However, because of the grounds set out in PD 31.5, the ability to seek 'train of enquiry' disclosure can be made in an application for specific disclosure. As always, such an application would need to be justified under the principles of the overriding objective, and be 'fair', 'just', and 'proportionate'.

Documents that need not be disclosed on a standard basis may well be disclosable on a specific disclosure order, which can extend the duty to 'a train of enquiry'.

Practical Considerations

The alternative order, for an expedited trial, needs to be considered with care, as it can leave the parties with the problem of preparing for a speedy trial which may not always be the best option.

KEY POINTS SUMMARY

- An interim application must comply precisely with the rule providing for it.

- The evidence supporting an interim application should, wherever possible, be given added 'weight' by the inclusion of material evidence.

- All interim applications must be justified within the terms of the overriding objective.

- Nearly all interim applications should be preceded with an informal request.

- Most interim applications that are listed for less than one hour will be heard by way of a telephone conference call.

- Interim applications, such as setting aside, default judgment, and summary judgment, are significant and important applications, because they can bring an end to proceedings if successfully defended or made. Make sure that your evidence is accurate, articulate, and persuasive.

- Always discuss the purpose of making or defending an application with your client, as well as the prospect of success, and costs incurred and/or recoverable.

- Ensure that you have specific instructions to proceed to make or oppose the application.

- Interim injunction applications carry severe risks and penalties if wrongly sought. Clients need to be fully aware of these responsibilities.

- Parties will need to file a costs schedule in Form N260 24 hours before any hearing.

Case Study *Andrew James Pike v Deep Builders Ltd*

Question 1

You have a witness statement of Andrew Pike dated 17 November 201? and an application notice dated 20 November 201?. You have also received a draft order and case summary. Assume that it is now 20 November 201?, and that the partner supervising the case has instructed you to attend to service of, and preparation for, this application. Consider the following:

- the purpose of this application and witness statement;

- the formalities relating to the making of the application, such as when and how you will serve the application;

- whether the statement is either necessary or adequate in terms of its compliance with any formalities and its substantive contents;

- determine whether the application complies with the requirements of the CPR and PD;

- what other preparations you would make for the hearing and what you would expect to be the outcome of the hearing.

Question 2

Assume that you are acting for the defendant in this matter. For the purposes of this stage, you are a legal representative with Rasputin & Co, and you have just received the application and witness statement. Your instructions from the insurer of the defendant are to resist the application with a view to ensuring that the claimant's application is refused or that any payment ordered is as small as possible. John Deep has told you that, at the time of the accident, he may have had 'a pint or two at lunchtime', and that he may possibly have been in a hurry to get to an appointment and so drove 'a little over the speed limit'. However, he is adamant that he was not over the centre lines and points out that he passed a breathalyser test. The accident was, in his view, the fault of the claimant, who was over the centre lines.

Draft a short witness statement to resist the application.

Question 3

What would happen at the hearing—for example, who would be present, in what order would things happen, and what matters may be discussed, apart from simply whether or not an order for a payment would be made? If you were to be present, what would you need to do at the end of the hearing and following the hearing?

What document will have been lodged at court (and served on your opponent) at least 24 hours before the hearing? What is the purpose of this document?

Case Study *Bollingtons Ltd v Mrs Elizabeth Lynch t/a The Honest Lawyer*

Question 1

You now have instructions to pursue the matter privately for Mrs Lynch. You have informed her that the judgment was entered correctly, but have advised that it will be necessary to apply to have judgment set aside if she wishes to defend the claim. What documentation will you need to prepare? Prepare the documents that you believe are appropriate for this type of application. If you believe that a defence is necessary, then, for the purposes of this exercise, you do not need to draft a defence, but you may wish to refer to one if you think that, in making the application, you would have prepared one.

Question 2

Consider the prospects of success of the defendant's application and the likely costs orders.

---

online resource centre

Any documents referred to in these case study questions can be found on the Online Resource Centre—simply click on 'Case study documentation' to access the documents that you need for Chapter 14 and to be reminded of the questions. Suggested answers to these case study questions can also be accessed on the Online Resource Centre when released to you by your lecturer.

15 PART 36 OFFERS

> Relevant parts of the CPR and its PDs: 36, 44, and 45

15.1 INTRODUCTION

Offers to settle pervade the practice of dispute resolution and litigation. Whilst this chapter is self-contained, the proactive legal representative should constantly be aware that it may be appropriate to make an offer to settle at any time.

ADR considerations

You should read Chapter 5 in conjunction with this chapter, on the basis that offers to settle may form part of the negotiation spectrum—usually as the first step in attempting to settle a claim.

It is extremely rare that a dispute is resolved or proceeds to trial without some type of offer being made. There does not, however, appear to be a limit on the number of offers that can be made, although credibility and common sense would indicate that offers to settle should be made purposefully, but not irrationally.

Over the years, Part 36 has undergone a number of revisions. In April 2015 the whole of Part 36 was revised to codify some of the more significant decisions of the court and

LITIGATION TRAIN: PART 36 OFFERS AND CONCLUDING A CLAIM

These are potential key points when P36 offers and/or ADR should be considered in an action.

its own automatic withdrawal at a certain date, rather than wait until the expiry of the relevant period and then withdraw it. The downside of including such a provision is that, if the offer is not accepted within the time stipulated, it will not have the consequences of Part 36 once it is withdrawn (CPR 36.17(7)).

- If a Part 36 offer is varied to make it *more advantageous* to the offeree, the original offer does not have to be withdrawn and the revised offer will be treated as the new offer (CPR 36.9(5)). The implications of this are twofold: firstly, if both the original offer and the revised offer turn out to be effective, the costs consequences will run from the first offer. Secondly, there will be a new relevant period when the revised offer is made.

 Example

If a defendant makes a Part 36 offer in the sum of £20,000 on 1 March with a relevant period for acceptance of 22 March and then on 1 June makes an improved offer of £25,000, the offer of £20,000 does not need to be withdrawn and there will be a new relevant period starting from 1 June. Further, if the claimant only secures £19,000 at trial then the costs consequences will run from 23 March.

Withdrawing or amending offers within the relevant period: If the offeree has not served a notice of acceptance and the offeror serves a notice of withdrawal of a Part 36 offer or of a change in its terms to make it *less advantageous* to the offeree before the end of the relevant period, then at the end of the relevant period:

- If the offeree has not served notice of acceptance of the offer in the meantime, the offeror's notice will take effect.

- If the offeree has served notice of acceptance, that acceptance will take effect unless the offeror applies for permission to withdraw the offer or change its terms within seven days of the offeree's notice, or before the first day of the trial, if earlier. The court will only grant permission if satisfied that there has been a change of circumstances and that it is in the interests of justice.

Withdrawing or amending offers outside the relevant period: The offeror can withdraw or amend the offer in writing to make it *less advantageous* to the offeree outside the relevant period without the court's permission, provided, of course, that the offeree has not accepted it in writing (CPR 36.10(4)). However, it is important to remember the provisions of CPR 36.9(5) discussed at the beginning of this section in relation to amending an offer to make it more advantageous: there is no requirement to withdraw that offer.

Please also note that if a Part 36 offer is withdrawn either within or outside the relevant period, then it will not have the usual Part 36 cost consequences (CPR 36.17(7)).

 Practical Considerations

In practice, the decision to withdraw a Part 36 offer is mostly case specific. However, tactics can play a large part in this decision. The withdrawal of a Part 36 offer is often done to put additional pressure on the opponent, as this can have the effect of altering the 'position of power' in negotiations. The withdrawal can be read as a signal that the party withdrawing the offer is taking the bolder negotiating position. Offers can always be 're-made', but clear client instructions would need to be taken if an offer is to be withdrawn. The dangers of leaving a Part 36 offer open for acceptance can be seen in the 'Professional Conduct' box. Best practice would suggest that all Part 36 offers are kept under close review at all times.

There are, however, provisions set out in CPR 36.11(3) and(4) in which, in specific circumstances, a Part 36 offer can only be accepted with the permission of the court. Perhaps the most significant one is where the trial is in progress (CPR 36.11(3)(d)).

 Professional Conduct

When making a Part 36 offer, make a diary note of when the relevant period expires. Consider with each offer made—both at this stage and periodically through to trial—whether the offer should be withdrawn.

By way of example, consider the situation in which you have been instructed to make, and have made, an offer on behalf of the claimant in a high-value personal injury claim based on a medical report. The relevant period elapses and the offer is not accepted. You do not withdraw or amend it. The litigation continues and, shortly before trial, you seek a supplemental report from your expert, which indicates that the claim for pain and suffering is more extensive than originally thought in the first report. The supplemental report is disclosed and, tactically, you make an increased Part 36 offer to reflect the greater damages potential recovery. The defendant accepts by letter the first offer, because it had not been withdrawn. This places you in potential conflict with your client.

The application of the costs consequences of a Part 36 offer has always been complex and this very complexity accounts for the vast amount of case law. There are two positions when the court will consider the application of an adverse costs consequence where an offer has been made:

- for a fully Part 36-compliant offer, Part 36 cost consequences will be enforced automatically, unless the court considers it unjust to do so;

- for any other offer, the residual discretion of CPR 44.2 can be applied.

Much of the next section is devoted to the provisions of CPR 36 generally. At this juncture we should highlight the fact that certain types of personal injury claims noted in paragraph 15.10 have their own specific rules in relation to Part 36 cost consequences and these should be noted separately.

15.7 **CLAIMANT OFFERS**

This section discusses what happens when a defendant receives a Part 36 offer made by a claimant. There are some helpful flowcharts at the end of this chapter to assist in the understanding of these complex rules.

15.7.1 **THE PROCEDURE AND COST IMPLICATIONS OF ACCEPTING THE CLAIMANT'S OFFER**

15.7.1.1 Procedure

Once the decision has been made by the defendant to accept the Part 36 offer, as stated in paragraph 15.6.1, this is simply done by letter or the notice of acceptance attached to the N242A. If proceedings have not yet been issued, then the defendant notifies the claimant in writing and the parties proceed to comply with the terms of the Part 36 offer. If proceedings have been issued, then the defendant sends a notice of acceptance, usually in letter form, to the claimant and files a copy with the court. The claim is then automatically stayed (CPR 36.14(1)).

The Part 36 offer and subsequent acceptance may not have been in respect of the whole claim, and any subsequent stay would therefore only affect the part of proceedings to which the Part 36 offer related (CPR 36.14(3)).

15.7.1.2 Cost Implications

By accepting the Part 36 offer within the relevant period, the defendant is liable to pay the claimant's costs up until the date on which the letter accepting the Part 36 offer is served on the claimant (CPR 36.13(1)). The claimant has an automatic entitlement to these costs, which are assessed on the standard basis (CPR 44.3(2) explains what this means).

So what happens if the defendant decides that he wants to accept the Part 36 offer, but outside the relevant period? CPR 36.13(4)(b) provides that the parties can try to agree liability for costs, but in the absence of agreement, the court must decide the liability for costs. CPR 36.13(5) further states that the court will decide, unless it is unjust, the following in relation to those costs: that the defendant pays the claimant's costs up until the end of the relevant period and the offeree—in this case, the defendant—will be liable for the claimant's costs incurred thereafter on the standard basis. In considering what is 'unjust' the court must take into account the factors listed in CPR 36.17(5).

15.7.2 THE PROCEDURE AND COST IMPLICATIONS OF REJECTING THE CLAIMANT'S OFFER

15.7.2.1 Procedure

If the defendant decides that he does not wish to accept the claimant's offer, he merely notifies the claimant in writing or simply fails to respond to the offer. The rejection of the offer by the defendant does not have the effect of withdrawing the offer. This can only be done by the claimant and must be done expressly by letter or notice. If this is not done, the offer will remain open for acceptance indefinitely.

 Practical Considerations

There is no requirement to give reasons for the rejection and it is unhelpful when the opponent simply fails to respond to the offer at all, although practically, to encourage further negotiation, there is no reason why the claimant cannot be informed of the reason for the rejection. It is in circumstances such as these that a without-prejudice chat over the telephone with the claimant's legal representative may be worthwhile. However, any proactive practitioner should be considering a Part 36 counter offer and alternative dispute resolution (ADR) when an offer is not acceptable.

15.7.2.2 Cost implications

The cost consequences for a defendant of rejecting a claimant's Part 36 offer are different from those of a claimant rejecting a defendant's Part 36 offer.

The current position is outlined at CPR 36.17(4), as follows. Where the defendant rejects the claimant's offer made more than 21 days before trial and the matter eventually proceeds to trial, if the claimant is successful and is awarded a sum that is the same or greater than his Part 36 offer, then the claimant is entitled to:

- interest on all or part of the damages, awarded at an enhanced rate of up to 10 per cent above base rate for some or all of the period from the date upon which the Part 36 offer's relevant period expired to the end of the trial;

- his costs, in respect of the period from the date on which the relevant period expired, to be assessed on the indemnity basis rather than the standard basis; and

- interest on those costs at an enhanced rate of up to 10 per cent above base rate.

If the claimant failed to equal or beat his own offer at trial, the costs will be decided in the usual way, in accordance with CPR 44.2. This would therefore make a claimant offer 'non-effective', save for being taken into account in a party's general conduct in an action.

15.7.2.3 Penalty damages

A payment of an additional amount of damages to a successful claimant also now forms part of the Part 36 regime in CPR 36.17(4)(d). These damages are based on percentages, which will be discussed shortly, and are payable in the following circumstances:

- the claimant has made a valid CPR 36 offer;

- the defendant has not accepted the offer; and

- the court has given judgment for the claimant which is 'at least as advantageous to the claimant as the claimant's offer'.

These new additional sanctions are calculated based on whether the claim is a damages-only claim, a mixture of monetary and non-monetary claims, or a non-monetary claim.

15.7.2.3.1 *Damages-only or mixed claims*

The amount to be paid by the defendant will be calculated as a percentage of the damages awarded to the claimant, as shown in Table 15.1.

TABLE 15.1 DAMAGES-ONLY OR MIXED CLAIMS

Amount awarded by the court	Prescribed percentage
Up to £500,000	Up to 10% of the amount awarded
Above £500,000	Up to 10% of the first £500,000 and 5% of the amount awarded above that figure

15.7.2.3.2 *Non-monetary claims*

In a non-monetary claim only the amount to be paid by the defendant will be calculated as a percentage of the costs ordered to be paid to the claimant, as shown in Table 15.2.

TABLE 15.2 NON-MONETARY CLAIMS

Costs ordered to be paid to the claimant	Amount to be paid by the defendant
Up to £500,000	Up to 10% of the costs ordered to be paid
Above £500,000	Up to 10% of the first £500,000 and 5% of any costs ordered to be paid above that figure

In these circumstances the amount to be paid is also subject to a cap of £75,000.

It is therefore interesting to note that in damages-only and mixed damages cases, the additional payment is likely to be received when the main damages payment is made to the claimant, whereas in non-monetary cases, the additional sanction is unlikely to be received until either costs have been agreed or formally assessed. This is usually sometime after the final hearing.

 Example

The claimant in an action for breach of contract made a Part 36 offer on 1 April in the sum of £75,000 shortly after the defence was filed. The defendant rejected the Part 36 offer and proceeded to a two-day trial on 1 December. Judgment was given to the claimant in the sum of £80,000. The claimant is therefore entitled to costs and interest as follows:

- Costs on the standard basis from date of first instruction to 22 April

- Costs on the indemnity basis from 22 April to 2 December

- Interest on £80,000 from 22 April to 2 December at up to 10 per cent above base rate

- An additional £8000 in damages

- Interest on costs from 22 April at 10 per cent above base rate

15.8 DEFENDANT OFFERS

This section discusses what happens when a claimant receives a Part 36 offer made by a defendant. There are also some helpful flowcharts at the end of this chapter to assist in the understanding of these complex rules.

15.8.1 THE PROCEDURE AND COST IMPLICATIONS OF ACCEPTING THE DEFENDANT'S OFFER

15.8.1.1 Procedure

Generally, where a claimant decides that he wants to accept a Part 36 offer made by a defendant, the procedure is the same as that set out in paragraph 15.7.1.1.

Where the Part 36 offer made by the defendant includes an offer to pay a single sum of money, in addition to there being a stay of proceedings, on acceptance of the lump sum, the defendant is obliged to pay the sum accepted directly to the claimant within 14 days of the date of acceptance (CPR 36.14(6)), failing which the claimant is entitled to enter judgment.

The parties can agree—usually in writing—an alternative time limit for payment of the monies, but the significant feature of this arrangement is that if the lump sum is not paid over to the claimant within the stipulated time frame, the claimant may enter judgment for the unpaid sum.

Where there are multiple defendants to an action and the claimant wishes to accept a Part 36 offer from one of them, the claimant needs to seek the court's permission to accept. CPR 36.15 sets out the criteria that the court will consider in granting permission, based on the nature of the liability of each defendant (joint and several, or just several) to the claimant.

15.8.1.2 Cost implications

The cost implications of a claimant accepting a defendant's offer are the same as those of a defendant accepting a claimant's Part 36 offer (CPR 36.13(5)), as set out at paragraph 15.7.1.2.

 Practical Considerations

There is some merit when acting for a claimant, in terms of adverse cost consequences, to accepting a Part 36 offer within the relevant period if at all possible. The information given to any claimant client when a Part 36 offer is made should include the possibility of adverse cost consequences if the offer is accepted after the relevant period.

15.8.1.3 The creation of a legally binding contract

The Part 36 offer of both a claimant and defendant and the letter of acceptance create a contractually binding arrangement between the parties. Consequently, should the receiving party not abide by the agreement, then it can be enforced within the same set of proceedings without having to go to the time and expense of issuing fresh proceedings on the breach of that agreement. The procedure is even simpler where there is a defendant offering a lump sum, as has been highlighted in paragraph 15.8.1.1.

15.8.2 THE PROCEDURE AND COST IMPLICATIONS OF REJECTING THE DEFENDANT'S OFFER

15.8.2.1 Procedure

As with paragraph 15.7.2.1, if the claimant wishes to reject the defendant's Part 36 offer, this is simply done in writing, and unless the defendant expressly withdraws the offer, it is open for acceptance at any time.

15.8.2.2 Cost implications

If the claimant makes the decision to reject the defendant's offer and proceed to trial, but fails to secure a judgment that is more advantageous than the defendant's Part 36 offer—that is, if the judgment is for an amount less than or equal to the Part 36 offer—then the court has a discretion to make the following orders unless it is unjust to do so (CPR 36.17(3)):

• award the defendant his costs on the standard basis from the date upon which the relevant period has expired; and

• award interest on those costs.

It is important to note here that the claimant has to do better than the Part 36 offer. What this means is that if the defendant offered £20,000 and the claimant rejected this, but at trial was only awarded £20,000, then the court may invoke the costs and interest penalties. Compare this to the situation in paragraph 15.7.2.2, in which the defendant rejects the claimant's Part 36 offer: in that case, the claimant only has to achieve a sum that is the same or greater. So if it was the claimant who had offered £20,000 and the defendant who rejected the same, and at trial the judgment of £20,000 was still made, the court has the discretion to award the costs penalties set out in CPR 36.17(4).

If the claimant beats the defendant's offer, even by the smallest of margins, then his costs will be decided in the usual way, in accordance with CPR 44.2. This would therefore mean that the defendant's offer has been 'non-effective', save for being taken into account in a party's general conduct in an action.

15.8.2.3 How can the court decide if a Part 36 offer has been beaten?

In many cases, due to the difference in the amount offered and the amount recovered at trial, the fact that a Part 36 offer has been beaten will be apparent. However, in cases in which it is a closer call—usually in unspecified sum claims—it may not be so easily ascertainable whether an offer has been truly beaten. This is usually either because the amount recovered in comparison to the offer is negligible (see paragraph 15.9 for a further discussion on this), or because of the interest awarded.

Remember that Part 36 offers are inclusive of interest and this is where the difficulty can sometimes lie. If this is the case, you may need to calculate the interest that would have accrued on the sum awarded at trial from the date on which the interest became payable up until the last date for acceptance of the Part 36 offer. Once calculated, you will need to add this to the amount of judgment and assess whether the sum awarded at trial is more or less than the amount of the Part 36 offer.

15.8.2.4 Part 36 and conditional fee agreements in non-personal injury cases (CFAs)

Consider the situation in which your claimant client, operating under a conditional fee agreement (CFA) with a success fee (either before or after 1 April 2013) and after the event (ATE) insurance, rejects a defendant's Part 36 offer and, at trial, is awarded less than the offer. In accordance with CPR 36.17(3), unless it is unjust to do so, the claimant will probably be ordered to pay the defendant's costs from the end of the relevant period to trial. It would follow that the claimant would pay his own costs for that period too and if the CFA post-dates 1 April 2013, then the claimant will have to pay the success fee and the ATE premium himself, not just for that period, but for the whole action.

Two issues arise here: firstly, because the claimant has ATE in respect of an adverse cost order, he will not be required to find the funds to pay the defendant, because his ATE insurers will pay—but, secondly, who will pay the claimant's own costs for that period? Unless the claimant purchased ATE to protect against him paying his own costs in this situation (which is unusual and expensive), the claimant will be responsible for payment of these to his legal representative in accordance with the terms of the CFA. This is because the CFA only stipulates 'no win, no fee' if the claimant fails to recover damages, but in this case, he has done so: he has just failed to beat a Part 36 offer.

Practical Considerations

As a practitioner, you will need to discuss this with your client, because the usual terms of CFAs allow the legal representative to use his discretion as to whether to claim back these base costs.

15.9 HOW THE COURT EXERCISES ITS DISCRETION ON COSTS IN 'UNBEATEN' PART 36 OFFERS AT TRIAL

It is important to remember that all costs awards made by the court, not only those in respect of Part 36 offers, are discretionary and that whilst CPR Part 36 may stipulate cost consequences for rejection of offers, it is for the court to decide whether it wishes to implement those sanctions or not.

Specifically in relation to CPR Part 36, the court will only award the penalties set out in CPR 36.17(3) and (4), unless it is unjust to do so, based on considerations set out in CPR 36.17(5). These are:

- the terms of the Part 36 offer;

- when the offer was made;

- the information available to the parties when the offer was made;

- the conduct of the parties in relation to providing information to enable the offeree to give proper consideration to the offer; and

- whether the offer was a genuine attempt to settle the proceedings.

The courts, in accordance with CPR 36.17(2), will decide whether to award the costs consequences where a claimant fails to obtain a judgment that is more advantageous than a defendant's Part 36 offer, or where judgment against a defendant is at least as advantageous to the claimant as the defendant's Part 36 offer. Sometimes it is not obvious when a Part 36 offer has been beaten, or if it has, by how much. Consequently, there has been a plethora of case law on how the court deals with awarding the costs sanctions in CPR Part 36 and the most noteworthy cases are as follows:

- *AB v CD and Ors* [2011] EWHC 602 (Ch) held that the claimant's purported Part 36 offer was not valid because the offer merely replicated the entirety of the claimant's claim and as such there had been no concession made by the claimant. If the offer were allowed to stand as a Part 36 offer, then every claimant could obtain favourable costs consequences simply by making an offer to settle, requiring total capitulation by the defendant. This was seen as so important that it formed the basis for one of the new Part 36 rules in CPR 36.17(5)(e).

- *Ted Baker Plc and another v AXA Insurance UK Plc and others* [2014] EWHC 4178 sets out what exceptional circumstances could be in deciding whether it was unjust to displace the general rule in CPR 36.17 where the overall result was that the claimants had failed to beat the defendant's Part 36 offers. The circumstances included the defendant's approach to the central issue, which left no stone unturned and increased costs hugely. The court also commented that the fact that a defendant may make a Part 36 offer did not give him 'carte blanche' to run any defence whatsoever so as to entitle him to expect that the Part 36 consequences would automatically apply.

- The case of *Bellway Homes Ltd v Seymour (Civil Engineering Contractors) Ltd* [2013] EWHC 1890 (TCC) held that due to all the circumstances of the case, it would be unjust to invoke the cost consequences under CPR 36.14(2) because the parties had not constructively engaged in settlement negotiations in a messy building dispute and had pursued a pointless litigation.

The case of *RXDX v Northhampton BC* [2015] EWHC 2938 (QB) has confirmed the correct application of 'unless it considers it unjust' in CPR 36.17(4), concluding that the court is entitled to consider for each of the separate sub-paragraphs, whether its application would be unjust in the circumstances of the case.

It should perhaps be mentioned here that if either the claimant or defendant to an action make an offer and they do not beat their own offer at trial, then it is of no consequence as far as cost sanctions are concerned.

15.10 PERSONAL INJURY LITIGATION AND PART 36

These provisions are pertinent to certain personal injury claims, but not all. The Rules are very specific and consequently, it would be prudent to review the nature and extent of any personal injury claim you handle in order to ascertain whether any of these Rules apply.

15.10.1 ADDITIONAL REQUIREMENTS TO THE CONTENT OF A PART 36 OFFER

15.10.1.1 Where the claim includes a future pecuniary loss claim (CPR 36.18)

Damages for future pecuniary loss in larger personal injury actions need to be particularized in a Part 36 offer if the offer is to be treated as a Part 36 offer with all the cost consequences that flow from such an offer. These future pecuniary losses are usually expressed to be paid by way of a lump sum, a periodical payment, or a combination of both. In terms of articulating this, the Part 36 offer must explicitly set out the amounts which relate to the lump sum and/or periodical payments, as well as the duration of the periodical payments. In addition, if the offer is accepted, not only must a written acceptance be provided to the opponent, but the claimant must also apply to the court for an order for an award of damages in the form of periodical payments within seven days of accepting the Part 36 offer.

15.10.1.2 Where the claim includes a provisional damages claim (CPR 36.19)

If the claimant's claim also includes a claim for provisional damages, as discussed in Chapter 7 at paragraph 7.6.3.6, a Part 36 offer must specify whether or not the offeror is offering to agree to an award for provisional damages. If this is the case, then the Part 36 offer must detail the damages offered in this regard, the medical conditions which could trigger a further claim, and the period within which the further claim could be made. Again, here, if the Part 36 offer is accepted, the claimant must apply to the court for an order within seven days of acceptance.

15.10.1.3 The CRU and Part 36 (CPR 36.22)

When drafting a Part 36 offer in a personal injury claim, the issue of deductible welfare benefits must be dealt with. For a discussion on the nature of these CRU benefits, see Chapter 7, paragraph 7.6.3.

The Part 36 offer can be made either without regard to any liability for the recoverable benefits (in which case the opponent will pay the benefits in addition), or the Part 36 offer can state that it is intended to include any deductible benefits.

Therefore, the Part 36 offer must state the gross amount of the damages before the CRU benefits are offset, the name and amount of any deductible benefit by which the gross amount is reduced, and the net amount after deduction. This information is essential, as it clarifies the exact figures sought under the Part 36 offer when it comes to ascertaining whether a Part 36 offer has been beaten. The crucial figures to 'beat' are those after the deduction of the benefits, i.e. the net figure offered.

As a final point here, if a claimant accepts a Part 36 offer after the relevant period has expired and the CRU repayment figure has increased (because the claimant has continued to receive a deductible benefit), the court has a discretion to deduct the additional benefits from the net offer.

15.10.1.4 QOCS and Part 36

The advent of QOCS (as discussed in detail in Chapter 4 at paragraph 4.2.3) and other April 2013 changes (such as the non-recovery of success fees and ATE premiums from the defendant) has had a significant impact on personal injury litigation for both claimants and defendants alike. As regards Part 36 offers, the balance continues to be attempted to be redressed, because now CPR 44.14 permits costs orders to be made against a claimant in a personal injury claim, subject to them not being unjust, where that claimant has failed to beat the defendant's offer to settle, including Part 36 offers. The likely costs order to be made will be that the claimant will be required to pay the defendant's costs (an adverse costs order) from the expiry of the offer, as well as paying his own costs. However, the adverse costs order will be capped at the level of damages and interest recovered by the claimant. Legal practitioners are therefore questioning the true benefit of QOCS to these claimants, as most defendants in personal injury actions will at some point make an offer of settlement of some sort, and if this is made early on in the dispute process, there is little comfort to be had from the QOCS regime.

 Example

The defendant in an action for personal injuries made a Part 36 offer on 1 April in the sum of £80,000 shortly after its defence was filed. The claimant rejected the Part 36 offer and proceeded to a 2 day trial on 1 December. The claimant was not funded and had not purchased ATE. Judgment was given to the claimant in the sum of £75,000. The costs and interest order that was made was as follows:

- The claimant was entitled to its costs on the standard basis up to 22 April.

- The claimant was ordered to pay the defendant's costs, as it was held not unjust to do so, from 22 April to 2 December on the standard basis. As the claimant had not purchased ATE the costs payment to the defendant would more than likely come from his £75,000.

- The claimant was ordered to pay his own costs from 22 April to 2 December on the standard basis. As the claimant was privately funding his claim these would have been paid monthly to his legal representative and therefore would not be reimbursed.

The defendant was entitled to interest on its costs at the standard rate of 8 per cent from 22 April onwards.

15.10.1.5 The pre-action protocol claims for low-value RTA, EL, and PL claims

These claims are looked at in Chapter 4 at paragraph 4.7.2 from a general costs perspective, and in Chapter 9 at paragraph 9.2.7 from a procedural perspective.

These processes do not escape the Part 36 regime. Part 36 needs to be considered in light of those claims that remain in the Portal up to and including Stage 3, and those that exit the Portal at an earlier stage.

In relation to those cases that reach Stage 3, CPR 36.25(1) requires the offer to be made to be called a 'Protocol Offer', and it will be a valid Protocol Offer in accordance with CPR 36.25(2) if it is set out in the Court Proceedings Pack (CPP) and contains the final total amount of the offer from both parties exclusive of interest. If the matter proceeds to a final assessment of damages hearing, there are three possible outcomes for the court to consider once the assessment has been made:

- If the claimant is awarded damages that are less than or equal to the defendant's offer, the court will order the claimant to pay the defendant's Stage 3 fixed costs and interest on those costs.

- If the claimant is awarded more than the defendant's offer but less than his own, the court will order the defendant to pay the claimant's fixed costs.

- If the claimant is awarded the same or more than his own offer, the court will order the following:

  - the defendant to pay interest on all of the damages at a rate not exceeding 10 per cent above base rate for some or all of the period, beginning on the date the offer was made;

– the defendant to pay the claimant's fixed costs and interest on those fixed costs at a rate not exceeding 10 per cent above base rate;

– the defendant to pay an additional 10 per cent of the amount awarded.

In relation to claims that exit the Portal, remember that Section III of CPR 45 contains costs provisions on a fixed costs basis, as mentioned in Chapter 4 at paragraph 4.7.2. Part 36 therefore also provides separately for these Protocol claims that have left the Protocol process before Stage 3. The Rules have been drafted to deal with the cost consequences of accepting a Part 36 Offer after leaving the Portal before Stage 3, and the cost consequences of rejecting a Part 36 offer and proceeding to trial.

15.10.1.5.1 *Cost consequences of accepting a Part 36 Offer—CPR 36.21*

These are divided into three different categories as follows:

- If the claimant accepts a Part 36 offer within the relevant period, the claimant is entitled to fixed costs, as set out in Section IIIA of CPR 45, but the level of those fixed costs will depend upon the date the Part 36 offer was accepted in relation to the stage reached in the Table of Fixed Costs in Section IIIA.

- If the claimant accepts the Part 36 offer outside the relevant period, the claimant is entitled to the fixed costs applicable at the date on which the relevant period expired, but the claimant will also be required to pay the defendant's costs from the date of expiry of the relevant period to the date of acceptance.

- If a Protocol Offer was made but only accepted after exiting the Portal, the claimant is entitled to Stages 1 and 2 Protocol fixed costs, but the claimant is also liable for the defendant's costs from the date on which the Protocol Offer was made until the date of acceptance.

15.10.1.5.2 *Cost consequences of a Part 36 Offer after judgment—CPR 36.29*

In these circumstances, the costs order made will depend on when the offer was made as follows:

- If the claimant failed to secure a judgment that was more advantageous than the defendant's Part 36 offer after the claim exited the Portal, the claimant is entitled to the fixed costs for the Stage reached at the point in time the relevant period expired, but the claimant is also required to pay the defendant's costs from the date on which the relevant period expired to the date of judgment.

- If the claimant failed to beat a defendant's Protocol Offer, the claimant is only entitled to Stages 1 and 2 fixed costs, but the claimant is also liable to pay the defendant's costs from the date on which the Protocol Offer was made until the date of judgment.

- If the claimant beats his own Part 36 offer and by virtue of CPR 36.21(1) becomes entitled to the enhancements in CPR 36.17, in particular indemnity costs, the Court of Appeal has recently clarified the position in the case of *Broadhurst and Anor v Tan and Anor* [EWCA] Civ 2016. Previous case law had concluded that the interaction of CPR 45.29A and CPR 36.17 was inconsistent with one case concluding that fixed costs did not apply where indemnity costs had been awarded as a result of the claimant beating his own Part 36 offer, and the other case deciding that costs did apply notwithstanding that the claimant beat his own Part 36 offer at trial. The Court of Appeal has decided that claimants who beat their own Part 36 offers are entitled to indemnity costs. It therefore appears that the provisions of Part 36 override the provisions of Part 45 in this regard.

- It is worth noting here that where the claimant is ordered to pay the defendant's costs as described in this section, these costs cannot exceed the level of fixed costs as set out in Section IIIA of CPR 45.

FIGURE 15.5 A TEMPLATE CLAIMANT PART 36 MONETARY OFFER LETTER

Dear Sirs,

Without prejudice save as to costs—Offer to settle under Part 36

(Heading of matter)

We refer to the above matter in which we act for . . . . Our client is confident that it has a strong case against your client, ..., and is entitled to substantial damages, [as set out in its particulars of claim OR as set out in correspondence OR for the reasons set out below]. Nevertheless, our client is [keen to resolve this matter amicably OR mindful that under the Civil Procedure Rules litigants are expected to try to resolve their disputes whenever possible]. We are, therefore, authorised by our client to make the following offer to settle under Part 36.

This Offer is intended to have the consequences set out in Part 36 of the Civil Procedure Rules. In particular, your client will be liable for our client's costs up to the date of notice of acceptance which must be in writing in accordance with CPR 36.10, if the offer is accepted within . . . . (the relevant period).

TERMS OF THE OFFER

Our client is willing to settle [the whole of the claim referred to above OR specify which part of the claim or issue the client is willing to settle] on the following terms:

- Your client to pay our client, within [14 or such other number as client is willing to accept] days of accepting this Offer, the sum of £ . . . . by [means of payment—e.g. electronic transfer] into [give account details] or [set out precise terms of offer in a non-money claim].

- This Offer [takes OR does not take] account of your client's counterclaim [or/and any other claims your client may have against ours] in this matter.

- The settlement sum does not include costs and, as mentioned above, your client will be liable to pay our client's costs on the standard basis, to be assessed if not agreed, up to the date of service of notice of acceptance if this Offer is accepted within the relevant period.

- The settlement sum is inclusive of interest until the relevant period has expired. Thereafter, interest at a rate of . . . .% p.a. will be added.

FAILURE TO ACCEPT THIS OFFER

If your client does not accept this Offer, and our client obtains a judgment which is equal to or more advantageous than this Offer, our client intends to rely on CPR 36.17. In other words, our client will be seeking an order in the following terms:

- Your client to pay our client's costs up to the expiry of the relevant period.

- Your client to pay our client's costs on the indemnity basis from the date on which the relevant period expired, with interest on those costs of up to 10% above base rate and interest on the whole or part of any sum awarded at up to 10% above base rate for some or all of the period starting from the same date.

- Your client to pay an additional amount of £xxx by way of an additional sanction.

If you think that this offer is in any way defective or non-compliant with Part 36, please let us know.

We look forward to hearing from you.

Yours faithfully,

16 DISCLOSURE AND INSPECTION

In non-PI multi-track claims parties will have to file the 'disclosure report' in Form N263. In this document the parties must state what relevant documents exist or may exist (as form N265 requires), but this report also requires the party to provide details of the likely cost of giving relevant disclosure. The parties are also required to discuss their report and, if possible, agree the scope of their disclosure obligations. If they cannot agree, the court will impose the extent of their disclosure obligations.

16.4.1 WHAT DOES 'STANDARD DISCLOSURE' REQUIRE A PARTY TO DISCLOSE?

'Standard disclosure' requires a party to disclose:

- documents on which it relies; and
- documents that:
  - affect its own case adversely;
  - affect the other party's case adversely;
  - support the other party's case; and
- documents that, in particular types of claim, are specified by the court.

This relates to all documents within a party's 'control'.

The question of whether a document should be disclosed is determined by reference to the issues raised in the parties' statements of case. Only those documents that have reference to the issues between the parties are to be disclosed. It is important, therefore, that where parties (or the court) limit the number of issues between them, the disclosure obligation will be reduced to meet only those issues remaining. In order to meet with the overriding objective—that is, the requirements of proportionality, fairness, and justice— parties are encouraged to be both realistic and reasonable in determining with which issues to proceed. It is often at the stage of disclosure—or later, at the stage at which witness statements of fact and expert reports are exchanged—that a party is able to determine more clearly the strengths and weaknesses of parts of (or the whole of) its case. Where a part of the case seems unlikely to succeed, it may be sensible for that party to seek to agree those parts, and in this way further restrict the amount of disclosure and documents to be referred to at trial. Obviously, if the reappraisal process determines that that party's whole case has been seriously undermined, then settlement of the whole should be sought.

Further examination of the definition of 'standard disclosure' reveals that:

- the obligation is a wide-ranging one and clients will usually need specific guidance on the extent of their obligation;
- it does not include documents, or classes of document, that are, in effect, documents that may simply lead a party on a 'train of enquiry'.

 Professional Conduct

A legal representative is under a professional duty to advise clients of their disclosure obligations. This advice should be given at the earliest opportunity to avoid clients removing documents from their possession that they consider to be harmful to their position. Where a client does deliberately remove or destroy harmful documents in their possession, the legal representative has further duties to the court. Principles 2, 6, and 7 should be upheld together with the Outcomes stated in Chapters Four and Five of the Code. These would expect him to advise the court and the other party in the disclosure process of the existence of the document so removed or destroyed, together with the circumstances of its removal or destruction. The court would be entitled to draw adverse inferences from the client's behaviour. If a client will not give instructions to give that information, the legal representative would be expected not to continue acting for the client. The professional duties relating to disclosure are onerous.

16.4.2 **THE MEANING OF 'CONTROL'**

The obligation to disclose documents includes those that are within a party's control. 'Control' extends to documents of which a party:

- has physical possession;
- has a right to possession, or to inspection, or to take copies;
- had, but no longer has.

This definition will mean, therefore, that a party has an obligation to give disclosure not only of documents that it has, but also of documents that it does not have, but which it has the right to reclaim or of which it has the right to obtain copies. This could include, for example, documents that are held by a party's accountants, or documents held by a subsidiary company in an action in which the parent company is a party.

It also includes the obligation of a party to disclose documents that it did have, but does not have anymore. At one end of the spectrum, this will include letters that have been sent, and at the other end of the spectrum, it can include documents that have been deliberately destroyed (see the 'Professional Conduct' box in paragraphs 16.4.1 and 16.5.1). In the case of 'letters sent', it is likely that a duplicate of that original letter is still retained by the party and that, also, is a document that must be disclosed. With the degree of electronically created documents and the extent to which these can be 'retrieved', the preparation of a party's list of documents in order to comply with its disclosure obligation can be very onerous indeed. However, some restriction on the potential scope of this obligation is provided by CPR 31.9(1)—that is, that 'A party need not disclose more than one copy of a document'. This rule would not apply, however, if any amendments or annotations were to have been made to the document in its exchanges to and fro, and the amendments on it met the definition of 'standard disclosure'.

16.5 **THE OBLIGATION TO MAKE A REASONABLE SEARCH FOR RELEVANT DOCUMENTS**

16.5.1 **THE OBLIGATIONS AND DUTIES OF THE PARTIES AND THEIR LEGAL REPRESENTATIVES**

Each party that has an obligation to give disclosure is required to make a reasonable and proportionate search for documents. The duty of a party in an action to disclose is qualified by the principles of 'reasonableness' and 'proportionality'.

Determining what is a 'reasonable and proportionate' search includes a review of the nature, the importance, and the value of the case. It also includes a consideration of the costs and the ease of retrieval of the documents.

Clients will need guidance on the extent of the search that the client should make so that he can make an honest and true 'disclosure statement or disclosure report'. A legal representative has an obligation to the court to ensure that his client makes proper disclosure.

When the client declares, when he makes disclosure, that he has conducted a 'reasonable search' for documents, he is saying that he *understands* the duty to disclose and that, to the best of his knowledge and belief, *he has discharged* that duty. The disclosure report that the parties will complete in non-PI multi-track cases includes a statement of truth. The declaration that he has carried out his disclosure obligation has a profound influence on the way parties should approach their obligations of disclosure. The client will therefore need to have a clear understanding of the issues of the case in order to carry out the search effectively. It will be for the legal representative to ensure that the client has this level of understanding. The case of *CMCS Common Market Commercial Services AVV v Taylor* [2011] EWHC 324 (Ch) confirms the risks for a legal representative who fails to undertake his disclosure obligations. In this case the court made a wasted costs order against the legal representative for their failure to supervise the client in undertaking their disclosure obligations.

Professional Conduct

As an 'officer of the court', a legal representative owes a duty to the court to have gone through his client's disclosure list carefully in order to make sure, as far as is possible, that no relevant documents have been omitted.

It is therefore good practice to give clients timely advice, both orally and in writing, about the types of document that are to be disclosed and the appropriate person in the client's organization to make the search, as well as advice concerning the retention, storage, and filing of documentation. The burden on the legal representative to ensure that he meets all of the professional obligations relating to disclosure is a heavy one.

16.5.2 'E'-DISCLOSURE AND THE ELECTRONIC DISCLOSURE QUESTIONNAIRE N264

PD 31B contains guidance for all e-disclosure.

'Documents' under the CPR include:

- emails and other electronic communications;
- word-processed documents;
- databases;
- documents readily accessible from computer systems, and other electronic devices and media, such as memory sticks, CDs, and mobile phones;
- documents stored on servers and back-up systems;
- electronic documents that have been deleted; and
- metadata.

PD 31B(10–13) provides guidance for the completion of the Electronic Documents Questionnaire (EDQ) in Form N264, which will be completed along with the List of Documents where electronic disclosure is undertaken. The purpose of the EDQ is to enable the parties to investigate, categorize, and agree the nature of electronically held documents that the parties must potentially disclose. Parties are expected to discuss and agree the extent of a reasonable electronic search before they undertake the search, and if they cannot agree, make representations to the court at the first CMC where the issue of the disclosure order is being dealt with. The potential extent of e-disclosure can be very great, so parties must take care to agree the extent of it such that it is proportionate. As technology develops this process will hopefully become more simplified by the development of predictive coding, which uses sophisticated technology to identify relevant documents and code them by issue.

The Technology and Construction Court has adopted the e-disclosure Protocol. Though the specific procedures in this specialist court are outside the scope of this manual it would be helpful for a legal representative to review this Protocol, which may act as guidance for the e-disclosure in their case. If these protocol guidelines are successful, the Protocol may be adopted by the courts in general.

Practical Considerations

Any legal representative engaged in the process of disclosure must think carefully about the range and extent of e-disclosure required of the client. There is a misconception that deleted files can very easily be retrieved; they can be retrieved—but not always that easily. Files often become fragmented when placed in the 'deleted files bin'. Does an isolated fragment found in an unallocated fragment or cluster on a disk constitute, for the purposes of disclosure, the document that is relevant to disclose?

online
resource
centre

Advising a client of their disclosure obligations and blithely stating that this includes 'deleted electronic materials' is likely to cause great consternation in the client's IT department, or, for a smaller company client, great concern because of the man hours, and expense, of complying with the advice given. Any early advice to a client about its obligations of disclosure in any action in progress or that might affect it in a possible future action should include advice that might result in its reviewing the way in which the company processes, stores, retains, or deletes data. This can be done in a standard 'disclosure letter' to the client. An example of such a letter appears on the Online Resource Centre.

There are additional questions that must be asked of the client that will assist them in complying with an order for e-disclosure. There are also further questions that will be asked in a review of a list of documents provided by an opponent. These might include the following:

- Has all equipment holding electronic data been searched?
- Are individuals (within the client's or opponent's workplace) able to store documents on their local hard drives, and have they been doing so?
- Is material on local hard drives routinely backed up onto the client's central server?
- What type of, and how many, servers are used? If they are web-based, does the client have 'control' of documents backed up this way?
- Do individuals have documents on their personal computers at home?
- Does the company operate a 'hot-desk' system, whereby employees may use more than one computer?
- How are documents backed up? (A full, detailed explanation is needed.)
- How is data stored? (A detailed explanation of the methods used is required.)
- Are mobile phones used to store documents and data?
- Do individuals use memory sticks, flash cards, external hard drives, CD-Rs, or DVD-Rs?
- What is the client's (or opponent's) email policy (particularly in relation to storage and deletion)?

Parties should meet early on in the litigation to discuss potential issues regarding electronic disclosure and that, where used, keyword searches should be agreed as far as possible. Where the extent of the search for e-documents is challenged by a party, the proper interim application to make is not one for specific disclosure, but instead should be an interim application for specific inspection.

The court may take the following matters into account when considering the correct level of e-disclosure to order the parties to undertake:

- the potential value of appropriate electronic searches to identify important documents that might otherwise be missed;
- but the rules do not require that 'no stone should be left unturned'; and
- it will be the court which ultimately decides what the scope of the e-search and e-disclosure should be.

16.6 FORM N265 AND THE 'DISCLOSURE STATEMENT', AND THE DISCLOSURE REPORT FORM N263

When a party complies with his obligation to give disclosure within the directions order made by the court in fast-track and PI multi-track cases, he will usually do so on Form N265. In non-PI multi-track cases the parties will complete a 'disclosure report' in Form N263 at least 14 days before the first CMC. So detailed consideration of the disclosure to be made will be looking to restrict the extent of disclosure wherever possible. The court has the power to dispense with disclosure altogether, to restrict it to specific issues, or to extend the scope of disclosure beyond 'standard disclosure', but only if it is considered proportionate, fair, just, and efficient to do so.

 Practical Considerations

The impact of the disclosure obligations and the requirement to give detailed information and proposals so early in the litigation means that parties and their legal representatives will need to consider 'documents' (for the case) very early on and require both to get organized. Legal representatives, and their clients, will also have to have regard for the estimated costs of the extent of the disclosure obligations they wish the court to impose, as they will need to give an estimate of these costs as part of the justification for their preferred option and in their costs budgets.

16.7.4 DISCLOSURE IS AN ONGOING OBLIGATION

The duty of disclosure continues until proceedings are concluded and this probably means after judgment, but before the judgment has been handed down (*Vernon v Bosley (No 2)* [1997] 3 WLR 683).

Often, the list of documents prepared and served or exchanged may be incomplete. This may be because investigations are ongoing. Where this occurs, the fact that further documents will be disclosed should be stated in the disclosure statement. It may be because documents come to light later. If the reason for a failure to disclose is because the client felt the document to be damaging, then this reason and the client's reluctance will need to be explained. A legal representative who is not given instructions to explain the failure or delay to disclose a document will have to cease acting.

 Practical Considerations

It is important to remind clients of the ongoing duties of disclosure, as well as of the disclosure obligations referred to in previous 'Practical Considerations' boxes. Clients should be reminded not only of the ongoing duty, but also of the possible consequences of a breach. Any costs implications of late disclosure should also be raised.

If additional material does come to light after the list of documents has been served, CPR 31.11(2) provides that the other party must be notified immediately. A supplemental list should be prepared and served. If there are only a small number of additional documents, these can be simply added to the original list. There is no prescribed form of the supplemental list, although Form N265 could be adapted for this purpose.

 Practical Considerations

If new material arises, it may be necessary to review your client's case again in the light of the new documents and then to update any advice to the client in the light of the new information. A further review of the documents listed should also be made to ensure that no further documents have slipped through the net of the 'reasonable search'.

16.7.5 THE ROLE OF THE LEGAL REPRESENTATIVE IN THE PROCESS OF DISCLOSURE

Part of the legal representative's role in the process of disclosure will be to ensure that the client understands their disclosure obligations and ensure that disclosure has been properly made and then to ensure that the organization of the documents is appropriate, so that the documents being disclosed are placed in the right part of Form N265.

16.7.5.1 Considerations of the Legal Representative when compiling a List of Documents
In relation to each document being considered, the following will need to be considered:

• Is the document, in principle, one that is to be disclosed?

• Does the client have the right (or a duty) to withhold inspection?

Thus, in the first part of the process, the documents that have been revealed by the 'reasonable search' may be sorted into five categories, as follows:

• **Documents that are to be disclosed, but disclosure of which is being withheld.** There will not usually be many documents, if any, in this category. If a document is to be disclosed, then few grounds will justify it *not* being contained within the list of documents being disclosed. One such reason might be a claim for 'public interest immunity'. This may happen, for example, in proceedings involving sensitive political or state information.

• **Documents that are to be disclosed, but inspection of which is being withheld.** These will most often be privileged documents. A full discussion of 'privilege' arises in paragraph 16.9. These documents will be listed in the middle section of Form N265. Some of the documents listed here may be withheld from inspection at the time that parties are ordered to 'disclose by an exchange of lists of documents' because they are, for example, privileged. However, the client may waive the privilege at a later stage and make the document available to the opponent. Thus, draft (or final) witness statements may be withheld from inspection, but will ultimately be made available to the opponents at the time at which the parties have been ordered to 'exchange witness statements' in the court's directions order made after allocation. This direction will usually be after the order for 'disclosure by list' (see Chapter 12).

• **Documents that are to be disclosed, and which will be disclosed and inspection of which will be permitted.** These are the documents that the opponent will be entitled to see once they exercise their rights of inspection. These documents may make up the bulk of the list and will be listed in the first section of the list. How the parties exercise the rights of inspection is detailed in paragraph 16.8.

• **Documents that are partly to be disclosed.** Part of such documents will be redacted. Privileged or irrelevant commercially sensitive material can be 'blanked out' of (that is, redacted from) a document that otherwise needs to be disclosed. The description of the document in the list should make it clear that it has been redacted (see also the case of *CMCS Common Market Commercial Services AVV v Taylor* [2011] EWHC 234 referred to at paragraph 16.5.1, a case concerning the redaction of documents).

• **Documents that are not to be disclosed.** The search for documents in an action may reveal documents that are either not relevant to the issues of the case and/or do not fall within the ambit of order to disclose. Most likely, it will be that they do not fall within the definition of 'standard disclosure', because that is the most likely definition of a party's duty to give disclosure (see paragraph 16.4).

 Practical Considerations

When documents are being sorted for disclosure, a file note should be made in respect of each document (or class of documents) of the reason for the category in which it has been placed. The transparency of the disclosure process in this way both shows that a proper consideration has been given to the process and will record the time spent on the process (and thus justify the charges applied to the process). A proper recording will also ensure that the whole team involved on the case is able to see the work done on the process, as well as the reasons for the categories into which the documents have been placed. The recording in this way will also be a starting point for dealing with any challenges that may be made to that party's disclosure or in responding to any application for specific disclosure. (For specific disclosure applications see Chapter 14, paragraph 14.5.)

When the documents have been categorized, sorted, and listed in Form N265, the client will be asked to sign off the prepared list and make the disclosure statement on the front page of the form. At this stage, the legal representative will indicate to his opponent that he is ready to effect exchange. Where both parties have been ordered to give disclosure—and this may not always be the case—when a party is ready to effect exchange he may write a letter, email, or fax to the opponent as follows:

> In accordance with the Order of [example: 'Mr District Judge'] made on the [date of the order] at paragraph [relevant paragraph of the order], we confirm that we are ready to effect exchange of our client's list of documents. Please confirm that you are ready to exchange your client's list.

16.7.5.2 Considerations of the Legal Representative when receiving a List of Documents

When a party receives the opponent's list, he will undertake the following:

- The legal representative should review the list. This review will initially compare each party's list to ascertain what documents both parties have and do not have. The revision will also need to consider whether there are any obvious omissions from the documents being inspected: perhaps a reference to another document is made in a document that has been disclosed for inspection, but which is not itself in the list. A review could reveal whether there are any surprises in the documents: for example, where a copy has been made available, but not the original. It could equally show up any queries of the scope of the search that has been made for documents or the extent of the documents that are held back from inspection (whether the claim for privilege can be justified, and whether it should be challenged). The review should include a review of the disclosure statement and whether any restrictions in the search for documents are reasonable. Has an appropriate person signed the disclosure statement?

- As a result of the review undertaken, that party's legal representative will prepare correspondence setting out any concerns and, at the same time, decide how they wish to exercise 'inspection', giving notice of same.

- The legal representative will serve a notice to inspect the documents available for inspection. The procedure for inspection is set out in CPR 31.15—that is, that a request to inspect should be given in writing and that the party disclosing the documents must permit inspection within seven days after receiving notice to inspect. The request to inspect may specify that the party requires copies and it is provided in the rules that they are also agreeing to pay the reasonable photocopying charges. It is good practice to seek to agree these charges.

- It is open to the inspecting party to inspect the originals either before or after receiving photocopies. There is no prescribed form of the 'notice to inspect'. Typically, the notice to inspect takes the form of a letter specifying the documents, or categories of document, inspection of which is sought—specifying whether this is by the provision of photocopies (or on disk) or by physical inspection.

 Practical Considerations

The process of inspection is often a paper exercise, with each party requesting certain documents from its opponent's list and agreeing to pay reasonable photocopying charges. It is therefore unusual for legal representatives and/or clients to attend inspection of the documents personally. But it should be remembered that it is the client's right to 'inspect' and that his legal representative is carrying out that right on the client's behalf. There may be situations in which it would be appropriate for the client to attend the inspection. Personal inspection will happen, however, when the numbers of documents to inspect are great and/or in a complex action, or where the list has been compiled in such a way as to make identification of specific documents difficult and unreliable.

If the list of documents for inspection is lengthy, it is important to ensure that the documents are made available to you to inspect in the order in which they appear in the list. If they are not, it can make inspection more time-consuming and therefore more costly for your client. Given the work that can take place in a review of a party's list of documents, the time limits are tight and should be diarized as a 'key date'.

16.8 INSPECTION

The time period for inspection of documents is invariably set out in the directions order and, as indicated earlier, is usually seven days after disclosure. If the time for inspection has not been fixed in the directions order, reference should be made to CPR 31.15, which contains default provisions on the timing of the provision of copies and inspection.

The place at which inspection should take place will often be at the offices of the disclosing party's legal representatives, but the court may order, or the parties may seek an order, that inspection should take place at another (more convenient) location.

When a party formally discloses a document in civil proceedings by stating that it exists, his opponent will have the right to inspect the document unless the disclosing party claims a right or duty to withhold inspection. Inspection means physically looking at the document, calling for a copy of it, or calling for a copy and then physically inspecting it. Specific provision should be made regarding inspection of electronic materials.

If the disclosing party is claiming a duty or a right to withhold inspection, the basis of that claim must be set out on the Form N265. If the disclosing party is claiming that it would be 'disproportionate' to make the document available for inspection, this reason should also be given. Any claim to withhold inspection may be challenged by the opponent.

Unless the list of the documents available for inspection states that they are 'copies', the assumption will be that the document available is the original. A document that has been amended in any way from the original is treated as a separate document.

 Practical Considerations

If there is any doubt about the authenticity of a document, it will be important to inspect originals. Important information can be observed by inspecting original documents, because they can reveal differing ink colours, the use of highlighters, pencil annotations, or other information that shows a transition in the form of the document. These additions to a document can provide valuable evidence when reviewing the documents.

CPR 32.19 provides that 'A party shall be deemed to admit the authenticity of a document disclosed to him under CPR Part 31 unless he serves notice that he wishes the document to be proved at trial'. Any notice under this provision must be served by the latest date for serving witness statements, or *within seven days of disclosure of the document*, whichever is later.

16.8.1 GROUNDS FOR WITHHOLDING INSPECTION

Under CPR 31.3, a party to whom a document has been disclosed has a right to inspect that document unless:

• the document is no longer in the control of the party disclosing it—in which case, the disclosing party is simply stating a fact that inspection of the document with them is not possible. In this situation, the opponent will need to consider the meaning of the word 'control' and determine whether examination of the document should be sought in the hands of another person, who may not be a party in the action (see paragraph 16.4). It may also involve consideration of an application for non-party disclosure under the provisions of CPR 31.17 (see paragraph 16.10.3);

- the party disclosing it has a right or a duty to withhold inspection of it—where a party claims a right to withhold inspection, it is usually on the basis (or ground) that the disclosed documents are 'privileged'. There are a number of different types of privilege, including:

- legal advice privilege;

- litigation privilege;

- common interest privilege; and

- without-prejudice privilege.

  A detailed examination of 'privilege' is contained in paragraph 16.9:

- the party disclosing it considers that it would be disproportionate to the issues in the case to permit inspection of it. This is in keeping with the overriding objective. Whether or not this claim will withstand a challenge from the opponent will depend on the facts of the case. A claim might be made to withhold inspection, for example when there are large numbers of documents held abroad, and it would be 'disproportionate' and little assist the court's ability to deal with the issues of the case 'fairly', 'justly', or 'expeditiously' to enforce inspection of these documents.

16.8.2 CHALLENGING THE EXTENT OF THE SEARCH AND CHALLENGING THE ALLOCATION OF DOCUMENTS TO THAT PART OF THE LIST THAT IS NOT 'AVAILABLE TO INSPECT'

Any party in receipt of another party's list of documents needs to undertake a careful review of the documents listed. The existence of the disclosure statement of the listing party does not mean that the receiving party has to take at face value the accuracy or the completeness of the list provided. Where you have identified concerns about the list provided, there are several steps that can be taken to ensure that an accurate or complete list is provided.

CPR 31.23 provides that proceedings for contempt of court can be brought against a party who makes, or 'causes to be made', a false disclosure statement without an honest belief in its truth. Such proceedings are quite rare and other options will usually be taken before contempt proceedings are considered. These 'other options' include the following:

- You might choose to set out your specific concerns by letter to your opponent's legal representative. This should include a full explanation of the reasons for your concerns, as well as, if possible, details of the documents that you feel are not included in the lists. The letter could have included in it advance warning that if an application has to be made to the court, then indemnity costs for the application will be sought.

- You might consider making a specific disclosure application (see Chapter 14, paragraph 14.5). Under CPR 31.12(2), the court may order a party to:

  - disclose documents, or classes of document, specified;

  - carry out a search as specified; and/or

  - disclose any further documents revealed by the search or as ordered.

- Any application for specific disclosure will need to consider the overriding objective: is the further disclosure *necessary* to do *justice* between the parties? Is it *proportionate* to the issues of the case? Is it *economic* to make the order for further disclosure?

- You might consider whether it is appropriate to serve a 'notice to admit facts' (see Chapter 17, paragraph 17.6.1). Under CPR 32.18(1), a party may serve another party with a notice requiring him to admit the facts or the part of the case that the party serving the notice states in the notice. The aim of the notice is to seek admissions on evidence or stated issues of the case, thereby avoiding the serving party having to prove the stated facts or issues set out in the notice. The provisions have the benefit of both narrowing issues and saving costs, both of which are important aspects of the CPR. The notice to admit facts can be used effectively to put pressure (usually costs pressure) on an opponent.

- In either of these applications, you should consider asking the court to include an 'unless order' that is intended to ensure that a party complies (see Chapter 13, paragraph 13.9). An 'unless order' is one that provides for a further step to be taken—usually to debar a party from proceedings with a step, or more critically, their action, if they do not comply with the initial part of the order. It would always be appropriate to seek an 'unless order' where the opponent has repeatedly failed to comply, or has unreasonably failed to respond to an early request, or when his good faith in not responding to the order is in doubt in some other way.

16.8.3 CHALLENGES MAY BE RAISED FROM A REVIEW OF AN OPPONENT'S LIST OF DOCUMENTS AND THE INSPECTION PROCESS

The following is a non-exhaustive list of the grounds on which challenges may be made to an opponent's list of documents:

- a failure to disclose a document referred to in documents that are disclosed and that have been inspected;

- that there are documents that, as a matter of common sense, should be in the list;

- in relation to documents that may be in the 'middle' section of the list and unavailable for inspection, but the claim for privilege of which can be challenged;

- that the disclosure statement has not been signed by an 'appropriate person';

- that the parameters of the search for documents are too narrow or otherwise too restricted either as to the search made or the period in which the search is made;

- in relation to e-disclosure (see paragraph 16.5.2), that the keyword search is too narrow, or the search has not been wide enough; or

- that the listing is too vague and is inadequate, and/or it is not possible to have a clear enough idea of the documents being listed.

In any request or challenge to a party's list of documents, consideration must be given to 'relevance', as well as to the aims of the overriding objective. The request and, especially, any application to the court should be supported with details of the likely cost (to the party) of complying with the application, so that the court can apply the concept of proportionality to the application, as well as the need for the further disclosure or verification in terms of fairness, justice, or expedition. Consideration can also be given to any alternative means of achieving the aim: for example, by CPR Part 18 requests if they would achieve a more efficient and cheaper, as well as fairer, outcome.

The CPR do not specify the format of most applications that may be made to challenge a party's list of documents. Most applications would include a written request first, then an application, either by letter or on Form N244, with supporting evidence.

 Costs

The process of scrutinizing your opponent's list of documents and inspecting the copies of documents that you request can be time-consuming, and therefore costly to your client. The time spent on this is regularly challenged at costs assessments (both summary assessment and detailed assessment). Make a careful note of the time spent and, with that note, your notes justifying the time spent. Inform your client before the cost is incurred in the larger 'document dense' cases, so that he is aware of the impact on proportionality and his overall costs, which he may not fully recover even if he is ultimately successful and secures a costs order in his favour.

16.9 **PRIVILEGE**

'Privilege' entitles a party to withhold evidence from production to a third party, an opponent in proceedings, or the court. Once privilege has been established, an absolute right to withhold the document in question arises. In litigation, 'privilege' entitles a party to withhold the 'inspection' of the privileged document; it does not provide a right not to 'disclose' the document. So privileged documents must still be contained within the list of documents, but they will be contained in the middle section of that part of Form N265 that lists the documents being disclosed but which are not available for inspection. However, some documents listed in this part may become available for the other party to see later in the action. An example of this is draft witness statements; these will not be disclosed to the other party until the date when the court has ordered exchange of witness statements. These statements may have been amended since the disclosure stage, but the final version will lose its privilege if the party relying on it wants to subsequently disclose it. Other documents may never be made available for the opponent to see.

Where privilege is claimed, neither the court nor the opponent can ask the court to draw adverse inferences by the exclusion of the document from the proceedings.

In paragraph 16.8.1, the types of privilege were identified as:

- legal advice privilege;
- litigation privilege;
- common interest privilege; and
- without-prejudice privilege.

The exclusion of privileged documents from the litigation process is extremely important—not least because the documents that are being withheld may be highly relevant to the issues of the case. In only four areas will documents be excluded from the court irrespective of the court's attitude to them:

(a) documents that are irrelevant;

(b) documents containing opinion evidence (save where expressed by an expert appointed for that purpose);

(c) where the document is privileged; and

(d) where public immunity interest applies.

Irrelevant documents—that is, area (a)—and opinion evidence that is not authorized by it being given by an appointed expert—that is, area (b)—are often included in a party's case, sometimes through mistake or, more commonly, because of a lack of good preparation by the legal representative. The courts do not exclude this type of evidence; they instead usually adopt the response of 'attaching very little or no weight' to such evidence.

However, in the case of evidence that is covered by privilege—that is, area (c)—or public interest immunity—that is, area (d)—the rights attaching to them for individuals amount, in practice, to an important personal constitutional right. These rights are underwritten by Arts 6 and 8 of the European Convention on Human Rights (ECHR). Accordingly, a person who has a (possibly highly relevant) document to which privilege or public interest immunity attaches may:

- refuse to give oral evidence or to produce the document to the court at any trial or hearing;

- refuse to disclose the information under any Pre-Action Protocol;

- refuse to answer a witness summons to answer questions or to produce documents relating to the privileged information;

- refuse to permit inspection of the document either pre action or during the action or at trial;

- refuse to give any access to the documents to any person with a search warrant or search order; and

- refuse to answer any questions relating to the privileged materials from a police officer or other investigator.

The importance of these rights cannot be overemphasized—especially because it is also to be noted that these rights may apply regardless of how relevant or otherwise admissible the materials might be, and, further, no adverse inferences can be drawn by the court from the exclusion of the material.

16.9.1 **LEGAL PROFESSIONAL PRIVILEGE**

Legal professional privilege includes 'legal advice privilege' and 'litigation privilege'. Privilege cannot be claimed unless the evidence in question is confidential, so where the information or the document has ceased to be confidential, the document containing it can no longer be subject to a claim for privilege. For the same reason, no privilege can attach to communications between opposing parties (unless they are subject to 'without prejudice' privilege). Equally, and for the same reason, when it is no longer 'confidential to one party', there can be no privilege in:

- transcripts of proceedings in chambers, in open court, or before arbitrators;

- attendance notes of meetings at which both parties were present; and

- telephone attendance notes of conversations between legal representatives of both sides. (The exception to this is if the notes contain additional notes by one party's legal representative that detail strategy, advice, or the merits of a party's case.)

The underlying purpose of legal professional privilege is to allow a party access to legal advice, to the lawyer's professional skill and judgment, without compromising his position with the opponent. In this context, 'lawyer' includes all members of the legal profession: solicitors; barristers; in-house lawyers, in part of their work; and foreign lawyers. It also covers supervised legal executives and trainees. The narrow definition of 'legal adviser' would probably exclude legal advice given by lay advisers at advice centres.

The position of in-house lawyers is more complex. Some of what they do is covered by legal professional privilege, but that part of their work that deals with business advice or administration will not be privileged. In-house lawyers should distinguish in their work between the giving of legal advice and work that, for example, ensures compliance with regulations for the business for which they work or which relates to their executive functions.

The case of *R (on the application of Prudential plc & another) v Special Commissioner of Income Tax & another* [2013] UKSC 1 has stated that such legal advice privilege relates to legal advice by lawyers, it cannot extend to *tax advice* given by accountants. However, in respect of such advice given by accountants and where litigation arises, the position will be different and, provided the 'dominant purpose' test is satisfied (see paragraph 16.9.2.2), an accountant's advice to his client will be privileged.

Legal professional privilege belongs to the client and it is therefore only the client, or an agent of the client with ostensible authority, who can waive the privilege applying.

16.9.2 **WHAT IS THE DISTINCTION BETWEEN 'LEGAL ADVICE PRIVILEGE' AND 'LITIGATION PRIVILEGE'?**

Legal advice privilege and litigation privilege are distinct types of legal professional privilege. See also Figure 16.1 at the end of this chapter.

16.9.2.1 Legal advice privilege

Legal advice privilege can apply whether or not litigation is pending or contemplated, whereas litigation privilege can apply only when litigation is pending or contemplated. 'Pending' or 'contemplated' means a real likelihood, rather than a mere possibility. A distinct possibility that sooner or later someone might make a claim, or a general apprehension of future litigation, is not enough.

Legal advice privilege protects against compulsory disclosure of all types of communication made between a client and his lawyer in which advice is sought or given within a relevant legal context. The subject matter of the advice sought or given is irrelevant, so long as it is in a legal context. Therefore, legal advice privilege protects advice sought by, or given to, a client in relation to both contentious and non-contentious matters. The key test of what constitutes 'legal advice' was considered in *NRG v Bacon and Woodrow* [1995] 1 All ER 976, in which Colman J stated that the advice must be 'directly related to the performance by the solicitor of his professional duties as legal advisor'. This position, although threatened in the Court of Appeal decision in *Three Rivers District Council v Governor and Company of the Bank of England (No 5)* [2002] EWHC 2730, was restored by the House of Lords in *Three Rivers District Council v Bank of England (No 6)* [2004] 3 WLR 1274, where it was confirmed that:

- legal advice privilege covers advice relating to public rights, liabilities, and obligations; and hence
- includes presentational advice given by lawyers to a party whose conduct might be the subject of public criticism; and
- would extend to advice and assistance given with reference to a range of enquiries, including coroners' inquests, and statutory and ad hoc enquiries; but
- if the lawyer became the client's 'man of business' advising across a wide range of non-legal topics, such as investments and other business matters, the advice might lack the relevant legal context to uphold the privilege; and
- there does not appear to be a 'dominant purpose' test as there is in litigation privilege.

The privilege does not apply in other types of 'confidential' discussion that a person may have with another person who is not their lawyer: for example, their doctor or priest. This applies even if the discussions with that person relate to legal matters. However, the court will consider the position carefully before compelling such persons to divulge the confidential information. This ability to include otherwise confidential information in proceedings has been held to apply in many situations in which the client may find it hard to understand, in the light of the absolute privilege that arises with legal advice privilege: for example, information held by personnel consultants (*New Victoria Hospital v Ryan* [1993] ICR 201) and industrial relations consultants (*M and W Grazebrook Ltd v Wallens* [1973] 2 All ER 868).

16.9.2.2 Litigation Privilege

Legal advice privilege does not, however, protect third-party communications—that is, a communication between either a client or his lawyer and a third party, such as a factual or expert witness. The latter privilege can only be protected within litigation privilege, and for that to arise, litigation must be pending or contemplated. A further distinction is that, where litigation privilege is being claimed but the document had more than one purpose, the courts will look at the dominant purpose of the document to determine whether litigation privilege applies. The 'dominant' purpose of the document must be to prepare for the litigation in progress or in contemplation.

Provided that the communication is made with one of the following as its sole or dominant purpose in relation to the actual litigation in process or in contemplation, the document will be privileged:

- giving advice; or
- obtaining evidence; or
- collecting evidence.

Once established as this, litigation privilege will attach to the communications themselves (for example, the letter of instruction to the expert, although this will be lost if that party intends to use that expert to give evidence at the trial of the action), the documents or materials used to provide the advice (unless those documents are already out in the open and no longer confidential), and the documents generated from the communications—that is, the reports that are prepared.

The 'dominant purpose' test is one of dominance and not exclusivity. Documents are frequently brought into existence for more than one purpose and close scrutiny of the purpose of the existence of the document will be made by the court to determine its 'dominant purpose'. The actual wording in the document may not be conclusive so, for example, if the document states on it that it was for the particular purpose of enabling litigation advice to be given, or was for another unrelated main purpose, the courts will look beyond the stated purpose of the document to determine its 'dominant' purpose.

The leading decision in seeking to define the 'dominant purpose' test is still *Waugh v British Railways Board* [1980] AC 521. The case involved the preparation of statements after a fatal rail accident. The courts decided that in order for litigation privilege to attach to a document, it must satisfy the 'sole dominant purpose' test. If the purposes for which the document were of equal weight, then the privilege would not attach. This decision has had significant repercussions for all compliance investigations, because as a result of the conclusions of this case, much of the collected material from enquiries and investigations will not attract litigation privilege. And it may not attract legal advice privilege as a result of the decision in *Three Rivers (No 5)*. In *Axa Seguros SA De CV v Allianz Insurance plc & Ors* [2011] EWHC 268 (Comm), the court again considered the extent and impact of the 'dominant purpose' test—and here concluded that the engineering reports in question had two purposes, one of which was to determine whether the highways in question had been constructed to internationally accepted standards. They concluded that the 'dominant purpose' test was not satisfied sufficiently to secure a finding of privilege. The test to claim litigation privilege is a high one and was restated recently in the case of *Tchenguiz & Anor v Rawlinson & Hunter Trustees SA & Others* [2013] EWHC 2297 (QB). In this case, the judge emphasized that the mere fact that a document is produced for the purpose of obtaining information or advice in connection with pending or contemplated litigation, or of conducting or aiding in the conduct of such litigation, is *not* sufficient for a claim to litigation privilege—it is only if that was the 'dominant' purpose of the document's creation.

The burden of proof in a claim for litigation privilege rests with the party seeking to assert privilege.

 Practical Considerations

Advising clients in this area is fraught with uncertainties and difficulties. It is important to give advice concerning the existence or not of 'privilege' to a document only after careful thought and research. Problems tend to arise in relation to documents not privileged in themselves and collected from the client or third parties, or copied during the course of preparing for litigation. The 'start point' for your considerations will be that all documents that are within the definition of standard disclosure or within the definition of any specific disclosure order that has been made, and that have, at any time, been within the client's control are to be disclosed and available for inspection *unless* privilege is available (or there is some other reason why it would be wrong to make it available—for example, that it is disproportionate to do so). The mere fact that the client seeks legal advice or that the document has been assembled for litigation does not cloak all otherwise unprivileged documents with privilege.

'Litigation' in this context means proceedings before the courts, but also before arbitrators and tribunals when exercising judicial functions. Thus, it will probably not apply in forums that are designed to be 'fact-finding', or those that are not 'adversarial'. Litigation privilege can normally be claimed in proceedings in which a judicial function is being exercised, but if the proceedings are merely fact-finding (for example, an inquiry under the Banking Acts—see the *Three Rivers* case again) or the tribunal has an administrative function, it is unlikely that litigation privilege can arise. The distinction is a fine one, because often an inquiry or inquest will result in litigation once the inquiry or tribunal has reached its conclusions.

The main difference between the two types of legal professional privilege is that litigation privilege enables the client or the lawyer to communicate under the protection of privilege with a third party, but is confined to situations in which litigation is in process (or contemplated). Legal advice privilege does not. On the other hand, legal advice privilege applies to communications between client and lawyer that may relate to both contentious and non-contentious matters.

Because legal professional privilege is a substantive right, it can be asserted in any situation and regardless of how old the document is (see *Calcraft v Guest* [1898] 1 QB 759, in which documents that were a hundred years old were still privileged).

 Practical Considerations

When advising clients of their disclosure obligations and the existence of legal professional privilege, it is important that both you and the client have an understanding of the consequences of actions taken. Being over-efficient can sometimes have unexpected and unwanted consequences, so, for example, take care in gathering evidence too early. If evidence is gathered before there is any reasonable prospect of litigation, then only 'legal advice' will be protected by privilege. Conversely, sending off a 'letter before action' or an early notice letter too early can equally have the effect of covering all of your opponent's 'fact-finding' steps as 'evidence gathering' covered by litigation privilege.

16.9.3 WHAT HAPPENS IF DOCUMENTS ARE 'COMMUNICATED' BY A PARTY WITHIN ITS ORGANIZATION?

So what happens if documents are communicated by a party within its own organization? Will this result in the document no longer being 'confidential' and no longer capable of attracting privilege?

The *Three Rivers* litigation has placed important practical limitations on the scope and availability of legal advice privilege where the client instructing the legal representative is a corporate entity (or similar). In *Three Rivers (No 5)*, the Court of Appeal decided that, in such circumstances, the client is not the corporate entity itself, but a narrow group of individuals employed by the entity charged with seeking and receiving legal advice on its behalf. Others outside this group of individuals who make communications related to the legal advice run the risk of exposing those communications, because they will not attract legal advice privilege (and they may not fit the criteria of litigation privilege either). This position applies even in relation to documents generated by employees (who are outside the group of employees defined as 'the client') that are necessary to provide information to the lawyers to advise (although here litigation privilege may apply).

Practical Considerations

Because of the practical effects of *Three Rivers*, there is a view that dissemination of advice given by the legal representative to others within the corporate entity should be made subject to appropriate confidentiality obligations. Consider whether your clients should be asked to exercise caution and accompany such notes disseminating legal advice with words such as 'privileged' or 'this communication does not amount to a waiver of privilege', and ask for an acknowledgement that the information will be held in confidence.

Designating the whole workforce of the organization as 'the client' is very unlikely to work; nor does it seem to be an answer to channel all communications through the in-house lawyer. Equally, it is impractical to construct an 'inner client' for every single legal issue that confronts any large entity. These very real problems, only very briefly highlighted here and the in-depth study of which is outside the scope of this book, are set out to alert any practising legal representative of the extent of the knowledge that they must have to advise clients about the complex issues of disclosure and privilege.

16.9.4 OTHER TYPES OF RELEVANT PRIVILEGE

16.9.4.1 Common Interest Privilege

Common interest privilege is a relatively new variant of legal advice privilege. It operates to preserve privilege in documents that are disclosed to third parties. It may occur in group actions, or in cases in which there is more than one claimant or defendant—that is, situations in which the group (who may not be parties to the action) or co-litigants have the same self-interest. All of these parties may collect information for the purposes of the litigation, and all may take copies of documents and relevant information.

The privilege is applied as follows: if party A has a sufficiently common interest in communications that are held by party B, then party A can obtain disclosure of those communications from party B even though, as against third parties, the communications would be privileged from production. In *Buttes Gas and Oil Co v Hammer (No 3)* [1981] QB 223, Lord Denning MR concluded that, for the purposes of disclosure, the court should treat all of the persons interested as if they were partners in a single firm. Each can avail himself of the privilege. Where common interest privilege applies, the document remains privileged in the hands of the recipient. The recipient can assert the disclosing party's privilege as against the world. For common interest privilege to be asserted, the common interest between the communicators must have existed at the time of disclosure between them. The principle of common interest privilege can apply in both arms of legal professional privilege: legal advice privilege and litigation privilege. Guidance as to when common interest privilege arises was given more recently in *Winterthur Swiss Insurance Company and Anor v AG (Manchester) Ltd and Ors* [2006] EWHC 839 (Comm).

Common interest privilege could be used as a 'sword' (to obtain disclosure), as well as a 'shield' (to prevent disclosure). It has been held to apply between companies in a group, insurer and insured, and agent and principal. However, the case law remains uncertain and each situation needs to be considered on its own merits.

 Practical Considerations

Because the case law is relatively uncertain in this quite modern form of privilege, it is best to be cautious when considering or advising clients about the disclosure of documents to third parties who could be considered to have a 'common interest'. If in doubt, consider disclosure only on the basis of express contractual undertakings that privilege in the document is not being waived.

FIGURE 16.1 LITIGATION PRIVILEGE AND ADVICE PRIVILEGE FLOW CHART

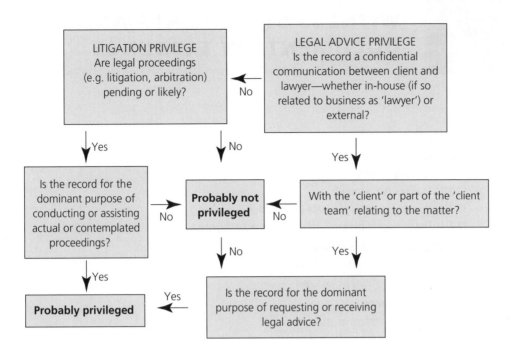

17 WITNESS STATEMENTS AND DOCUMENTARY EVIDENCE

Relevant court forms relating to this chapter:
- Forms N266 and N268

Relevant parts of the CPR and its PDs: 3, 13, 22, 32, 33, and 35

17.1 INTRODUCTION

A case can readily be won or lost on the strength of witness evidence at trial. Similarly, important applications may fail if a witness statement does not adequately deal with all of the issues. A legal representative must therefore understand both the underlying theory behind the use of witness evidence and documentation during the course of litigation, including the rules on hearsay, as well as the practical requirements and challenges encountered in the preparation of witness statements.

LITIGATION TRAIN: WITNESS STATEMENTS AND DOCUMENTARY EVIDENCE

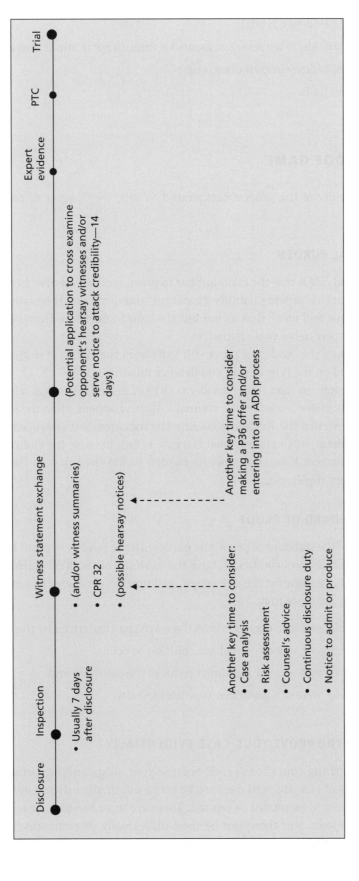

The relevant parts of the CPR are Parts 32 and 33. The governing statute is the Civil Evidence Act 1995.

This chapter covers:

- the use of evidence at trial;
- the preparation of witness statements for interim applications and at trial;
- the use of hearsay in civil cases; and
- evidential tools.

17.2 **THE PROOF GAME**

As a reminder of the general background to this, see Chapter 6, paragraphs 6.4.2.3 and 6.4.3.6.

17.2.1 **THE LEGAL BURDEN**

The general rule is that the claimant has to prove every element of his case. In most claims, this will include proving liability, causation, and quantum. If he fails to prove any part of his case, that will mean that he has lost the issue in question. However, what part does the defendant play in the proof game?

Sometimes, the burden of proof will shift from the claimant to the defendant, and this will depend on the type of case and defence raised.

For example, in road traffic accidents (RTAs), defendants often raise allegations of contributory negligence against the claimant. If this happens, then the claimant will initially have to prove that the accident was caused by the defendant's negligence (primary liability). If the claimant fails to do so, then the case is lost, because the claimant's burden has not been discharged. If he succeeds, the burden would then pass to the defendant to prove contributory negligence.

17.2.2 **THE STANDARD OF PROOF**

In terms of the standard of proof, the party with the burden of proof has to prove his claim on a balance of probabilities. Taking the example of the RTA again, the claimant, when proving his case against the defendant, will need to persuade the judge at trial that it was more likely than not that:

- the defendant drove negligently in the way(s) particularized by the claimant;
- those negligent actions caused the collision to occur;
- the injuries were caused as a direct result of the collision; and
- the injuries were of a particular type and severity.

17.2.3 **HOW DO YOU PROVE YOUR CASE EVIDENTIALLY?**

When preparing your client's case, because your allegations are being formulated in your statements of case, thought needs to be given simultaneously to how each of those allegations is going to be proved or refuted. There are three methods of proving a case evidentially, as follows, and these can be used individually or cumulatively in respect of each allegation made:

- by oral evidence at trial—that is, lay witness evidence, based on written witness statements, or expert evidence, based on experts' reports;
- by the provision of documentary evidence at trial—that is, a contract, expert's report, or hospital notes; and/or
- by real evidence being available at trial—for example, a faulty machine or defective car.

However, as can be seen from paragraph 17.3, the court can control whether or not you are allowed to use a type of evidence at trial. This chapter concentrates on lay witness evidence and documentary evidence. (For a discussion of the use of expert evidence, see Chapter 18.)

17.2.4 THE CONCEPT OF PROPORTIONALITY AND WITNESS EVIDENCE

The concept of proportionality may influence the decisions that you make concerning the collection of witness evidence. The lower the 'value' of the action, the more likely it will be that you will have to undertake some considered 'pruning' of the numbers of witnesses that you wish to use. This will be more prevalent with the proportionality test in CPR 44.3(5). Please see Chapter 4, paragraph 4.3.2.4.

17.3 CAN ALL TYPES OF EVIDENCE BE USED AT TRIAL?

A party to litigation is at liberty to obtain any type of evidence to prove or disprove the case against him. However, whether that party will be permitted to use and rely on that evidence at trial will depend on mandatory requirements and the court's discretion.

17.3.1 EVIDENCE THAT MUST BE EXCLUDED

In your early practice as a legal representative, it is unlikely that any of these exclusionary rules will be problematic. However, you are required to know that the following categories of evidence cannot be used or relied upon at trial:

- irrelevant evidence, such as some similar fact evidence and previous judgments or convictions;
- opinion evidence, except from that of an expert in his field;
- privileged evidence;
- without prejudice communication (this includes any Part 36 offers); and
- evidence protected by public interest immunity.

(See Chapter 16 for a fuller discussion on privileged evidence, without prejudice communications, and public interest immunity.)

17.3.2 EVIDENCE THAT MAY BE EXCLUDED

The court has a discretion to exclude evidence that is ordinarily admissible and its powers to do so are derived from the CPR. The most common areas are as follows:

- The court's discretionary powers under CPR 32.10, CPR 32.12, and CPR 35.13, regarding lay and expert witness evidence, respectively, permit the court to exclude the use of oral witness evidence at trial, and to rely on experts' reports and oral testimony at trial. Therefore, where the party wanting to use the evidence has failed to disclose it in accordance with directions set by the court, the court can exclude it altogether.
- The court's powers under CPR 32.1 are general and far-reaching, to the extent that the court can exclude evidence that would otherwise be admissible—for example, a second witness statement attesting to the same facts as appear in another witness statement obtained by you.

• The court's case management powers specifically under CPR 3.1(2)(m) mean that the court can take any other step or make any other order for the purpose of managing the case and furthering the overriding objective.

 Practical Considerations

In practice, you are far more likely to have material evidence excluded as a result of the court exercising its discretion under any one of these parts of the CPR. It is therefore advisable to raise the admissibility issue with your client before you incur the fee or cost of obtaining the evidence, so that he is aware that there is a possibility that the court may disallow it.

17.4 WITNESS STATEMENTS

This section deals with some early considerations of which a legal representative should be aware in order to ensure that witness statements are well prepared and presented in the correct format, whether the statements are for use at an interim hearing, at which the witness is not generally required to attend, or for use at trial, at which the witness is obliged to attend.

17.4.1 WITNESS STATEMENT OR AFFIDAVIT?

In most aspects of High Court and County Court litigation, evidence at interim hearings and at trial is given by way of witness statements. However, Practice Direction (PD) 32.1.4 sets out the occasions on which an affidavit must be used—most notably, in applications for search and freezing orders, parts of insolvency proceedings, and in applications for contempt of court. These applications fall outside the scope of this book (but see the Additional Chapter 'Injunctions and Other Equitable Remedies' on the Online Resource Centre).

 online resource centre

17.4.2 WITNESS STATEMENTS FOR TRIAL

17.4.2.1 First steps

The preparatory work that is needed to prepare an effective witness statement of fact for trial starts well in advance of the issue of proceedings. For example, if you act for the claimant, you will want to obtain a proof of evidence (a 'warts and all' record of what was first said by your client or witness, including a full commentary on any documents) to help you to draft your letter of claim and statement of case. Conversely, if you act for the defendant, you will require your client's proof of evidence to assist in the response to the letter of claim and the preparation of the defence.

17.4.2.2 Preparing the witness statement

With this in mind, once you are in a position to commence the preparation of the witness statements for trial, which may be many months after you have taken the proof, there are a number of important points to note, as follows:

• You only need to refer to facts that are in issue. Therefore, review the statements of case, and assess which facts are agreed and which are not agreed.

• Decide which party has the burden of proving those facts.

• Assess which witness(es) can prove which facts, and if there is more than one, assess which witness is in the best position to prove the fact in issue.

• If you have not already made contact with a witness, do so, explaining who you are, who you represent, and why you would like to speak to them.

• Arrange a meeting and send any key documents in advance.

- At the meeting, let the witness tell his story and take him through the relevant documents, ensuring that you ask questions to clarify his evidence.

- After the meeting, prepare the witness statement as soon as possible. This must be in the witness's own words, not yours. The statement may take some careful drafting to achieve this. Remember that the witness can be cross-examined on any part of his witness statement and so be sure how the witness would respond on cross-examination.

- Send the statement in draft to the witness, with a covering letter inviting him to make any amendments, approve, and sign the statement of truth. This may need to be explained to the witness.

 Practical Considerations

The witness statement may need to be passed between the witness and yourself many times before it is finalized. Once a final draft has been signed, create a witness statement section in your paper or electronic file. Any witness who is not your client may have no interest in the outcome of the trial, and so treat them with respect and keep them fully informed of their impending attendance at trial.

 Professional Conduct

There is no 'property' in a witness; therefore, you may approach any witness who has already been approached by your opponent, asking them to talk to you and to provide a witness statement. Whilst interviewing the witness, it would therefore not be sensible to give the witness a view of the merits of the case or details of your tactics. However, you must never try to persuade the witness to change his evidence (The Code, Principles 1, 2, 3, and 6, Outcomes 5.1, 5.2, and 5.4, and IBs 5.7(a), 5.10, and 5.11). There may be a risk, if you do decide to interview your opponent's witness, that such allegations will be made. Therefore, to avoid this, either record the interview or ask the other side to attend.

 Practical Considerations

Discuss with your client, at the outset of the claim or defence of the claim, which facts need to be proved and how. If your client is to give evidence in the form of a witness statement, then he should be aware of the fact that his statement will contain a statement of truth. Remember that a list of witnesses and the facts/issues to which they will be attesting is to be inserted in the Directions Questionnaire, although, in practice, it is often too soon to have the identities of all of your witnesses at this early stage. The more up-to-date list of witnesses will go in section B of the pre-trial checklist.

17.4.2.3 Formatting the witness statement

Every witness statement must contain certain information to make it compliant with CPR 32 and its Practice Direction. If it is not in the required form, then, in accordance with PD 32.25.1, the court may disallow the use of the evidence and the costs arising from it. It is therefore important that you are aware of these basic formalities that appear in PD 32.12–20, starting from the beginning of the statement as follows:

1. The top right-hand corner of the witness statement must include five points and these are usually numbered for ease:

   (a) the party on whose behalf the statement is made;

   (b) the initials and surname of the actual witness;

    (c) the number of the statement for that particular witness in the litigation—that is, is it the first statement, second statement, etc;.

    (d) the initials of the witness and the number of exhibits attached to the statement; and

    (e) the date on which the statement was made.

2. The statement must be headed with the title of the action. This can be obtained from an indorsed claim form or the particulars of claim. The heading stays the same even if, for example, it is the defendant who makes the interim application.

3. The statement should set out in heading form, usually in bold, the full name of the witness. This is helpful to the parties to the action and the court when sifting through large numbers of statements, because it makes it easily identifiable.

4. The maker of the statement must then set out his name (again), address, occupation, and whether he is a party to the proceedings or employed by a party to the proceedings.

5. Numbered paragraphs must also be used throughout.

6. The statement will be in the first person.

7. A standard introductory paragraph must be used for all witness statements for trial and includes the following:

    (a) who the maker of the statement is in relation to the claimant or defendant, if not a party to the action;

    (b) that the witness, if not a party to the action, has authority to make the statement on behalf of that party—remembering that, if a party is a limited company, it will always need a representative to speak for it and so 'the authority point' will need to be dealt with;

    (c) the witness must declare that the information he will give in the statement is either from his own knowledge and are matters of information of belief, or from the source stated (and then, when appropriate, to say in the statement the source of a particular fact—that is, 'I am informed by xxx that ...').

8. A statement of truth must conclude the witness statement as required by CPR PD 22.2: 'I believe that the facts stated in this witness statement are true ...'

The importance of a legal representative's compliance with these rules is paramount. The High Court has criticized witness statements for failing to state that the witness was speaking from his own knowledge, the source of the information, and the relevant facts. In the case of *Brownlie v Four Seasons Holdings Inc* [2014] EWHC 273 (QB), the court indicated that it was unacceptable for legal representatives to breach the rules and directed that in such circumstances, an application for permission to file a defective witness statement under PD 32.25.2 should have been made along with a detailed explanation as to the need for such an application. Otherwise, the statement should not have been filed at all, as non-compliant statements waste time and costs, and could attract sanctions.

17.4.3 WITNESS STATEMENTS FOR INTERIM APPLICATIONS

In order to be successful at an interim hearing, you will need to prepare evidence to prove your case. This very often takes the form of a witness statement. The party making the application is called the 'applicant' and the party opposing the application is known as the 'respondent' (but they may also be referred to as if 'claimant' or 'defendant' is their title in the action). Many of the points in paragraph 17.4.2.3 also apply to witness statements prepared for interim applications. However, there are also a number of additional considerations. It may also be helpful to refer to Chapters 13 and 14 when considering the drafting of witness statements for interim applications.

17.4.3.1 Preparing the witness statement

17.4.3.1.1 *Facts or Submissions*

Whatever type of interim application you are preparing for or opposing, it is very likely that you will be outlining facts to the court at the hearing, having regard to the order that you are asking the court to make or oppose. You will also be making written submissions in relation to your legal arguments to be put to the court to persuade the district judge or master to grant or dismiss the order.

For example, if you act for a defendant who has had default judgment entered correctly against him in an alleged debt action, an application to have that judgment set aside under CPR 13.3 can be made on his behalf. A factual background will need to be set out in the witness statement to highlight the fact that the defendant does not believe it to be an undisputed debt case, but a contested dispute. Those facts can then be drawn upon when the written submissions are made in relation to the requirements of CPR 13.3.1 being 'a real prospect of successfully defending the claim', or 'another good reason why the defendant should be allowed to defend the claim'. In essence, there must be a marrying up of the facts to the legal submissions (see Chapter 14 for further discussion).

17.4.3.1.2 *Who should make the statement?*

In light of the fact that an interim application is likely to contain both facts and submissions, you will need to give some thought as to in whose name the witness statement should be: you as the legal representative, the client, or another witness. This will depend on who is best placed to give first-hand evidence on the information that you intend to place before the court.

Where detailed legal submissions are to be made, it is more usual for the legal representative to make the witness statement, but this still leaves the problem of the factual submissions in relation to which the client or another witness may have first-hand knowledge. If this is the case, there are two options: either prepare two witness statements for the application, one being a factual statement for the client or witness, or a carefully worded statement from the legal representative covering both facts and submissions. The latter is the most common way of dealing with this problem and how to achieve this is highlighted here.

17.4.3.1.3 *Where the legal representative makes the statement*

The following important features will also need to be included where a legal representative makes the witness statement:

- In relation to the point made in paragraph 17.4.2.3, rather than state whether you are a party to the proceedings, it is more usual to state that you are the legal representative for the claimant or defendant, and include your firm's address.

- In addition to the points raised in paragraph 17.4.2.3, as a new legal practitioner, you are required to state that you 'have the care and conduct of the matter on behalf of the claimant (or defendant), subject to the supervision of [your] supervising partner'. Obviously, on qualification, the supervision point can be relinquished.

- It is important to remember that where you, as the legal practitioner, are making reference to the factual background to the case, you must use the words 'I am informed by …', or 'the claimant/defendant has informed me that …', to ensure that you are relaying the source of your knowledge to the court.

17.4.3.2 Formatting the witness statement

Much of paragraph 17.4.2.3 applies to witness statements for interim applications, but the following additional features should be noted:

- The second paragraph of the statement should inform the court of the purpose of your witness statement. As with the earlier example of the application to set aside default judgment, an appropriate sentence to achieve this would be: 'I make this statement in support of the defendant's application to have default judgment set aside.'

- In terms of formatting the structure to the statement, subheadings may be useful—especially to identify any relevant factual background and any legal submissions. Alternatively, when opposing an application, your witness statement in response may flow better if you respond to the witness statement in support, and, where appropriate, make additional relevant factual and legal arguments.

- It is helpful, when you come to making the written submissions in the statement, to state the part of the CPR (if there is a relevant part to your application) under which you are seeking the order, such as CPR 13.3.

- After the introductory statements and declaration of what the witness statement seeks to achieve (to make or oppose an application), it is usual for the applicant to set out a brief chronology of the relevant facts or the progress of the case. This should, in effect, make it clear that the application has been made at the correct time. Unless this is contested by the respondent to the application, the respondent will be able to agree this brief chronology.

- Once you have completed your submissions, conclude by repeating what it is that you are requesting: 'I therefore respectfully ask this honourable court to set aside default judgment in accordance with the terms of the draft order annexed to this application.'

- Finally, the statement of truth is as in paragraph 17.4.2.3, but because you are not a party to the action, this statement must be qualified with an authority sentence as follows: 'I am duly authorized to make this statement on behalf of the claimant/defendant ...'

 Practical Considerations

When setting out the persuasive elements of your client's case, you can be as articulate as you like, making reference to parts of the CPR. Here, you are seeking to persuade the district judge that he should make the order sought. The degree of persuasion needed may vary with the particular interim application or ground under the CPR on which the case relies. Another way to look at how these 'persuasive' elements of the witness statement should be drafted is to consider the discretion that the district judge or master has in relation to the application and, in effect, draft arguments that enable the district judge or master to make the order that you seek within the remit of his discretion.

Figure 17.1 at the end of this chapter is a template for a witness statement for an interim hearing.

17.4.4 EXHIBITS TO WITNESS STATEMENTS

A witness statement for trial or for an interim application can refer to documents. If this is the case, the documents must be exhibited to the witness statement. Reference to the number of exhibits is made at point (4) in the information given in the top right of the front page of the statement itself.

When referring to an exhibit in the body of the witness statement, the witness should state, 'I refer to [description of the document including a date] marked "TS 1/2/3 etc."'. Detailed provisions relating to exhibits can be found in PD 32.11–32.15. Each exhibit, or bundle of exhibits, should have a covering sheet featuring (or should have expressly written upon it) the court heading, the name of the witness, and that 'this is the exhibit marked "TS 1/2/3 etc." referred to in the statement of ... '.

17.4.5 DISCLOSURE AND SERVICE OF WITNESS STATEMENTS

17.4.5.1 Witness evidence for trial

Witness statements for use at trial must be disclosed to your opponent (CPR 32.4), in default of which a party will be unable to rely on such evidence and call the witness to trial. The court has, unsurprisingly, a discretion to allow a party to rely on new evidence at trial even where that evidence has not been disclosed in accordance with the case management directions on exchange of witness statements. The criteria which must be satisfied for an application to rely on and adduce such evidence at trial is set out in *The Nottinghamshire and City of Nottingham Fire Authority v Gladman Commercial Properties* [2011] EWHC 1918 (C). The terminology for this is 'exchange of witness evidence'. This must be done in accordance with the directions

17.5.3.2 Where the evidence is contained in a witness statement of a person who is not giving oral evidence

Remember from paragraph 17.5.1.2 that a written statement from someone who will not be attending trial is also classed as hearsay evidence. If this is the case, then a separate formal notice should be served with the witness statement, identifying the hearsay evidence, confirming that hearsay evidence will be relied upon at trial, and giving reasons why the witness will not be called.

There is no guidance given in the CPR as to the exact format of the notice. We would suggest that the template found in Figure 17.2 at the end of this chapter be used as a starting point for a hearsay notice. Please also see the hearsay notice in the Andrew Pike case study in the Online Resource Centre.

 Practical Considerations

In practice, very few legal representatives serve a notice, and even fewer will ever raise the point. Failure to serve the notice does not affect the admissibility of the hearsay evidence, but the court may exercise its discretion on the question of costs.

17.5.4 **WHAT ARE YOUR CLIENT'S OPTIONS IF HEARSAY EVIDENCE IS BEING USED AGAINST HIM?**

If, in the course of litigation, you receive a hearsay notice, you will need to consider the effect that the weight of the hearsay evidence will have on your case and whether there is anything constructive that you can do about it.

In terms of the effect of the weight of the hearsay evidence, this will very much depend on the strength of your own evidence, the type of hearsay evidence against you, the strength and type of any other evidence against you, and the six factors listed in paragraph 17.5.2.

Constructively, the best that you can hope to do, where you believe the hearsay evidence to be effective for your opponent, is to try to reduce any weight that the trial judge may attach to it. This can be done in one of two ways: either by calling the maker of the hearsay statement to court to be cross-examined, or by attacking the credibility of the maker of the hearsay statement in his absence.

17.5.4.1 Cross-examination

Section 3 of the 1995 Act allows a party who has been served with a hearsay notice to apply to the court for an order to call the maker of the hearsay statement to court to be cross-examined. The application is effected in the usual way, with a Form N244 plus witness evidence in support of the application. CPR 33.4 requires that the application be made no later than 14 days after service of the hearsay notice.

 Practical Considerations

Applications of this nature would only be used in cases in which the whereabouts of the witness is known, because the court is unlikely to make the order if the witness has disappeared. In practice, consideration should be given to cross-examination orders where your opponent has obtained and served a witness statement, but decides not to call the witness to give oral evidence at trial, relying on the statement of the absent witness as hearsay. You are permitted to apply to cross-examine. If you do succeed and cross-examine your opponent's witness, there is a risk that the witness may be uncooperative and this may damage your client's case.

17.5.4.2 Attacking credibility

Section 5(2) of the 1995 Act permits a party who has been served with a hearsay notice to attack the credibility of the maker of that hearsay evidence. This is done by serving a 'notice to attack credibility' on your opponent within 14 days after service of the hearsay notice under CPR 33.5. There is no guidance on the form of the notice in the CPR, but it usually follows the format of the hearsay notice and will include an outline of the reasons why you seek to attack the witness's credibility.

 Practical Considerations

When trying to identify the reasons for attacking a hearsay witness's credibility, try imagining that the witness is, in fact, in the witness box at trial and consider what questions you would put to him to discredit him. Go on, then, to consider what trait it is about the hearsay witness's character that you are trying to highlight to the judge: is he biased, untrustworthy, or unreliable? It is these character defects that need to be included in the notice to attack credibility, not the questions that you would have put to the witness had they attended court.

In practice, trial judges place limited weight on hearsay evidence.

 Practical Considerations

You may wish to consider taking both of the steps in paragraph 17.5.4.1 or 17.5.4.2, because they both operate under the same time limits—particularly if you are trying concurrently to trace the hearsay witness. If you are unable to locate them by the time that your application comes to a hearing, you have the option of withdrawing the application—but be mindful of any costs consequences. Alternatively, you may not wish to take either step. This would probably only be the case if you were to feel you have a sufficiently strong case, but care should be taken, because if you do choose to do nothing on receipt of the hearsay notice, then, at the trial, you will not be permitted to make any representations to the judge on the character or credibility of the hearsay witness.

17.6 USEFUL TOOLS IN THE EVIDENTIAL BATTLE

Usually, at a point after disclosure and exchange of witness statements, when reviewing your client's case generally and conducting your risk assessment, as illustrated in the 'litigation train' diagram at the start of this chapter and that at the start of Chapter 16, there may be facts or parts of the case that could usefully be admitted by your opponent with a view to putting some pressure on your opponent and saving costs. There are two methods available to you, as follows.

17.6.1 NOTICE TO ADMIT FACTS

online resource centre

In order to ensure that the court's time at trial is not wasted in having to determine facts and issues that could be reasonably admitted, consideration should be given to serving a 'notice to admit facts' in Form N266, in accordance with CPR 32.18. This can be served at any time, but no later than 21 days before trial. See the Online Resource Centre for a copy of the form.

If an admission in relation to the fact or issue sought is not forthcoming from your opponent, then you have the burden of proving or disproving the fact at issue at trial. If you are successful on that issue, then your opponent may be asked to pay your costs of proving or disproving those particular facts or issues, irrespective of the overall outcome of the case.

The use of the notice to admit facts is, perhaps, best explained by way of an example.

FIGURE 17.1 TEMPLATE FOR A WITNESS STATEMENT FOR AN INTERIM HEARING

1. Claimant/Defendant

2. T. Solicitor

3. 1st/2nd etc.

4. TS 1/2/3 etc.

5. Date

IN THE COUNTY COURT AT   **CASE NO**

BETWEEN

MR   **CLAIMANT**

AND

MR   **DEFENDANT**

WITNESS STATEMENT OF TRAINEE SOLICITOR

Witness name: insert name of trainee solicitor

Witness address: insert firm's address

Witness occupation: insert the fact that you are a trainee solicitor and that you act on behalf of either the Claimant or the Defendant

1. I am a trainee solicitor and have the care and conduct of this matter subject to the supervision of my supervising partner. I am duly authorized to make this statement on behalf of the Claimant/Defendant. I make this statement from my own knowledge, belief and from the information given to me by the Claimant/Defendant/someone else.

2. I make this statement in support of (or in opposition to) the Claimant/Defendant's application for . . . .

Chronology/facts/procedural events

Insert any relevant background here in numbered paragraphs 3-?

Submissions

Insert your legal arguments here repeating the wording of a relevant part of a CPR part if appropriate in consecutive number paragraphs.

    Conclude your submissions with 'I therefore respectfully ask this honourable court to make the order as asked in accordance with the terms of the draft order annexed to this application'.

Statement of truth and authority

I believe that the facts stated in this witness statement are true. I am duly authorized to make this statement on behalf of the Claimant/Defendant.

FIGURE 17.2 TEMPLATE FOR A HEARSAY NOTICE

IN THE COUNTY COURT AT   **CASE NO**

BETWEEN

                                                               Claimant

                            and

                                                     Defendant

NOTICE OF INTENTION TO ADDUCE HEARSAY EVIDENCE

Take Notice that at the trial of this action the Claimant/Defendant intends to give in evidence the statement made in the following document, namely the statement of . . . . dated . . . . a copy of which is annexed hereto.

And further take notice that the particulars relating to the said statement are as follows:

1. It was made by . . . .

2. It was made to . . . . of the Claimant/Defendant's solicitor.

3. The said statement was made on . . . . at . . . .

4. It was made in the following circumstances, namely that the Claimant/Defendant's Solicitor obtained the witness name from . . . . and attended . . . . for the purpose of obtaining a statement from him/her

And Further Take Notice that the said . . . . .cannot be called as a witness at the trial because . . . .

To: The Claimant/Defendant

Dated . . . .

18 EXPERTS AND EXPERT EVIDENCE

LITIGATION TRAIN: ACTING FOR A DEFENDANT, RESPONDING TO THE CLAIM, THE CONSEQUENCES OF FAILING TO RESPOND

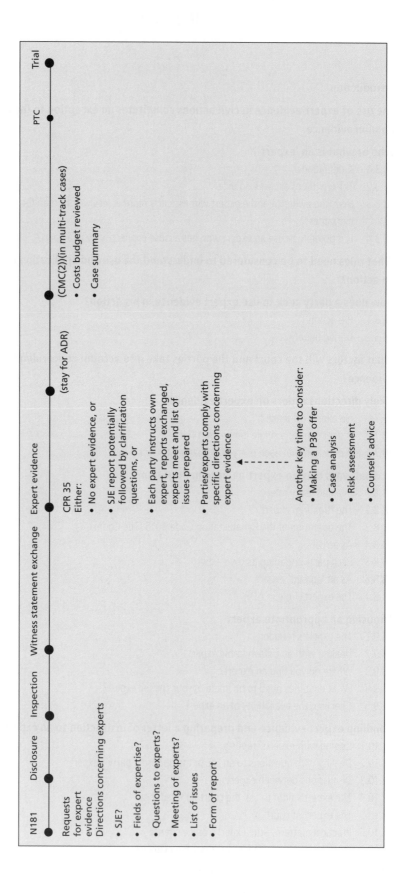

expert to assist in the litigation process. The Civil Justice Council has stated that experts should 'provide opinions which are independent, regardless of the pressures of litigation. In this context a useful test of 'independence' is that the expert would express the same opinion if given the same instructions by an opposing party. Experts should not take it upon themselves to promote the point of view of the party instructing them or engage in the role of advocate. Provided this very 'independence' can be shown, the courts have concluded that, in certain circumstances, using an expert who has a close connection to a party may not always be a bar to instructing the expert. In *Gallagher International Ltd v Tlais Enterprises Ltd* [2007] EWHC 464 (Comm), the judge permitted the use of an expert who was employed by the claimant. The defendants in this case had applied that the claimant's employee should be debarred from giving expert evidence. Aitkens J agreed with and adopted the reasoning set down in an earlier case (*Armchair Passenger Transport Ltd v Helical Barr plc* [2003] EWHC 367 (QB)) of the circumstances in which it may be appropriate to permit a person to give expert evidence despite a close connection with a party.

The reasons given in the *Gallagher* case were as follows:

- The fact (of the expert's employment with the claimant) was openly declared.
- The terms of engagement of the expert have been clearly defined within the provisions of the CPR, and the claimant had done as much as it could to 'isolate and separate' the expert from the affairs of the company in the litigation and his duties as an expert in the proceedings.
- The expert had relevant experience and was wholly aware of his duties to the court.
- Experts in the field were scarce—and further, the timescale before trial indicated that it would be unfair for the claimant to have to try to seek another expert in the field at the late stage of the proceedings.
- The expert would be open to cross-examination.
- The claimant bore the risks that the weight of the expert's evidence may be reduced by the judge at trial because of the connection to the party calling him.

Clearly, these reasons would not apply in many situations and the principle remains that an independent expert should be sought whenever possible.

The case of *Smolen v Solon Co-operative Housing Services* [2003] EWCA Civ 1240 can be distinguished from the *Armchair* and *Gallagher* cases because it was not clear, in that case, that steps had been taken to ensure the impartiality of the expert (who had previously worked for a party), and experts in that field were not so difficult to find. It is also clear, though, that, in the circumstances listed, 'a close connection with a party' will not automatically render the evidence of that expert as inadmissible.

The case of *Edwards v Bruce & Hyslop (Brucast) Ltd* [2009] EWHC 2970 (QB) is a reminder of the need for the expert to maintain his impartiality. In this case, communications between the appointed SJE and the defendant (that had not been revealed to the claimant) had 'tainted' the expert's impartiality and his position as SJE was untenable.

18.4 WHAT RULES NEED TO BE CONSIDERED TO UNDERSTAND THE USE AND APPLICATION OF AN EXPERT IN AN ACTION?

CPR Part 35, its supporting Practice Direction (PD), and the Guidance Note are the rules that govern the use of experts in litigation.

However, CPR 32 also needs to be considered, because this provides the power for the court to control the evidence before it and this will include the control of expert evidence.

18.5 **HOW DOES A PARTY SEEK TO USE EXPERT EVIDENCE IN HIS ACTION?**

18.5.1 **PRE ACTION**

A party can decide himself when and how to use an expert in the pre-action stage. This may be to help him to formulate his case, or to add strength and weight to his arguments.

Protocol—whether it is one specifically designed for the action or within the Practice Direction on Pre-Action Conduct and Protocols (PDPACP)—sets down guidelines for the use of expert evidence at paragraph 7.2–7.11 of the Action Protocol for Personal Injury Claims. Some specialist proceedings may be covered by other specific rules (CPR 49) but these are outside the scope of this manual. The aim in Protocol is that parties should seek to agree how to use an expert and who to use. However, the ultimate decision will lie with the claimant. The legal representative's role will be to ensure that the client has given instructions to engage the expert and that he understands the costs implications of engaging the expert. There is no certainty that the courts will allow any costs recovery of the fees of retaining the services of an expert in the pre-action stage.

18.5.2 **DURING LITIGATION**

If the action does not settle in the Protocol stage and proceedings are issued, any future use of evidence will be strictly controlled by the court under CPR 35 and parties may only use expert evidence at trial if given permission to do so. The court will also define the way in which expert evidence will be used (see paragraph 18.6).

Where a party has defined a need to use expert evidence in his action, he should make a request for that evidence as soon as is practicable. The request must include an estimate of the costs involved. The arguments for permission to adduce expert evidence will usually be set down in the Directions Questionnaire (DQ) and at a later stage, regarding oral evidence of the expert, in the pre-trial checklist (see Chapter 12). Any further requests for the permission of the court to define the use of expert evidence by the parties further, or for permission for additional expert evidence, must be made by an interim application or at a subsequent case management conference (CMC).

18.6 **WHAT FACTORS WILL THE COURT AND THE PARTIES TAKE INTO ACCOUNT CONCERNING THE USE OF EXPERT EVIDENCE?**

The court will consider at the first opportunity—usually on receipt of the completed DQs—whether expert evidence will be required. Both parties' legal representatives should have considered their requirement for expert evidence in the action and should have justified their request in their completed Form N180 or N181 (the DQs), or come prepared to address the court on their reasons for expert evidence and the extent of it at a subsequent CMC. No expert evidence may be adduced without the permission of the court (CPR 35.4(1)), so any perceived need for it must be fully set out as 'necessary' within the aims of the overriding objective. CPR 35.1 provides that expert evidence should be restricted to that which is reasonably required to resolve the proceedings.

Expert evidence may be sought for actions in any of the tracks, but clearly issues of proportionality will apply and therefore, for cases in the small claims track, careful consideration will have to be made about the use of expert evidence. CPR 27 restricts the cost of any expert permitted in a small claims track case to a maximum of £200 for each expert (CPR 27.7.3). However, in any of the tracks the court will consider a 'cost capping' provision stating the sum that may be spent on any expert evidence permitted. Any request for permission to have experts to provide evidence in a case should be accompanied by an estimate of the cost of it.

Expert evidence may be central to issues of liability and causation, and/or quantum. Although parties are expected to cooperate in the preparation of their cases, the need for expert evidence is often one area in which the parties are unable to agree. The disagreement may concern:

- whether expert evidence is needed at all;
- whether expert evidence is needed in a particular field;
- whether an SJE should be used; and
- the cost of it.

The case of *(1) Kenneth Alex Wattret (2) Laurie Grace Wattret v Thomas Sands Consulting Ltd* [2015] EWCH 3455 (TCC) highlights the degree of consideration by the court as to whether an expert is *needed* in an action. The case highlights the need in any application by a party, or the parties, for an order that expert evidence may be permitted in the action, the parties should not only seek to *justify* why expert evidence is needed but also should identify exactly what *issues* the expert should cover.

18.7 LIKELY DIRECTIONS ORDERS ON EXPERT EVIDENCE

If the court concludes that expert evidence may be adduced at trial, the following are examples of directions orders that may be made.

18.7.1 NO EXPERT EVIDENCE

No expert evidence being necessary, no party has permission to rely on expert evidence.

18.7.2 A DIRECTION FOR A SINGLE JOINT EXPERT (SJE)

In the small claims track or fast track, any permission for expert evidence to be adduced will *normally* only be given to call expert evidence on a particular issue from one expert (CPR 35.4(3A)). This is intended to provide consistency and directly refers the courts to PD 35.7, which sets out the criteria to apply when the court considers whether to direct the use of expert evidence in a matter. However, in the multi-track also the question of *proportionality* will be at the forefront in the consideration of expert evidence and the use of a SJE will always be a consideration.

Any direction order for an SJE must use the term 'single joint expert'. A direction for an SJE could include some or all of the following directions:

- 'Permission is given to the parties to rely on the written evidence of an SJE in the field of [specify field], instructed jointly by the parties on the issue of [specify issue], and the parties have agreed to use [name expert].'
- 'If the parties cannot agree who the SJE should be, any party may apply to the court to obtain further directions.'
- 'In the event that the parties cannot agree the identity of the SJE by [date], the parties shall, on or before [date], apply to [specify who—for example, the President of the Royal Institute of Chartered Surveyors] to nominate a suitable SJE.'
- 'The claimant shall inform the court, in writing, when the SJE has been appointed.'
- 'Instructions are to be provided to the SJE by [date], and the report is to be simultaneously served by [date] on both parties.'
- 'The parties are to serve any written questions on the SJE and the other party by [specify timescale—for example, within 28 days of receipt of the expert's report], and the SJE shall

file and serve the answers to any such questions on both parties by [time—for example, 28 days thereafter].'

- 'Unless the parties agree in writing or the court orders otherwise, the SJE's fees and expenses shall be paid by the parties [equally or in the proportions agreed or ordered], and the total amount of the SJE's fees and expenses shall be limited to £x [amount].'

- 'The evidence of the SJE shall be given at trial by [written report *or* oral evidence of the SJE].'

- Where more than one expert is giving evidence the court may direct that some or all the experts give their evidence concurrently (PD 35.11.1). The court may make further directions concerning the use of multiple experts at a trial in accordance with PD 35.11.2.

18.7.3 A DIRECTION THAT EACH PARTY MAY INSTRUCT ITS OWN EXPERT

A direction that each party may instruct its own expert might include the following options:

- 'Where, at the first CMC, the parties have decided in principle that they will want experts, but have not yet decided on the area of expertise [for example, whether it should be expert evidence of a quantity surveyor or a chartered surveyor], a further CMC can be held to deal with expert evidence [and any other outstanding matters], to be fixed for the first available date after [date], and to be reserved to [specify master or district judge], if possible.'

- Where the parties have decided that they each want to rely on their own expert:

  – 'permission is given to each party to rely upon the written evidence of [specify number of] in the field of [specify field] expert(s) addressing the following issues [list issues]. [Specify which party] intends to use [name expert] and [specify other party] intends to use [name expert]';

  – 'the parties shall exchange their lists [of issues] and the experts of both parties shall consider both parties' issues in their reports';

  – 'the experts' reports shall be exchanged simultaneously by [date]', *or* 'there shall be sequential exchange of experts' reports, the claimant's [specify field] expert's report to be served by [date] and the defendant's [specify field] expert's report to be served by [date]';

  – 'written questions may be put to the experts on their reports within [number of days— usually 28 days] of the report being served. The experts are to respond to the questions in writing within [number of days] of being served the questions';

  – 'the reports are to be agreed if possible';

  – 'if not agreed, the experts shall hold a without prejudice meeting for the purpose of identifying the issues, if any, between them and, where possible, reaching agreement on those issues. The experts shall by [specify date] prepare and file [at court] and serve a statement showing:

    – those issues on which agreement has been reached; and

    – those issues on which they have not agreed, with a summary of the reasons why they disagreed.'

- 'All supplemental experts' reports shall be limited to [specify number of] pages, excluding supporting documentation and appendices, and shall be served by [date].'

- 'No party shall recover from any other party more than £[amount] for the fees and expenses of an expert.'

18.8.4.2 Instructing an SJE

Once an SJE has been selected, CPR 35.8 and paragraph 20 of the Guidance Note give guidance on the instructions to the expert. It is clear that both parties are at liberty to send separate instructions to the expert, although they must send a copy of their instructions (and of any other communications that they may have with the expert) to the other party in the action. Ideally, the letter of instruction to the expert should be agreed, because this is more likely to create a clearer list of the issues on which the expert is being asked to report. If any instructions are given by telephone or in person, then the content of the instructions should be confirmed in writing. All communications from the SJE should be addressed to all parties.

The instructing parties are jointly and severally liable for the SJE's fees unless the court directs otherwise. The court will often also direct that the sum of the SJE's fees shall not exceed a certain figure (that the court will set) and further direct the proportion of those fees that each party should pay. This is often an equal division. The court also has the power to order either or both parties to pay that sum into court (see also *Smolen v Solon Co-operative Housing Services Ltd* [2003] EWCA Civ 1240).

 Costs

> The direction by the court as to how the SJE's fees should be divided between the parties does not decide the issue of which party will ultimately bear the costs of the expert—this will depend on the ultimate order for costs that the court makes. The earlier direction indicating the share each party should pay of the SJE's fees merely ensures that the expert gets paid. Any party seeking expert evidence must, in their request, provide the court with an estimate of the costs of doing so.

When sending instructions for a report, it is necessary to ensure that the expert is aware of all of the issues in the case, where the burden of proof lies, and what the relevant standards of proof are. This will ensure that the expert produces the right kind of report.

18.8.5 EACH PARTY ENGAGING ITS OWN EXPERT

For each party to be able to adduce its own expert evidence at the trial of an action, a direction for each party to have its own expert must be made.

Given that there is so much emphasis on the use of SJEs in actions, when would it be appropriate to oppose the appointment of an SJE and seek instead an order that each party may instruct 'its own' expert?

The use of more than one expert may be justified if:

- there are several tenable schools of thought on the relevant issue;
- the issues on which the expert will be advising are very complex;
- the issues on which the expert will be advising are so important to the likely outcome of the case that the parties should be allowed to instruct their own expert;
- the value of the claim is sufficiently high that the appointment of separate experts would not be disproportionate;
- the parties have already appointed their own experts before proceedings began and it will be more cost-effective to continue using them, and to try to resolve the expert evidence issues through written questions and experts' discussions, rather than to appoint a new SJE; or
- the expert is being asked to report on difficult issues of liability and causation. It is more difficult to persuade the court of the need for separate experts where the issue to be addressed is quantum only, unless those issues are particularly complex and substantial.

Where the court has made an order that each party should have its own expert, it will normally wish to state the purpose or field of expertise required.

Practical Considerations

If a specific expert is named in the order for directions, it will not be possible to use a different expert in that field without seeking the court's permission. If only the *field of expertise, not a named expert in that field* is referred to, it will not be necessary to obtain permission to use a different expert. However, if more than one expert's report is obtained in the field directed and a party decides to rely on the later report, that party is likely to have to disclose the original expert's report—especially as the instructions are very likely to have referred to the first expert's conclusions.

18.8.6 AS AN 'AGREED' EXPERT

The distinction of what is an 'agreed' expert is not an easy one to define and the word is perhaps used by legal representatives without clearly defining what they mean by it, and where they are, in reality, referring to an SJE.

For clarity, an 'agreed' expert (otherwise referred to as a 'jointly selected expert' or a 'mutually accepted expert') is one proposed by the Personal Injury Protocol and is an expert retained in the pre-action phase. Under the Protocol, an expert (or a list of experts) is proposed by one party (usually, but not always, the claimant) to his opponent. If an expert is 'agreed' from that list, the expert remains that party's own, solely instructed expert, but the other party has the right to raise questions. If the expert is not 'agreed', the parties may instruct experts of their own choice.

18.8.7 THE EXPERT'S ROLE IN ADR

An expert may have a relevant and positive role to play in any ADR process—particularly in any mediation into which the parties enter. The parties may agree, or the mediator may require, that some areas of expertise be one of the areas that require examination in a mediation. If both parties have retained experts, they can be asked to explain their differences in a joint session in the mediation, so that all participants can get a better understanding of the different points of view. The expert's role in a mediation may be helpful in assisting the decision-making processes. Any legal representative in the process should also be aware of the difficulties that can arise in the use of experts in mediation: they could create further divisions; they may make admissions or concessions that may damage the strength of a party's negotiating position; costs will be increased; and issues of privilege may arise if the mediation does not result in a settlement and litigation proceeds. It is also worth noting, however, that using experts in ADR may have consequences in any subsequent proceedings on the issue of privilege. In *Aird v Prime Meridian Ltd* [2006] EWCA Civ 1866, the Court of Appeal held that a joint statement by experts used in a mediation could be disclosed and could be ordered to be produced within the proceedings, and concluded that it was not privileged just because it was used in the mediation.

18.9 CHOOSING AN APPROPRIATE EXPERT

It is important to choose an expert wisely, but equally it is important to select an expert who is available in the timescale that the court directions have allowed. A failure to find the right expert and instructing one who proves to be unable to deliver his report in time can be disastrous, (see paragraph 18.3.3) and the court will not readily permit extensions of time for the preparation of a report, or to attend to questions, or to attend a meeting between experts without regard to the overriding objective.

18.9.1 THE EXPERT'S RETAINER

PD 35 and paragraphs 16–20 of the Guidance Note contain useful advice on appointing an expert. The terms of the retainer with an expert are suggested to include:

- the capacity in which the expert is to be appointed (that is, as an SJE, an expert adviser, or an expert for one party);

- the services required (that is, to prepare a report, answer questions, have a meeting with any other expert appointed, participate in the preparation of an expert's schedule of issues, attend court, etc.);

- the time for the delivery of the report; and

- the basis of the expert's fees, and how disbursements will be dealt with and whether any cancellation charges have been agreed. How and when the expert will be paid and whether his fees will be subject to assessment by a costs officer.

 Practical Considerations

It may be helpful to set out the terms of the retainer with the expert separately from the letter of instruction to that expert. If this is done, the expert should be asked to acknowledge the retainer letter and confirm that he accepts the terms of appointment. A sample letter of retainer is available to lecturers on the Online Resource Centre.

18.9.2 DEALING WITH AN UNFAVOURABLE EXPERT

Because of the need for impartiality of the expert evidence, it can be difficult to deal with the expert who proves to be unfavourable, whether this is an SJE or an expert for one party only. Where this happens, any application to the court for permission to obtain an alternative expert report or for leave to appoint a new expert is likely to be met either with an order refusing permission (because it would not be within the provisions of the overriding objective to give permission), or, where permission is being granted, an order that the earlier report also be disclosed with the alternative expert's report. On the basis that any subsequent expert is likely to have had sight of the earlier report and have been asked to comment on it, any privilege attaching to the earlier report will be lost. The recent decision of *Odera v Ball* [2012] EWHC 1790 (TCC) highlights the court's view that when a further expert is being sought by a party, any permission for a further expert to be used should be conditional on the first expert's report being disclosed, but that view is not 'fixed in stone' and the courts will look at the facts of the case when deciding whether to order disclosure of the first report. *Guntrip v Cheney Coaches Ltd* [2012] EWCA 392 has also confirmed that an expert whose report is unfavourable is not 'good reason' to seek permission for an alternative expert to be appointed.

18.9.3 WHERE DO YOU FIND AN EXPERT?

One of the most effective ways of selecting an expert will be by recommendation, and in this, your client (possibly with the exception of personal injury claims) may be an obvious starting point. They will have a feel for who is rated in their industry. However, whenever taking the client's views, it is important to ensure that there is no possibility of a conflict arising for the expert or a finding that the expert is not sufficiently impartial (but note the special circumstances referred to in paragraph 18.9.2).

However, a search for an appropriate expert may also be made by:

- reviewing any lists of experts previously used that your client may hold—usually with an assessment of that expert and whether it is worth using them or not;

- consulting Judicial College publications;
- consulting the Expert Witness Institute; or
- consulting the Academy of Experts—which advances the role of expert evidence in the following ways:
  - it keeps and provides a directory of members, categorized according to discipline and experience;
  - it develops and maintains the standards of excellence—vetting all applicants for practising membership; and
  - it is cooperating with, and making representations to, judicial and legal authorities, government departments, official enquiries, and tribunals to ensure that the best use is made of experts' advice;
- following the recommendation of other lawyers working in that field, colleagues, opponents, the Association of Personal Injury Lawyers (APIL), counsel, and other experts.

Clearly, the 'type' of expert needed will be indicated by the nature of the case and the issues on which the expert will be expected to comment: for example, in a case needing technical expertise in manufacturing, an engineer may be what is required; on accounting matters, an accountant. It is necessary to be clear of exactly what the expert is needed for and this may not necessarily be directly related to the subject matter of the cause of action.

It is also important that the retained expert is well respected in his field. Notoriety, or a person who has a reputation for novel and untested theories, is not what is needed.

Additionally, the expert will ideally be a person who has some experience of being an expert witness—that is, a person who will not be undermined or intimidated by the judicial process or by cross-examination (see paragraph 18.3.3). Although it is perfectly proper to advise your expert of the *form* of their report and thereby assist them with the judicial process, it is not in any way acceptable to make any attempt to guide or influence the expert as to his *findings and conclusions*.

18.9.4 WHAT ENQUIRIES NEED TO BE MADE OF YOUR CHOSEN EXPERT?

Your chosen expert will need to provide you with a curriculum vitae (CV) and references before they are engaged. In February 2015 the Academy of Experts' Judicial Committee published a model form of CV for expert witnesses. This is not a standard form, but it offers useful guidance to legal practitioners and to experts in the provision of the expert's CV.

You will also need to assess whether they have the required experience for your case. One way in which you can do this is to give brief details of the case in which they will be expected to act as expert and to ask directly whether they think they have the requisite experience. Alternatively, you can make enquiries of them regarding details of:

- in which courts they have previously appeared;
- the nature of the cases in which they have previously been engaged; and
- their previous court experiences—for example, whether they have been cross-examined.

You will also need to ensure that there is no conflict of interest with engaging your chosen expert. To ensure this, you will need to advise the expert of the names of the other parties in the action, any other experts that have been engaged, and the names of the other party's legal representative, asking the expert to confirm that he has no conflict of interest. It has also been suggested that an expert should be required to make an additional statement at the end of his report in relation to conflicts of interest, although there is no formal requirement for this (see *Toth v Jarman* [2006] EWCA Civ 1028 for detail of the Court of Appeal's recommendation on this point).

of Appeal considered the meaning of 'clarification' and concluded that it did enable a party to put a question to the expert that would have the effect of extending his report—that is, a question may be put on a matter not covered in the report. However, if the questions put to the expert are oppressive, in number or content, the court will not hesitate to disallow or restrict the questions asked.

18.10.3 **DISCUSSIONS BETWEEN EXPERTS**

Experts' discussions may take place at any time by arrangement between the parties, but they are usually ordered by the court in a directions order (see paragraph 18.7) (CPR 35.12). The court may also direct that the experts produce a statement after their discussions, setting out those areas on which they agree and those on which they do not. In the areas in which they disagree, they should give reasons.

 Practical Considerations

> The CPR do not specify exactly how meetings of experts should be set up. The Guidance Note, at paragraphs 70–83, and the Practice Direction on Experts and Assessors, at paragraph 18, sets out guidelines on how the parties and their legal representatives should cooperate in preparing an agenda, and making all of the necessary arrangements. It specifically states that instructing solicitors must not seek to restrict these discussions in such a way to 'avoid reaching areas of agreement on areas within their competence', but they can be reminded not to disclose certain confidential information of their client's. Equally, the legal representative must not instruct the expert to submit any schedule of agreed issues for 'approval' before it is finalized.

The Practice Direction on Experts and Assessors states, at paragraph 18.8, that legal representatives should not be present at the meeting of experts unless all parties and their experts have agreed, or the court orders the presence of legal representatives. In practice, many meetings of experts take place over the telephone for convenience and costs reasons.

18.10.4 **THE EXPERT'S RIGHT TO ASK THE COURT FOR DIRECTIONS**

Experts are entitled to ask the court for directions to assist them in carrying out their responsibilities and duties to the court, and where they feel that they need assistance. If the expert does ask the court for directions in this way, he is required to let his instructing party have a copy of his request to the court at least seven days before filing it at court, and all other parties, at least four days before his request is filed (these times can be varied by the court in the directions order that it makes concerning expert evidence).

 Practical Considerations

> It may be a good idea to include in your terms of engagement with the expert a provision concerning the notification of any request to the court for directions. This will give the legal representative the chance to explore with the expert whether it is possible to resolve the difficulties that the expert has identified, and if it is not possible to resolve the issue that the expert has identified, to assist him in formulating the request to the court.

18.10.5 **THE EXPERT AT COURT**

Oral evidence at trial can only be given with the court's permission, and this includes expert oral evidence. In the fast track, the court is more likely to order that expert evidence be adduced in writing and that there is no oral expert evidence. Where oral expert evidence is provided for, the order will probably not be given until after the pre-trial checklist, which will be after the conclusion of experts' meetings and the preparation of the schedule of issues between the experts. If a party seeks an order for expert oral evidence, he will be expected to establish all, or one, or some, of the following:

- that the expert oral evidence is likely to have an impact on the outcome of the case;
- that the expert oral evidence will assist the judge;
- that there is a risk of injustice if the expert evidence is not tested at trial; or
- that the costs of expert oral evidence are not disproportionate.

Under the provisions of PD 35.11 the court will consider whether multiple experts in an action should give their evidence concurrently and, if so, will make orders as to how this will be achieved.

 Practical Considerations

If your expert is giving oral evidence at trial, it is important that you make the necessary arrangements concerning the expert's availability (that is, serve a witness summons—see Chapter 19, paragraph 19.4.1), and that he is aware what to expect and of the likelihood of cross-examination. If the trial is listed for several days, consideration should have been given in the trial timetable to provide on which day(s) the expert should be available. It is important, though, that the expert is in court not only for the time of his own oral evidence, but also for the time during which other evidence is being given that is within his area of expertise, so that he is able to comment on it and explain its significance. A single expert may assist his instructing party in the cross-examination of a witness or expert of the opponent. If the expert is not giving oral evidence or is not in court when judgment is given, as a matter of courtesy, make sure that you inform the expert of the outcome of the case.

18.10.6 PRACTICAL MATTERS—THE EXPERT'S ORAL EVIDENCE

Prior to attending court to give evidence, you need to ensure that the expert being called as a witness is aware that he will be expected:

- to speak clearly, briefly, and in simple, non-technical terms, where possible;
- to look at the judge, rather than the legal representative;
- not to be evasive, obstructive, hostile, or obstinate when his opinion is shown to be wrong—particularly if the point is not detrimental to the client;
- to be detached and concerned for the truth at all times, and not to be perceived as always allied with only one side;
- to be positive and assured about having his experience tested under cross-examination and not be resentful or antagonistic;
- not to become emotionally involved with the client;
- to stay within the boundaries of his own expertise and experience;
- to come up to proof;
- to be well prepared and as knowledgeable about the case as possible, including his opinion on prognosis; and
- not to be misled by omissions—you need to ensure that he has, and has considered, all of the material facts.

18.10.6.1 Concurrent expert evidence: 'Hot-Tubbing' PD 35.11

The Guidance Note at paragraph 83 supports the court's power to order that where there is more than one expert giving oral evidence, that evidence may be given 'concurrently' where appropriate. This is known as 'hot-tubbing'. Judges are likely to direct the 'hot-tubbing' of multiple experts where they consider it would be beneficial in terms of justice and efficiency.

18.10.7 PRACTICAL MATTERS—THE EXPERT'S WRITTEN EVIDENCE

If experts look for and report on factors that tend to support a particular proposition, the report should still:

- provide a straightforward, not misleading, written opinion that the court will readily understand;
- be objective and not omit factors that do not support the expert's opinion—remembering that you may find that the expert has to give an opinion that is adverse to your client, and if this occurs, you need to consider how to inform the client;
- be properly researched—if the expert considers that insufficient data is available, then he should say so and indicate that his opinion is no more than a provisional one.

Where an expert's report contains opinion evidence (that the expert is not qualified to give), the view has been that those parts of the report should be redacted. This view has been questioned by the High Court in *Hoyle v Rogers* [2014] EWCA Civ 537, with the suggestion that applications to redact are unnecessarily expensive—the whole document should be admitted without redaction and the judge can ignore that which is inadmissible.

18.11 THE EXPERT AND HIS IMMUNITY FROM SUIT

The common law concept of witness immunity is that all witnesses, including expert witnesses, are immune from civil suit, in that 'no action lies against parties or witnesses for anything said or done, although falsely and maliciously and without any reasonable or probable cause, in the ordinary course of any proceedings in a court of justice' (*Dawkins v Lord Rokeby* (1873) LR 8 QB 255, 264). However, the justification for giving immunity from suit has been questioned in recent cases. In the judgment of *Jones v Kaney* [2011] UKSC 13, the Supreme Court, by a majority decision, has concluded that the immunity from suit that experts have had in the work they undertake in legal proceedings should be abolished. This was probably an inevitable decision, as a barrister's previously enjoyed immunity was abolished several years ago (*Arthur JS Hall & Co v Simons* [2002] 1 AC 615, 740). There were dissenting judgments (Lord Hope and Lady Hale, who felt there was no justification, on the facts, to remove the immunity from suit), so we cannot be sure that the case is the final word on this. However, the judgment may well mean that experts can be expected (and directed) to be more careful when preparing their opinion and report.

18.12 EXPERTS AND PRIVILEGE

An expert's report, which is prepared for the purpose of contemplated or pending civil actions for obtaining or giving legal advice, is privileged. There is no obligation to disclose a report on which the party does not intend to rely at trial. Provided that a report is not used as a source of evidence, it may be used in cross-examination of the other side's expert—to test the strength of his opinion. However, once a report has been disclosed by a party, notwithstanding any later decision not to adduce it as evidence at trial, the opponent is permitted to rely on it if he so wishes. This is because once a report has been disclosed, it loses its privilege.

Any advice given by an expert acting in an advisory role for a party will be privileged (*Carlson v Townsend* [2001] EWCA 511) provided the dominant purpose test is satisfied (see Chapter 16, paragraph 16.9.2.2).

In *Aird v Prime Meridian Ltd* [2006] EWCA Civ 1866 (see also paragraph 18.8.7), the Court of Appeal concluded that the joint experts' statement produced as a result of their meeting and ordered by the court as part of its general directions order under CPR 35.12(3) was not privileged, even though it was prepared in advance of a mediation. The court concluded that it was not appropriate to 'look behind' the case management order. The court reasoned that, viewed objectively, the order had been made as part of its standard case management directions concerning the use of expert evidence and that, on that basis, it would not be privileged. It concluded that the statement did not become privileged because the statement was used in the 'without prejudice' forum of mediation.

18.12.1 **WHEN WILL EXPERTS' REPORTS BE DISCLOSED?**

In personal injury claims, the claimant must disclose a report when issuing proceedings. Any further use of expert evidence in personal injury actions will be controlled by the court in the normal way (see paragraph 18.3).

In all other cases, the courts will usually make orders detailing the exchange of experts' reports as part of its case management directions. Usually, reports will be ordered to be exchanged after an appropriate period of time, but usually after disclosure and exchange of witness statements. Generally, disclosure of expert evidence should be simultaneous. PD 29.4.11 provides that if it appears that expert evidence will be required both on issues of liability and on the amount of damages, the court may direct that the exchange of those reports that relate to liability will be exchanged simultaneously, but that those relating to the amount of damages will be exchanged sequentially.

KEY POINTS SUMMARY

- The key provisions of CPR Part 35 are:

  - CPR 35.1—there may be no experts at all;

  - CPR 35.2—expert evidence defined;

  - CPR 35.3—expert's duty to court prevails;

  - CPR 35.4—court control;

  - CPR 35.6—questions to experts;

  - CPR 35.9—sharing unilateral expertise;

  - PD 35.11—'hot-tubbing' provisions;

  - CPR 35.12—experts' discussions;

  - CPR 35.14—experts applying to the court.

  - Experts have a variety of roles (and uses) in litigation—be sure to understand the distinctions.

- Expert evidence can only be adduced in litigation with the permission of the court. Essentially, it will only be permitted if it can be shown to be probative, useful, and cogent, and the cost of obtaining it must be proportionate. Any request for expert evidence must be accompanied with a statement of the costs of having it.

- The duties and obligations of the expert to the court take precedence over any obligations that he may feel to the party who engages or is paying him. Remember the three 'i's of an expert: integrity; independence; and impartiality.

- A legal representative may influence and guide the expert of the form of his report, but not its content or the conclusions reached by the expert. There must be complete transparency of communication between expert and legal representative.

19.6.4 UNFORESEEN EVENTS

On the eve of the trial, or even on the morning of the hearing, certain matters often arise, the most common of which are new evidence and attempts to amend statements of case on the part of your opponent. If something does arise, it is important to discuss it with counsel and your client, taking the time to assess the potential impact on your client's case, and whether and to what extent the late change should be opposed.

Occasionally, the trial will need to be adjourned, but this is really a last resort. When this happens, costs orders will need to be considered. If the trial is to go ahead, then you may wish to make the appropriate costs representations to the judge if the unforeseen event has an impact on your own client's costs, such as a new witness, which extends the length of the trial, or an amended particulars of claim, which requires an amended defence to be prepared.

19.7 AFTER THE TRIAL

There are a number of considerations that you will need to bear in mind when both parties have made their closing submissions and the trial has effectively finished. These are in relation to the judgment, costs, and appeals.

19.7.1 JUDGMENT

Fast-track trials or trials that have been relatively straightforward are more likely to have judgments available immediately after the completion of the closing submissions. In these cases, the judge may retire to his rooms to consider his judgment before coming back into the court to 'hand it down' to the parties' advocates. Once judgment has been given in these circumstances, then representations are made to the judge on the question of costs (see Table 4.2 in Chapter 4 for the different types of costs order) and for permission to appeal. These are discussed in paragraph 19.7.2.

In most other cases, judgment is not usually handed down on the last day of the trial, because the judge requires time to evaluate all of the evidence heard and review any legal authorities. After closing submissions, the judge will inform the court that he will reserve judgment, and will fix a date, there and then, with the court clerk and the parties for the formal handing down of the judgment, which is frequently several weeks—or even months—from the completion of the trial.

 Practical Considerations

In some cases, clients have been waiting a long time for their case to come to trial. It is sensible to manage their expectations not only of the trial procedure itself, but also as to when they are likely to know whether they have substantially won or lost. The trial day(s) are the most expensive part of litigation and whether your client is under a conditional fee agreement (CFA), is paying privately, or is funded by insurance, there may be additional legal fees and disbursements relating to the trial that need to be paid out before the judgment is handed down. A well-informed client is more likely to be patient and content during the period between trial and judgment.

Once the judge has prepared his judgment and the date that has been fixed for the formal handing down approaches, the judge may release his draft judgment to the parties. Draft judgments are technically confidential and should not be released to your client, although the judge may not, in every draft judgment, attach an embargo in this regard. PD 40E contains provisions dealing with how draft judgments should be treated.

Judgments are sometimes released in draft a day before the judgment is to be delivered to allow the parties time to consider whether they wish to seek any consequential orders or permissions to appeal, and to identify any typographical errors or other minor errors before the formal handing down, which is when the judgment becomes effective.

At the handing-down hearing, the judge will sit and recite his judgment, after which the parties can make various representations to the court on the question of costs.

 Practical Considerations

In order to be prepared for the handing down of judgment hearing, which is only a short hearing, revisit the Court Guides on draft judgments and handing down, and be clear about what potential orders you may be required to apply for.

19.7.2 COSTS

Your client should have been given the requisite information on costs at the outset of your retainer with him and at appropriate intervals throughout his case. This information would include funding the litigation, the extent of costs recovery against the opponent, and the various costs orders that can be made by the court, including the basis upon which those costs are assessed. (See Chapter 3, paragraph 3.2, and Chapter 4, paragraph 4.3, for full details of your duty to your client in this regard.)

Therefore, by the time that the judgment is handed down, the costs consequences of winning or losing should come as no surprise to your client, even if the terms of the judgment do. The important feature here is to ensure that, at the hearing, you are in a position to do your best for your client when counsel is making representations to the judge on costs, either asking for an order for costs, or opposing an order for costs.

 Practical Considerations

You may wish to prepare in advance of the hearing a bundle for your counsel containing all of the Part 36 offers or Calderbank offers that have passed between the parties in the event that, should your client be successful, you have to hand information to help the judge decide what costs order to make (whether this is for standard or indemnity costs) and whether any costs and interest enhancements should be made; conversely, should your client have effectively lost, the bundle may assist the judge in deciding whether any penalties should be imposed as a result of your opponent not beating an offer.

Remember that, if it is a fast-track trial, you should have prepared a statement of costs in a form similar to Form N260, as a summary assessment will be made. Fixed costs usually apply to fast-track trials (see Chapter 4, paragraph 4.7.3, and CPR 45, Section VI, 45.37– 45.45.40).

19.7.3 APPEALS

19.7.3.1 Introduction

Where a party is unhappy with a court judgment or order at either a final or interim hearing, including a costs order, that party may be entitled to appeal that judgment or order. The practice and procedure is the same for appeals in the County Court, the High Court, and the Court of Appeal which are all governed by CPR 52 and its recently revised PDs. The PDs have now been subdivided into five separate PDs as follows:

- PD 52A Appeals general provisions;
- PD 52B Appeals in the County Court and the High Court;
- PD 52C Appeals to the Court of Appeal;
- PD 52D Statutory Appeals and appeals subject to special provision; and
- PD 52E Appeals by way of case stated.

The Court Guides are also very useful to help you to prepare for these types of appeals and should be consulted in addition to CPR 52 and the relevant PD. Legal representatives should, however, remember that the main procedure governing appeals is contained in CPR 52 and that the purpose of the PD is only to supplement CPR 52.

It is, however, very different in the Supreme Court, which has its own rules: Supreme Court Rules 2009, SI 2009/1603.

We will cover here the basic provisions relating only to appeals in the County Court and the High Court, as these are likely to be the most common appeals to those new to legal practice.

19.7.3.2 To which court do you appeal?

The identity of an appeal court is contained in the destination of appeals tables found in PD 52A.3.5 as follows for civil matters:

TABLE 19.1 DESTINATION OF APPEALS

Court	Deciding judge	Nature of claim	Interim/final	Destination
County Court	DJ	Part 7 Claim	Interim	CJ (CC)
		Part 7 Claim (not MT)	Final	
		Part 7 Claim (MT)	Final	CA
		Part 8 Claim	Interim/final	CJ (CC)
		Other	Interim/final	
		Specialist	Interim	
			Final	CA
	CJ	Part 7 Claim	Interim	HCJ
		Part 7 Claim (not MT)	Final	
		Part 7 Claim (MT)	Final	CA
		Part 8 Claim	Interim/final	HCJ
		Other	Interim/final	
		Specialist	Interim	
			Final	CA
High Court	Master	Part 7 Claim	Interim	HCJ
		Part 7 Claim (not MT)	Final	
		Part 7 Claim (MT)	Final	CA
		Part 8 Claim	Interim/final	HCJ
		Other	Interim/final	
		Specialist	Interim	
			Final	CA
	HCJ	Any	Interim/final	CA

It is also possible to 'leapfrog' to a different court or judge and the rules relating to 'leapfrogging' are set out in CPR 52.14.

To assist in the understanding of terminology, the 'lower court' is the court whose decision is to be appealed and the 'appeal court' is the court which will hear the appeal.

19.7.3.3 Permission to appeal

In virtually all cases of appeal from a County Court and the High Court, you must obtain permission to appeal. This can be undertaken in a number of ways. Firstly, by way of oral submission when the judgment you wish to appeal has been handed down in the lower court (CPR 52.3(2) and PD 52A.4.1); secondly should that submission be unsuccessful (or simply not made), then permission must be sought by way of paper application known as an Appellant's Notice plus the application for permission to the relevant appeal court within 21 days after the date of the decision of the lower court, unless of course the lower court orders further time (CPR 52.4(2)(b)). The Appellant's Notice and the application for permission are usually heard without an oral hearing. Where permission is refused, then thirdly, there is a further right to have the decision refusing permission reconsidered at an oral hearing (CPR 52.3(4) and PD 52B.7.2), the time limit for which is seven days after service of the notice that permission had been refused.

Permission will ultimately only be granted if the appeal has a real prospect of success or there is some other compelling reason why the appeal should be heard.

 Practical Considerations

Should your client lose the trial, it may be worth considering making an application for permission to appeal in any event after judgment, even if you are unsure whether the appeal will eventually be lodged—it is more difficult and costly to apply for permission to appeal out of time.

19.7.3.4 Grounds for appeal

There are only two grounds for appealing the decision of a lower court: the decision was wrong, either in fact, law, or in the exercise of the court's discretion; or it was unjust because of a serious procedural or other irregularity in the proceedings.

 Practical Considerations

In drafting your grounds for appeal, it is helpful to set out the reasons why one or both of the grounds apply and specify whether the ground raises an appeal on a point of law or against a finding of fact. However, PD 52B.4.2 states that all grounds of appeal must be concise.

19.7.3.5 Documents for appeals

The appellant must prepare the Appellant's Notice (Form 161) plus a court fee. Skeleton arguments are not, however, automatically required in every County Court and High Court appeal. There is also now no express requirement for the appellant to file a bundle at the same time as the N161 although some documents will still inevitably need to be filed and bundled at a later stage. All that is required at this stage is:

- three copies of the N161 and one additional copy for each respondent;

- a copy of the sealed order under appeal;

- if permission was not granted or applied for, the application for permission to appeal and the grounds of appeal.

The 21-day time limit already mentioned commences from the date of the judgment or order and not from the date it was drawn up.

The Respondent's Notice (Form 162) is only required to be filed if the respondent wishes to seek permission for a cross appeal from the appeal court (the same rules as to permission will apply) or he wishes to ask the appeal court to uphold the decision of the lower court for different reasons to those given by the lower court (and as such no permission is required). If the Respondent merely wishes to maintain the decision of the lower court for the reasons given, then there is no requirement to file an N162. If an N162 is to be filed, it must be filed within 14 days of receiving the N161 unless the court orders otherwise.

It should also be noted here that if the case had been allocated to the small claims track, the correct form for the Appellant is the N164.

may also disapply the default costs rule here. The recent case of *Nelson's Yard Management Company and others v Eziefula* [2013] EWCA Civ 235 has held that the defendant should only pay a proportion of the claimant's costs on discontinuance because there had been an abject failure to reply to any pre-action correspondence. One wonders if the same decision would have been reached by the Court of Appeal if there had been late or inadequate responses.

KEY POINTS SUMMARY

- Issue and serve witness summons, and liaise with witnesses directly before trial.

- Book and brief counsel, and consider whether a pre-trial conference is appropriate with the client and any experts or witnesses.

- Allow plenty of time to prepare accurate and user-friendly trial bundles. Keep a spare one at court and at the office.

- Ensure that you are familiar with every aspect of the case before the trial commences.

- Put administrative arrangements in place for the smooth running of the trial.

- Keep in close contact with counsel and the client in the days running up to the trial.

- Be clear as to the arrangements for the handing down of judgment, and if a draft judgment is released, adhere to any embargo placed on it by the judge.

- Know the new Appeals procedures and the strict time limits for appeals, and instruct counsel to be prepared to seek permission or to oppose an application for permission to appeal when the judgment is handed down.

- Understand the mechanics of settling before and after the issue of litigation.

- If settlement is concluded by a non-Part 36 offer, ensure that the correct consent order is agreed and drafted.

Case Study *Andrew James Pike v Deep Builders Ltd*

All of the directions have now been complied with, and the PTC has been filed and served. You have now received a notice of hearing, listing the trial for three days. Acting for Andrew Pike, consider the following questions.

Question 1

On whom should you serve a witness summons and why?

Question 2

Is it necessary to have a conference with counsel at this stage? Give reasons for your answer.

Question 3

If Andrew Pike does not beat Deep Builders' Part 36 offer of £20,000, what are the likely cost consequences for each party and how will the court deal with this?

Question 4

You have been instructed by your supervising partner to help prepare a trial bundle index for the trial of this matter. He informs you that all special damages have been agreed subject to liability, although medical evidence has not been agreed, because the defendants obtained an order seeking their own evidence. There is no order for expert oral evidence at trial.

The young practitioner who was helping your principal has departed on annual leave, but has left you his notes on what he would include in the bundles. These may or may not be of assistance to you. These appear on the Online Resource Centre.

Based on your knowledge of the case for Andrew Pike and the information that your colleagues have provided, draft the trial bundle index.

Case Study *Bollingtons Ltd v Mrs Elizabeth Lynch t/a The Honest Lawyer*

Question 1

The fast-track trial has been listed. As the day of the trial approaches, Mrs Lynch is getting nervous and asks you to attend the trial with her. What costs advice would you give her?

Question 2

Mrs Lynch lost the fast-track trial both on the claim against her and her counterclaim, the judge indicating in his judgment that he preferred the evidence of Mr Green. Permission to appeal was obtained. Consider what advice you would give to her on the prospects of successfully appealing and the costs implications.

online
resource
centre

Any documents referred to in these case study questions can be found on the Online Resource Centre—simply click on 'Case study documentation' to access the documents that you need for Chapter 19 and to be reminded of the questions. Suggested answers to these case study questions can also be accessed on the Online Resource Centre when released to you by your lecturer.

FIGURE 19.1 TEMPLATE CONSENT ORDER

IN THE HIGH COURT OF JUSTICE   201?-P-3003

QUEEN'S BENCH DIVISION

        DISTRICT REGISTRY

Between

                                                        Claimant

                            and

                                               Defendant

                            CONSENT ORDER

Upon the Claimant and Defendant having agreed to settle this matter

By Consent it is ordered that:

1. The Defendant do pay the Claimant the sum of £ . . . . by Friday 25th January 201? in full and final settlement of his claim.

2. The CMC listed on 14th December 201? be vacated.

3. The Defendant do pay the Claimant's costs of the action to be the subject of a detailed assessment if not agreed.

We consent to the terms of this order

. . . .

For the Claimant

. . . .

For the Defendant

Dated . . . .

FIGURE 19.2 TEMPLATE TOMLIN ORDER

IN THE HIGH COURT OF JUSTICE   **201?-P-3003**

QUEEN'S BENCH DIVISION

       DISTRICT REGISTRY

Between

Claimant

and

Defendant

TOMLIN ORDER

Upon the Claimant and Defendant having agreed to the terms set out in the Schedule attached,
By Consent it is ordered that:

1. All further proceedings in this action be stayed on the terms set out in the attached schedule to this order, except for the purpose of carrying the said terms into effect and for that purpose there is permission to apply.

2. Each party shall have permission to apply to the court to enforce those terms without the need to bring a new claim.

3. There be no order as to costs **OR** each party shall bear its own costs **OR** the claimant **OR** the defendant shall pay the defendant's **OR** the claimant's costs on the standard **OR** the indemnity basis to be subject to a detailed assessment in default of agreement.

Schedule

1. The Defendant do pay the Claimant the sum of £xxx within xx days of the date of this order.

2. The order is made in full and final settlement of claims subsisting or capable of subsisting between the parties.

3. In the event of late payment, the Defendant will pay interest on the sum of £xxx . . . . . . or any part thereof at a daily rate of xx . . . .%.

> Relevant parts of the CPR: 44, 45, and 47

20.1 INTRODUCTION

This chapter is primarily concerned with the practical considerations and procedures involved in assessing costs once the litigation is concluded. It should, however, be read with reference to the underlying costs principles, formulas, and likely costs orders that were discussed in Chapter 4 on 'The Nature, Extent, and Recovery of Legal Costs'.

The client must understand that, despite receiving a costs order in his favour, agreeing a liability to pay, or being ordered to pay costs, if the amount of costs cannot be agreed between the parties, then further proceedings and costs are incurred before a resolution is secured.

 Practical Considerations

A 100 per cent costs recovery is very rare even if a party was wholly and fundamentally successful in his case and obtained a 'cost of proceedings' order from the court. While there is nothing set in stone, practitioners adopt an unwritten guide when advising clients on the amount of cost recovery that a successful party usually recovers between 65 per cent and 80 per cent of what they have been charged and, in privately paying cases, have also paid their legal representatives. It is important to highlight this with the client, as they need to understand that what they are responsible for paying to you as their legal representative is not likely to be covered by any amount that they recover from their opponent. Eliminating enhanced expectations of costs recovery at an early stage will avoid additional time and further costs in negotiating with your opponent the figure your client is prepared to accept.

This chapter will cover:

• the procedures for the assessment of costs;

• costs only disputes.

Practical Considerations

Up until any detailed assessment proceedings commence, there is no requirement to disclose to your opponent your client's CFA with a success fee as entered into before April 2013 (or detail of the success fee) with either yourself or with Counsel. In detailed assessment proceedings, only the relevant details of the success fee must be served on the opposing party, but this does not mean the actual CFA needs to be disclosed; a 'statement of reasons' for the percentage increase will do. However, the court has a discretion to ask the receiving party to elect to produce a copy of the CFA to help it reach its decision on costs at the hearing. There is still, however, no compulsion.

20.3.5.2 Points of dispute

After the notice of commencement has been served with supporting documents, your opponent is entitled by CPR 47.9 to dispute any item in the bill by serving points of dispute on the receiving party within 21 days of service of the N252. This time period can be extended by agreement between the parties.

The points of dispute should be concise and follow Precedent G in the schedule of costs precedents in PD 47. It is helpful when completing the points of dispute to identify each item in turn, explain why you object to it, and suggest a reasonable alternative. For example, you may object to the grade of fee earner dealing with part of a case at a particular hourly rate. You would therefore give a reason, such as the claim was relatively straightforward, and put forward your own suggestions.

The points of dispute must be signed by the paying party or his legal representative.

20.3.5.3 Default costs certificate

If the paying party fails to serve points of dispute, CPR 47.9(4) permits the receiving party to file at court, along with a court fee, Form 254, requesting a default costs certificate. On receipt of this, the court will deem that the paying party has no objection to the bill of costs and issue Form N255, which is the default costs certificate. The amount specified to be paid will be the total amount stated on the bill plus interest and must be paid within 14 days.

The default costs certificate can be set aside if there is good reason as set out in CPR 47.12.

The whole default costs certificate procedure can be likened to a default judgment (although there is a fee required for the default costs certificate request) and potentially having that judgment set aside in the main action (CPR 12 and 13).

20.3.5.4 Replies to points of dispute

CPR 47.13 permits the receiving party to reply to the points of dispute within 21 days after service. This is entirely optional. Some legal representatives believe there is little point in conceding items in the replies, as it is better to do this in separate negotiations where concessions can be made. Others believe that if an item cannot be substantiated, it is better to get it out of the way early on.

20.3.5.5 Requesting a detailed assessment hearing

Settlement negotiations can take place at any time. It is usual to try to negotiate costs as soon as the draft bill has been prepared right up until the hearing itself. If negotiations have failed and the steps detailed in paragraphs 20.3.5.1–20.3.5.4 have been completed, then it is time to proceed to a final hearing.

This is done by filing at court (this is the court's first involvement in the detailed assessment procedure) a Request for Hearing (Form N258), the bill of costs plus receipts and court fee, the points of dispute, any replies, any costs budgets, and a hefty cheque. This must be done within three months of the expiry of the first three-month time limit discussed in paragraph 20.3.5.1. Form N258 requires the receiving party to give a time estimate for the hearing and careful consideration must be given to this.

Again, there are sanctions for missing the second three-month time limit as follows:

- If the receiving party misses the second three-month time limit and the paying party issues an application to compel a Request for Hearing to be sought, unless it is sought by the receiving party within a revised time limit stipulated by the court, all or part of the receiving party's costs and/or interest may be disallowed.

- If the receiving party misses the second three-month time limit and the paying party does nothing, there is no automatic sanction imposed. Although, if matters are left too long the court may disallow all or some of the receiving party's costs and interest.

Once the N258 plus supporting documentation and cheque have been filed with the court, the court will fix a hearing date and serve the opponent. It is, therefore, important to ensure that you have filed enough copies of the requisite documentation with the court.

When serving the Notice of Hearing Date, the court will usually request that the receiving party lodge its full file of papers with the court seven days before the actual hearing.

20.3.5.6 Provisional Assessment of Costs

This paper-based part of the process applies to any detailed assessment proceedings commenced after 1 April 2013 where the costs claimed are less than or equal to the amount set out in CPR 47.14.1 being £75,000.

The provisional assessment will commence after all the documents have been filed at court in accordance with PD 47.14.3, as set out in paragraph 20.3.6.5, save for the fact that a sealed envelope marked 'Part 36 or similar offers' containing any such offers made by any party must also be filed at court. The court will try to conduct the provisional assessment on paper within six weeks, and once assessed, it will return the points of dispute with the court's decisions noted thereon to the parties. The parties must then agree the total sum due to the receiving party based on the court's decisions. CPR 47.15 permits the court to list the case for a detailed assessment hearing where it believes the matter is not suitable for a provisional assessment. It also allows either party to request an oral hearing to challenge the provisional assessment with 21 days of the return of the points of dispute. If no such challenge is made, the provisional assessment is binding on both parties.

20.3.5.7 Interim costs certificate and final costs certificate

20.3.5.7.1 *Interim costs certificate*

The detailed assessment hearing will usually be listed at least 14 days in advance of the hearing itself. If it is evident that the matter is contested and the hearing is in fact some time in the future, CPR 47.16 permits the court to issue an interim costs certificate and PD 47.16 permits a party to also apply by way of a Part 23 application for an interim costs certificate.

20.3.5.7.2 *Final costs certificate*

This can be issued at two separate points:

(1) If settlement is achieved between the request for the hearing and the detailed assessment hearing itself, the parties draft a consent order. This is to be signed by both parties and filed at court along with a court fee for approval, with a view to obtaining a final costs certificate.

The procedure on the final costs certificate is akin to the manner in which a main action can be concluded by consent.

(2) If the parties proceed to the final hearing, at the conclusion of the hearing, the receiving party has 14 days to complete the bill with the figures ordered by the costs or regional costs judge and return it to the court. The court will serve the final costs certificate once this is received.

20.3.5.8 What happens at the detailed assessment hearing?

Persons with a thorough knowledge of the file should attend the hearing. In practice, costs draftsmen frequently attend. A costs draftsman may have prepared the bill, but his ability to argue on your behalf for the work undertaken can only be as good as the instructions and information that you give to him, so it is important to engage with issues raised on the bill. The court will go through each and every item claimed in the bill that is in dispute from start to finish and allow both parties to make submissions on these issues. This process is laborious and time-consuming, and detailed assessment hearings can take half a day or more, even in smaller cases.

The court's powers at the detailed assessment hearing, in terms of what it will take into account, have already been set out in Chapter 4 at paragraph 4.3.2. In addition to this, in considering the level of costs to award, the court will also take account of costs budgets filed at the directions stage of the main action, as a result of which such budgets have been approved in accordance with PD 4 at paragraph 3.

However, this practice direction only sets out the impact of costs budgets on detailed assessment proceedings where a costs management order (CMO) has not been made under CPR 3.15. Remember, in many cases, CMOs are not routinely made. It states that if, on assessment, there is a difference of 20 per cent or more between sums claimed and the costs budget filed by the receiving party, the receiving party must provide with his bill of costs, a statement of reasons for the difference. If the paying party reasonably relied on the exceeded budget, then the court may restrict those costs to a lesser amount than appears in the bill or to the amount of the original costs budget, especially where the court does not believe the receiving party has supplied a satisfactory explanation for the difference. It is, therefore, crucial that costs budgets are prepared carefully so that they do not adversely affect any later costs recovery.

In cases where there has been a CMO, the court will have regard to the party's last approved or agreed budget and will not depart from it unless satisfied that there is a good reason to do so. At present, there is little guidance as to what that good reason would be, and the authors await further cases on this point.

20.3.5.9 Costs of the detailed assessment hearing
The costs are usually awarded to the receiving party unless the costs or district judge feels that the detailed assessment proceedings had been conducted unjustifiably or where a CPR 36 offer had been validly made and beaten.

The amount of the costs of the detailed assessment proceedings are summarily assessed and the receiving party should provide details to the court and opponent, although there is no requirement to serve a statement of costs in N260.

The costs are usually ordered to be paid within 14 days of the final costs certificate. Should payment not be made, then orders for costs can be enforced in the usual way as money judgments. Please see the Additional Chapter on 'Enforcement of Judgments' on the Online Resource Centre.

 online resource centre

20.3.5.10 Interest
As already stated in paragraph 20.2.3, interest on costs of the main action accrues from the date of the final judgment or order if over £5,000. Similarly, interest on the costs of the detailed assessment hearing begins to run on the same basis from the date of the order.

20.4 COSTS ONLY PROCEEDINGS

These are governed by CPR 46.14 and PD 46 and were developed to deal with the situation where, before proceedings are issued, the parties had settled the dispute and determined who should pay the costs, but could not agree on the level of costs to be paid. The procedure allows the parties to quickly and relatively cheaply obtain an order for costs which can then provide the basis for those costs to be assessed.

This simple procedure is a CPR 8 claim seeking an order for costs (see Chapter 9 on 'Starting your Claim' at paragraph 9.3.6 for the procedure on CPR 8 claims) followed by a detailed assessment of those costs.

The court will consider the basis of the costs to be assessed and will usually order that the costs of the application are to be in the assessment, i.e. the party in which the court holds favour makes an order for costs at the end of the detailed assessment proceedings and will be entitled to the costs of this application.

Once an order for costs has been made, there are no short cuts to a detailed assessment final hearing and CPR 47 will apply.

KEY POINTS SUMMARY

- Advise your client at the outset of the nature of costs recovery proceedings and the likely percentage recovery to be made.

- Ensure your client file is well documented to enable you to prove each item of work done that is being claimed for.

- Understand the procedures for summary and detailed assessment of costs.

- Prepare accurate costs budgets.

- Do not forget to claim interest on costs of the main action and of the detailed assessment proceedings.

SELF-TEST QUESTIONS

1. What form is generally used for a summary assessment of costs?

2. When must a Detailed Assessment commence?

online resource centre

Suggested answers to these general questions can be accessed on the Online Resource Centre.

FIGURE 20.1 DETAILED ASSESSMENT FLOWCHART

APPENDIX 4

PARTICULARS OF CLAIM

IN THE COUNTY COURT BUSINESS CENTRE   **CLAIM NO. BY2LY87650**

BETWEEN:

SALEMARSH INVESTMENT LIMITED

<u>Claimant</u>

-and-

(1) MR SIMON HILL
(2) MRS PATRICIA HILL

<u>Defendants</u>

PARTICULARS OF CLAIM

---

1.   The Claimant company advanced to the First and Second Defendants sums of monies pursuant to three Private Loan Agreements made in writing as follows:

   1.1.   Private Loan Agreement for £65,000.00 dated 20 November 200? ('the first Loan Agreement');

   1.2.   Private Loan Agreement for £15,000.00 dated the 20 April 200? ('the second Loan Agreement');

   1.3.   Private Loan Agreement for £2,000.00 dated the 29 May 200? ('the third Loan Agreement');

   Copies of these three Agreements are attached to the Particulars of Claim.

2.   The following were express terms of the first Loan Agreement:

   2.1.   The loan of £65,000.00 was in respect of an interest only Agreement subject to capital repayments being made by the First and Second Defendants following refinancing by themselves at a date after the 20 February 200? being the review date;

   2.2.   Interest was to accrue on the £65,000.00 at a rate of 7% gross per annum payable monthly in arrears directly to the Claimant company's bank account.

3. The following were express terms of the second Loan Agreement:

   3.1. The loan for £15,000.00 was an interest and capital repayment loan over a period of 48 months commencing on the 20 April 200?;

   3.2. The interest was to accrue on the balance at 7.5% gross per annum payable monthly in arrears directly to the Claimant company's bank account.

4. The following were express terms of the third Loan Agreement:

   4.1. The loan for £2,000.00 was an interest and capital repayment loan over a period of 48 months commencing on the 29 May 200?;

   4.2. The interest was to accrue on the balance at a rate of 7.5% gross per annum payable monthly in arrears directly to the Claimant company's bank account.

5. The First and Second Defendants have made the following payments:

   5.1. In respect of the first Loan Agreement, the First and Second Defendants have made no payments in respect of the capital amount of the loan in the sum of £65,000.00. However, interest payments in the sum of £379.16 per month were made until October 200? after which no further payments were received by the Claimant company save for a 'one off' payment of £500 on 17 December 200? which was allocated to outstanding interest by the Claimant company;

   5.2. In respect of the second Loan Agreement, the First and Second Defendants made five capital and interest repayments between May 200? and September 200? each in the sum of £362.68. No further payments have been received by the Claimant company;

   5.3. In respect of the third Loan Agreement the First and Second Defendants made four payments between June 200? and September 200? each in the sum of £48.36. No further payments have been made.

6. In respect of the first Loan Agreement, the Claimant company has made a number of requests since the 29 February 200? requesting repayment of the capital loan of £65,000.00 but no payments have been made. However, as stated in paragraph 5.1 above some interest payments have been made in respect thereto. As regards the second and third Loan Agreements, the loan period of 48 months has now expired and as detailed in paragraph 5.2 and 5.3 above no further payments have been made in respect of capital or interest since those dates. Consequently, the First and Second Defendants are indebted to the Claimant company in respect of the following sums:

PARTICULARS

6.1. <u>First Loan Agreement</u>

Capital sum outstanding	£65,000.00
Interest at a monthly rate of £379.16 from October 200? to date (less a payment of £500.00 made towards interest in December 200?)	£ 9,737.32

6.2. <u>Second Private Loan Agreement</u>

Capital sum outstanding as a result of payments set out in paragraph 5.2	£13,437.50
Interest at a rate of £50.18 per month from October 200? to date	£ 1,254.50

6.3. <u>Third Loan Agreement</u>

Capital sum outstanding as a result of payments set out in paragraph 5.3	£ 1,833.32
Interest at a monthly rate of £6.69 from October 200? to date	<u>£ 167.25</u>

Total of capital and interest due to date of issue   £91,429.89

7.   Further, the Claimant company is entitled to continuing interest on the said capital sums of £80,270.82 at the contractual rates as set out in the three private Loan Agreements at a daily rate of £14.53 until judgment or sooner payment. Alternatively, the Claimant company will seek interest pursuant to Section 69 of the County Courts Act 1984 at a rate of 8% per annum from the date of issue until judgment or sooner payment.

AND the Claimant claims:

(1)   £91,429.89;

(2)   Interest from date of issue to judgment or sooner payment at a contractual rate of 7% in respect of the first Loan Agreement and a contractual interest rate of 7.5% per annum in respect of the second and third Loan Agreements or pursuant to Section 69 of the County Courts Act to be assessed.

STATEMENT OF TRUTH

I believe that the facts stated in these Particulars of Claim are true.

I am duly authorised by the Claimant company to sign this Statement of Truth.

Signed ……………………………..

Director of Claimant company

Dated ………………………………

Address for receiving documents:

LPC and CO
27 Leek Road
Stoke on Trent
Staffordshire
ST1 8ED

Ref: KE.SJW.Sal3/1

10. By no later than 4 p.m. on Monday 18ᵗʰ March 201?, the parties must file with court their availability for trial, preferably agreed with a nominated single point of contact. They will be notified of the time and place of trial.

11. Not more then seven and not less than three clear days before trial, the claimant must file at court and serve an indexed and paginated bundle of documents which complies with the requirements of CPR 39.5 and PD 39A. The parties must endeavour to agree the contents of the bundle before it is filed. The bundle will include a case summary, chronology with list of issues and a trial timetable.

12. The parties must file at court and exchange skeleton arguments at least three clear days before trial by email.

13. Costs in the case.

The parties are reminded of the provisions of the Practice Directions to CPR 28 or 29 concerning variation of directions and failure to comply with directions, and that in particular such applications must be made without delay. They should not be left until the filing of pre-trial checklists.

Each party must inform the court immediately if the case is settled whether or not it is then possible to file a draft consent order to give effect to their agreement.

APPENDIX 7

DISCLOSURE STATEMENT

List of documents: standard disclosure

Notes

- The rules relating to standard disclosure are contained in Part 31 of the Civil Procedure Rules.
- Documents to be included under standard disclosure are contained in Rule 31.6
- A document has or will have been in your control if you have or have had possession, or a right of possession, of it **or** a right to inspect or take copies of it.

In the	
The County Court at Brighton	
Claim No.	**7TG23510**
Claimant (including ref)	**Mr David Anderson**
Defendant (including ref)	**South Meadow Holidays Limited**
Date	**2nd November 201?**

Disclosure Statement

I, the above named

[ ] Claimant   [ ] Defendant

[x] Party (if party making disclosure is a company, firm or other organisation identify here who the person making the disclosure statement is and why he is the appropriate person to make it)

> Stewart Coaster, Managing Director of the Defendant Company. Individual with the relevant knowledge and authority in this litigation

state that I have carried out a reasonable and proportionate search to locate all the documents which I am

required to disclose under the order made by the court on (date of order)   5th JULY 201?

[x] I did not search for documents:-

[x] pre-dating   October 200?

[x] located elsewhere than
> South Meadows Holidays Ltd's Head Office

[x] in categories other than
> The circumstances surrounding the contract for the adventure holiday

[ ] for electronic documents

I carried out a search for electronic documents contained on or created by the following:
(list what was searched and extent of search)

> The desk top computers at South Meadows Holidays Ltd's head office in Cambridge. All emails and documents created in respect of the holiday contract and information.

| x | I did not search for the following:-

| x | documents created before | October 200? |

documents contained on or created by the | | Claimant | x | Defendant

| | PCs | x | portable data storage media
| | databases | x | servers
| x | back-up tapes | x | off-site storage
| x | mobile phones | x | laptops
| x | notebooks | x | handheld devices
| x | PDA devices

documents contained on or created by the | | Claimant | x | Defendant

| | mail files | | document files
| x | calendar files | x | web-based applications
| | spreadsheet files | x | graphic and presentation files

I certify that I understand the duty of disclosure and to the best of my knowledge I have carried out that duty. I further certify that the list of documents set out in or attached to this form, is a complete list of all documents which are or have been in my control and which I am obliged under the order to disclose.

I understand that I must inform the court and the other parties immediately if any further document required to be disclosed by Rule 31.6 comes into my control at any time before the conclusion of the case.

| | I have not permitted inspection of documents within the category or class of documents (as set out below) required to be disclosed under Rule 31(6)(b) or (c) on the grounds that to do so would be disproportionate to the issues in the case.

Signed | Stewart Coaster   **Date** | 2nd November 201?

Defendant's Representative

List and number here, in a convenient order, the documents (or bundles of documents if of the same nature, e.g. invoices) in your control, which you do not object to being inspected. Give a short description of each document or bundle so that it can be identified, and say if it is kept elsewhere i.e. with a bank or solicitor

I have control of the documents numbered and listed here. I do not object to you inspecting them/producing copies.

1. Emails from Claimants to Defendant dated 05.01.?? – 09.04.??
2. Customer enquiry form undated
3. Sales invoice dated 14.04.??
4. Agreement Terms Summary dated 31.03.1??
5. Sales invoice dated 11.10.??
6. Statements of Case in this action
7. Correspondence and copy correspondence between the Claimants' and Defendant's solicitors
8. Correspondence and copy correspondence between the Claimants' solicitor and Defendant

---

List and number here, as above, the documents in your control which you object to being inspected. (Rule 31.19)

I have control of the documents numbered and listed here, but I object to you inspecting them:

1. Confidential correspondence and copy correspondence and communications and attendance notes written by the Defendant's solicitor for the Defendant for the purpose of giving legal advice relating to this action.
2. Statements and proofs of evidence, drafts and copies thereof.
3. Documents brought into existence solely for the purpose of this action.

Say what your objections are

I object to you inspecting these documents because:
They are privileged by legal professional privilege and/or litigation privilege

---

List and number here, the documents you once had in your control, but which you no longer have. For each document listed, say when it was last in your control and where it is now

I have had the documents numbered and listed below, but they are no longer in my control.

The originals of any correspondence referred to above. The originals were last in the Defendant's possession on the dates when they were posted to the recipients at the address noted.

Medical Report dated 5th October 201?
Professor M Harris

The plate is still in place and he has been told that it could be removed. He has decided to leave it in place however. I asked him about hobbies and sports but he tells me that although he played cricket many years ago he no longer does any sport or hobbies and did not do so at the time of the accident.

<u>MEDICAL RECORDS</u>

I have seen photocopies of the 336 pages from the hospital records and the General Practitioner notes-including-x-rays.

All sections within quotation marks are verbatim. Comments in square brackets are mine. I will only refer to the entries that I consider relevant to this report.

I cannot find any reference to any significant pre-existing condition affecting his left knee.

21-3-1?   A letter from Mr Dawson, Consultant Orthopaedic Surgeon states "Mr Smith was admitted yesterday. He was between two cars and caught between the bumpers of the car in front and the car behind. When the car behind was started it was in gear and lurched forward crushing his tibia. He has a small abrasion in the distal third of his tibia. He has sustained a fracture of his proximal tibia which is minimally displaced. There is some extension of the proximal posterior tibial component. There is a significant coronial split."

The options of management have been discussed with Mr Smith and he wishes to consider surgical intervention by way of a left proximal lateral tibial plate.

8-4-1?   A letter from Mr Dawson, Consultant Orthopaedic Surgeon states "Surgical wound has healed. He has a good range of motion of the knee . . . radiographs . . . show that the fracture is in a good position. Whilst he was here he mentioned pain over the left thigh. There is clinically nothing abnormal to find. He may have sustained a strain of his quadricep muscles".

18-5-1?   A letter from Mr Jones, Consultant Neurologist states ". . . as you can see you have a relatively mild acute partial left femoral nerve lesion which will either be related to the accident itself or possibly be related to your diabetes. From our last conversation I understand that the pain was beginning to resolve and I would expect things to gradually improve . . ."

13-6-1?   A letter from Phillippa Griffiths, Physiotherapist states "He has full active movement in his left knee but has had tightness in his ilio-tibial band. These issues have settled with massage. He can straight leg raise but has weak quads which will need further work . . ."

Medical Report dated 5th October 201?
Professor M Harris

2-9-1? A letter from Mr Dawson, Consultant Orthopaedic Surgeon states "Radiographs show that the proximal tibial fracture appears to be well on its way to healing with good callus formation at the fracture site. He is mobilising independently without a stick now with a good range of motion. The alignment clinically is satisfactory and the plate is prominent proximally. He wishes to have this removed, this can be arranged in 12 months.

Review in one year, with x-rays on arrival for a final check . . ."

EXAMINATION

I interviewed and examined Mr Smith on 5th October 201? at The Nuffield Hospital, Benjamin Lane, South Manchester. He was not wearing any form of support or bandage on the left leg and walked without a stick or crutch but had a noticeable limp.

Left Leg

There was a curved antero-lateral surgical scar over the proximal left tibia measuring 10 cms in length. There were three 1 cm scars more distally from insertion of the percutaneous screws of the LISS plate. The proximal end of the plate is easily palpable just under the skin. It is not tender. The knee is cool and there is no effusion. There is no deformity and he has a normal valgus angle I could not detect any significant ligament laxity. The knee flexes and extends fully but there is some crepitus palpable through parts of the range of movement. Some of the crepitus appears to be patello-femoral but some may becoming from medial or lateral compartments.

RADIOLOGIAL EXAMINATION

I have examined the x-rays and all the relevant x-rays are of the left knee and tibia.

18-3-201? X-rays taken on admission show a long oblique fracture of the proximal left tibia extending proximally into the tibial plateau. The fracture line runs up between the tibia plateau and into the lateral plateau. CT scans confirm an unusual fracture pattern as there is a very long oblique component to the fracture. The proximal fragment is continuous with the postural part of both tibial plateaux but there is a separate anterior fragment which is displaced. There is some comminution or shattering laterally.

20.3.201? Post operative x-rays show that the fracture has been nicely fixed with two inter-fragmentary screws and a bridging anterior – lateral locking plate. There are six screws approximately and three screws distally in the plate.

The most recent x-rays taken on 2nd September 201? confirm the fractures have all healed and are in good alignment.

Medical Report dated 5th October 201?
Professor M Harris

PROGNOSIS AND OPINION

Mr Smith describes how he was standing behind his own car when the car behind him suddenly reversed striking the back of his legs. He felt two impacts before he started to collapse. He was caught by some friends who lowered him to the ground. He was immediately aware that he had injured his leg.

He was taken by ambulance to the University Hospital of South Manchester where he was admitted and told that he had sustained a left tibial plateau fracture.

He underwent an operation three days later in which the fracture was internally fixed with an LISS plate. He was discharged from hospital after 12 days with a plaster cast on his leg and used crutches for several months.

He found it very difficult to get around and was unable to return to his work as a General Practitioner. He underwent nerve conduction studies due to the fact that there does not appear to have been any direct crushing of the part of the thigh where the femoral nerve lies. It is more likely that the abnormalities and the femoral nerve identified by the conduction studies are due to diabetes than to the trauma.

Mr Smith has undergone physiotherapy and the movement in his left knee has slowly improved. The pain initially has improved but it has not settled completely. After 5 months he was able to return to driving. After 6 months he started work again as a General Practitioner.

I would suggest that the time absent from work was perfectly reasonable in view of the nature of the injury and the treatment which it necessitated.

Mr Smith still suffers from aching in the left knee which tends to be worse when he is resting. The pain often wakes him in the night. When I examined him on 5th October 201?. I found that he had regained full movement in the knee although there was some crepitus as he flexed and extended his knee. This crepitus is likely to becoming from the arthritic patello femoral joint. As explained earlier, the degenerative change in the patello femoral joint is likely to have pre-dated the accident and was not made worse by the affects of the accident.

It is likely that the residual aching in his knee will improve over the next 2 ½ years. By 3 years from the date of the accident the aching will have become mild and intermittent.

The articular surfaces of the tibial plateau have been nicely restored by the internal fixation. The injury has not therefore thereforeincreased any risk of arthritis in the knee. It has not increased the rate at which any pre-existing degenerative changes will progress.

The plate can be felt quite prominently into the skin but he is not keen to have it removed at the moment. There is no absolute reason for the plate to be removed but if the protruding proximal

Medical Report dated 5th October 201?
Professor M Harris

end starts to irritate him then he could have the plate taken out at a later stage. Removal of the plate would require a further operation under general anaesthetic.

When Mr Smith was seen by Mr Dawson in Clinic on 2nd September 201?, it was decided that matters would be reviewed in 12 months hence when a final decision would be made about whether to remove the plate.

DECLARATION

I understand that my overriding duty is the Court both in preparing this report and in giving oral evidence. I have set out in my report what I understand from those instructing me to be the questions in respect of which my opinion as expert is required. I have done my best in preparing this report to be accurate and complete. I have mentioned all matters which I regard as relevant to the opinions I have expressed. All of the matters on which I have expressed an opinion lie within my field of expertise.

I have drawn to the attention of the Court all matters which I am aware which might adversely affect my opinion. Wherever I have no personal knowledge I have indicated the source of factual information. I have not included anything in this report which has been suggested to me by anyone including the lawyers instructing me without forming my own independent view of the matter.

Where in my view there is a range of reasonable opinion, I have indicated the extent of the range in the report. At the time of signing the report I consider it to be complete and accurate. I will notify those instructing me if, for any reason, I subsequently consider that the report requires any correction or qualification.

I understand this report will be the evidence I will give under oath subject to any correctional qualification I may make before swearing to its veracity.

I confirm that I have made clear which facts and matters referred to in this report are within my own knowledge and which are not. Those that are within my own knowledge I confirm to be true. The opinions I have expressed represent my true and complete professional opinions on the matters to which they refer.

....

PROFESSOR M. HARRIS MB. FRCS(Ed)
Consultant Orthopaedic Surgeon
University Hospital of South Manchester

Section A — Claimant's details

☐ Mr. ☐ Mrs. ☑ Ms.

☐ Miss ☐ Other

Claimant's name

Claire Peakston

Address

57 Oakes Town Centre Street
Oakes Town
Near Chester

Postcode C H 2 5 7 G K

Date of birth

1 3 / 0 4 / 1 9 8 0

Is this a child claim? ☐ Yes ☑ No

National Insurance number

N B 2 2 1 3 7 8 Y

If the claimant does not have a National Insurance
number, please explain why

Occupation

Teacher (Part time)

Date of accident

2 4 / 0 7 / 2 0 1 6

If exact accident date is not known please select the
most appropriate date and provide further details in
Section B 1.1

Section B — Injury and medical details

1.1 Please provide a brief description of the injury
sustained as a result of the accident

Bruising to her left hip, thigh, arm, elbow and cheek. Small laceration to her left forehead. Left black eye.

this section continues over the page ⇨

1.2 Has the claimant had to take any time off work as a result of the accident? ☑ Yes ☐ No

1.3 Is the claimant still off work? ☐ Yes ☑ No

If No, how many days in total was the claimant off work? `3`

1.4 Has the claimant sought any medical attention? ☑ Yes ☐ No

If Yes, on what date did they first do so? `2 4 / 0 7 / 2 0 1 6`

1.5 Did the claimant attend hospital as a result of the accident? ☐ Yes ☑ No

If Yes, please provide details of the hospital(s) attended

1.6 If hospital was attended, was the claimant detained overnight? ☐ Yes ☑ No

If Yes, how many days were they detained?

Section C — Rehabilitation

2.1 Has a medical professional recommended the claimant should undertake any rehabilitation such as physiotherapy? ☑ Yes ☐ No ☐ Medical professional not seen

If Yes, please provide brief details of the rehabilitation treatment recommended and any treatment provided including name of provider

Physiotherapy. Ultra Sound.
Shore Side Physiotherapy Clinic.

2.2 Are you aware of any rehabilitation needs that the claimant has arising out of the accident? ☑ Yes ☐ No

If Yes, please provide full details

See section 2.1 above.

Section D — Accident time, location and description

3.1   Estimated time of accident (24 hour clock)

> 11.15

3.2   Where did the accident happen?
Please provide sufficient detail to identify
the precise accident location (e.g. road name,
house number, permanent location feature,
grid reference etc.)

> Cotters Playground, Oakes Town.
> CH25 7JK

3.3   Please give a description of the accident and
provide a sketch or photograph, if appropriate

> The claimant's daughter had been using one of two swings. The other swing was also occupied by a child.
> When the claimant's daughter had finished her swing, she and the claimant walked away from the swings
> (but not directly behind the other swing). As they walked away the other swing suddenly detached itself
> from the swing frame and flew through the air hitting the claimant and knocking her to the ground. The
> claimant's child was not hit.

3.4   Was the accident reported?   ☑ Yes   ☐ No   ☐ Not known

If Yes, please confirm the date the accident was
reported and to whom it was reported (if known)

> By telephone to Mrs Cotter on the 24th July 2016 shortly after the accident.

Section E — Liability

4.1 Why does the claimant believe that the defendant was to blame for the accident?

Cotters Playground (the premises) is in breach of its statutory duty under section 2 of the Occupiers Liability Act 1957 (the Act) and/or is negligent in that the firm:
1. Failed to take any or any reasonable care to ensure that the claimant would be reasonably safe on the premises
2. Caused or permitted unsafe swings to be used
3. Failed to institute or enforce any or any adequate system for the inspection and/or maintenance of the equipment at the premises, notably the swings
4. Failed to any or any adequate care for the safety of the claimant
5. Exposed the claimant to a danger and foreseeable risk of injury
6. In the circumstances, failed to discharge the common duty of care to the claimant in breach of the Act

Claim notification form (PL1)

Low value personal injury claims in
public liability accidents (£1,000 - £25,000)

Compensator response

Section A — Liability

Please select the relevant statement

Defendant admits: Accident occured

Caused by the defendant's breach of duty

Caused some loss to the claimant, the nature and extent of which is not admitted

The defendant has no accrued defence to the claim under the Limitation Act 1980

☐   The above are admitted

☐   The defendant makes the above admission but the claim will exit the process due to contributory negligence

If the defendant does not admit liability please provide reasons below

Section B — Services provided by the compensator - Rehabilitation

Is the compensator prepared to provide rehabilitation?   ☐ Yes   ☐ No

Has the compensator provided rehabilitation?   ☐ Yes   ☐ No

If Yes, please provide full details below

Section C — Response information

Date of notification   ☐☐ / ☐☐ / ☐☐☐☐

Date of response to notification   ☐☐ / ☐☐ / ☐☐☐☐

Defendant's compensators details

Address

Contact name

Telephone number

E-mail address

Reference number

HPS Personal Injury Solicitors
12th Floor HPS House
High Street
Chester CH1 2DF

Tel: xxxxx 23456
www.HPSsolicitors.co.uk

e-mail:sj@HPSsolicitors.co.uk

20 August 2016

Cotters Playground

Oakes Town

Near Chester

CH25 7JK   ref: SJ/CP.12/2106

Dear Mr and Mrs Cotter,

Ms Claire Peakston   Accident 24th July 2016

We refer to the above accident and enclose a copy of the Claim Notification Form.

Under the Civil Procedure Rules, 'Pre-action Protocol for Low Value Personal Injury (Employer Liability and Public Liabilty) Claims Portal' you must confirm receipt of the Claim Notification Form by email within 1 day of receipt of this letter. You must also provide us with your insurers full details including your policy number.

We look forward to receiving the above details along with your confirmation that your insurers have been sent a copy of the enclosed Claims Notification Form. A duplicate of the form is enclosed for this purpose.

Yours faithfully

HPS Personal Injury Solicitors

Enc: Two copies of PL1.

HPS Personal Injury Solicitors
12th Floor HPS House
High Street
Chester CH1 2DF

Tel: xxxxx 23456
www.HPSsolicitors.co.uk

e-mail:sj@HPSsolicitors.co.uk

25 August 2016

Cotters Playground

Oakes Town

Near Chester

CH25 7JK

ref: SJ/CP.12/2106

Dear Mr and Mrs Cotter,

Ms Claire Peakston   Accident 24th July 2016

We refer to our letter dated 20th August 2016.

We note that you have failed to provide your insurer's details to allow us to submit this claim to them via the Portal. You are now in breach of rule 6.10 of the Civil Procedure Rules 'Pre-action Protocol for Low Value Personal Injury (Employer Liability and Public Liabilty) Claims Portal' and we are consequently entirely justified in commencing court proceedings against you.

However in an attempt to avoid costly litigation, we will provide you with a further 7 days to provide us with your insurers details, with policy number.

Your reply is awaited in that time.

Yours faithfully

HPS Personal Injury Solicitors

HPS Personal Injury Solicitors
12th Floor HPS House
High Street
Chester CH1 2DF

Tel: xxxxx 23456
www.HPSsolicitors.co.uk

e-mail:sj@HPSsolicitors.co.uk

31 August 2016

Cotters Playground

Oakes Town

Near Chester

CH25 7JK   ref: SJ/CP.12/2106

Dear Mr and Mrs Cotter,

Ms Claire Peakston   Accident 24th July 2016

We refer to your letter dated 27th August 2016, with enclosed response.

We note that you are seeking to deny our client's claim. As a result of this the claim will enter the Pre-Action Protocol for Personal Injury claims and the Claims Notification Form sent to you under cover of our letter dated the 20th August 2016 will act as the Letter of Claim within that Protocol.

Under the provisions of the Pre-Action Protocol for Personal Injury claims you now have 3 months from the date of your acknowledgment (27th August 2016) to provide us with a decision on liability. We calculate that date to be 27th November 2016.

As you have chosen for the claim not to be dealt with under the Portal, the relevant costs shall apply.

We look forward to hearing your detailed response on liability by 27th November 2016.

Yours faithfully

HPS Personal Injury Solicitors

HPS Personal Injury Solicitors
12th Floor HPS House
High Street
Chester CH1 2DF

Tel: xxxxx 23456
www.HPSsolicitors.co.uk

e-mail:sj@HPSsolicitors.co.uk

20thNovember 2016

Cotters Playground

Oakes Town

Near Chester

CH25 7JK   ref: SJ/CP.12/2106

Dear Mr and Mrs Cotter,

Ms Claire Peakston   Accident 24th July 2016

We refer to our letter dated 31st August 2016 and write to remind you that your decision on the issue of liability, in accordance with the Pre-Action Protocol for Personal Injury claims (the protocol) falls due on the 27th November 2016.

We expect compliance with the Protocol and we give you notice that, in the event that your decision is not provided by the due date (27th November 2016), or if liability continues to be denied and you do not simultaneously provide disclosure, we shall make an application, without further notice, for pre-action disclosure pursuant to Civil Procedure Rules 31.16.

For the avoidance of any doubt, we shall be seeking disclosure of the following documents:

1. Accident report Form
2. Accident report
3. Risk assessments
4. Inspections records for the relevant area (the swings) of your playground for 1 month prior to our client's accident
5. Copies of any warning signs and markings present in the relevant area
6. Records of similar (or any) accidents in the playground for the 12 months prior to our client's accident
7. Records of any complaints made of any facilities within the playground for the 12 months prior to our client's accident
8. Details of the frequency and type of inspections taken place of the equipment in the playground in the 12 months prior to our client's accident

In the event that an application does become necessary, we shall draw to the attention of the court your breach of the Protocol and, in addition to an order for disclosure of the above documents, we shall be seeking payment of costs on the indemnity basis.

We look forward to hearing from you.

Yours faithfully

HPS Personal Injury Solicitors

INDEX